SAIL POWER

SAIL POWER

The Complete Guide to Sails and Sail Handling

by WALLACE ROSS
with Carl Chapman

Adlard Coles Limited   London

Granada Publishing Limited
First published in Great Britain 1975 by Adlard Coles Limited
Frogmore St Albans Herts AL2 2NF and 3 Upper James Street London W1R 4BP

ISBN 0 229 22545 4

Manufactured in the United States of America

FIRST EDITION

ALL PHOTOGRAPHS IN THE BOOK ARE BY THE AUTHOR EXCEPT THOSE LISTED BELOW:

Figures 1–6, pages 4–5 by Eric Twining
Figure 90, page 117 by UPI Telephoto
Figure 91c, page 119 by John Hopf
Figure 94c, page 123 by Jim Evans
Figure 100, page 133 by Stanley Rosenfeld
Figure 128c, page 185 by Dick Wall
Figure 131b, page 191 by Stanley Rosenfeld
Figure 137, page 199 by Stanley Rosenfeld
Figure 141a, c, d, pages 206–7
  by Stanley Rosenfeld
Figure 142c, page 209 by Stanley Rosenfeld
Figure 144a, page 214 by Diane Beeston

Figure 144b(1), page 214
  by Fusanori Nakajima
Figure 144b(2), page 214 by Dan Hightower
Figure 144c, page 215 by Bill King
Figure 158b, page 233 by Stanley Rosenfeld
Figure 163, page 239 by Stanley Rosenfeld
Figure 167d, page 245 by John Hopf
Figure 170a, page 250 by Stanley Rosenfeld
Figure 170b, page 250 by Joe Crampes
Figure 178a, page 270 by David McChesney
Figure 179c, page 274 by Sue Cummings
Figure 212c, page 329 by Jim Evans

Contents

Acknowledgments

About five years ago, Regina Ryan, an editor for Alfred A. Knopf, Inc. stopped by our sailmaking and hardware booth at the New York Boat Show and asked about the possibility of my writing an all-encompassing book on sails and sail handling—including related subjects, such as hardware selection, deck layout, measurement procedures, and perhaps something about the handicap rules.

My immediate reaction was that this is so vast a field, without source material in many areas, that it would be a back-breaking job which could take several years to complete. The thought was intriguing, however, and, since business brought me in close contact with hundreds of boat owners each year—through talks and seminars at various yacht clubs—I took the opportunity to find out whether there was a need for such a book.

Obviously, only a small portion of information could be covered during a two- or three-hour evening, and the thirst for more knowledge was constantly evident. It was also evident that in each group there were many different levels of sail-handling knowledge, so that one small segment on the total subject was not adequate. It had to be presented in its entirety—from the simple basics to the most sophisticated sail-trimming procedures—in a logical sequence, so that one could see the many variables involved. But the thought of compiling all of this was awesome and seemed close to impossible. In sail handling, one statement seems to lead to new questions and this process is continuous.

A year went by and another Boat Show arrived; and Regina, still determined, stopped by once more to pursue the matter of the book. She was undaunted by the dire predictions that, because of the complexity of the subject, she might end up doing much more editing than she had bargained for. The source material from aerodynamicists, naval architects, hydrodynamics engineers, and other highly skilled persons often involved formulations and highly technical terms which had to be translated into simple, clear language that could be understood by the layperson but respected by the professional. The writing was further complicated by the fact that the sailors' lingo and terminology varies from area to area. Another problem was the fact that the world of sailing is advancing technically by leaps and bounds. To avoid including material that would be quickly outdated, we decided to stick to fundamental principles as much as possible. Inevitably, however, there will be some changes by the time the book is published.

As predicted, the book was over four years in preparation. An incredible amount of help was required to bring it into being; Bob Carrick put the vast array of notes and accumulated data into an initial word platform from which I worked. Carl Chapman, a young aerodynamicist-engineer was of great help in checking the technical discussions. Carl dedicated himself to the project and, with his uncommon intelligence and zeal, made a very important contribution to the book.

There were many others who contributed to the book in important ways. To mention only a few, there was Rich McCurdy who built all the electronic equipment for *Courageous* and shared much of this experience for the chapter on Speed Made Good; Dick Bewley, Jim Armitage, and many others on the Kenyon Marine staff who helped in the research of different alloys and plastics in the hardware chapter; Bill Ficker and Bill Cox who made many helpful comments after reading the manuscript. There were a number of artists: Bob Smith, Carol Evans, Bob Sorries, Charles Hurley, and especially Cathy Boyd, who did at least a third of the drawings and worked tirelessly until three and four in the morning to meet final deadlines; the typists, Nancy Dimasi, Otsie Obrig, and Judy Griffin, not only typed the manuscript but helped organize myriads of paper. And last but not least, Regina, who spent—as predicted—many evenings, holidays, and weekends alone and with me on a seemingly endless critique and revision, until the book was right.

Ideas have been provided by sailors from all over the United States, Canada, Europe, and even the Far East. However, I realize that many other sailors have done more extensive research in particular subjects than we knew about or had the space to cover. I especially hope all sailors will contribute their thoughts about what is written here, because the exchange of ideas is what this book is all about.

Wally Ross
November, 1974

Introduction

This book represents the first attempt to gather together and explain the scores of factors—from the deck up—which can affect boat speed. Sail shape, sail trim, the rig and fittings, all can be varied in many ways creating endless combinations. The wind and sea varies also. To get maximum boat speed, the sailor has to choose the right combination for the particular wind and sea condition in which he's sailing. Our objective in this book is to show you the whys and wherefores of sails, rig, and equipment so that you will understand the underlying principles and, on the basis of this knowledge, have guidelines that will enable you to cope with all the variables successfully.

The first four chapters cover aerodynamics and sail design, and are necessary to lay the groundwork for the remainder of the book. However, they are sometimes quite detailed and technical. You may find it easier to begin with the practical sections of the book—starting at Chapter 5. Then, as questions arise, you can go back and find the answers in the early chapters.

In the chapters on sail handling and hardware, reference is made to both ocean racers and one-design boats. You will probably be more interested in one than the other, but keep in mind that the differences in sail handling on the large boats and the dinghies have been narrowing in recent years. For instance, ball-bearing travelers were found only on one designs for a long time, but recently have been adopted as indispensable equipment for the ocean racers. Conversely, new accomplishments in the cruising boats are being scaled down to accommodate the one-design needs. You will soon come to realize that a large boat requires the same sail-handling techniques as a small boat but with varying applications of crew weight and strength, relating to the job to be done.

One thing to remember: there is no substitute for getting to know your own boat. This takes a lot of time and patience. It takes a steady crew. It takes sail testing. It takes tuning, and, if you race, it takes the detailed recording of the sail-handling adjustments that work for *your* boat.

Perhaps more important than any of these is a steady and well-trained crew. Look at the leading sailors. Most of them have done exactly what is outlined above—the skipper and crew have put a lot of time and practice into one boat. Of course, some new designs win races right away, but if you look beneath the surface, you will undoubtedly find a very experienced crew who have worked together on other boats. Each crew member, having done his particular job many times before, knows his objectives. The skipper, as leader of the crew, must be as knowledgeable in all areas as each crew member is in his particular job. Generally, the more experienced the crew in working together, the quieter and more efficient the boat will be. You will find it a pure delight when an emergency situation occurs and everything happens properly and hardly a frustrated word is spoken. Practice will give you the ability to act fast so you can seize any opportunity which will put you ahead. This is what wins the race. Good luck!

Part One

THE SCIENCE OF SAILS:
Technical Background

Chapter 1

If You Could
See the Wind . . .

If you could see the wind and how it envelops your boat with complex patterns of air flows and eddies, you would have a better understanding of just about everything that follows in this book. But wind is invisible. You *can* see the physical effects of wind on a sail, but that is all. You *cannot* see what a sail does to the wind and the environment around your boat. However, since wind is a fluid, it behaves much like water, which indeed is visible and photographable. Consequently, the closest approximation to seeing the wind is seeing the water and how "sails" affect it.

Eric Twiname at the Fluid Mechanics Laboratory at Imperial College in England set out to show just this; the result was this dramatic series of photographs (Figs. 1–6). The arrows indicating the direction of flow and the hull shape are superimposed on the photographs, which illustrate how "sails" made of curved rectangles of aluminum deflect a steady stream of water. A floating powder was scattered upstream on the surface of the water and then illuminated and photographed from above. The aluminum sails were coated with a liquid to minimize surface tension.

Although these tests broke no new ground in sail research, their value is that they illustrate clearly and accurately a good deal of what is known about the wind flow around sailing rigs. Whether you are an expert sailor or a beginner, these revealing photographs should help you see the wind and understand what it does to your sails, your boat, and the boats around you.

4   Sail Power

Fig. 1
This will help you visualize what the wind
does around your sails on a dead run. It
approaches the boat in parallel flow lines
which are split by the mainsail. The flow
lines attempt to resume parallel flow
forward of the mainsail. The pressure
build-up on the windward side of the sail
is clearly shown. Where flow lines are
compressed, there is a definite increase in
flow velocity.

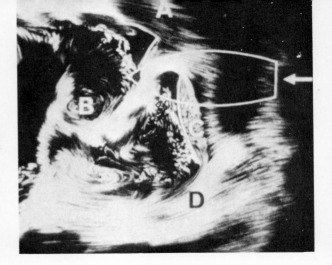

Fig. 2
With the wind abeam and sails properly
trimmed, flow lines build up as they are
deflected by the windward surface of the
mainsail; as they pass the leech, they tend
to resume their normal flow direction.
There is relatively smooth flow on the
leeward sides of the sails and few eddies.

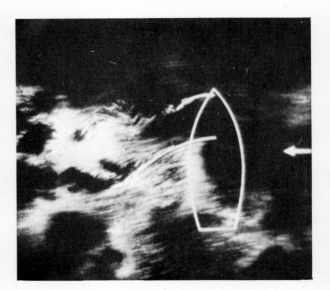

Fig. 3
What happens when you have the wind
abeam and remove the jib? Without the
slot effect, the smooth flow on the leeward
side of the mainsail is broken up by large
eddies, which stall out the sail. This
interruption of flow reduces the
aerodynamic forces acting on the sail and
decreases its driving power.

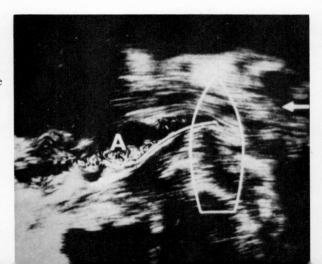

Fig. 4
When you overtrim the mainsail in a beam wind, eddies destroy most of the flow on its leeward surface, and the whole sail is virtually stalled. There is less disturbance on the lee side of the jib, which is not overtrimmed. However, by overtrimming the main, you might prevent a competitor from passing you to leeward, where there is a "hole" in the wind. Compare this area with Figure 2.

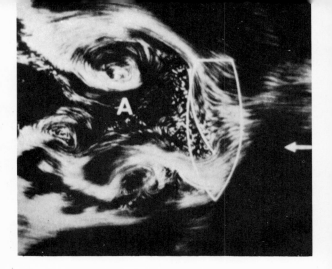

Fig. 5
Going to windward, there is smooth air flow on the leeward side of the mainsail and jib. Notice the "bad" air or disturbed flow, which would affect a boat overtaking to leeward. Also, there is a definite deflection of air flow off the windward quarter, which would give a competitor there a continual header.

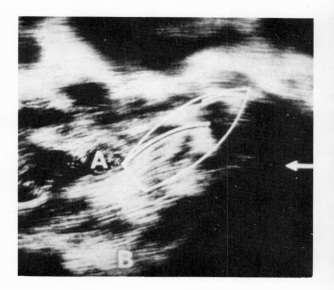

Fig. 6
Going to windward with the jib removed creates a situation comparable to that in Figure 3. Disturbed air near the leech disrupts the air flow on the leeward side of the main and reduces the efficiency of the sail. This illustrates the value of the slot, which helps increase air flow on the lee surface of the main. It is interesting to note that the wind is bending even before it reaches the sail.

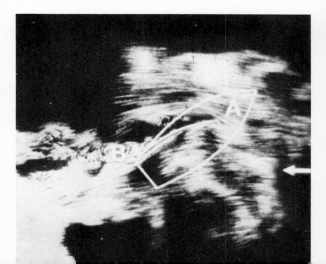

Chapter 2

How Sails Work

There is only one thing better than just plain sailing, and that is the satisfaction you get from knowing you are driving your boat as fast as she will go under existing conditions of wind and sea. But you cannot reach this level of expertise unless you understand how the interaction of wind and sails imparts motion to your boat.

The first thing to learn is what makes a boat go to windward. Once you have understood this, it is easier to assess what happens when you are reaching and running. To start with, think in terms of only one sail. (Two or more sails create local wind-flow conditions that interact with each other. These will be explained once you understand basic aerodynamic concepts.)

A boat is moved ahead in a windward direction by a total force acting on the sail. This total force is a combination of negative surface force (or suction force) on the lee side of a sail and positive surface pressure (or pushing force) on the windward side of the sail (Fig. 7). Both act on the sail in the same direction, and contrary to what some people think, it is the negative force on the leeward side that does the biggest job.

Since this is the most important force, let us see first how it is developed. Negative pressure results from an increase in the velocity of air flow over the lee side of the sail. Such an increase in air-flow velocity in

Fig. 7

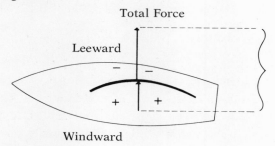

relation to the velocity of the surrounding free air steam causes a decrease in pressure within the faster-flowing air—a phenomenon discovered in 1738 by Daniel Bernoulli (Fig. 8).

Fig. 8

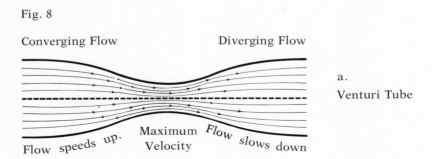

Converging Flow　　　　　　Diverging Flow

a.
Venturi Tube

Flow speeds up.　Maximum Flow slows down
Velocity

b.
Leeward Side of Sail

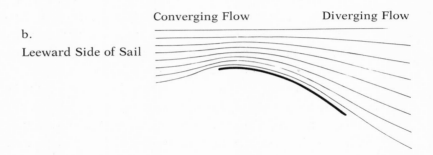

Converging Flow　　　　　　Diverging Flow

Among the many attempts to explain why the velocity of air flow increases on the convex or lee side of the sail have been those which equate a sail with an airplane wing. This widespread theory holds that the air has to travel faster over the greater length of the wing's curved upper surface in order to rejoin the air on the underside of the wing, thus causing increased velocity of flow over the upper surface. This is not a valid explanation for either the sail or the wing. It conveniently ignores the fact that some wings are symmetrical; although the air has the same distance to travel both on top of and underneath the wing, the velocity of flow over the upper surface is faster than that over the underside. Actually, when any wing is operating at peak efficiency, the air particles that split at the leading edge do not rejoin at the trailing edge; the particle traveling over the upper surface arrives at the trailing edge well before the particle on the underside of the wing. The same thing happens around a sail.

What is the real explanation of this phenomenon? First, you must understand certain facts about the behavior of air.

1. The free air stream normally flows in straight parallel lines, but the flow is attracted toward low-pressure areas and repelled by high-pressure areas.

2. Air at low speeds (under 126 m.p.h. at sea level) is considered incompressible.

3. Although it generally resists changing its parallel flow direction, an air stream *will* adhere to the convex side of a curved surface, providing the curve is not too divergent to the direction of the free stream. If the curvature becomes too deep, the air stream will rejoin the parallel flow.

4. Air speeds up as it flows through a restricted area, as G.B. Venturi discovered in experiments with constriction tubes.

Using these principles, here is why the velocity of flow increases on the convex or lee side of the sail or aerodynamic shape. The flow adheres around the outside of the curved shape and, in order to follow the curve, has to bend out toward the free air stream. But the free air stream has a small amount of inertia and tends to maintain its straight, parallel flow. This can be thought of as a kind of wall or barrier to the outward curving air. The combination of the bulge of the convex shape and the inertia of the free air stream creates a narrow channel through which the initial volume of air has to travel. But air is essentially incompressible and cannot compact. And so, in order to get the same volume to flow through this narrower space, it speeds up. This is the reason why the velocity of flow increases on the lee or convex side of a sail.

Once this happens, Bernoulli's theorem applies: an increase in air-flow velocity in relation to the surrounding free air stream causes a decrease in pressure where the faster air flow occurs. Thus a low-pressure field forms on the lee side of the sail. This low-pressure area is not only the source of the negative or suction power acting on the sail, it also sets up an important aerodynamic chain reaction which leads to the forming of even greater negative pressures. New air approaches the leading edge of the sail where it must split; when it does, more of this air mass is attracted to the newly formed low-pressure area on the lee side (Fig. 9). Thus, an even greater mass of air must travel faster to pass through the same gap. This results in greater decrease in pressure, which, in turn, attracts even more of the air mass. The chain reaction continues to build until the maximum flow velocity for the existing wind condition is reached, and a maximum low-pressure area is created on the lee side of the sail. This low-pressure area is the strongest aerodynamic force acting on the sail. It is important to understand that the flow is speeded up only until it reaches the deepest point of the curved shape. Up to this point there is converging flow and increasing velocity. Beyond the deepest point of the curve, there is diverging flow and the velocity slows down until it is again the same as the free air stream.

Fig. 9
Progressive Building of Flow Patterns

1. The flow begins.

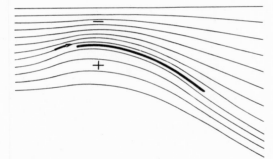

2. The flow builds in strength.

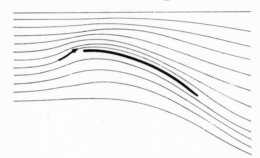

Once the flow pattern begins, a greater percentage of the approaching air mass is attracted to the negative pressure area and repelled by the barrier effect caused by the positive pressure on the windward side. Thus, the point at which the air mass splits in front of the sail changes location until, when maximum flow is developed, it is a good bit farther to windward than when the flow pattern began.

3. The flow reaches its maximum.

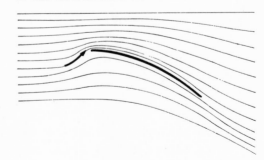

On the windward side of the sail, just the opposite is happening. As more volume flows over the lee side, there is less of the air mass remaining on the windward side to flow through the expanded space between the concave side of the sail and the free air stream. Thus, the velocity of the air flow slows down, and since it is traveling at a lower speed than the free air stream, it creates a positive pressure area on the windward side of the sail. This action can be compared to the flow outside the constricted area of the Venturi tube (Fig. 10).

Fig. 10

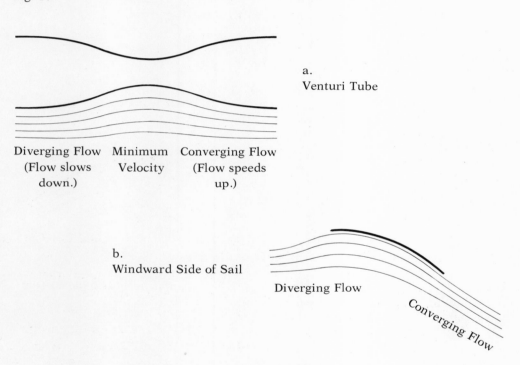

a.
Venturi Tube

Diverging Flow   Minimum   Converging Flow
(Flow slows   Velocity   (Flow speeds
down.)   up.)

b.
Windward Side of Sail

Diverging Flow

Converging Flow

To put it simply, on one side of the sail you have more air going through a narrower opening, increasing in velocity, and decreasing in pressure, while on the other side you have less air going through a wider gap, resulting in a decrease in velocity and an increase in pressure. The end result is a strong negative pressure or suction force on the lee side of the sail and moderate positive pressure on the windward side, both acting on the sail in the same direction (Fig. 11).

Fig. 11

Leeward side=negative pressure
Air is squeezed.
Velocity increases, pressure decreases.

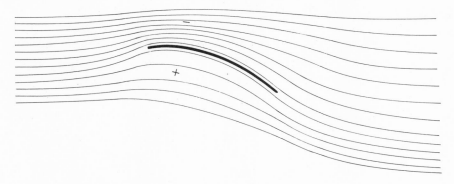

Windward side =positive pressure
Air spreads out.
Velocity decreases, pressure increases.

You now have a theoretical total force that consists of the combination of aerodynamic forces on both sides of the sail. But how, in practice, do you develop these forces? Basically, what you must do is establish a relationship between the sail shape and the wind (angle of attack) that allows the wind flow to both speed up and adhere to the convex curve of the sail most easily, thus developing maximum aerodynamic forces.

To achieve this, your sail must first of all have a curved shape. This is built in by the sailmaker, but it takes a certain amount of wind for the curvature to fill out. The sail must also be pointed at a certain angle to the wind. As you can see in Figure 12a, if the sail is pointed directly into the wind stream, the wind splits evenly on either side, there is no curvature, and no differential in pressure is obtained. The sail will flap like a flag in the breeze. However, the moment you angle the sail to the wind to just the right degree, two things happen: one, the sail fills away, taking its curved shape; and two, you get the natural phenomenon of the wind flow attaching to the lee side, clinging to the curved surface, and speeding up. This point is the critical angle of attack, and it is very precise. Beyond two or three degrees of the optimum angle, the aerodynamic forces deteriorate rapidly; if the sail is pointed too close into the wind, it will start to flag (luff); if it is at too wide an angle to the wind, the flow lines detach from the lee side of the sail (separation), and a stall zone consisting of haphazard eddies develops, reducing the aerodynamic forces. As the flow that develops the increase in velocity is interrupted in the separated area, velocity drops and the pressure begins to return to that of the free air stream; the low-pressure build-up is destroyed. Separation starts at the leech; this is because a sail's curvature will always cause the aft end of the sail to be at a greater angle to the wind than the leading edge. As the sail's angle of attack to the wind widens, the point of separation moves forward, leaving everything behind a stall zone.

Fig. 12
Sail at Different Angles of Attack

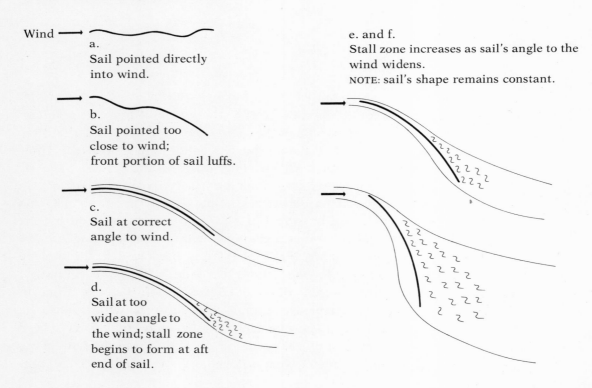

Wind

a.
Sail pointed directly
into wind.

b.
Sail pointed too
close to wind;
front portion of sail luffs.

c.
Sail at correct
angle to wind.

d.
Sail at too
wide an angle to
the wind; stall zone
begins to form at aft
end of sail.

e. and f.
Stall zone increases as sail's angle to the
wind widens.
NOTE: sail's shape remains constant.

Not only must the leading edge of the sail be angled properly—to allow the air flow to pass smoothly onto the sail—but the flow must remain attached all along the sail. Thus, the sail must have the right amount of curvature all the way aft. If the curvature is too slight, the air flow will not bend out, and therefore you will not get the squeezing effect that causes the increase in velocity of flow (Fig. 13a). On the other hand, if the curve is too deep, the flow will not remain attached: an air flow will adhere to a curved surface only if the curved surface is not too divergent from the direction of the normal air flow (Fig. 13b). Thus, separation will also occur if the sail is too full. It's very important, therefore, not to have too little or too much curvature in the sail. Figure 12c shows the right amount of fullness as well as the correct angle of attack. How you manage this is discussed in detail in Chapter 5, Draft Control.

Fig. 13
How the Wind Flow Is Affected by the Sail

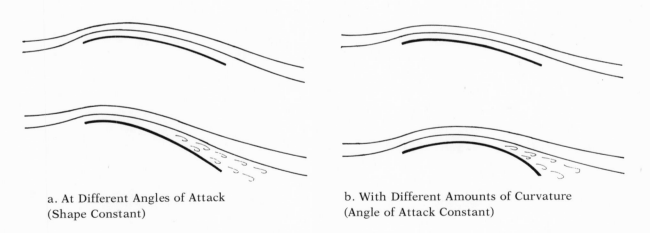

a. At Different Angles of Attack
(Shape Constant)

b. With Different Amounts of Curvature
(Angle of Attack Constant)

Do not confuse the words "separation" and "turbulence." (See Fig. 14.) The attached flow on the lee side of a sail can be either laminar (smooth) or turbulent (non-smooth), or a combination of both; sometimes, turbulent flow is purposely induced as it will adhere to an irregular surface better than laminar flow. In either case, whether the flow is smooth or turbulent, if it remains attached, the highest aerodynamic forces can be developed and this is exactly what you're aiming for in any windward sailing. Therefore, the sail must be angled to just the right degree—no more and no less, and the sail must not be too full or too flat.

Fig. 14
Types of Flow

Attached flow on the lee side can be either laminar (smooth) or turbulent (non-smooth).
Both produce effective forces; in fact, the turbulent flow is sometimes more desirable, as it will adhere to a rougher surface.

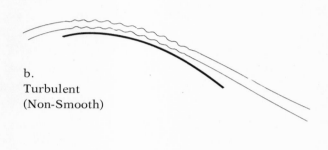

b.
Turbulent
(Non-Smooth)

a.
Laminar
(Smooth)

SAIL-FORCE STRENGTH

Now we have seen how the pressures on the sail are developed theoretically and practically. But how do these pressures work on the sail, how strong are they, and how are they translated into forward motion of the boat?

In the first place, air pressures are real and measurable. Take the low-pressure area, for example. At sea level there is a constant pressure of 14.7 pounds per square inch or 2,116 pounds per square foot. If the faster flow on the lee side of the sail drops the pressure to 2,112 pounds per square foot, you have an average negative force of 4 pounds per square foot acting on your sail. If your sail area is 500 square feet, you have a force of 2,000 pounds on the lee side, "pulling" or "sucking" the boat forward. As we have seen, this suction force is the major component of the total force acting on the sail.

There is also a positive force on the windward side of the sail. Assume that this averages 2 pounds per square foot. Add this to the 4 pounds per square foot of negative pressure on the leeward side. Regardless of the positive and negative signs, both forces are working in the same direction. There is an average force of 6 pounds per square foot or a total force of 3,000 pounds working on the entire sail (Fig. 15).

Fig. 15

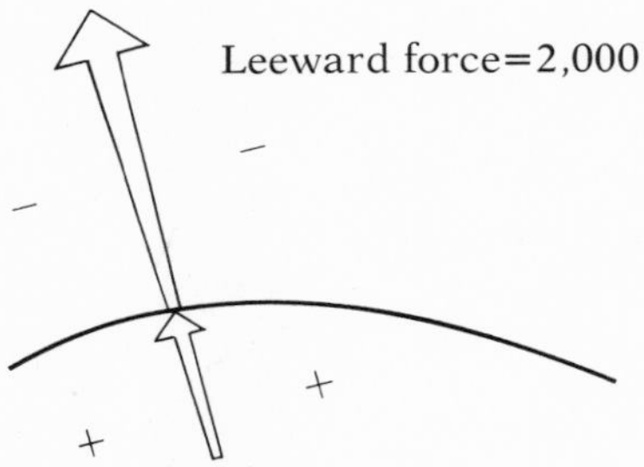

Total force=3,000 lbs.

Leeward force=2,000 lbs.

Windward force=1,000 lbs.

Fig. 16
Local Sail Forces at One Level of the Sail
from Fore to Aft

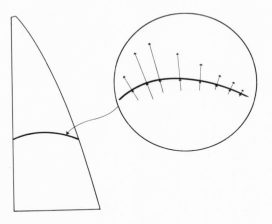

These are only average figures because, in actuality, the pressures are different at each point on the sail. Remember that the lee flow increases in velocity as it approaches the deepest point of the curve—with a corresponding increase in force; after the deepest point, the velocity of flow slows down until, at the trailing edge, it is near the speed of·the free air stream. The forces here are negligible. Figure 16 shows the varying strengths of the individual forces on the sail at one level from fore to aft. But that's not all: you also get different pressures at different heights on the sail, since the velocity of flow increases with height above water—as the air is less and less affected by the surface friction of the water. This is called the *wind velocity gradient*. Also, the fullness of the sail can vary at different heights and this too varies the pressure.

These individual pressures on each unit of sail area not only have strength, but, as you can see, each has direction as well: at every point in the sail, the force is perpendicular to the sail's surface.

The very strong forces in the forward third of the sail are also in the most forward direction. As you move back toward the middle of the sail, the forces grow weaker and they are not in as forward a direction; they contain a larger heeling component. As you move even farther aft, the heeling or sideward forces become more predominant. You may even get backward or drag forces because of the sail's adverse angle in this area. However, the forces are minimal at this point.

Of course, the directions of force (forward drive, heel, and drag) are only meaningful when you relate them to the boat. And then, the directions are modified by the angle at which the sail is trimmed in relation to the centerline of the boat. If you trim the sail outboard, all the forces will be in a more forward direction than if you trim the sail to the centerline (Fig. 17).

Fig. 17

The direction of the forces on the sail changes with changes in sail trim.

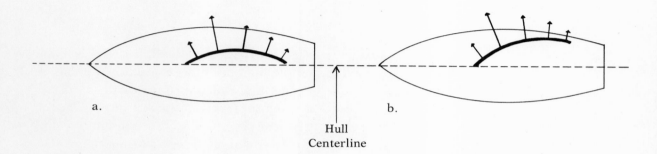

a.

b.

Hull
Centerline

Finding the Components of Force

Each force on the sail can be broken down and diagrammed into its component parts to show how much forward drive, heel, or drag it contains. First, one draws a vector representing the strength of the pressure force over the unit of sail area (Aerodynamicists use vectors as illustrative simplifications. Vector lengths are arbitrary but proportionate.) (1)

Then, from the point on the sail where the vector originates, a line is drawn perpendicular to the centerline. This line will represent heel (2).

Fig. 18

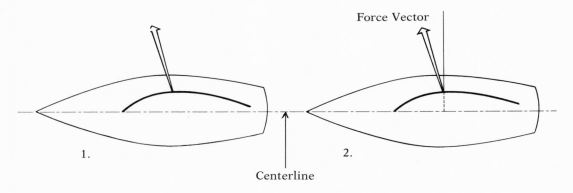

To find out how long the heel line should be, draw a line parallel to the centerline from the tip of the force vector, to the perpendicular; where they intersect, the heel line ends (3).

To find the amount of forward drive, a line is drawn parallel to the centerline and passing through the point on the sail where the vector originates (4).

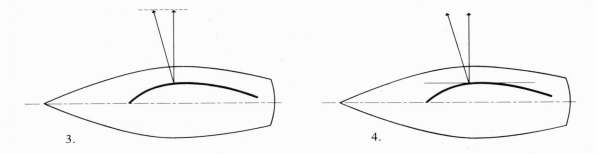

To find its length, a perpendicular line is drawn from the centerline to the tip of the vector; the drive vector ends where the perpendicular intersects the parallel line (5).

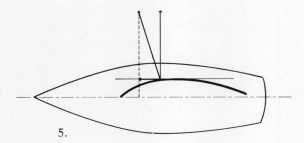

5.

Finally, one cleans up the drawing so that only the three vectors are left, representing the forward drive component, heel component, and total force. (If the force vector goes aft, one simply reverses this procedure. The same procedure is also applied to the forces on the windward side of the sail.) (6,7)

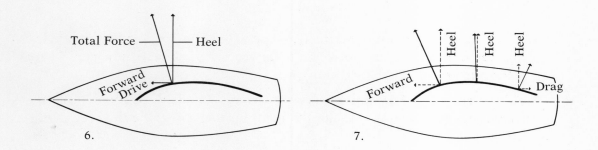

Total Force —— —— Heel

Forward Drive

6.

Heel Heel Heel

Forward   Drag

7.

By analyzing the sail forces from fore to aft in this way, you can get a very good idea in what direction the different forces act and what relative strength they have. You can see, for example, that the most efficient part of the sail is the forward portion. That is why it is important not to let your sail luff even slightly, unless, of course, you are overpowered in heavy air and need to carry a luff to keep the boat on its feet.

Total Sail Force

Given all these different forces acting on different parts of the sail in different directions, how do you find the strength and direction of the *total* force? Obviously, the strength of the total force will be the sum of the strengths of all the individual forces on both sides of the sail that act in the same direction (whether windward or leeward, all forces are perpendicular to the sail's surface). But the direction of the total force has to be calculated by weighting the direction of the individual forces according to the strength of each. Since the forward forces are also the strongest forces, they will predominate. Therefore, the total force will have a slightly forward direction, unlike the individual force that is perpendicular to the sail's surface. The total force can be diagrammed into its component parts in the same way the individual forces were plotted. For the sake of clarity and simplification, wherever possible from now on individual forces will not be drawn; instead, the total force vector will be used to indicate sail force (Fig. 19).

As you can see, most of the force acting on the sail is in a sideward direction when going to windward. The sideward component will usually be many times greater than the forward component. As a result, when you increase the power of the sail to get more forward driving force, you also

Fig. 19
The total-force vector represents the total
of windward and leeward vectors.

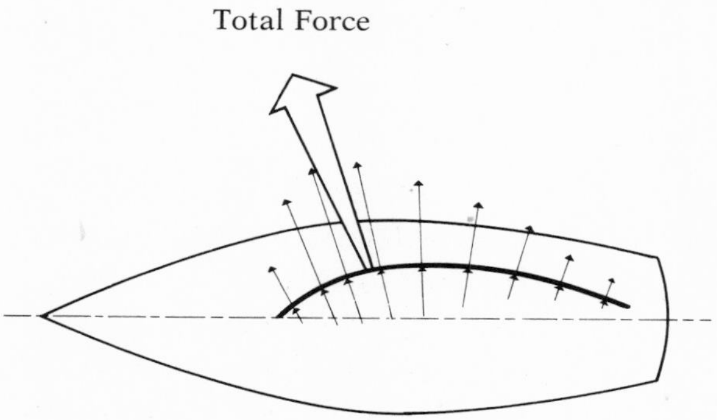

Total Force

get a great deal more heeling force. (See Fig. 20.) Crew weight and hull stability are the major counterbalances to this, and set the limit to how powerful a sail you can carry. Obviously, this limit doesn't apply to light air, where you're not in danger of being overpowered, which is why, over the years, fuller sails in light air and flatter sails in heavy air have become standard.

Fig. 20

Medium Sail   Fuller Sail

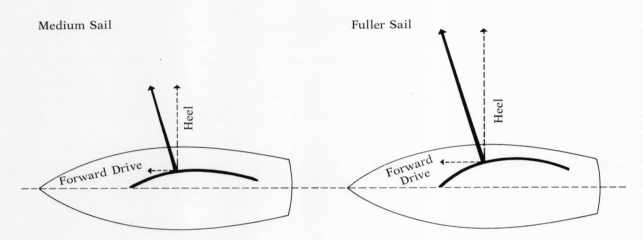

How Sail Force Moves the Boat

Now we have a total force acting on the sail in a general direction. How is this force on the sail translated into forward movement of the hull?

First, the direction of the total force will be almost directly perpendicular to the sail's axis or chord—the imaginary line drawn from luff to leech at any one height. Now, if, as in Figure 21a, the chord of the sail is directly parallel to the centerline of the hull, you can see that the main force is almost completely to the side. The lateral plane of the boat (its hull and centerboard or keel) will resist these sideward forces, but the steady perpendicular thrust pushes the boat slowly sideward. The boat "crabs" slowly to leeward as the keel or centerboard resists the side thrust of the sail.

If you angle the sail just a little so that the sail force is in a slightly more forward direction, the boat will immediately move forward (Fig. 21b). The reason behind this rather puzzling phenomenon is simple: the lateral plane resists sideward movement to such a degree that forward movement is the course of least resistance. You can see this happen quite commonly in everyday life: take a mop. If you push straight down on the handle, the mop won't go anywhere. The moment you angle the handle even slightly, the mop slides across the floor easily. (The mop can give you another graphic example of a sailing principle: the more slippery the mop, the faster it moves. The same applies to a boat's hull—if it is encrusted with barnacles, for example, it is a lot harder to move than a sleek, slippery hull would be.)

This explains how a boat, with most of the force to the side when

Fig. 21

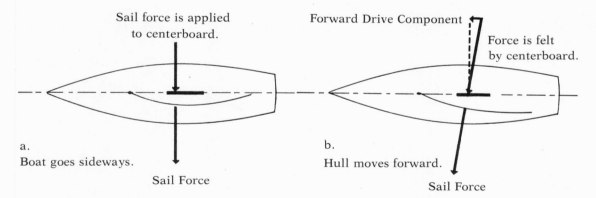

Sail force is applied to centerboard.

Forward Drive Component

Force is felt by centerboard.

a.
Boat goes sideways.

Sail Force

b.
Hull moves forward.

Sail Force

the sail is close-hauled, moves to windward. As you go farther and farther off the wind—and the sail is angled more and more out from the centerline —more of the force is in a forward direction, and there is less and less side or heeling force, until, when you are heading dead downwind, all the force is in a forward direction—that is, in the same direction as the hull is moving. This would seem to be the most efficient and, therefore, the fastest point of sailing—all the forces are pushing you in the direction in which you want to go. However, like almost everything else in the theoretical part of sailing, things are not that simple. In fact, in average wind conditions, you may go faster to windward than downwind. One reason is that in going to windward, the total force on the sail is developed from aerodynamic flow and is very much stronger than the force resulting from the simple drag of the sail to the wind on a run. Another reason is the difference in *apparent-wind* velocity. This is the wind the sails "feel," which is indicated by the telltales. It is a combination of the true-wind velocity and boat speed. When you are heading into the wind, boat speed is added to the true-wind speed, resulting in a greater velocity of flow over the sail, thus producing greater forces. However, downwind, the fact that the boat is moving in the same direction as the wind decreases the apparent-wind velocity over the sail. Boat speed is subtracted from the true-wind velocity; the velocity of the apparent wind operating on the sail is less than the true-wind speed, and the already weaker total force is weakened even further. (See Fig. 27 for a detailed explanation of apparent wind.)

Thus, going to windward, the stronger sail force at a poorer angle produces more forward drive than sailing off the wind with the weaker force at a more favorable angle (Fig. 22).

Fig. 22

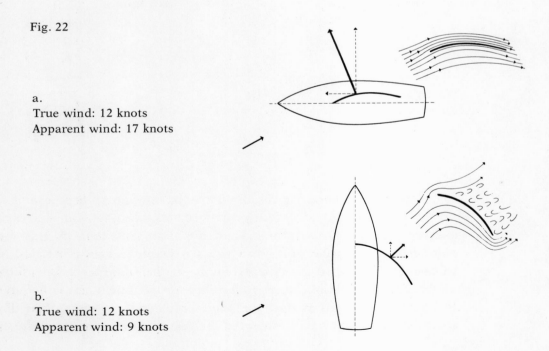

a.
True wind: 12 knots
Apparent wind: 17 knots

b.
True wind: 12 knots
Apparent wind: 9 knots

Fig. 23
As the boat rotates under the sail onto a reaching angle, the forces are less to the side and gradually more forward—which is the favorable direction. In addition, as the reaching angle widens, leeward suction decreases and windward pressure increases.

True wind: 12 knots

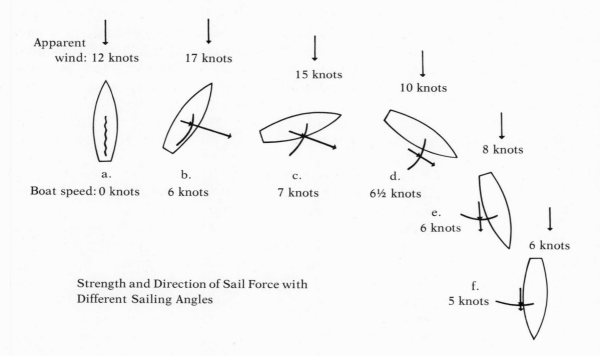

Strength and Direction of Sail Force with Different Sailing Angles

Examine Figure 23 to see what happens as you head off the wind: as the boat goes from a windward point of sailing to a close reach, the sail remains trimmed to approximately the same angle of attack to the apparent wind as when going to windward. In other words, the sail remains in basically the same position in relation to the wind, but the hull rotates underneath it. Most of the driving power is still developed by aerodynamic forces on the lee side of the sail, where attached flow is maintained. However, as you go farther off the wind to keep the proper angle of attack, the sail has to be angled more and more to the centerline until, on a broad reach with the wind coming from well aft, it is no longer possible; the shrouds prevent the sail from going any farther. Thus, you can no longer achieve the proper angle of attack, and the flow on the lee side begins to break down. Finally, on a run with the wind directly astern, the force is almost entirely derived from the weaker pressure on the windward side; the sail simply blocks the air. Because the negative force on the lee side is so much stronger, it is important that as you head off the wind you make every effort to keep lee flow attached as long as possible (see Chapter 6, Sail Trim).

Thus, in Figure 23, you can see that the fastest point of sailing is generally a beam reach (Fig. 23c) because the sail still maintains good aerodynamic flow, the force is at a more favorable angle, and the apparent wind is still strong, therefore developing strong forces on the sail.

INTERACTION OF SAILS

So far, the explanation of how sails work has been confined to one sail. Now we will see what happens when a jib or genoa is added to the rig.

We have already shown that air flow speeds up in a constricted area. Look back at Figure 8b, where the convex curve on the lee side of the sail creates a narrow channel between the sail and the free air stream, thus causing the air mass to accelerate. This produces a decrease in pressure, which is the major force in moving the boat to windward.

When you add a genoa that overlaps the lee side of the mainsail, the most widely accepted theory has been that you introduce an even stronger leeward side barrier than the free air stream; there is more squeezing of the air between the after portion of the genoa and the convex, lee surface of the mainsail, and the result is a greater decrease of pressure. This constricted area is known as the "slot" and the phenomenon is described as the "slot effect."

If the main and genoa are too close, the main will luff or become backwinded (Fig. 24b), reducing its drive. If these sails are too far apart, there is no constriction, and the air flow does not attain the maximum increase in flow velocity (Fig. 24c). However, when the main and genoa are properly trimmed, the slot operates effectively (Fig. 24a), and air flow

Fig. 24

b.
Slot Too Closed—Too Much Squeezing

c.
Slot Too Open—Not Enough Squeezing

a.
Correct Slot—Just Enough Squeezing

Fig. 25

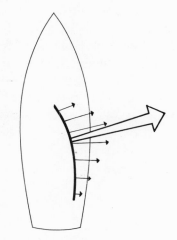

a.
Without Headsail

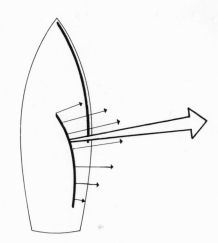

b.
With Headsail

from the windward side of the genoa adds even more speed to the flow on the lee side of the main, thus altering the forces developed by the mainsail. Comparing Figures 25a and 25b, you will see that the changes in flow velocity in the area of the overlap cause the forces on the forward part of the main to change in strength and direction.

On small boats with working jibs, there is no overlap at all, but the jib redirects the air flow toward the mainsail in the same way, although to a lesser extent. This also increases the flow velocity over the lee side of the main and augments the forces. The photographs in Chapter 1 show this quite graphically.*

In addition to increasing the forces developed by the mainsail, the jib and genoa obviously create driving forces of their own. In fact, the genoa, which can be trimmed more outboard near the rail of the boat, provides a force with more forward direction than the main. The forces acting on the genoa and the forces acting on the main are combined into one total force acting on the boat's centerboard or keel to produce forward motion.

By now you should have a basic understanding of the theory behind your sails and how sail force is developed, how it is translated into forward movement, what happens on different points of sailing, and, in a general way, how sail shape and trim affect your boat speed. Virtually all the remaining chapters will be devoted to showing you how to put this theory into practice and how to use it to get the most out of your boat and sails. The first step toward this goal is having the right sails for your boat and for your particular needs, and so we will begin with a discussion of sail design.

*See Figure 148 for the latest explanations of aerodynamicists concerning the slot effect.

Chapter 3

Sail Design

The overall linear dimensions of a boat's sails, as well as the number and kind of sails a boat will have, are established by the naval architect who designs the boat. This is true of a one-design racing boat as well as an individually designed cruising boat, although in the case of a one design, these specifications are generally modified and controlled by class rules. On cruising boats the naval architect has much more leeway and decides how big a mainsail and headsail you need, and whether the boat will be sloop-rigged or set up as a yawl or ketch. In order to decide this, he takes into consideration a number of factors, such as the kind of sailing you want to do—whether you are interested in long-distance racing or just comfortable cruising, in sailing alone or with a good-sized crew. On a custom boat, he will consider the prevailing winds in your waters and adjust sail area accordingly: for instance, when reaching is a more common point of sailing, the sail area will depend heavily on reaching sails and spinnakers.

In determining the height of the sail plan, the naval architect will be influenced by the wind and sea conditions in which the boat is normally sailed. If you sail in an area with predominantly light air, the architect will design a rig that will get more sail area up higher. This is because the wind velocity gradient (or increase in velocity of wind aloft) is much more pronounced in light air. Therefore, there is an advantage under these conditions to getting the sails up higher so that you will have more area in the stronger velocity of flow. Conversely, in heavier air, the higher rig will work against you, since it moves the center of effort up (the calculated point where the total sail force is exerted; see Chapter 7 for a detailed discussion). This increases the heeling moment and makes the boat tender. A taller mast can also add a good deal of weight up high, lowering the stability and increasing pitching movement in heavier seas.

The essential consideration in determining a sail plan is *the amount of sail needed to move the boat efficiently to windward in the average amount of wind and sea the boat is to be sailed.* The reason the naval architect is primarily concerned with going to windward is that the windward sails set the fixed rig in the boat—the mast, the boom, the headstay and shrouds—which is difficult to change. For offwind sailing, the headsails and spinnakers, if used, can be increased in size to fit your particular needs without changing the fixed rigging.

In order to move the boat efficiently to windward, the naval architect has to carefully consider the total sail force versus the resistance of the hull: the sail force cannot be so great as to overwhelm the boat, nor can it be so little that the hull will not move through the water at or close to designed speed.

First of all, remember that the forces on the sail going to windward are in both a forward and a sideward direction and that the most predominant component by far is to the side. Thus, in order to increase the forward force, you automatically have to increase the side force—and in a proportionately much greater amount. The result of this fact of life is that a sail that generates too much force will first overwhelm the stability of the hull, making the boat heel excessively and gradually slide sideways. At the same time, the angle of heel will reduce even further the amount of lateral plane resisting the side force, and a vicious circle is set up, one effect enhancing and magnifying the other. The result is a boat that will have excessive leeway and decreased boat speed. Thus, the forward or drive force is limited by the amount of side force the boat can handle or, in other words, how much heel from the side force the boat can resist.

The naval architect (and later the sail designer) has to try to get the most forward force he can, while not exceeding the side force that the boat can handle. Usually the naval architect can calculate this on the basis of experience with other boats; he knows generally what total force is needed to move one of his designs through the water, what force will overwhelm the boat, and what sail area is required to produce this total force in a given amount of wind.

He then plots a sail plan and presents the sailmaker with the specifications: what sails there are to be, and the height and linear dimensions of each (including the amount of genoa overlap, if any).

The sailmaker then must take this flat sail plan and give it three-dimensional shape by designing the depth and curvature of each sail. In other words, his main concern is *draft*. And, since this is the source of sail power going to windward, he must create enough draft to generate the force needed to move the boat to windward as per the naval architect's calculations. Theoretically, then, the sail power generated by draft should match the total-force figure calculated by the naval architect. Practically speaking, however, since there is no way to measure these forces precisely — either on the sail or on the boat — the sailmaker must also take into account the same factors that the naval architect has considered when laying out the sail plan. He must keep in mind the stability of the hull, and what the boat will primarily be used for and in what kind of seas, among many other things. All these factors will remain in the back of his mind, influencing his decisions as he goes along.

Given all the information he needs, the sailmaker sets out to make the best sail shape he can for windward work: one that will generate the greatest allowable drive force for that particular boat, with the lowest cost in terms of heeling or drag. This sail will have the fullest draft possible (to maintain adequate speed) while still allowing the boat to point to windward as high as it can (allowing the boat to cover the shortest practical distance in the least possible time when tacking to windward).

The first real limit on sail fullness is the pointing ability of the boat, which, for the sailmaker, is measured in terms of the *pointing angle* (Fig. 26). This is the angle between the centerline of the hull and the apparent-wind direction and is entirely dependent on boat speed. The apparent wind, the wind the sail "feels," is indicated by shroud telltales or the masthead

Fig. 26

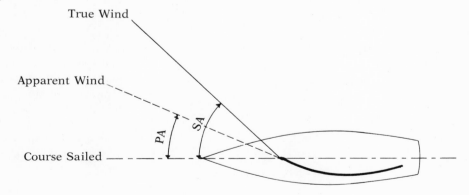

Pointing angle (apparent-wind angle)=PA
Sailing angle (true-wind angle)=SA

fly; it is the wind direction that results from the combination of the true wind and the wind the boat creates by itself as it moves at a certain speed through the water. The *sailing angle,* in contrast, is the angle between the centerline and the true wind.

You can see how apparent wind is developed quite clearly on a windless day: the flag on a motorboat at anchor will droop listlessly, but once the boat starts up, the flag will fly straight back in the breeze—the breeze created by the boat moving through the air. If a wind suddenly comes up, blowing across the boat at a 45-degree angle, the flag would be affected by both breezes and would fly in a direction somewhere in between the two. The faster the boat goes in relation to the true wind, the more it is making its own wind and the more the wind that passes over the boat will come from the direction of the bow (Fig. 27c). Conversely, the stronger the true wind in relation to the boat speed, the more the apparent wind will approach the true-wind direction (Fig. 27d). Thus, the direction of the apparent wind depends on how fast the boat is moving in relation to the velocity of the true wind, and the boat speed, in turn, depends on the design characteristics of the boat.

Fig. 27
Apparent Wind.   Apparent-wind direction and strength can be obtained by drawing one line parallel with the boat's centerline, whose length will represent boat speed (S), and another line, whose length and direction represent the true wind (W). Complete the parallelogram by drawing equal and parallel sides (SL and WL). The direction and relative velocity of the apparent wind can then be found by connecting the opposite corners of the parallelogram.

31   Sail Design

a. Finding Apparent-Wind Direction and
Velocity

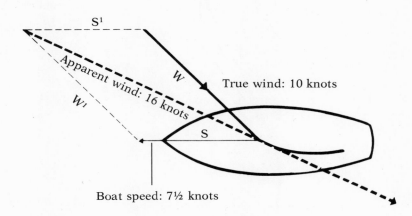

b. Changes in Apparent-Wind Velocity
with Changes in Sailing Angle

Close Reach

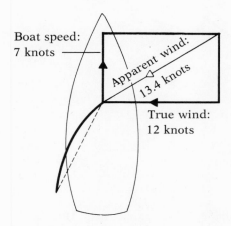

When the true wind is abeam, the
combination of boat speed and true-wind
velocity produces an apparent wind that
has a greater velocity than the true wind.

Downwind

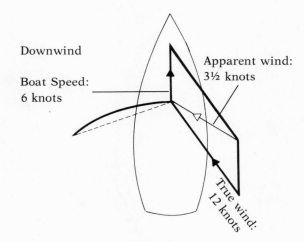

As the true wind moves aft, the wind the
boat "feels" is decreased by the speed of
the boat. Thus, the diagonal representing
the apparent-wind velocity is much
smaller. This decrease in apparent wind is
one reason why, under normal conditions,
boat speed decreases downwind unless a
good deal more sail area is added.

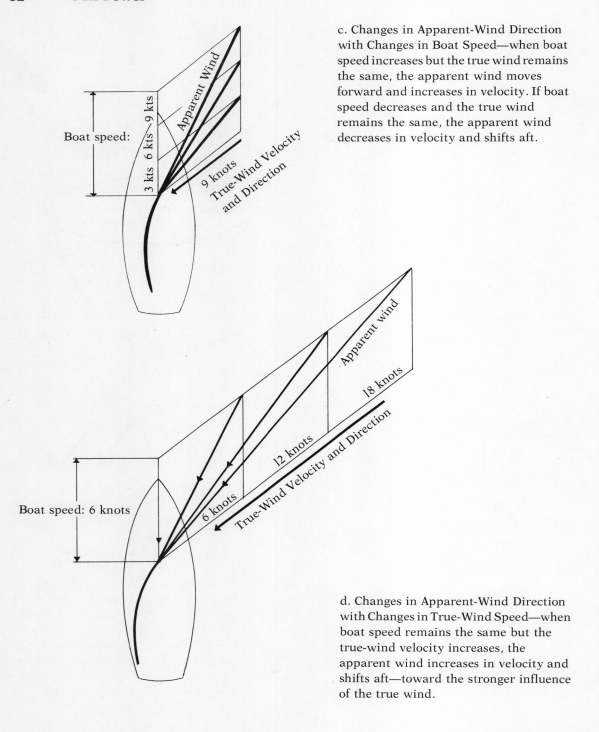

c. Changes in Apparent-Wind Direction with Changes in Boat Speed—when boat speed increases but the true wind remains the same, the apparent wind moves forward and increases in velocity. If boat speed decreases and the true wind remains the same, the apparent wind decreases in velocity and shifts aft.

d. Changes in Apparent-Wind Direction with Changes in True-Wind Speed—when boat speed remains the same but the true-wind velocity increases, the apparent wind increases in velocity and shifts aft—toward the stronger influence of the true wind.

The pointing angle, then, is different for different types of boats, and it will also change for each boat at different wind velocities and/or in different sea conditions. The naval architect can supply the boat speed figure for a certain velocity and sea condition on the basis of testing and experience, and with this figure in hand the sailmaker can plot the apparent-wind direction for that boat, but only for that particular velocity and sea condition. Clearly, sea conditions can have a great effect on boat speed; in many one-design classes it has become common practice to have a flat-water sail and a rough-water sail. On cruising boats, different genoas are used for different conditions because the genoa is easily changeable whereas the main is not. Furthermore, class and handicap rules in most cases make it illegal to change the main.

How does the pointing angle affect draft? The wider the pointing angle, or angle created by the apparent wind, the fuller the sail can be; conversely, the narrower the pointing angle, the flatter the sail has to be (Fig. 28). The reason is simple: at no point can the curvature of the sail exceed the line of the apparent wind as it comes over the boat. The wind will not allow the sail to bend outward beyond the direction of the apparent

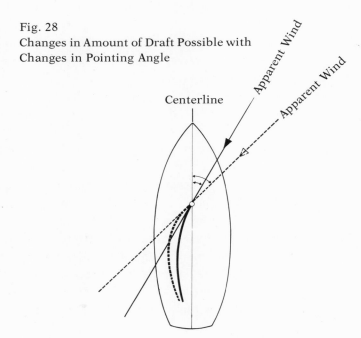

Fig. 28
Changes in Amount of Draft Possible with
Changes in Pointing Angle

wind; where the sail's curvature is too full, it will simply be blown down-stream like a flag until it reaches the point where the curvature is within the limit of the apparent-wind direction.

Thus, the apparent wind sets the outer limits to the fullness of the sail. But it also limits the curvature in other ways. The leading edge of the sail—that is, roughly the first 10 per cent of the sail—obviously cannot be outside the line of the apparent wind or it will luff, but neither can it be too far inside. If it is, it will be too divergent from the direction of the air stream, the air will not cling to the lee surface of the sail, and aerodynamic flow will not develop. These are the limits, and you have only a margin of a few degrees between them to gain greatest efficiency (Fig. 29). What this means, in effect, is that the leading edge has to be virtually parallel with the apparent wind and neither to one side nor the other. The need for the air to enter easily upon the sail also demands that the leading edge be virtually a flat plane for at least a short distance. Thereafter it has to have some curvature to build up forces, but the curvature cannot be too great or the flow will separate. Thus, the apparent wind directly affects the fullness and the flatness of the entire sail. This very real limit on the sail's shape cannot vary unless something is done to the hull configuration to increase its speed through the water, thus changing the apparent-wind direction.

The apparent-wind factor is one of the major reasons the sailmaker can build a sail only to one specific wind velocity and sea condition, although, through sail-handling techniques, the sailor can adjust the sail to work properly in a limited range on either side of this designed velocity. It is also the reason why flat sails do not work on some boats while they do on others. The boat that points close to the wind operates in a narrow angle of attack and requires a flatter sail. Conversely, the boat that does not point as well—i.e., has a wider apparent-wind angle—requires a fuller sail. So it is important that the sailmaker be given accurate information on the boat's characteristics as well as on the average wind and sea conditions for which he is to design the sail.

The apparent-wind direction, then, is a boundary line. But it is a boundary line that will be different all the way up the sail because of the wind gradient: the increase in wind velocity with height above water. The change in apparent-wind direction from the bottom of the mast to the top can be as much as 7 or 8 degrees and therefore must be calculated in the sailmaker's plans. Since the true-wind velocity increases aloft while boat

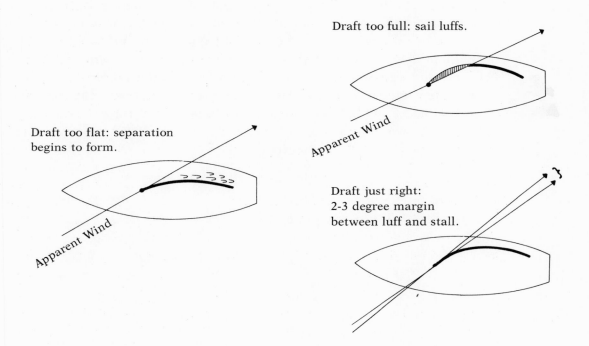

Fig. 29
How Angle of Apparent Wind Determines
Draft of Sail

Draft too full: sail luffs.

Draft too flat: separation
begins to form.

Draft just right:
2-3 degree margin
between luff and stall.

speed remains constant, the apparent wind will come more from the true-wind direction the higher up you go. Therefore, the angle will be wider and the sail can be a good bit fuller aloft than at deck level (Fig. 30). In addition, as the wind velocity changes, the wind-gradient values change: in light air, the velocity aloft will be proportionately stronger than that at deck level, and the sail aloft should be correspondingly fuller.

The wind-gradient factor is obviously an important element in sail design, but it is also the reason that wind-tunnel testing of sails has so far proved to be useful only for one sail section at one level at a time. There is no way as yet to reproduce the wind gradient to any reliable degree of accuracy in the small proportions of a test model in a wind tunnel. Until a way is found to do this, the only real test of a whole sail will be on the boat itself, under the conditions for which it was designed.

Another modification of the apparent-wind direction has to be taken into consideration: the change due to the interrelationship of the sails. The headsail is the leading sail, operating in what appears to be free air but is not. Each sail has a local air-flow system whose overall shape is created primarily by the wider local apparent-wind angle at the luff (uplift) and the more inboard local apparent-wind direction at the leech (downwash). These local air flows around the luff and leech affect the overall air-flow pattern immediately around the sail and to a lesser extent at a considerable distance both in front of and behind the sail. As a result, the genoa in front of the main can be operating in a flow altered by the mainsail, and the main can be operating in a flow altered by the genoa.

Fig. 30
Wind-Gradient Effect on Apparent Wind.
The arrows represent the increasing angle
of the apparent wind with height above
water. The corresponding increase in
draft or fullness is indicated by the curved
lines at each point. You can see this
increase in draft quite clearly in the jib of
Windigo (Fig. 31B).

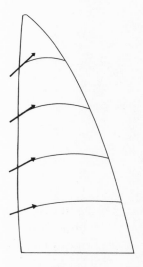

The amount that the mainsail's apparent wind is deflected depends on the type of headsail; a working jib will not cause as much as a genoa with a small overlap, which in turn will not cause as much as a genoa with maxi-·mum overlap. Since the mainsail affects the headsail—but in the opposite way—the amount that the apparent-wind-flow pattern is altered over the

Fig. 31A
Varying Apparent Winds on Successive
Sails

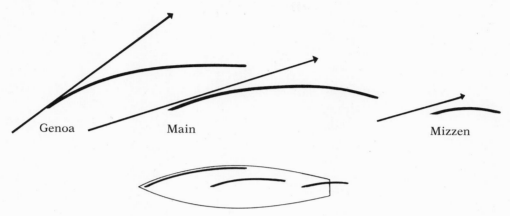

Genoa   Main   Mizzen

Fig. 31B
Windigo.   This aerial shot of the yawl
Windigo illustrates several key points—
1. *The apparent wind becomes more acute on each successive sail aft.*The genoa creates a narrower wind angle for the main and the main creates an even narrower wind angle for the mizzen. The main is flatter and trimmed in closer to the centerline than the genoa, and the mizzen is flatter and trimmed in closer than the main.
2. The wind-gradient factor is quite apparent—as the height above water increases, the true-wind velocity increases and the apparent-wind angle is wider. The leading planes of both the genoa and main are angled more and more toward the true-wind direction as height increases. This allows the sail to have more fullness aloft.
3. Leech twist or leech sag is also apparent in the main and genoa. As the leading sail, the genoa operates in the widest wind angle and has the most twist.

headsail depends on the type of mainsail; a small main will not cause as much of a deflection as a large one.

Generally the relative size and proximity of the sails determine how they affect one another. The amount that the apparent wind is deflected over the mainsail is also dependent on how far inboard or outboard the headsail is trimmed, and, conversely, the mainsail trim affects the headsail's apparent wind. The height of the headsail has a significant effect: if the genoa or jib goes only two-thirds of the way up the mast, the mainsail above that point will be operating in free air and will have a much wider effective apparent-wind angle. (See Fig. 43.) All this must be determined by the sailmaker before he can design the draft of any of the sails.

THE DESIGN PROCESS: The Headsail

The process of sail design normally starts with the headsail. To begin to work out the actual design on paper,* the sailmaker first draws in a line representing the luff of the headsail. This will not normally be a straight line: the pressures acting on the sail almost always cause the jibstay to sag somewhat, and the stronger the wind velocity, the more the sag. The sag is due to the tremendous pressures working on the sail going to windward, and the reason that it is unavoidable to a certain extent is that neither the hull nor the rigging of a boat will stand up to the enormous pressures that would have to be applied to the stay to counteract the force on the sail. Because jibstay sag has a negative effect on the shape of the sail, causing the entire sail section to move farther aft, it has to be taken into account by the sailmaker. (For a discussion in greater detail, see Chapter 5, Draft Control.) The amount of sag can be gauged for a boat in a particular wind velocity on the basis of the experience the sailmaker has had with other, similar boats and sails (Fig. 32).

Once the luff is established, he draws in the apparent-wind direction at various heights in the sail. And, since he knows that the leading edge of the sail has to be a plane almost parallel to the apparent wind, he can now

*The following description of how a sailmaker works is simplified for the sake of illustration. The basic considerations will always be the same, although the procedure may vary from sailmaker to sailmaker.

Fig. 32
Jibstay Sag. Although the backstay exerts countertension to reduce luff sag, it is nearly impossible to remove sag entirely.

Fig. 33
Apparent wind determines leading edge.

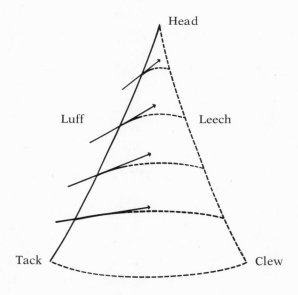

establish the leading edge or plane constituting the front portion of the sail (Fig. 33).

Next, the sailmaker works on the after plane of the sail. This is trickier for several reasons. First of all, the leech is unsupported and, because of the long distance from head to clew, if it is not stiffened in some way, it is probably going to flap or flutter or curl. If the sail doesn't overlap the mast or only has a slight overlap, as in a working jib, battens are used to support the leech. With considerable overlap, as in a genoa, battens can break when coming about and thus are not used. The alternative method is to scoop out the leech. In broad terms, the excess material that flutters is taken away, which results in a negative curve from head to clew. Under sheet tension, this negative curve tries to assume a straight line, and gives the leech the added stiffness or support it needs. This is one of the most difficult parts of the sail to get right and each sail designer has his own theory on how much negative curvature is needed in a sail (Fig. 34).

Fig. 34
Different Kinds of Leech Cut

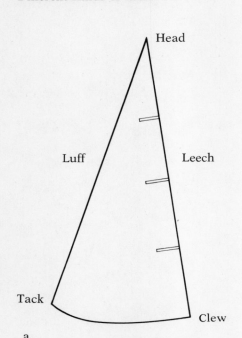

a.
Working Jib—the straight-line leech is supported by battens.

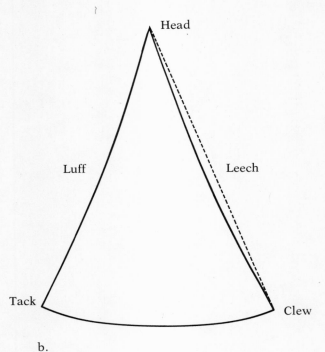

b.
Genoa Jib—negative curvature in the genoa leech helps to prevent fluttering or curling.

Once the linear leech shape is determined, the designer turns to a problem that involves the cross-sectional shaping of the sail. This complication is known as *leech twist*. In medium and heavier airs the tremendous pressures on the sail actually cause the leech to sag or fall off in more and more of a curve to leeward as it rises from deck level (Fig. 35). As with jib sag, this is also unavoidable to a certain extent; you can have a force of as much as 2,000 pounds on a medium-size genoa going to windward, and almost half this force is working on the after portion. Imagine a bolt of cloth strung between two tall posts 40 feet apart: simulate 1,000 pounds hanging from the cloth, and you will have an idea of what is happening to the leech of a sail going to windward. On the mainsail, the leech is, in effect, suspended between the masthead and boom end; on the genoa or jib, it is between the headstay (where the head of the sail is fastened) and the sheet lead on deck; and both sails are controlled by their respective sheets. The more the sheet is tightened, the straighter the leech will be from head to clew.

In heavier airs, there is no way to keep the free-standing leech from sagging or twisting somewhat. This distortion is predictable for a given wind velocity, and the sailmaker has to allow for it in his design. If the leech

Fig. 35
How Pressures on Sail Cause Leech Sag

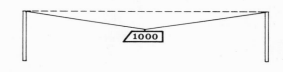

a.

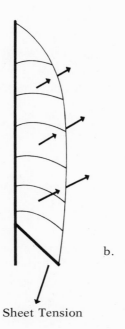

b.

Sheet Tension

c.
Photograph of Mainsail, Looking Up
Leech from Boom.   Twist is greatest
two-thirds of the way up.

twist is not considered in the design of the sail, it will be blown into the leech as soon as the sail is used in any kind of wind. Built-in leech twist is also important because it moves the leech of the sail more outboard—an effect that increases with the height of the sail—this compensates for an apparent-wind angle which is wider aloft. This is particularly important in light air, where the wind gradient is more pronounced. Thus, twist is designed into every sail, and once it is, it should not be trimmed out. It is important to remember this in light air, when it is easier to overtrim and remove the twist. The sailmaker should tell the boat owner what amount of twist is designed into the sail. The boat owner should maintain it, or the whole curvature of the sail will be changed, and the sail will be partially stalled out.

Once the sailmaker has plotted the leech twist at various points in the sail, he connects the points into a curved line from clew to head. Although the clew position can vary inboard or outboard, depending on the designer's choice, the amount of leech twist for a genoa or a working jib will remain approximately the same for a given wind condition (Fig. 36).

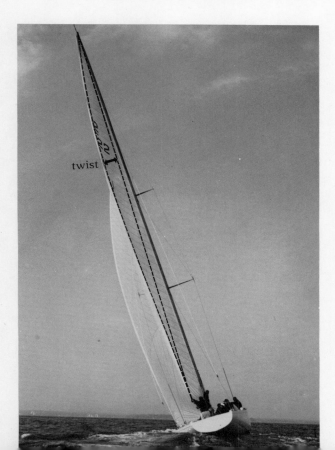

Fig. 36
Main and Jib Leech Twist.   In this photograph it is easy to see the twist in the genoa leech and to a lesser degree in the smaller main. The tremendous pressures on the sails are causing the free-standing leeches to fall off to leeward. This is more evident in the genoa because of its larger size. It is also more evident on a larger boat because the taller rig encounters a greater change in wind velocity (wind gradient).

Fig. 37
Angle between chord and line parallel to straight-line foot equals the amount of twist. After the amount of leech sag or twist is determined and drawn in, it is then related to the leading edge of the sail by the chord at each height.

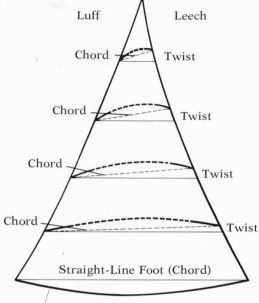

Foot roach is added to gain extra area.

The sailmaker's next step is to connect the leech with the front portion of the sail (Fig. 37). Since the linear dimensions of the sail have been given to him by the naval architect, the sailmaker knows the distance from luff to leech at every point; this distance, in the form of an imaginary horizontal line, is the chord. Chords are the baselines from which he works to develop draft at each level; they compose, in effect, the skeletal structure of the sail onto which is modeled curvature, until the shape is right. Because each chord terminates at a different outboard point along the leech twist, each chord traveling up the sail will be at an increasingly wider angle relative to the chord at the foot. Each chord will also be the base for a different shape, depending on the angle it makes with the apparent wind. Eventually, as we shall see, the curvature from each chord at selected heights is filled in and connected to make a smooth and flowing overall shape for the sail. (See Figure 40.)

The third side of the sail, the foot, is determined next. Here, the designer can usually add a little extra sail area below the straight line from tack to clew. This is called *foot roach*. Although it is unsupported, it will hold its shape because of gravity. However, with increased sheet tension in medium or heavy airs, the foot roach will curl up if it is excessive. The amount of roach that will stand well depends on the wind range of the sail. It is also limited by some one-design class rules.

Determining the Trim Point

So far, we have been talking about the sail as if it were suspended in mid-air. Now that we have an entity with three sides, and a chord connecting two of them, we can relate this to the boat. Since we know where the luff has to be placed—on the jibstay—the question at this point is where the clew will be fastened. In other words, how far outboard or inboard will the sail be trimmed in relation to the boat's centerline? This has to be decided by the sail designer because it will determine the angle the chord makes with the apparent wind all the way up the sail and therefore determines how much curvature the sail can have. If the sail is trimmed in close to the centerline, there will be more room between the chord and the apparent wind for fullness of curvature, while if the sail is trimmed outboard, where it will be closer to the planned apparent-wind angle, there will be less room for curvature, and the sail will have to be much flatter (Fig. 38).

The trim point, therefore, affects the fullness of the entire sail and also determines the direction of the forces acting on it. Remember that when the forces acting on the sail are averaged out, they will act on the sail in a general direction that is slightly forward of the perpendicular drawn to the chord. Since the trim point determines the position of the chord in relation to the centerline, it controls the direction of the forces on the sail. The farther outboard the trim point, the more forward the forces will be; the more inboard the trim point, the more the forces will be to the side until, when the chord is parallel to the centerline, they are mostly to the side.

Basically, in deciding the trim point of a headsail, the sailmaker must weigh the advantages of a fuller sail against the increase in side forces, and come up with a trim position that will balance the two most favorably. Again, his decision will depend to a great extent on the lateral resistance and stability of the boat and the wind and sea conditions in which it will be sailed.

Fig. 38
With the apparent-wind angle remaining
constant, changes in trim point affect
fullness of the jib and the resultant
strength and direction of forces generated
by the sail.

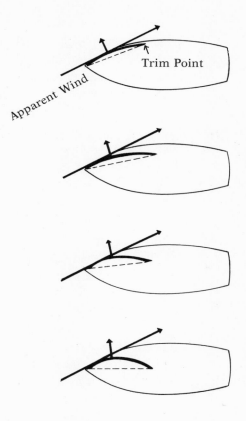

Since the headsail will be operating in free air, it usually will have a wide enough apparent-wind angle to allow it to be trimmed in an outboard position and still have adequate curvature to develop strong forces. Since most of these forces will be in a favorable direction, the jib or genoa is a valuable driving sail, something that is often overlooked despite the fact that some genoas can be over twice the size of the main.

Since the genoa is so large, it has to go *outside* the shrouds as it comes aft to be trimmed; the point at which it passes the shrouds is usually the farthest inboard point to which the sail should go and is often established as its trim point. A genoa with its clew trimmed farther inboard than the shroud position will normally result in negative curvature from the shrouds aft, unless, as on some of the latest one-design boats and offshore racers, the fuller-cut genoa is trimmed inboard and the sheet is eased;

this permits the leech of the sail above the foot to fall into increased twist. But a genoa with an inboard lead and trimmed in too much may close up the slot. It may also divert the apparent wind into such a narrow angle that the mainsail will have to be so flat that it will only develop minimal forces (see Figs. 8–14).

The genoa trim position is also limited by the beam of the boat and the deck layout, although these considerations are taken into account by the naval architect when he suggests the amount of overlap a boat can carry. If the boat has its greatest beam forward near the shrouds, it will not be able to carry a genoa with so much overlap that it has to be trimmed well aft, where the boat is a good deal narrower. This will be gone into in more depth in Chapter 10, Headsails; for the moment, it is sufficient to note that these factors limit the genoa trim point and must be considered.

Choosing the trim point of the working jib presents a different problem. Since it does not pass around the shrouds, it can be trimmed farther inboard. Also, the more forward the leech of the headsail is in relation to the mainsail, the more open the slot, the less the deflection of the apparent wind, and, again, the more inboard the sail can be trimmed. In practice, the sail designer picks a trim point for the working jib that is as inboard as possible while still not permitting the apparent wind to be directed toward the mainsail at too narrow an angle.* At the same time, no trim point should be so outboard that the after end of the sail has to curve in sharply to be trimmed, since this creates negative force aft.

Determining Draft

Once the trim point of a headsail is decided upon within these limitations and considerations, the sailmaker can begin to fill in the curvature for each chord. He knows that the leading edge will be a fairly flat plane parallel to the apparent wind. And he knows that the after end—approximately the last 10 or 15 per cent of the sail—should be in a straight run and, when possible, should not be too much inward of a line parallel to the centerline of the boat, so that the wind can exit smoothly off the sail (Fig. 39).

Thus, given the chord at a certain level, the apparent-wind direction

---

*These trim points may be changed later as a result of the sailmaker's and sailor's testing for increased speed in actual races.

Fig. 39
Luff plane and leech plane are determined
first.

Fig. 40
The luff and leech planes are then
connected as smoothly as possible to form
draft. Arrows represent apparent-wind
angle.

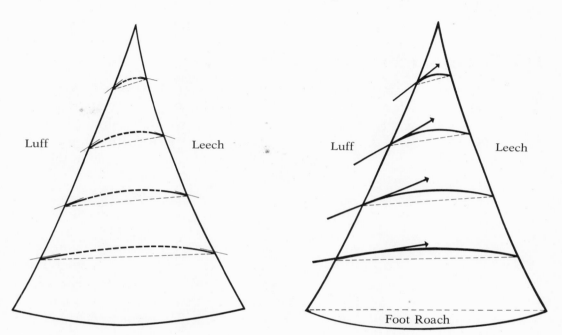

Luff   Leech

Luff   Leech

Foot Roach

at that height, and the trim point, he can fill in the leading and, tentatively,
the trailing edges of that sail section.

Then he can fill in the curvature between these points, bearing these
principles in mind: first, *to develop maximum aerodynamic forces, the
point of maximum curvature should be approximately 33 to 40 per cent
of the way aft;* and second, *the maximum amount of draft that works aerodynamically is a camber ratio between 10 and 15 per cent.* (See page 55
for an explanation of camber ratio.) If the draft is any fuller, the flow
will detach from the sail. This maximum can be achieved only where the
apparent-wind angle is very wide, usually in the upper portion of a sail
acting in free air. Third, *the leech curving inward increases the amount
of total draft but also increases negative forces aft in the sail* (Fig. 40).

And so, at various heights in the sail, the sailmaker fills in as much draft as he can for each chord at each selected height, making the curvature as smooth as possible without any sharp divergences. He then connects the curvature vertically so that the sail has a smooth flowing shape from top to bottom.

THE DESIGN PROCESS: The Mainsail

Once the headsail is designed, the sailmaker can begin on the mainsail. He can now calculate the way the headsail is going to deflect the wind over the main, and thus determine its apparent-wind angle. Although the deflection will make the apparent-wind angle very narrow, this angle will open up higher in the sail because of the wind gradient. And, also, if the headsail goes only partway up the mast, the mainsail above that will be acting in free air and can be much fuller than at deck level (see Fig. 43).

Once the redirected apparent wind is determined all the way up the mainsail, the procedure is the same as for the genoa or jib. First, the luff is drawn. As with the jib, this will not always be a straight line. Some masts today are designed to bend, the idea being that in a good breeze the mast will bow forward, thus flattening the sail forward. In any case, whether mast bend is intentional or not, the designer has to take it into account, gauging it as he does jib sag for the particular wind velocity. Otherwise, as with stay sag, the shape of the sail will change when it is put on the boat under actual sailing conditions (Fig. 41).

Next the leech twist is plotted, and the chords are drawn. Then the trim point is selected. Because of the very narrow apparent-wind angle in which the lower part of the main usually has to operate, the inboard-outboard range within which the trim point can be located is often very limited. In fact, in order to allow for any fullness at all, the sail frequently has to be trimmed to the centerline, particularly in powerful racing machines that have very narrow pointing angles to begin with. This obviously causes more heeling force, and how far inboard you trim the sail depends on the stability or "stiffness" of the boat.

Another difficulty results from the boom being trimmed right at the centerline: there is no way to avoid negative leech direction low in the sail. The curvature of the lowest sail section starts at the centerline and

Fig. 41
Kinds of Mast Bend

a. With no rigging, as in Finn, there is free mast bend.

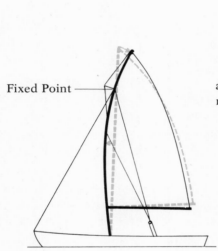

Fixed Point

b. Mast bends above and below a fixed jibstay position, (a).

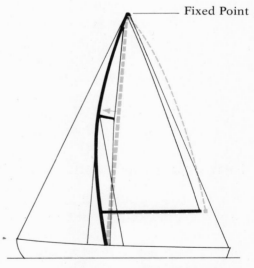

Fixed Point

c. Mast bows forward from a fixed masthead position.

terminates at the centerline, thus causing negative forces in the after end of the sail. This, again, would seemingly create forces only to the side or even backward. However, two things save the situation: first, twist quickly moves the leech to leeward as height increases; and second, as we have seen, the forces in the forward part of the sail are always much stronger than the aft forces, and they are made even stronger by the increased velocity of flow in the slot between the headsail and the main. Therefore, the force gained by creating additional draft through trimming the boom at the centerline and allowing negative direction in the leech more than offsets the side force created. The resultant total force will be in a forward direction. Even if the boom is not trimmed right at the centerline, the sailmaker may not be able to get enough draft in the lower part of the mainsail without hooking the leech in toward the centerline.

In summary, it is a choice between making the sail section fuller, with the leech curving inward at a negative angle, or making the sail section flatter and keeping the leech as nearly parallel to the centerline as possible (Fig. 42). This question will arise more often in the lower portion of the sail; because of the wind-gradient factor and leech twist, the apparent-wind angle will open up more and more, higher in the sail, allowing sufficient curvature to be developed without resorting to this inward-curving leech. A mainsail with a negative curvature high in the leech is generally undesirable, except in light air.

The curvature of the leech has a noticeable effect on sail performance, controlling the direction and amount of total force in the sail, and it is how this curvature is handled that separates the men from the boys in sailmaking. Once again, it is another variation of the constant dilemma facing the sailmaker: whether to make the sail fuller and have more force, or to make the sail flatter, with the forces in a more favorable direction.

Determining Maximum Draft Locations

The location of maximum curvature in the main has to be handled quite differently from that of the headsail, and the reason again has to do with the extremely narrow angle of the apparent wind. The rule for the location of maximum draft in the genoa or jib (or any sail operating in clear air) is simple: for maximum aerodynamic efficiency, the point of maximum draft has been established by testing at 33 to 40 per cent of the way aft.

Fig. 42
Near boom level, the leeches of both sails
have a negative direction. The more the
leech is curved inward, the more the
increase in negative area and, therefore,
the greater the draft; the total-force vector
will have more strength but will be in a
less forward direction. In lighter airs,
draft is more important, so the sail is
made fuller by addition of curvature. In
heavier airs, negative leech is detrimental
because it adds to the heeling force, so the
leech curve is generally decreased,
making the sail flatter.

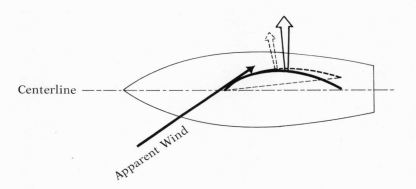

Centerline

Apparent Wind

But if you stuck to this rule for the main (where the headsail affects it),
you simply could not build enough draft into the sail to create sufficient
power. The apparent-wind angle is so narrow that there is very little room
for curvature between the chord and the apparent wind until you get a good
bit farther aft. Thus, for the low or overlapped portions of the main, you
strive to put the point of deepest draft as far forward as you can while still
getting adequate curvature. On the average, this will be about halfway
back, although in extreme cases, such as a 12-Meter with a high pointing
angle and maximum overlap, it might have to be back as far as 60 per cent.
In the upper portion of the main, however, where there is either little overlap
or none at all, the apparent-wind angle opens up and the maximum draft
can be farther forward (Fig. 43).

Fig. 43
The location and amount of maximum draft in the main depend on how the headsail deflects apparent wind.
NOTE: draft or fullness will be indicated in two ways throughout this book—as a curve above the chord or as a curve below the chord (as below), depending on which illustrates the point more graphically and clearly.

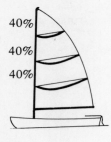
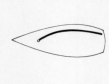

40%
40%
40%

a.
With no overlap,
draft is fullest possible
and only about 40 per cent of the
way aft.

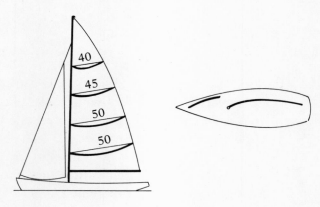

b.
Working jib deflects air to a certain degree, causing draft in main to be flatter and farther aft.

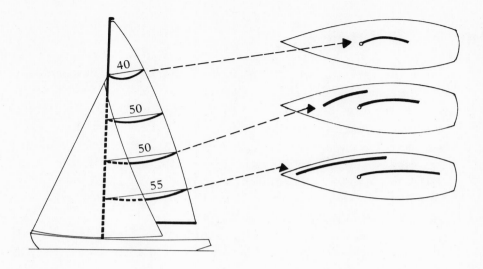

c.

Above the genoa, the mainsail operates in free air and draft can be 40 per cent of the way aft. With increasing overlap, draft decreases and moves farther aft.

d.

With a masthead genoa, the apparent wind is deflected to the greatest degree. The main will be flatter and the point of maximum draft will be farther aft as the overlap increases.

Testing the Sail Design

Once the curvature is figured for each chord and connected up and down the mainsail, the design is completed, and the sail is built accordingly. Now comes the big test: will the sails create the desired total force? Usually, if the sailmaker has carefully considered every problem and has brought into play the experience gained from other sails on boats with similar characteristics, the sails will be successful. But the proof is in the sailing: the best way to tell whether the sails are right or not is from performance data gained in competition with similar boats over a period of time. If the sails do not appear to be competitive, what then? First, the sail designer will check carefully to see that the design has been executed properly and that draft controls and sail-trim settings on the boat are correct, so that the shapes of all the sails are right. This can easily be done by visual inspection. If the sail designer cannot spot anything wrong with the way the sail has been made or with the amount and location of draft, an alteration in the sail plan might be necessary, and a consultation with the naval architect would be in order.

If the sailmaker cannot come aboard to check the sails, he will ask you to tell him what the sail looks like, how much draft there is at various levels, and where it is located. It is difficult for most people to convey this information accurately because they do not have the technical vocabulary or ability to describe what the sailmaker needs to know to analyze the problem. The simplest and best solution, therefore, is to photograph the sail, so that draft can be measured and analyzed. (See Fig. 60.)

HOW DRAFT IS MEASURED

Because draft is curvature, it is described and measured in terms of a proportion — between the depth of the curve and the length of the chord of the sail — which tells you the relative depth of the curve. The chord is a straight line drawn horizontally from the luff to the leech at any height in the sail (Fig. 44).

Depth is measured by drawing a perpendicular from the chord to the deepest point of the curve at that height.

Fig. 44

a.

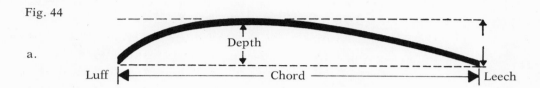

When you relate the two, you get a proportion or camber ratio which expresses the rise of the curve—in other words, how relatively deep or shallow the curvature is. For example, if the depth is 1 foot and the chord is 8 feet, the camber ratio is 1:8. This amount of camber would give you a medium-to-full sail. The maximum camber ratio for effective aerodynamic build-up in a sail is 1:5.5 and the minimum is around 1:20.

Depth=1 ft.
Chord=8 ft.

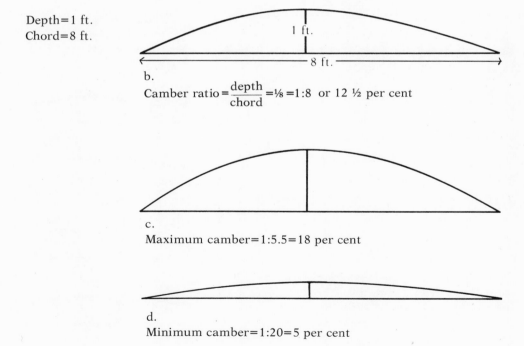

b.
Camber ratio = $\dfrac{\text{depth}}{\text{chord}}$ = ⅛ = 1:8 or 12 ½ per cent

c.
Maximum camber = 1:5.5 = 18 per cent

d.
Minimum camber = 1:20 = 5 per cent

Camber ratio can also be expressed as a percentage; this is obtained by dividing the depth by the chord. The greater the depth in relation to the chord, the higher the percentage. Thus, the fullest possible sail—with a camber ratio of 1:5.5—would be expressed as 18 per cent. The practical minimum of 1:20 would be expressed as 5 per cent.

A camber ratio is the measurement for only one curvature at one height in the sail, defining a *sail section:* the cross-sectional shape at a given level. Different sections of the sail can have different camber ratios: a 12-Meter, for instance, might have a 17 per cent section high in the main (where the apparent wind allows fullness) and a 7 per cent section low.

Sail sections with the same camber ratios could have different fore and aft shapes; camber ratio is only descriptive of the depth of draft, not the shape it takes or where the maximum draft is. The deepest point of draft might be 33 per cent of the way aft in one section, and 50 per cent of the way aft in another; yet both might have a camber ratio of 12½ per cent. It is not possible to talk in terms of relative depth only. Even if the points of maximum depth were at the same place, it would be possible for the curvature to be handled differently for each, depending on what the sailmaker is trying to accomplish (Fig. 45).

Fig. 45
Various Cross-Sectional Shapes with
Same Camber Ratio

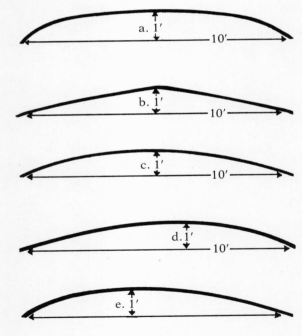

All the draft curves have the same camber ratio. In addition, (a), (b), and (c) have the point of maximum draft at the same place, yet the shapes vary widely.

How to Photograph Draft in Your Sail

Here are some hints to help you get the best photographs of the amount and location of draft in your sail:

1. Use black and white film—not color.
2. Face the windward side of the sail, just aft of the mid-point of the foot.
3. Be sure the light on the sails is such that the seams show up well.
4. Shoot upward, from below the foot, if you can.
5. Get at least the entire upper half of the sail in the picture, from luff to leech. The more you can get in, the better.
6. Photograph the main and jib or genoa separately.
7. Make pictures under various wind conditions: for a medium-weather sail, you might take one set at 6 to 10 knots, one at 12 to 15 knots, and one at 20 knots.
8. Mark each set with all pertinent information including approximate wind velocity, mainsheet traveler setting or boom angle, the position of draft control mechanisms (sheet, Cunningham hole, etc.), and what headsail is being used.

From these photographs your sailmaker should have enough information to analyze the problem. However, for your own information, you may want to carry this procedure a step further and actually plot the draft onto the photographs yourself.

Plotting Draft

Draft should be calculated at a minimum of three heights: one quarter, one half, and three-quarters of the way up the sail but, if you're working on a photograph, you will only be able to plot it at one half and three-quarters of the way up because of the limited range of the camera. First, outline the seam from luff to leech at each height. Then, draw the chord from luff to leech at the points where the seam begins and ends. Now you have established a sail section at each height. The next step is to take four depth readings for each section: at one quarter, one half, three-quarters of the way aft, and at the point of maximum draft (Fig. 46). Now you can see with some exactitude just where the draft is located at each height in the sail. To get the camber ratio, measure the depth of a section and the length of its chord with a ruler, and divide the depth by the chord. Even though you will calculate camber ratio in inches, it will be the same as if you had actually measured it on the sail itself.

Using photographs of your sails and plotting draft on them in this manner can be a very valuable tool for most sailors, particularly in analyzing your draft setting in different conditions. It is a procedure worth mastering.

Fig. 46
Recording of Amounts of Draft from Photographs.   Each cross-sectional shape can be plotted to show the amount of draft at the ¼, ½, and ¾ points, from luff to leech. The heavier arrow shows the amount and location of maximum draft.

a. Main

b. Genoa

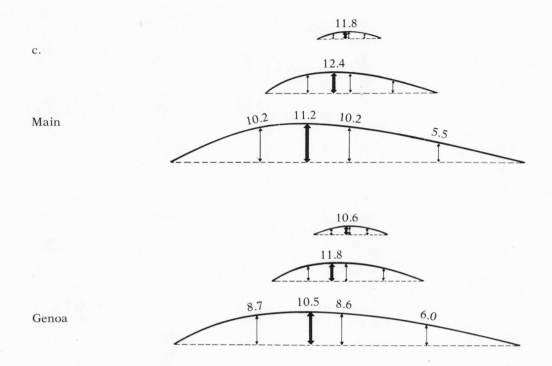

c.

Main

Genoa

Sail design, as you can see, is complex. Today, however, thanks to the computer, sail design is becoming more organized and scientific. It may even be possible one day to feed the computer hull and rig characteristics, plus wind and wave conditions, and have the computer tell you exactly what shape sails are needed and how sails should be cut to produce these shapes. In the one or two most advanced computer systems, much of this can already be done, although the difficult and complex process of designing the pressure distributions throughout the sail must be done by hand. The computer can, however, take the pressure distribution calculated by hand and produce the best overall sail shapes and the best trim angles for the sails. It can also serve as a memory bank in which all the latest research and performance data on different sails in different conditions can be stored, helping the sailmaker to make more and more precise judgments as he designs a sail. Nevertheless, it is still these judgments—based on skill and experience—that make the difference in the success or failure of a suit of sails. There is still a great deal of art left in the science of sailmaking.

Chapter 4

Making the Sail: Cloth and Construction

Once the sailmaker has settled on the shape of the sail, he must then realize this design through the medium of sailcloth, a material so tricky to handle that it is fair to say it's easier for an engineer to build the right shape into the wing of a supersonic aircraft than it is to build a sail. The wing is made of metal and does not change shape in use, so it can be counted on to perform as designed. The sail, however, is made of material which is not only flexible but stretches under pressure. The amount of stretch varies, not only from one type of cloth to another but sometimes from one bolt of the same type to another, particularly when one weight is made by several different finishers. Within any single piece of cloth, stretch varies in a different way—according to the direction and strength of the weave and the direction of the greatest tensile loads.

The sailmaker, therefore, has to understand his material—and must have sophisticated devices to measure the stretch in all directions—so that he can accurately correct for it in cutting the cloth and/or use it to help him produce the shape he wants in the wind velocity for which the sail is designed.

The stretchiness of sailcloth occurs for several reasons. First of all, the thread itself can stretch out: the threads actually lengthen under load. Although we are using the word "stretch" to cover a number of similar problems, this, in fact, is what is technically meant by stretch. It takes a lot of force to stretch out the fiber in this way, and when it does happen, it causes a major change in sail shape, which after a certain point might be permanent. Usually, however, the sailmaker will have chosen a cloth with a thread strong enough for a certain wind range, so that this is not as much of a problem as the other kinds of stretchiness. These are caused by the fact that sailcloth is woven, and stretchiness is inherent in the geometry of woven cloth.

The weaving process consists of threads going over and under each other in an interlaced pattern. The *warp* threads are the long threads going the length of the cloth, across which the *weft* or *fill* threads are woven at right angles (Fig. 47). The threads do not lie flat as they cross over and under each other: in effect, a thread curls up and over one thread, then dives down below the next, then up and over again, and so on. This is called *crimp* from the old Dutch word meaning "to shrivel." It is crimp (Fig. 48) that causes one kind of troublesome stretchiness: when a load is put on the cloth in either the warp or fill direction, the crimp in the direction of the strain will be pulled out and the threads that had been curled over and under will straighten out, lengthening the cloth in that direction. It is rather like what happens when an accordion is pulled all the way: the "pleats," like crimp, straighten out, allowing the accordion to expand. Technically, this is known as geometric *elongation*. Nevertheless, the result is stretchiness in the cloth.

Fig. 48
Cloth Cross-Section

No Crimp

Medium Crimp

High Crimp

Super Crimp

Fig. 47
Bolt of Cloth

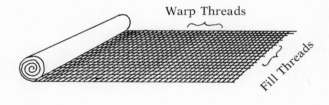

Warp Threads

Fill Threads

There is no way to avoid this elongation because of the way cloth is woven: the threads simply cannot pass over and under each other without some crimp occurring along both the warp and the fill. You can, however, put more crimp in one direction than another, depending on what the cloth is to be used for. This is where cloth design comes in. In the case of a mainsail, for instance, you would want a cloth with heavier fill thread and less fill crimp, giving you less elongation and stretch across the width of the cloth panel. The cloth would then be laid out with this stronger direction in the line of the greatest strain—in this case, along the freestanding leech. The warp, which contains most of the crimp, will be at right angles to the leech, where it will be subject to less strain and, therefore, elongation. On the other hand, cloth for a genoa usually has threads of equal strength and stretch in both warp and fill directions because, unlike the mainsail, the strains on the sail go in all directions. This is called balanced construction; in unbalanced construction, one thread direction is stronger than the other. Thus, the sailmaker chooses the cloth with the crimp in the direction that suits his needs. Generally, however, putting more crimp in one direction increases another kind of stretchiness: elongation across the bias.

Bias elongation presents an even more difficult challenge to the sail-maker. It is due to the geometric distortion of the weave under pressure, and is much more dramatic and easier to see than either crimp interchange or stretch (Fig. 49). If you take a handkerchief and hold it at the two top corners, when you pull them apart you will notice a small amount of give. This is due mainly to the crimped threads straightening out, and to a slight amount of thread stretch as well. But when you pull the handkerchief from diagonally opposite corners, it will stretch out to a much greater degree. This is what happens to your sail whenever a load is applied in any direction other than along the fill or warp threads. What actually happens is quite simple: the warp and fill form a lattice-work pattern. The threads cross each other at right angles and are, in a sense, fastened at every juncture of warp and fill. The pattern is strong in the direction of thread line and weak on the diagonal. When the cloth is pulled across the diagonal or bias, the whole lattice pattern shifts, and the threads are no longer at right angles to each other. You may have seen children making the same kind of lattice with ice-cream sticks: at the slightest pressure the whole construction will shift from a square to a diamond shape. This is exactly what happens when a load is applied along the bias of a cloth: the threads pivot over one another, causing the lattice pattern to expand in one direction and contract in another until, after considerable elongation, the threads reach the point where they can no longer contract because they are so packed together. At this point, they are "locked," and there will be no further elongation, but this is a severe alteration not generally found in a sail.

Obviously, then, the more loosely woven the cloth, the more easily it will elongate on the bias. Threads woven and packed very tightly will not twist over one another as easily and will form a locked pattern under diagonal loading much sooner. However, the more tightly woven the threads are, the steeper the crimp will be, and the greater the possibility for crimp interchange or elongation along the thread line. Similarly, if you put more crimp in one direction than in another, the cloth will elongate on the bias more easily. You are in a bind: eliminate stretch in one direction and you get more of it in another. There is simply no way to get rid of cloth stretchiness through alteration of the weave.

In an attempt to stabilize the cloth and particularly to overcome bias elongation, fillers are often applied to the cloth after it is woven. The fillers are literally pressed into the minuscule spaces in the weave pattern to

Fig. 49

c. Load on Bias
When cloth is pulled on a diagonal, there is little to prevent distortion of the weave pattern, so the threads slide over one another to form a parallelogram.

a. Normal Weave

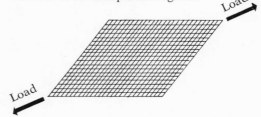

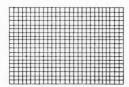

b. Load on Threadline
Only a small amount of elongation occurs when cloth is pulled along the threadline.

d. Locked Pattern
After considerable bias elongation, the threads pack against one another and can go no farther; they are locked in place.

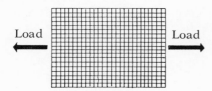

prevent the threads from sliding over one another. Fillers brace the square configuration of the weave and can reduce the bias elongation to only a third of what it was before. This is a partial answer, but, unfortunately, cloth treated this way has a firm, stiff finish that makes it harder to handle. This does not affect the small-boat sailor using lighter-weight sails to any degree, but it does make the heavier-weight sails on larger boats difficult to furl and stow.

There is no way to eliminate stretch or elongation entirely. All you can do is choose the cloth with the best qualities for the particular sail. It must have low stretch on the primary stress line, which normally will be parallel with the leech (usually the fill threads), and it must have low bias stretch. What you are looking for is a cloth with good balance—that is, with low stretch and only small differences in the amount of stretch in all different directions. This is an idealistic goal, because no perfect sailcloth yet exists, and may never exist so long as it is woven and has to be flexible.

Balance is a function of weaving, but it is also a result of the finishing process. After the cloth is woven, it is sewn into 1,000-yard bolts. It is scoured by passing it through very hot water and detergent to remove dirt and impurities. Then it is dried and made ready for heat-processing. This involves heat-setting to stabilize and shrink the fabric. The shrinkage may amount to 8 per cent in some cases, and the direction in which the cloth shrinks will depend on where the most crimp is. When the cloth is thus stabilized, the sailmaker will be able to predict the stretch with a good deal of certainty; thus, this is a crucial step in the production of good-quality cloth.

The next step is the application (if desired) of fillers and/or finishes. A sail can have both a filler and a finish or coating. Fillers, as we have seen, are used to stabilize the cloth. One of the most common fillers is a resin called melamine, which is used primarily in the lighter-weight cloths for one-design sails. Finishes or coatings reduce porosity in the cloth, which usually improves sail performance, most noticeably in sailing to windward in a stiff breeze. They reduce bias elongation as well, but they also contribute to the perishability of the more fragile nylon sails by making them easier to tear. There are a variety of polymers used to finish sailcloth: an acrylic finish is used for Dacron and a polyurethane finish is used on nylon.

After the application of fillers and finishes, the sail is ready for the final process, which is calendering. A calender consists of two rollers that apply heat and tons of pressure to the sailcloth. The pressure, which may be as high as 150 tons, is determined by the desired type of finishing. Calendering straightens and smooths the fabric. If sailcloth has a very high sheen, it probably has been calendered many times.

All cloth manufacturers have variances in production because of the very involved finishing processes. Consequently, it is necessary for a sailmaker to have the technical equipment that will help him select the most consistent cloth and also enable him to measure the stretch in the cloth. A stretch correction factor is then incorporated into the design of the sail.

By the same token, one-design sails cannot be produced over a period of years simply by cutting sails from the same pattern and having the same men fabricate the sails. Over a short period of time, and particularly over a period of years, the cloth characteristics will change, generally through improvements. Therefore, the sails will seldom, if ever, be identical unless each lot of cloth is tested before it is cut and the differences in stretch incorporated into the design. The definition of identical sails is not necessarily that they are made from the same pattern. They are identical only if, under sail in the same wind velocity, they have identical cross-sectional shapes at various heights.

THE SYNTHETICS

Today, synthetic man-made fibers are exclusively used in sailmaking instead of the natural fibers such as cotton and flax that were once used for sailcloth. Dacron and nylon fibers are extruded filaments like fiberglass; they are spun into threads which vary in size and in other qualities. Each synthetic has some advantages over the others; the one you choose will depend on your needs.

Dacron

Dacron cloth is used for mainsails, genoas, jibs, certain staysails, mizzens, and heavier drifters. Its biggest advantages over the other synthetics are its lower stretch and its good resistance to sunlight deterioration.

Dacron cloth is superior to other synthetics for another important reason: it will not shrink or get stretched out of shape through use. Old-time sailors will remember the break-in periods that cotton sails required. Long hours of careful sailing in moderate breezes were necessary to get the sails more or less stabilized, with the cloth shrinking and stretching into what one hoped was a reasonably good shape. Thanks to Dacron, the correct shape can now be built in by the sailmaker; the sailor can keep it as designed through draft controls and sail-trim devices as well as through proper care. Dacron has also made it possible for the sailmaker to reproduce a sail shape more closely than before.

But Dacron has also led many racing sailors into a trap: everyone always wants the lightest-weight sailcloth for his racing sails, and because Dacron has such a good reputation for strength, sailors insist on using it in lighter and lighter weights. But lightweight Dacrons are effective for light-air situations only. If the cloth is too lightweight, once you are in any kind of breeze the sail will begin to stretch out. You sacrifice Dacron's main advantage: high resistance to stretch. It is better to avoid the whole problem by using cloth with an adequate weight, particularly for the new tall, narrow rigs which produce high cloth loading.

Most one-design sails are made from Dacron cloth weighing between 3½ and 5 ounces.* All-purpose mainsails for small cruising boats (around 30 feet) are usually made from 5½- to 6½-ounce cloth, mains for medium cruising boats (35–40 feet) from 6½- to 7-ounce cloth, and those for large cruising boats (over 50 feet) from cloth weighing up to 12 ounces. These weights will give the non-racing sailor the best possible all-purpose sails, combining durability, good shape retention, and ease of handling.

Genoas can be made from cloth that is anywhere from 2 to 10 ounces, depending on what is needed. If a lighter genoa is needed, say under 2 ounces, it might have to be made from nylon, because Dacron is not made in the lighter weights.

Nylon

Nylon is used for spinnakers, lighter drifters, and light staysails. It is stronger than Dacron but has appreciably more stretch and changes dimen-

---

*Sailcloth weights refer to the weight of a "yard" that measures 36 inches by 28½ inches, as specified by the American Bureau of Standards. A cloth yard amounts to about 80 per cent of a normal 36-inch yard.

sion with heat and humidity. The advantages of this cloth are that not only is it stronger than Dacron but it can be made in lighter weights (under 2 ounces), is easy to dye, and has good mildew resistance.

Nylon's weak points are its deterioration in sunlight, its stretch, and its poor balance. Compared to Dacron, the bias has far more elongation than the warp or fill.

Nylon cloth is available in ½-ounce, ¾-ounce, 1.2-ounce, 1½-ounce, 2½-ounce, and 4-ounce weights. A reaching or downwind sail needs some elasticity to support the shock of strong gusts; hence nylon is good for spin-nakers—in fact, better than Dacron. This is why a 2½-ounce nylon rather than a 2-ounce Dacron would be used for a heavy-weather spinnaker. The lighter weights of nylon are deceptive in their usage. The ½-, ¾-, 1.2-ounce, and 1½-ounce weights do not have large differences in stretch characteristics on the warp or fill; they do have increasing diagonal stretch as the weight gets lighter. But the differences are not as great as might be expected. As a result, ¾-ounce nylon has proved strong enough to be used as the all-purpose spinnaker weight not only on one-designs, but on 50- to 60-foot cruising boats. The ½-ounce spinnaker is used on all sizes of boats only as a special light-air broad-reaching or -running spinnaker, and since closer-reaching spinnakers are usually under greater strain, they are made in 3¾-ounce cloth for boats up to 30 to 35 feet, in 1½-ounce cloth in the medium-size cruising boats, and 2½-ounce cloth in larger cruising boats. This procedure has practically eliminated the need for 1.2-ounce cloth. The new star-cut spin-nakers used with the apparent wind well forward are usually 1½- or 2½-ounce.

Other Synthetics

Orlon, one of the original synthetics, was used successfully for relatively small working sails. However, it is no longer used because the fibers are not readily available. There have been numerous attempts to produce cloth from other synthetics; this research will continue until an improved product is discovered. For now, there is no commercial replacement for Dacron. The mylars and some polymers, for example, have problems of uncontrolled cold stretch and no resistance to shock caused by pitching in heavy seas. A new material, Kevlar 29, or Fiber B, by Du Pont, is being used by a number of cruiser-racers as a mainsail fabric but is still in the experimental stage.

It has a very low stretch on the fill but fairly high bias elongation. For now, a composite weave of Kevlar on the fill and polyester on the warp is being used.

SAIL CONSTRUCTION

Since cloth generally has more strength in one direction than another, many problems arise when the cloth is laid out for the sail. To compound the imbalance further, cloth has, as we have seen, different amounts of stretch and/or elongation in almost every direction. Thus, the layout of the sailcloth will depend on the lines of greatest stress in the sail.

On mainsails the cloths are laid so that the strongest thread line (normally the fill) is parallel to the leech drawn as a straight line (Fig. 50). The luff and foot are reinforced on the edge by the tabling (a double or triple

Fig. 50
An exaggerated weave shows thread directions.

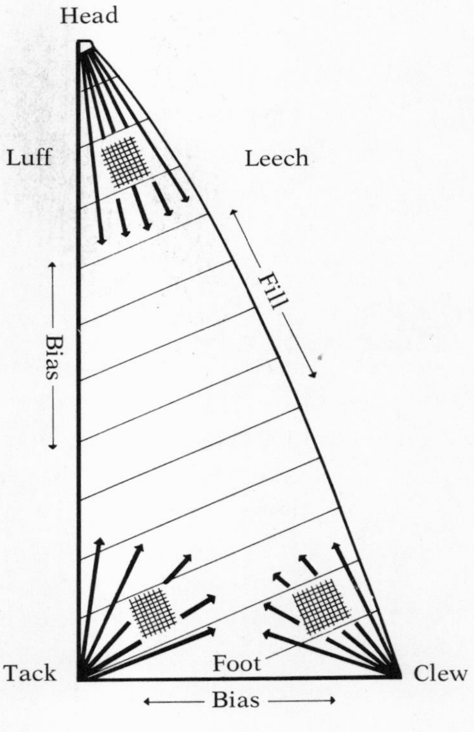

Mainsail

hem along the edge of the sail) and additional rope or tape. Then the edge is further aided by being attached to a spar; but the leech is a freestanding span and all the support necessary to counter stretch has to come from the cloth alone. (Battens only help support the leech roach.)

The jib or genoa is more difficult to make because it has two unsupported edges, the leech *and* the foot. If the leech and the foot meet in a 90-degree angle, as they do on some working jibs (Fig. 51), there is no problem: if the panels are laid out as below, one edge will be on the fill and the other will be on the warp, which, although not so strong, is still stronger than the bias. But as soon as the clew angle is larger than 90 degrees (as in a high-clewed working jib) or smaller than 90 degrees (as in genoas), if the fill is parallel to the leech, the foot will be on the bias.

Fig. 51

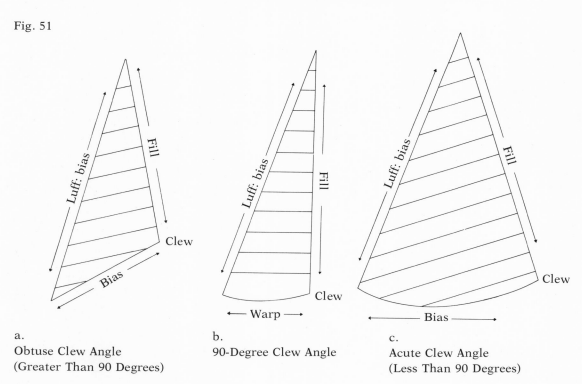

a.
Obtuse Clew Angle
(Greater Than 90 Degrees)

b.
90-Degree Clew Angle

c.
Acute Clew Angle
(Less Than 90 Degrees)

In order to get the fill parallel to both free edges, sailmakers have used a miter in which sailcloth panels are set with the fill parallel to the foot and to the leech (Fig. 52). Stretch along the foot and leech is reduced to a minimum because the strain is on the thread line. This cut looks at first like a good solution, but you can get some bias stretch along the miter line. A strong wind will put a bulge in this area (Fig. 53), causing excess fullness

Fig. 52

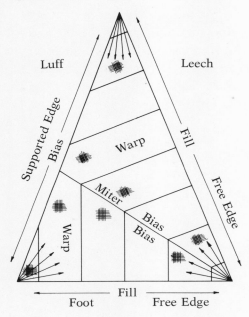

Fig. 53
Conventional Miter-Cut Genoa.   When loaded, area under bias loading along the miter will have more stretch than strains across the warp or fill, such as along the leech and foot. Stretch allows increased local curvature and imbalance of shape. (Photograph taken from clew of the genoa.)

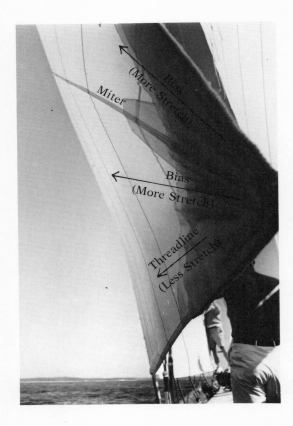

in the center of the sail. There are no answers to problems of stretch although sailmakers continually experiment with different panel configurations in an effort to equalize stretch in various directions (Fig. 54).

Fig. 54
Various genoa cuts have been devised to
deal with the problems of stretch.

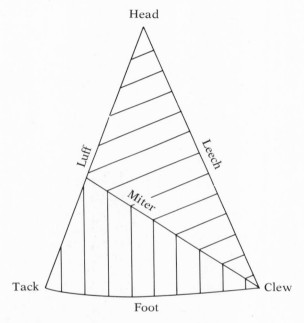

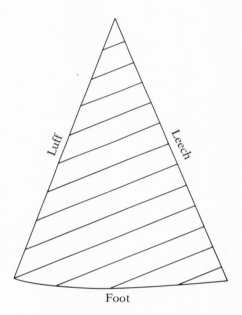

1. Miter-Cut—the cloths are square to both the leech and foot, placing the stronger fill directions parallel with these unsupported edges. However, the cloths are on the bias along the miter line. The luff has two different bias angles, one in the panels above the miter and another in the panels below—each with different stretch ratios.

2. Cross-Cut—the luff has a constant bias angle; the fill of the cloth is parallel to the leech, but the foot is on the bias.

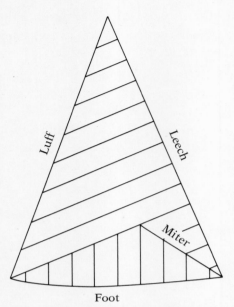

3. Mini-Miter—the fill is parallel to both the leech and foot; the luff has the same bias angle all the way.

4. Radial-Cut—this alternative aims at keeping the loads radiating out of the clew on the same threadline direction of the cloth. In this case the warp is parallel to the load direction, but the luff has many different bias angles.

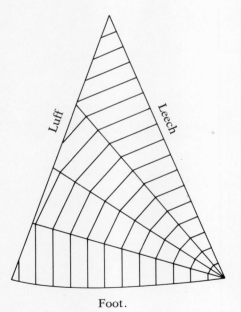

5. Spider Web-Cut—the principle is the same as the radial-cut, but the cloths are rotated 90 degrees, so that the fill is parallel to the leech and foot and other directions of stress radiating out of the clew. It is a stronger but more difficult and complicated layout and hard to execute into a smooth shape.

Spinnakers give even more complex problems, since they are unsupported on three sides. The various attempts to solve this problem will be covered in Chapter 9, Spinnakers.

Nevertheless, no matter what variations are tried, in any panel only the one fill line and, to a lesser extent, the warp line have minimum stretch. The rest of the cloth is on the bias, with the result that the cloth will stretch in these areas to varying degrees. Lay any sail on a flat surface and you can see strain lines radiating out of the corner. Look at the angle at which the strain lines cross the seams (Fig. 55). The strains cross the cloth on a perpendicular in only one direction from the corner; all other strain directions cross over the cloth on the bias. This is where your sail will stretch, and the lighter your cloth weight relative to the loading on the sail, the more of a problem it becomes.

The reason stretch is so serious is that under load it causes draft; and the stronger the wind force, the more draft is created.

The more the stretch in a particular fabric, the greater the problem. Stretch is what causes the draft to move aft in the sail under increased loading in heavier winds. If the cloth had no stretch, there would be no shifting of designed draft location.

For these reasons, a good sailmaker must be able to measure the stretch in all directions in the cloth he uses and have a design system sophisticated enough to use the correct amount of stretch allowance throughout

Fig. 55
a.
Corner Loads in Sails

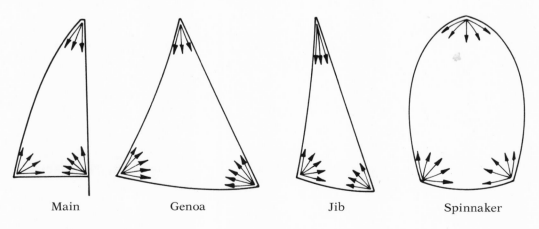

Main   Genoa   Jib   Spinnaker

b.
Mainsail Head

c.
Genoa Clew

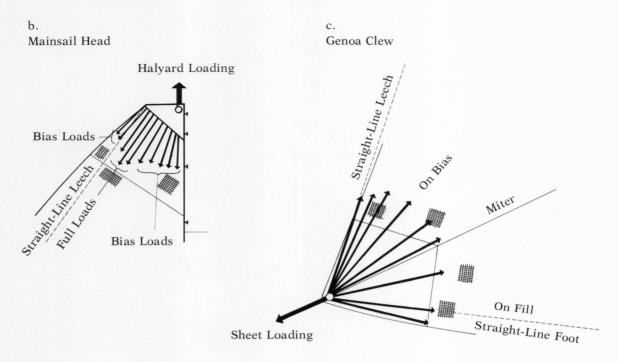

the sail. To put it another way, the greater the stretch, the flatter the sail (stretch correction) has to be, so that when it is under load the stretch will form exactly the amount of fullness needed—no more and no less. Obviously, this must be precisely calculated. Even then, however, the stretch allowance can be for only one wind velocity, because more or less loading than the designed range will need a different correction. Again, the more overall stretch in the cloth, the more this problem is magnified and the more limited the range of the particular sail, because even a small loading change puts it quickly out of the designed shape.

Construction of Draft

Basically, deeper draft or a fuller sail is created by putting more sailcloth over a given span, and conversely, shallower draft is created by designing less cloth over a given span, such as between the luff and leech. If there is no excess cloth beyond the minimum needed to span the distance between two points, the cloth will be flat as a board; without some excess cloth, curvature cannot form.

Over the years, sails made of cloth with considerable stretch were traditionally made by the *edge-cut* system (Fig. 56). By this method, mainsail panels are laid flat on the floor and excess cloth is added in a curve along the luff and the foot. These curves assume a straight line when the sail is fastened along the mast and boom, and the extra cloth lies along the spars in a curl. When the wind fills the sail, pressure is exerted on the central area, pulling this excess cloth from along the edge of boom and mast to form the draft. The same thing happens with a jib or genoa.

The edge-cut method is dependent on bias elongation, since the additional cloth cannot move from the luff and foot into the sail without a change in weave configuration. Bias elongation is greater in the soft-finish cloths, because the threads change in their angle to one another more easily, and the weave configuration in bias loading moves from its rectangular form to a parallelogram. (See Fig. 49.) With this kind of sail, draft will change more with variations in the wind velocity. The stronger the wind, the farther aft it pushes the draft in a sail. This is the reverse of what you want: the more it breezes up, the more you want the draft to stay forward. Here, as in most cases, stretch is the enemy.

Generally, you cannot use the edge-cut method with low stretch material because there is not enough bias stretch to allow the draft to work into the sail. Therefore, draft is built into a sail by a method of curving and shaping individual panels called *seam dilation* (Fig. 57). A convex curve in the edge of a panel provides the extra cloth when the panels are sewn together. The sail is designed with the extra cloth in a specific location, and since there is little bias movement, the draft stays put. Increases in wind velocity will not shift the draft appreciably, and the sail retains its designed shape over a range of wind velocities.

Smaller boats in the one-design classes do not have high loadings, and so there is not enough wind pressure to force the draft into a sail made by the edge-cut method. Wind force has less effect on the shape through stretch, and the sail fills with a minimum of air. In fact, most sails today are made by a combination of both methods, but with different proportions of the edge-cut and seam-dilation methods.

Once the sail is made, you cannot change the actual amount of cloth

Fig. 56
Edge-Cut Method

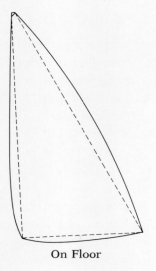

On Floor

a. The excess round in front of the straight line (which will become the mast line) is forced back into the sail by the wind to form draft. If you press your finger in the center of the drawing, you can visualize how the wind pushes the excess cloth into the sail to form draft.

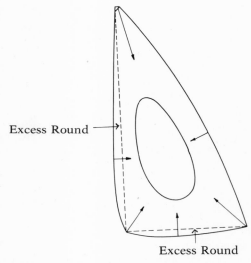

Excess Round

Excess Round

b. On Spars—when the sail made by this method is placed on the spars, the excess cloth (under pressure from the wind) moves back into the sail to form curvature.

Fig. 57
Seam-Dilation Method.   The curved seams are sewn together, producing draft.

Fig. 58

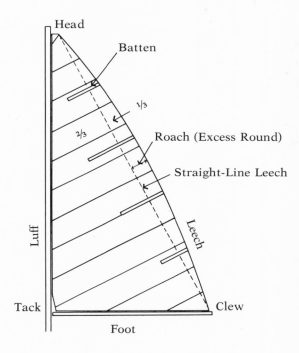

Head
Batten
1/3
2/3
Roach (Excess Round)
Straight-Line Leech
Luff
Leech
Tack
Clew
Foot

Fig. 59
With an excessive roach (50 per cent or more of batten length), the leech is very difficult to support.

between two points, but you can adjust draft by using the same principles: if you move the two points closer together by, for example, moving the main outhaul or headsail clew in toward the luff, then the same amount of cloth covers a shorter span, and the additional cloth will form curvature. Draft control will be fully discussed in Chapter 5.

Increased hull weight places an increased loading in the sails. As boats get larger, the sail loadings increase greatly. However, sail weights do not increase in the same proportion. A 4½-ounce cloth for a 700-pound Lightning is adequate, so cloth stretch is at a minimum under sail. A 60-foot, 70,000-pound boat should use a cloth of 12 to 15 ounces to have the same relative stretch. But, larger boat owners seem far more conscious of weight aloft and use sails made from a lighter cloth, around 9 ounces, producing a greater relative stretch. Because of the extra stretch in the cloth of the larger sails the edge-cut method is used to create draft in the sail.

In the smaller sail, with its lower cloth stretch, the draft must be built in. If cut by the edge-cut method, the extra cloth in the edge-cut curves will just hang against the luff or foot and not work into the body of the sail, so draft would not be correctly formed.

The adequate weight low-stretch sailcloth allowing built-in shape produces the most stable, consistent shape.

Battens

Battens serve two basic purposes: first, they stiffen the long, free edge of a sail to prevent it from curling or fluttering, as in a working jib; second, they are necessary to support the fair curve of leech roach. (Roach is a curve in the edge of a sail out beyond the line from masthead to clew point.) As shown in Figure 58, there is considerable round beyond the straight-line leech, and this would simply flop over without any support from battens. As a general rule, for each inch of batten extending into the roach (beyond the straight-line leech), you should have approximately 2 inches of batten *inside* the straight-line leech. If the batten were set so that half was in the roach and half in the triangular sail area, then the leech would have a cantilever or seesaw motion and be very unstable, as shown in Figure 59. This is the problem that some one-design classes encounter—where big roaches are allowed but the battens are restricted.

Part Two

BASIC SAILS:
Handling and Trim Techniques

Chapter 5

Draft Control

Draft control enables you to create and keep the best aerodynamic shape in your sail when you are going to windward and relying entirely on aerodynamic forces for your driving power. The farther off the wind you sail, the more the power comes from the simple resistance of the sail to the wind, and the less you have to worry about holding the perfect aerodynamic shape, although draft controls can help here, too.

Remember that the sailmaker can design the aerodynamic shape of the sail for one wind velocity only, as we have seen in Chapter 4. He will put the right amount of draft in the right place for a breeze of, say, 5 knots or 9 knots or 18 knots or whatever meets your need. Once the wind force changes, however, the sail's shape—because of cloth stretch—will also change. Not only does the draft get fuller as the wind gets stronger, but the greater pressure from the wind pushes the draft aft; conversely, as the wind force decreases, the draft may move too far forward and the sail will flatten out. If, as generally happens, the proper shape of the sail is altered by changes in the force of the wind, countermeasures called draft controls must be applied to keep the correct amount of draft in the desired location (Fig. 60).

These draft controls can increase the effective range of the sail to 3 or 4 knots above and below the designed velocity. Thus, a medium- to light-air sail might be designed for 8 knots, but could have a range of between 4 and 12 knots through draft-control techniques. The limits of a sail's range are determined largely by the stretch in the cloth: the more stretch, the more a small change in wind velocity will adversely affect sail shape.

But draft controls cannot do the impossible: with sail designed for 8 knots, you probably would not be able to get the sail full enough below 3 or 4 knots to have it function as effectively as desired; while in heavy winds, when neither cloth weight nor designed shape is right for this condition, the sail might very well be damaged if you have to apply excessive force on a

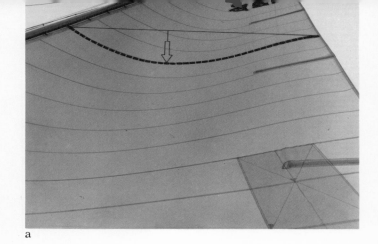

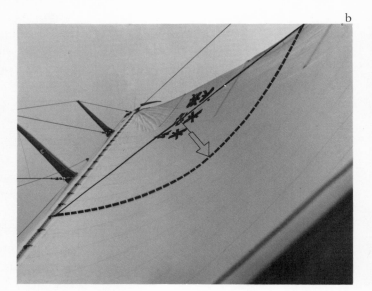

Fig. 60

This series—(a), (b), (c)—shows quite
dramatically the need for proper draft
control. The same sail is shown in each
photograph, with the same medium-air
draft control setting in each. Only the
strength of the wind is different—but look
at the dramatic change in sail shape. In
the light winds of 6-8 knots (a), the draft is
too far forward and the sail is too flat. In
the medium breeze of 12 knots (b), the
fullest point of draft is just where it should
be—in this case almost halfway
back—but the leech is a little tight. In the
heavy-air photograph (18 knots) (c), the
draft has been blown far aft, where it will
cause excess heeling and a decrease in
forward driving force—just the opposite
of what is desirable for this condition.

a

b

c

particular control to contort it into the shape you want. The same warning applies to using these controls to work a poorly cut sail into a more effective shape.

Thus, although controls are a great help, you must use a sail built to the wind range in which you are sailing. If you have only one suit of sails, you have to manipulate draft as best you can, taking care not to destroy the sail by pulling the cloth beyond its elastic limits and causing permanent distortion.

As a general rule of thumb, for windward work, draft should be located approximately 33 to 40 per cent of the way aft in a jib or genoa and about halfway aft in a mainsail. However, remember that the right location of draft in a mainsail can be affected by the headsail used. The more genoa overlap there is, for example, the farther back the draft has to be (because of the genoa's major effect on the apparent-wind angle). With maximum genoa overlap, you might have to keep the draft as far as 55 per cent of the way aft, while if you have no jib at all, as in a catboat, the draft need be only about 40 per cent of the way aft or in approximately the same position as you would have it in a jib or genoa (Fig. 61). The height of the genoa also has to be taken into consideration: if the genoa is masthead high, then the entire main is affected, while a low-cut genoa will affect only the lower portions of the sail. In this case, the draft in the upper portion of the main can be much farther forward than that down low. A working jib will have less effect on the location of draft, since it has little or no overlap and therefore affects only the leading edge of the main.

Keeping mainsail draft in proper relation to genoa overlap is one of the main functions of draft control. The mainsail is usually built to match the overlap of the maximum size or No. 1 genoa. However, as the wind increases, you have to use a smaller genoa. This genoa will have a shorter luff and less overlap; consequently, the genoa leech will be farther forward, and the redirection of the apparent wind will not be as acute over the mainsail. The mainsail draft can therefore be slightly farther forward, and you have to move it forward artificially, with draft controls.

Once the proper location of draft has been determined, draft controls should keep it there—in every strength of wind—up to the physical limits of the sail as described. The amount of draft, on the other hand, should be varied according to wind velocity. Draft is the source of the driving power of the boat: the more draft you have, the more power in the sail—up to prac-

Fig. 61
Ideally, the point of maximum draft should be 33 to 40 per cent aft in the genoa and approximately halfway back in the main.

Genoa

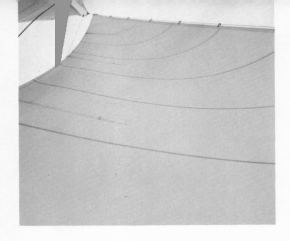

Main

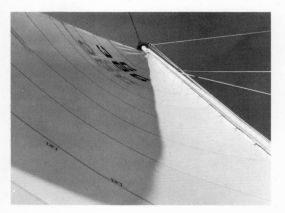

tical limits: until the point where the sail luffs or, in heavy weather, where the boat is overpowered, and neither crew weight nor hull stability can keep the boat on its feet. In either case, you have to make the sail flatter by decreasing the draft. In light air, when you want to get as much driving power as possible, try to get as much draft as you can while still holding the optimum pointing angle.

PUTTING ON THE SAILS

The first step in draft control is to bend on your sails so that the draft is where it was originally designed to go. A great help in first setting up your sails would be a drawing showing the approximate cross-sectional shapes your sail should have at three different heights for the specified sailing con-

Fig. 62
Example of Cross-Sectional Sail Shapes
Showing Hypothetical Setting for a
Specific Rig in Medium Air.   Each
individual boat will have different
requirements.

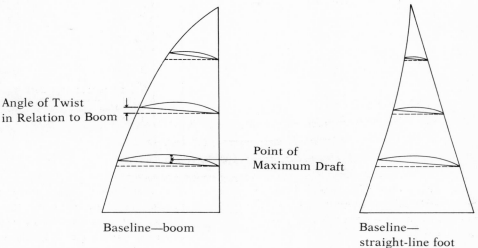

Angle of Twist
in Relation to Boom

Point of
Maximum Draft

Baseline—boom

Baseline—
straight-line foot

dition (Fig. 62). If you cannot get a drawing like this, then use the basic rule
of thumb mentioned above.

It is important to check the position of the attachment points of the
sails, particularly the tack and the clew. The corners are the main stress
points on the sail and must be in their designed positions to take the load
evenly. Unless the fittings dictate otherwise (see below), the corners of the
sail should be on a straight-line projection of the luff or the foot. This means
that the corners should be the same distance from the spar or headstay as
all the other points along the same edge of the sail (Fig. 63).

If the corner of a sail is out of its designed position, the loading is
transferred to the point of attachment nearest the corner. This distorts the
balance of the sail and affects the draft. Imagine that you have put on the
main with the tack attached too far aft on the boom. All the load transfers
to the first slide on the mast or to the point where the sail leaves the groove.
This flattens the whole lower corner of the sail by removing any edge-cut or
built-in curvature. Conversely, if the tack is moved farther forward than
designed, it leaves excess sailcloth around the lower slide or base of the

Fig. 63

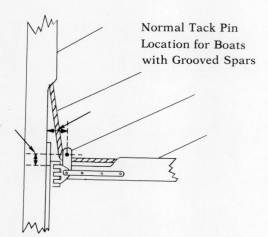

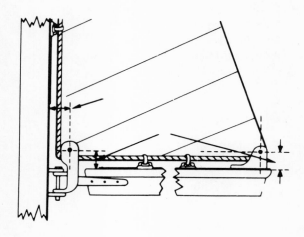

Normal Tack Pin Location for Boats with Grooved Spars

a. Tack Position for Boats with Grooved Spars—the sail has to be cut back from the base of the mast groove to match the aft tack position.

b. Proper Tack and Clew-Pin Locations for Boats Using Sail Track—the pins are located so that the rope or tape in the luff and foot is the same distance away from the track at all points (indicated by arrows).

groove; this excess cloth forms extra draft forward just where it isn't wanted. The same problems occur with a clew position that is too high or too low, or with a headboard position that is too close or too far away from the mast (Fig. 64).

If the boat's rig has some special fittings, the sailmaker adjusts the sail so that the corner is properly located in relation to the rest of the sail. For example, if your boat is fitted with roller reefing, the tack fitting can be as much as 7 or 8 inches aft of the mast (Fig. 65). Therefore, the lower part of the luff, instead of being attached close to the mast, has to be cut back to prevent distortion in the shape of the sail. With the use of the Cunningham hole, the tack position is not as critical. This luff control is explained fully later; but, in brief, when tensioned, it relieves the load on the tack pin so that the alignment is not so vital.

With your attachment points squared away, the next question is how

Fig. 64

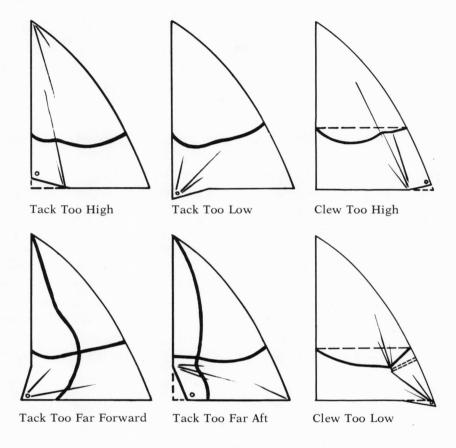

Tack Too High   Tack Too Low   Clew Too High

Tack Too Far Forward   Tack Too Far Aft   Clew Too Low

Fig. 65
For roller reefing, the tack is cut back to
allow the sail to roll up around the boom.

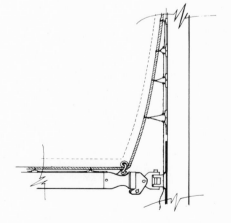

tight to pull out the mainsail foot. The clew is generally restricted by either the boom length itself or a maximum legal limit indicated by a black band. In a good breeze you will probably want as much tension along the foot as you can get, and so it should be pulled to the maximum setting. If the air is light, you may want to ease the outhaul fitting 1 or 2 inches so that the excess cloth along the boom has a chance to work up into the sail and increase draft.

   With the jib or genoa snap hooks secured to the stay, you are now ready to hoist the main and jib. Now comes the question of how far up or how tight to pull the halyards. On one-design boats the main halyard often terminates at a halyard lock aloft, or the halyard wire has an eye at its end which is fastened by a hook near the deck level. In either case, no variation is possible and the top of the main will always be at the right height (Fig. 66). But in general, it is standard practice to take up the main halyard as high as is practical, so that the headboard still has freedom to go from side to side without hitting the backstay. However, on cruising boats and on many one designs, the setting of the tack and head of the main may be governed by black bands at the top and bottom of the spars, indicating the limits between which the luff should be set. (On cruising boats the band limits are established at the time the boat is measured for her racing

Fig.66

a. Main Halyard Locks Used on One Designs—there are similar locks for the jib halyard.

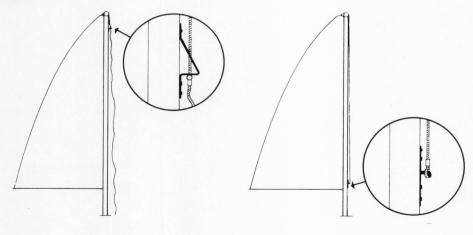

b. Jib Halyard Locks

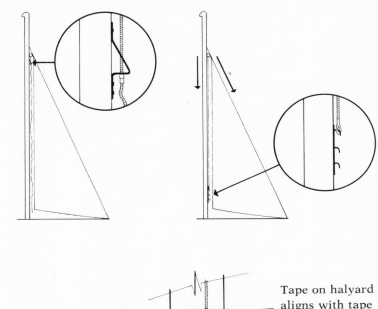

Fig. 67

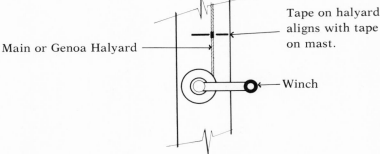

Main or Genoa Halyard —————

Tape on halyard
aligns with tape
on mast.

Winch

certificate, while the one-design bands are established by class rules (see Chapter 18, Measuring Sails). Many yachtsmen still go through the procedure of raising the mainsail and looking up from the stern or yelling over to another boat to find out if the head of the sail is "at the band." Actually, the easiest method is to put tape on the wire halyard and a mark or tape on the mast near the winch; when these marks line up (Fig. 67), the mainsail is at its limit aloft.

Steps for raising the jib or genoa halyard vary somewhat. On a one design, a halyard lock or halyard wire and eye are ordinarily used. In this case, the backstay (if there is one) generally has to be released to create a forward rake in the mast, giving enough slack in the halyard wire to get the lock or eye engaged (or, conversely, unlocked). Then, as a rule, the mast is supported between the jib luff wire and the secured backstay and/or mainsheet.

Most cruising-boat genoas have stretchy rope luffs to allow adjustment for different wind conditions, and so it is a good idea to mark the halyard for each condition so that you can quickly see the setting. This will be a good starting point from which to make your fine adjustments. There are no restricting bands governing the cruising-boat genoa luff, and if the limits are not marked you might pull the halyard wire splice right into the sheave and damage the sheave. Without the guide marks it is difficult to know how much more you can pull the halyard up before this danger point is reached.

DRAFT CONTROLS UNDER SAIL

Let us examine ways to adjust sail shape for different conditions once the sails are raised. One of the basic principles of sail adjustment is that the shape of a sail is affected by changes in tension on any of its three sides: luff, foot, and leech. When you tighten the edge of a sail, the cloth near the tensioned area is pulled into a straight line and, in the process of changing from a curved to a straight-line configuration, cloth is drawn from the central areas of the sail. In other words, tension on the edge of a sail pulls the sail over a longer distance and draws sailcloth away from the central areas, thus reducing draft. When overdone, this excess cloth is held in a curl next to the spar. This is called a *tension curl* (Fig. 68). Easing the tension allows the cloth to work back into the sail, creating curvature or draft.

MAINSAIL DRAFT CONTROL

Luff tension controls the fore and aft location of the draft. The tension is changed by moving the whole boom up or down on a sliding gooseneck or by keeping the tack in a fixed position and using a device such as the Cunningham hole (see Fig. 69) in the sail above the tack. If the draft in the

Fig. 68

a. The Cunningham hole, or any luff-tensioning device, pulls the draft forward when tightened (to counter the wind force driving the draft aft) and, when eased, allows the draft to move aft.

b. The photograph shows luff-tension curl from too much Cunningham trim in light air.

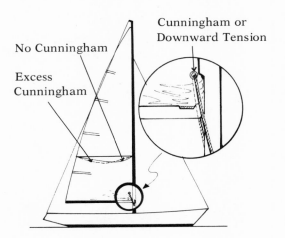

No Cunningham

Cunningham or Downward Tension

Excess Cunningham

Fig. 69
The Cunningham hole consists of a line run through a hole in the mainsail luff which is trimmed by pulley arrangement. By marking the mast off in inches, you can easily duplicate the proper Cunningham setting needed to get the draft in the right place for a particular condition. The Cunningham allows you to ease the luff tension without raising the boom as you would have to when using a downhaul system. This allows you to have the advantage of a longer luff and, therefore, more sail area in light air.

mainsail is forced aft by increased wind, it can be moved forward again by putting tension on the luff. If the draft is too far forward, and sometimes it can be, then ease the tension on the luff (Fig. 70).

Foot tension controls the amount of draft in the lower half of the sail: by easing foot tension you create more draft, and by tightening it you flatten the sail (Fig. 71). This is handled by the outhaul.

Fig. 70
Tightening the luff tension moves draft forward; easing it allows draft to move aft.

a. Excess Luff Tension (Tension Curl)

b. Moderate Luff Tension (Draft Still Too Far Foward)

c. Proper Luff Tension (Draft in Center)

Fig. 71
The Effects of Outhaul Tension.

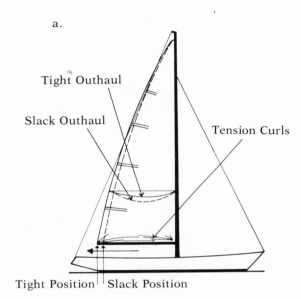

b.

Tightening the outhaul removes draft (b).

Easing the outhaul, and moving the clew
forward, adds draft to the lower portion of
the sails (c).

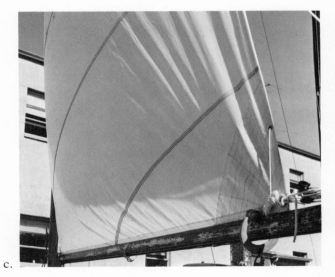

c.

Sheet tension controls the leech. This is perhaps the most overlooked factor in draft control. If the leech is loose, it removes curvature from the after portion of the sail, rendering it relatively ineffective. A loose leech also decreases the total amount of remaining draft and causes the deepest point of draft to move forward. The opposite is true of a tight leech: a tight leech curves the leech to windward, thus increasing draft in the after portion of the sail, making the deepest point of draft farther aft. In the extreme, either of these conditions will produce a bad aerodynamic shape, the flow patterns will be greatly disrupted, and the effect on boat speed will be dramatic (Fig. 72).

Fig. 72
Effects of Leech Shape

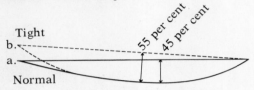

In a tight leech condition, the leech moves to windward. When the new chord from luff to leech is drawn, you can easily see the results of a tight leech: the sail is appreciably fuller and the draft is farther aft.

In a loose or soft leech condition, the leech falls off. The new chord from luff to leech shows that a soft leech produces a much flatter sail; the deepest point of draft is fairly far forward and there is almost no draft aft.

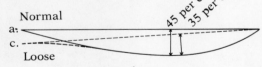

d.
Remember that in both conditions the sail shape is identical until trailing edge. The plane of the leech alone accounts for the very large differences shown; section (b) has almost twice the depth of section (c). The leech plane is a result of the way the sail was made or of the way the sail is being trimmed—by the mainsheet in particular.

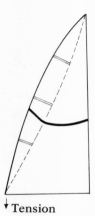

↓Tension

1. Tight Leech

2. Loose Leech

Fig. 73

a. Slack Leech—as the sheet is eased too much, the boom moves up toward the masthead, decreasing support for the leech. With a slack leech, draft is removed from the after portion of the sail. The forces are forward, but the total force is reduced.

NOTE: once the sheet setting is correct, then the traveler can be varied effectively.

b. Fair Leech—the leech is neither too tight nor too loose. Forces are forward and the total force is stronger than with a slack leech.

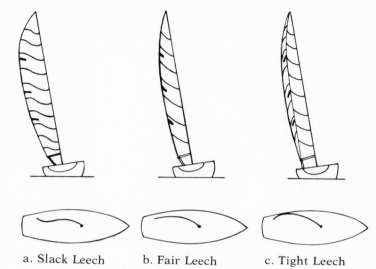

a. Slack Leech   b. Fair Leech   c. Tight Leech

c. As you tension the mainsheet, the leech moves to windward and is in more of a straight line. With a tight leech, the draft moves aft. The total force is strongest but more to the side.

Without proper battens and the proper cut in the sail in the batten area (both of which are up to the sailmaker), you cannot have good leech control. However, once these are right, the sheet will allow you to control the leech. Looking at the sail from astern, you will see that if you tighten the sheet, the leech tends to become a straight line from head to clew. As you ease the sheet, the leech falls off to leeward more and more, realigning each fore and aft horizontal section of the sail to the wind (see Fig. 73). This fall-off or twist is usually greatest at a point about three-quarters of the way up the leech.

A certain amount of twist is necessary because, as mentioned earlier, wind velocity increases with height above water, and therefore the angle of attack has to change correspondingly. As the wind velocity increases, the closer that section of the sail can be pointed toward the wind. Twist allows you to change the angle of attack of any vertical section of the sail to correspond to the wind velocity at that level. Since there is such a slight margin between luffing and stalling—only a few degrees under most conditions—and since, at times, the sail section aloft should be pointed an average of about 5 degrees closer to the wind than the sail section near the foot, you can see how important twist control is in keeping the whole sail working efficiently. However, again because the margins between luffing and stalling are so small, you have to be very careful that you do not ease the sheet too much and allow excess twist. Just the smallest error here in sheet trim can make the sail luff or stall aloft. If you have the right amount of twist, and the foot and luff tensions are right, the entire leading edge of the sail should backwind or luff just about simultaneously. Take a look at Figure 74 to see what a well-set leech should look like.

How does leech control actually affect draft? When you tighten the leech by tensioning the sheet, the leech stiffens or curves around to windward and the sail automatically has more curvature or draft (this is the opposite of fall-off). As with twist, the effect is greatest about three-quarters of the way up, and so this is where you get the most additional draft. Conversely, easing the sheet flattens the sail aloft as twist becomes excessive. (This is also an anti-heeling device, which will be discussed in Chapter 8.)

This is the way sheet tension normally works. However, when you are doing very fine tuning in light air, there is something else to consider. If the sheet is overtrimmed so that the leech is virtually a straight line, the small amount of stretch in the leech area is pulled out, making the sail flatter. If you ease the sheet a few inches, the stretch is alleviated, allowing some draft to re-form. So in this one instance, easing the sheet for the first few inches *increases* draft. Beyond this point, however, easing the sheet causes the leech to fall off excessively, and the sail will as usual be flattened in the maximum twist area.

Although the sheet is the primary leech control, another valuable aid is the *leech line*, a kind of drawstring running from head to clew inside the tabling of the leech, which, when it is tensioned, stiffens the leech. The leech line is particularly helpful in light air when you need to tighten the leech and you do not want to trim in the sheet too much. It is used with increasing effectiveness as you go farther and farther off the wind; that is, from the moment the end of the boom is no longer over the boat and the sheet is not pulling straight down. (At this point, you also need a vang, which is discussed in Chapter 6.) Remember that the leech line is a secondary control which adjusts only the outer rim of the sail. It must be coordinated with mainsheet tension, which affects the whole after third of the sail.

When permitted, another factor to consider in draft control is mast bend, which is used mostly on small boats. This removes draft from the forward portion of the sail. When the mast bends, the luff of the mainsail moves farther away from the leech and flattens the sail in the forward area. This flattening is most noticeable where the greatest bend in the mast occurs. Actually, though, the flattening is greatest on a line between the point of maximum mast bend and the fixed clew (Fig. 75). Because the clew is fixed, when the mast is overbent the sail can be stretched taut like a wire

Fig. 74
A Well-Set Leech

Fig. 75
Flattening Effects of Mast Bend

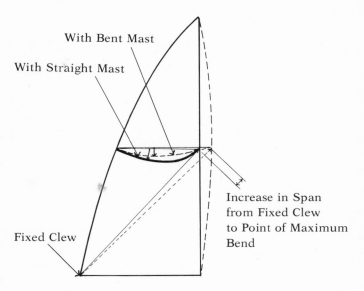

With Bent Mast

With Straight Mast

Fixed Clew

Increase in Span
from Fixed Clew
to Point of Maximum
Bend

between these two points. This causes "hard lines," as shown in Figure 76. Since mast bend removes draft from the forward areas of the sail, along the luff, the cross-sections become flat in the forward half, causing the point of maximum draft to move aft. The Cunningham hole, or downhaul, generally will have to be pulled tighter to bring the point of maximum draft forward and reinstate the smooth curvature to the front half of the sail.

Since sails are made for specific amounts of mast bend, there has to be a way for the sailor to check the amount of bend he has at any given time. One method is to mark the sail as shown in the photograph of *Columbia* (Fig. 77). These marks should go on the sail at the estimated point of maximum bend or, if the rig is such that you can control bend at different heights, the series of marks should go at two vertical heights so that relative bend in the top and the bottom can be measured. A smaller boat will probably only need marks 1 inch apart; a larger boat with a bendy rig may need them as far apart as 3 or 4 inches. When you sight up the luff of the main (Fig. 78), these marks will tell you how many inches the mast has bent forward of the straight line of sight from tack to head. Thus, you can tell if you have 3 inches of mast bend, or 8 inches, or however many inches are indicated by the number of marks from the mast to your line of sight.

On boats with a flexing mast and jib-headed rig, the stronger the wind, the more the mast bends. Consequently, mainsails for these boats are cut with extra cloth on the edge to allow for the bend so that the sail does not flatten out too severely. However, when the wind lightens and the mast gets straighter, the extra cloth hangs in the forward area of the sail. When this happens, easing luff tension will usually allow most of the cloth to work aft in the sail; however, if the air is very light, to make the sail fit properly it may be necessary to bend the mast artificially by whatever devices you have available, such as a backstay, a movable deck partner or step, or on a larger boat, by tightening of the forward shrouds to pull the mast forward in the middle.

If you have no way to make the mast bend in light air—for example, if you have a 5-0-5 with a jib-headed rig and no backstays—the only way to cause the mast to bend is to put more pressure on the sheet, but this is undesirable in light air. There really is no solutiom to this problem and, as a result, many of the one-design boats where this situation occurs are now using less flexible masts, thus avoiding the problem: there is less mast bend in heavier air, and the sail does not have to be cut with as much excess cloth.

Fig. 76
When the mast is overbent, as in this photograph, the leech can move forward to absorb some of the excess bend, thus keeping a little draft in the sail. However, the line from the maximum bend point to the clew has fixed extremes since the clew can't move forward. Therefore, as the luff bows out, hard lines form along the line of maximum strain between clew and point of maximum bend. In most boats, mast bend is controllable and the sail is cut to fit the amount of bend that should be used. In this picture, excessive bend at the spreader level could have been controlled by lower backstays.

Fig. 77
Mast-Bend Marks on Sail

Fig. 78
Line of Sight from Tack to Head.
Mast-bend measurement is taken from a line of sight from the after face of the mast at the tack to the after face of the mast at the head.

The ideal spar is difficult to make. It will, however, be one that will bend very readily in light air but will become quite stiff and resistant in medium airs and will not bend beyond a set amount in heavy air. All kinds of devices have been created to try to achieve this. On some bendy 12-Meter booms, for example, crossed wires were strung internally; they were slack until a set amount of bend took place in the spar, at which point the wires were tensioned, preventing further bending. But this system was too complicated and expensive for general use.

Another draft-control device on the main is a zipper from tack to clew along the foot. You simply zip up the excess draft down low in the sail when you do not want it moving up into the center of the sail. The sail is zipped up going to windward and then unzipped for reaching or downwind work and once in a while for light-air windward work when you want fullness. The only problem with zippers is that they sometimes break—and then you are stuck with a highly inefficient sail going to windward (Fig. 79).

Fig. 79

a.

Zipper Foot In

b.

Zipper Foot Released

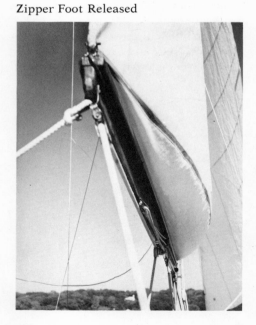

JIB AND GENOA DRAFT CONTROLS

The principles of draft control are generally the same for jib and genoa as for the main: luff tension controls the fore and aft location, foot tension controls the amount of draft in the lower portion, and leech tension controls the draft at various heights. However, unlike the main, where all the controls are separate and independent, on the headsail things are complicated by the fact that the foot and leech tensions are controlled by only one line—the sheet. You cannot change one without affecting the other. There is a way, though, to emphasize the tensioning of one side rather than the other: the trick is in the positioning of the deck lead through which you first run the sheet after it leaves the sail.

Moving the sheet lead aft puts tension on the foot and is similar to tightening the outhaul on the mainsail; it flattens the lower portion of the sail. At the same time, there is a corresponding decrease in tension on the leech, causing more leech curvature or twist and thus flattening the upper portion of the sail. Moving the sheet lead forward has just the opposite effect: it tightens the leech and creates more draft high in the sail. At the same time, there is less foot tension, so that the lower portion of the jib is affected as if an outhaul had been eased, forming more draft in the lower portion of the sail (Fig. 80).

If the sheet lead is too far forward, the sail will be so full at the bottom that it will luff there while the upper portion is still full and drawing. If the lead is too far aft, the upper portion of the sail will fall off into excess twist, and the sail will then luff aloft first. To get the best out of your sail, it is important to avoid either of these extremes; the only way to do this is to keep fiddling with the lead until the sail luffs evenly from head to foot. In addition, there should be an even balance, so that, as the sheet is eased, the desired draft increases in amount proportionately throughout the sail.

Here is a rule of thumb to help you find the initial location of the sheet lead from which to start your fine adjustment. Since the leech and foot are both free spans, both depend on sheet tension for support. If the leech and foot are both the same length, they require equal support; the longer one edge is in relation to the other, the more support that edge needs. To give you a starting point, if both leech and foot are the same length, the sheet should be led from the sail in a direction that if projected upward through

Fig. 80
Fore and aft positions of the sheet lead
affect both the foot and leech shape.

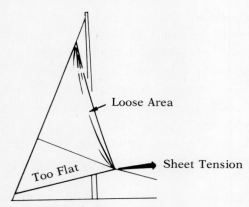

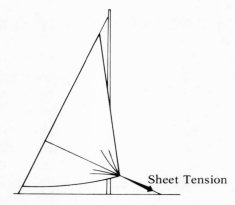

a. Sheet lead aft increases tension on foot
and eases tension on leech.

b. Sheet lead at correct setting; leech and
foot are properly shaped.

c. Sheet lead forward eases tension on
foot, adds tension on leech.

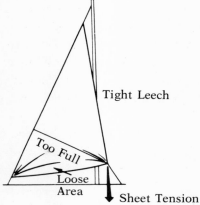

the clew to the luff of the sail would divide the clew angle in half and reach
the luff at the mid-point. (This projection should start at the bottom of the
sheet lead sheave.) As the leech gets longer than the foot, the sheet has
to be led in a more downward direction to support the leech, and therefore the lead is moved further forward. A line projected from the top of the
sheave would reach to 60 per cent or more up the luff. On a tall, narrow
working jib or a tall, thin decksweeper jib (see Chapter 10, Headsails) the
projected line through the clew might reach 70 to 75 per cent up the luff
(Fig. 81).

Fig. 81
Headsail Trimming Block Position.

Longer spans require higher tension to control twist and curvature. If the leech and foot are of different lengths, the lead must be angled toward the longer free side. The angle increases as the difference between the leech and foot lengths becomes greater.

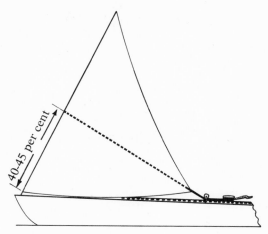

a. Leech is 20 per cent longer than foot (approximately 180 per cent genoa). Lead position is a line projected from about 40-45 per cent up luff through clew to trimming block.

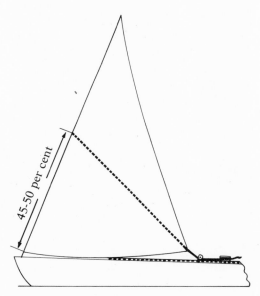

b. Leech is 50 per cent longer than foot (approximately 150 per cent genoa). Lead position is a line projected from about 45-50 per cent up luff through clew to trimming block.

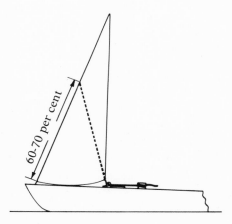

c. Leech is 2½ times the foot length (approximate proportions of a working jib). Lead position is a line about 60-70 per cent up luff through clew to trimming block.

The location of draft in the jib or genoa is controlled by adjusting the tension on the luff, either by halyard, downhaul, or Cunningham hole (see Fig. 84). If the draft is too far back, tightening the luff pulls it forward. This will also flatten the sail a little. However, when you put tension on the halyard, you lift the head of the sail, which raises the clew at the same time. This makes it necessary to move the sheet lead aft and readjust the sheet tension to maintain the balance between leech and foot tension (Fig. 82). Using the downhaul or Cunningham hole avoids having to change the lead, because the clew remains in the same place—only the tack is affected.

Fig. 82
When halyard is raised to pull draft forward, clew is also lifted, requiring a change in sheet block position.

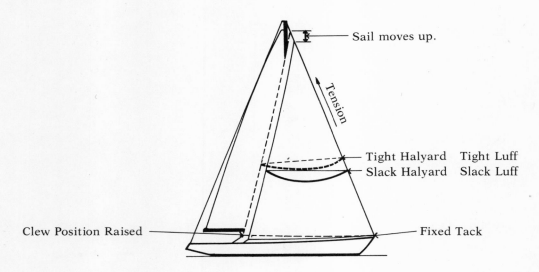

Sail moves up.

Tension

Tight Halyard   Tight Luff
Slack Halyard   Slack Luff

Clew Position Raised

Fixed Tack

Luff tension controls the location of draft. Note raised clew position with halyard raised.

One form of downhaul used by one designs to keep the draft in the right place is the jerk-string method (Fig. 83). The jib is attached at the head and fixed in position by a halyard lock. The sail's leading edge is actually a sleeve that fits around the luff wire. By pulling on a line attached to the cloth at the tack, the entire luff of the sail slides down over the wire. This practical system also eliminates the friction from the halyard block and makes adjustment easier. And, of course, you do not have to change the jib leads, because the clew again remains in the same position. The only problem is that to be able to pull the tack down, it has to be some distance above the deck to start with. This raises the foot of the sail, and if it is too high, the decksweeper effect of the jib is reduced when the luff tension is eased (see Chapter 10).

Another form of downhaul used on cruising boats is the Cunningham hole on the genoa (Fig. 84). In order to use it, the wire halyard fixes the head

Fig. 83
Jerk String or Vary Luff Jib.

Jib luff wire is tensioned inside luff tabling. Jib is secured at head but can be stretched over its own wire by pulling jib tack down by means of downhaul control line, which terminates in cockpit.

Fig. 84
Cunningham Hole for Genoas.

The Cunningham pulls the genoa or jib down just above the tack, tensioning the luff and producing a flatter sail with the draft farther forward.
Clew stays in same position.

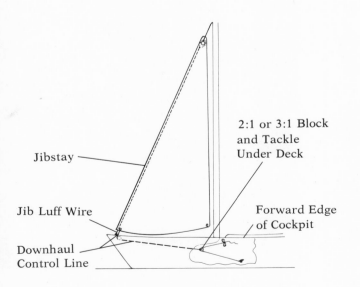

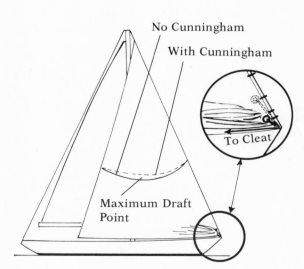

of the sail at the maximum height; luff tension is then applied by tensioning the Cunningham hole. To do this, you need the elasticity of a rope luff instead of a wire luff in the sail.

Another device to control shape in the genoa is a leech line similar to that used on the main. The leech line runs inside the leech tabling of the genoa and either goes through the clew hole and ties back on itself—which requires a lot of tying and untying for each adjustment—or can go through the clew hole and up to a point on the sail where it is laced in a figure-eight pattern around a pair of stiff leather buttons (Fig. 85).

The genoa leech is perhaps the most difficult edge of any sail to keep smooth and in a straight run without a curl or hook to windward. In working jibs, the leech is stiffened by battens, but in a genoa, the leech is reinforced only by tabling, or extra cloth along the free edge. But the tabling, with its double or even triple layers of cloth, will stretch less than the cloth in front of it. Therefore, when pressure from the wind creates draft, the cloth in front of the edge will stretch, but the tabling will not, producing a cupped leech (Fig. 86). This will create resistance on the trailing edge because the air cannot exit smoothly off the sail. One way around this problem is to put the tabling on very loosely with a lot of slack. Thus, as wind velocity increases and the cloth in front of the tabling stretches out, the two become equal. However, in light air this technique causes the leech tabling to be quite floppy, and you must use a leech line to support the leech. Then, in

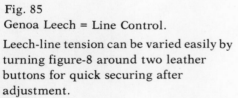

Fig. 85
Genoa Leech = Line Control.

Leech-line tension can be varied easily by turning figure-8 around two leather buttons for quick securing after adjustment.

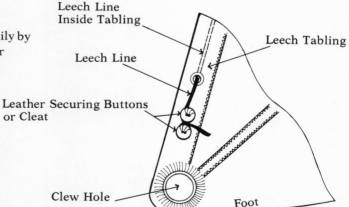

Fig. 86

Shape with Excess Wind Pressure

Normal Shape

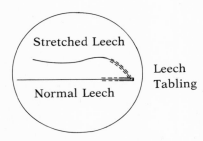

a. Leech curl adds to the drag of a genoa and ruins efficiency.

b. Curled Leech in a Genoa Caused by Tight Tabling

increasing air, the leech line can be eased so that the sail and the tabling can move into balance. You have to adjust the leech-line tension for each velocity of wind. A general rule is to ease the leech line until the sail flutters and then pull it in until the flutter just stops, and no more. Remember, too, that every time you trim the sheet your leech may be elongated or shortened, so that you may have to adjust the leech-line tension then, as well.

Another factor in draft control is jib- or genoa-stay sag. As we saw in Chapter 3, this is a phenomenon which occurs as wind velocity increases. The stronger wind exerts greater pressure on the center of the sail, forming more draft. The cloth to form this draft comes primarily from the luff, which is pulled aft and which in turn pulls the stay to which it is attached aft, thus causing sag (Fig. 87). The way to prevent sag is to increase tension on the jib- or headstay to which the luff is fastened. On a cruising boat, this is usually done by tightening the backstay; on a one design that has no backstay, it is done by mainsheet tension. However, the amount of tension you can exert on the headstay is limited: if you exert too much pressure, you may break your mast through overcompression, or you may pull up the ends of the boat (bend the hull) and cause damage to the hull structure.

Fig. 87
Effects of Jibstay Sag on Sail
Shape.   Luff sag increases as wind
velocity increases, and creates two
problems. First, the luff moving aft
creates more draft in the sail just when a
flatter sail is needed. Second, the luff
moving aft allows the entire central
section of the sail (except for the fixed
head and clew) to swing aft and, at the
same time, move to the side of the boat. As
a result, the forces on the sail are less
forward and more to the side. The genoa
has, therefore, more draft at an increased
sideways angle.

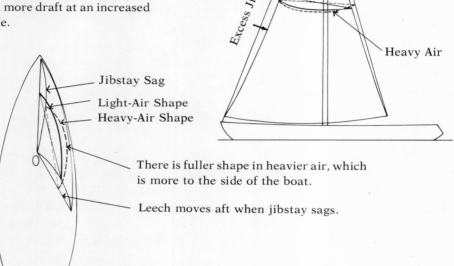

a. Plan View

Leech moves aft
in heavier air.

Excess Jibstay Sag

Light Air

Heavy Air

Jibstay Sag

Light-Air Shape

Heavy-Air Shape

There is fuller shape in heavier air, which
is more to the side of the boat.

Leech moves aft when jibstay sags.

b. From Above

To help you understand the enormous amount of tension needed
to keep luff sag to a minimum, the same kind of example used to demon-
strate leech twist will help. Imagine a wire stretched between two posts,
50 feet apart. If you hung a 100-pound weight in the center of the wire, it
would be virtually impossible—with any devices available to boat owners
today—to put enough tension on the ends of the wire to make it assume a
straight line. Now turn this example on its side so that the wire parallels

the luff, with one end fixed on the mast and one end on the bow. The difference is that the weight would be more like 1,600 pounds—the pressure on, for example, a 400-square-foot genoa in a stiff breeze. Thus, tremendous tension is needed to keep sag to a minimum, but you have to apply it within the limits of your boat and rigging.

Before attempting to exert the kind of tension needed to counteract sag, you should first check with the builder or designer of your boat to find out just how much load you can put on the headstay. (In many cases, the makers of class cruising boats offer a custom mast that withstands higher compression loadings as an option for racing where control of jibstay sag is very important.) You must also check your equipment to be sure that you have the control devices such as a hydraulic backstay or high-speed turnbuckle to apply this amount of tension.

Jibs or genoas are generally cut with an allowance for the boat's particular stay sag; nevertheless, a stay will always sag more as the wind increases. Beyond a certain point the only solution is to change to a flatter and usually smaller genoa or jib, which is cut to allow for increased sag and will thus be more efficient in the stronger wind conditions.

You now know the major ways and means to control draft in your sails when going to windward. Before giving you some examples of how you would apply this theory in practice, there is one extremely important point to remember that affects almost everything we have talked about in regard to controlling draft, and that is that just as sailcloth stretches with increased pressure, so will rope sheets stretch. Although the head of the sail is generally secured by a wire halyard, and the tack is fastened to a fixed point, the clew is usually trimmed with rope. As the pressure increases in the center of the sail, load on the rope sheet increases, and it can stretch, allowing the clew to move forward and form more draft, just as if you had eased the sheet. Therefore, a low-stretch sheet is almost as important as low-stretch sailcloth; if you have one without the other, it is somewhat self-defeating. Stretchy sheets only compound your trim problems.

DRAFT CONTROLS IN PRACTICE

Since the headsail is the leading sail and operates in clear air, and since it has such a great effect on the mainsail, it should be adjusted first. Then, once the genoa is correct, you have to set the mainsail draft to complement the genoa setting, so that, in effect, they form a team—one working with the other. However, since everything is interrelated, you should never change one control without inspecting the sail shape to see whether other changes might now have to be made.

Increasing Winds

Suppose that the wind velocity increases. First, tension the luff of the genoa or jib to hold the draft forward and flatten the sail. If you have raised the halyard to do this, the clew will also be raised, and you will have to change the sheet lead. Next, check the main. Because of the increased wind velocity, the draft has probably moved back too far, and so you should tighten the downhaul or Cunningham hole to get it back where it belongs. Next, if the genoa is backwinding the main and if you can reach the main outhaul, tighten it to flatten the sail. If you cannot adjust the outhaul, or if you tighten it and the sail is still being backwinded by the genoa, you may have to move the traveler farther inboard or the genoa farther outboard. However, this inboard setting may make the boat heel too much; you may then have to live with a little luffing to prevent excess heel. (These are questions of sail trim and will be covered in the next chapter; and see Fig. 115.)

If, however, you have done all these things and the sail is still luffing forward, it may be because of excessive twist from the combination of sailcloth stretch and sheet stretch, which have decreased leech control. To counteract this, you have to trim the sheet until you get the proper amount of twist. (Any one of these changes, particularly the setting of the traveler, can affect the balance of the helm; this problem also will be taken up in the next chapter.) This example shows how to use draft controls in an increasing breeze. What happens when the wind decreases?

Decreasing Winds

Suppose you are sailing in a breeze that has increased from 10 to 15 knots. You have been gradually adding more and more tension on the luff of the headsail and on the luff and foot of the main. Suddenly the wind goes down to 8 knots. You have to make some quick changes. Without the pressure of

Fig. 88

a. In very light air, the Cunningham and outhaul are eased to increase the draft and move it back into the center of the sail. You can see the location of draft by the seam lines on the sail.

b. With an increase in wind speed, the loading in the center of the sail is increased. If the downhaul and outhaul are slack, there will be too much draft, too far aft. You can see the loading pulling the sail from the mast, increasing the wrinkles in the sail. The leech also hooks to windward. Notice also that the fuller draft has created a fairly strong side force, causing the boat to heel.

c. When the sail is adjusted, the Cunningham is tensioned, the outhaul is tensioned and the sheet adjusted if necessary. The sail is flatter and the draft moves from aft of center back to the middle, where it should be. The boat also has less heel.

the wind on the sails, everything is overtrimmed. First, the headsail luff tension has to be eased. The sheet is overtrimmed, making the sail much too flat; with a genoa, the leech and foot will probably be hard against the shrouds. So next, the sheet has to be eased to let some draft flow into the sail. Then, in the case of a genoa, the leech line will have to be eased slightly. Now turn to the main, which is also overtrimmed. The leech will be almost a straight line. The foot of the main will have a big curl just above the boom where excess cloth has been pulled from the lower half of the sail by foot tension. (Since the pressure on the center of the sail is decreased, the edge tension now predominates and the cloth responds to this.) There is another bulge of excess cloth just behind the mast. (See Fig. 68b.) The mainsheet is trimmed in too tight and the traveler is too far outboard (where it has been set to relieve heeling).

To correct all this, you should first ease the luff tension until the draft moves back toward the center of the sail, and at the same time, reduce mainsheet tension to ease the leech. Then ease the foot until the excess cloth feeds into draft curvature. After this is done, you may find that you cannot point very well. This is probably because the traveler is still in an outboard position and should be brought inboard to a spot where it belongs in 8 knots of wind.

Draft too far forward in light air is just as bad as draft too far aft in stronger winds. So easing luff and foot tensions along with sheet tensions in lighter air is just as important as concentrating on tightening them as the wind velocity increases.

Off the Wind

So far, we have discussed draft control only when sailing to windward, because this is the point of sailing where aerodynamic flow is the main driving force. As you sail farther and farther off the wind, the driving force comes more and more from the sail's sheer resistance to the wind, and less and less from aerodynamic flow. When the wind is forward of the beam on a close reach, the windward aerodynamic principles still apply, and any resistance or drag is bad and should be kept to a minimum. However, as the reach becomes broader and the wind goes aft, any resistance created by the sail will be an asset, since the resistance or drag force is now going in the same direction as the boat (see Fig. 23f, Chapter 2). Thus, when the wind is aft, the location of draft will not be as important. Instead, you should concentrate on presenting the maximum sail area to the wind.

Since wind pressures are minimal on the sail, there is very little stretch. Edge tensions, therefore, have to be eased so that valuable area is not used up in tension curls along the luff and foot. Ease the outhaul to add draft along the foot of the sail. Slack luff tension by easing the tension on the Cunningham hole or by raising the gooseneck slide and locking it in an *up* position so that it will not be pulled down when tension is applied by the vang.

Because a curved surface offers more resistance than a flat one does, the sail should have an overall curve to it. However, too much curvature is undesirable because it will reduce the surface area you present to the wind. By the same token, if the leech is not firm, the sail will fall off into an "S" shape, and the air, instead of being met with resistance, will spill off the leech. (See Fig. 89.) You can stiffen the leech by tightening the leech line and applying the vang.

Summary

Now you know the ways to control draft in the mainsail and headsail: luff tension controls the fore and aft location of draft (tightening the luff moves draft forward; easing it allows draft to move aft). Tension on the foot controls draft in the lower half of the sail (tightening it flattens the sail; easing it creates more draft). Adjusting sheet tension affects draft in the upper portion of the sail (tensioning the sheet creates more draft aloft; easing it flattens the sail aloft). And in the case of the headsail, adjusting the fore and aft location of the sheet lead controls the tension on foot and leech (moving it forward increases draft; moving it aft flattens the sail).

When you adjust one control, check your sails to see whether you should adjust the other controls; they are all interrelated. Then, once you are satisfied with the shape, you have to manipulate the entire unit inboard or outboard to the best angle of attack. This is called *sail trim* and will be discussed next.

Fig. 89
Downwind Mainsail Setting

Upwind, luff tension counters strong wind
pressures and prevents the draft from
moving aft. Offwind, the pressure of the
wind is much weaker, so if no adjustment
is made to luff tension, it will be
overpowering, pulling the draft toward
the mast. In addition, since the end of the
boom is no longer over the boat, there is
no downward loading on the sheet, so the
leech falls off from lack of tension.

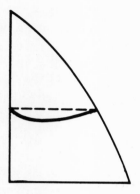

a. Proper Upwind Trim

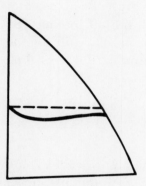

b. If downhaul or Cunningham is not
eased downwind, draft will be held near
the mast and the center will be flat. The
leech falls off because there is no
downward sheet tension.

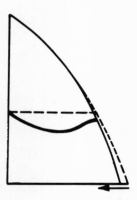

c. Ease outhaul to add draft in lower leech
area.

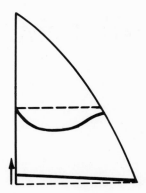

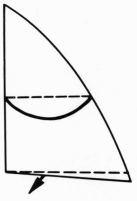

d. Raise downhaul or ease Cunningham to add draft forward.

e. Apply vang to lighten leech. All this will produce a good downwind shape.

Chapter 6
Sail Trim

You now know some of the elements of sail design and why a sail is shaped the way it is. You have learned where draft should be and have an idea of how much draft you should have in different wind velocities. You have also seen how to adjust draft by various controls that regulate the tension on the edges of a sail. The next thing to understand is how to aim the sail toward the wind: how to give it the proper angle of attack. This is a matter of trim. The sail designer specifies the trim point for each sail for one velocity of wind. For any other wind velocity within the sail's range, and for different sea conditions, you have to establish the proper point by trial and error, working from the originally designated spot as a starting point.

Imagine, for a moment, that your sails are rigid airfoils with the right amount of draft in the correct place for the particular conditions under which you are sailing. These sails pivot on their leading edges, and the angle of attack they have with the wind is regulated by devices that control the athwartship (side-to-side) movement of the sails without affecting their shape in any way. This is exactly what you are doing when you trim your sails to the wind.

The reason this is possible is that the trim devices are separate in operation from the draft-control devices. Formerly, the sheet controlled the sail's trim or position in relation to the centerline as well as the shape and tightness of the leech; the sail was moved outboard to a different angle of attack by "cracking the sheets," which probably resulted in more change in leech tension and sail twist than anything else. But with the advent of the traveler for the main, and similar devices for working jibs on some one designs, it is now possible to change the sail's inboard or outboard trim position by moving the traveler carriage, without touching the sheet tension.

Fig. 90
Travelers

a. The Ultimate Traveler—because of the width of the outriggers on *Pen Duick IV* (the 70-foot trimaran sailed by Alain Colas in the *London Observer* Singlehanded Transatlantic race in 1972), a traveler could be installed that allowed the mainsail's angle of attack to be adjusted 180 degrees without a change in mainsheet tension.

TRIM CONTROLS

The main traveler* (see Fig. 90) consists of a carriage mounted on a track that is located on deck below the sheet block on the boom. The mainsheet passes through the traveler block by one system or another, and is locked at a certain tension. The traveler carriage has controls which regulate its side-to-side movement. Consequently, the carriage can be positioned any-where on an athwartship track from a spot to windward of amidships to the leeward extremity of the track. This enables you to control the angle of the boom to the centerline of the boat without any sheet adjustment.

* The placement and technical information on all these devices is covered in Chapter 15, Deck Layout and Fittings.

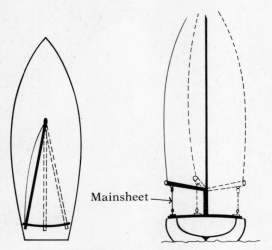

Mainsheet →

Standard Traveler

b. On the average boat, however, the traveler is restricted to the width of the hull, and the scope of the traveler may be only 20 to 30 degrees because, traditionally, the traveler is located in the stern area of the boat.

c. The mid-boom traveler (or mid-boom horse) is gaining popularity because of the increased use of high-aspect rigs with shorter booms, which are not long enough to reach the cockpit. This type of traveler provides a wider swing, but less leverage because it is farther forward. It also causes boom bend, which may or may not be desirable depending on how the sail is cut.

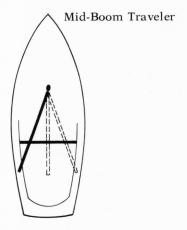

Mid-Boom Traveler

When sailing farther off the wind with the boom no longer over the deck but out over the water, the boom vang substitutes for the mainsheet to control the leech twist, the mainsheet replaces the traveler (Fig 91a) and controls trim.

On a close reach the traveler carriage will be at the most outboard setting because the angle of attack of the mainsail is so broad. As you sail even farther off the wind, you want to set the carriage even farther outboard, but you have reached the end of the track. At this point, the vang takes over. The vang should be presecured so that when you have to ease the mainsheet to allow the sail to go farther outboard, you still have a firm control over the leech (Fig. 91).

Vangs are very important for one-design class boats when travelers are not allowed. There is no real substitute for a traveler—the Crosby rig, used on Lightnings, allows some athwartship control but only for a short

Fig. 91
Vangs

Conventional Vang

b. The pivoting boom vang, unlike the conventional vang, is fixed, pivoting on the after face of the mast. Therefore, it doesn't require adjustment as the boom moves in or out. This type is commonly used on medium-size one designs.

a. If the boom needs to be trimmed farther outboard than the scope of the traveler, the mainsheet must be eased, thus reducing leech tension and control over leech twist. To avoid this, you need a traveler-like block-and-tackle system called a vang. The vang is mounted forward along the boom at the point that will still be over the deck when the boom is as outboard as possible. The conventional vang is secured to the deck, and as the trim angle of the mainsail is changed, the point of attachment on the boom and on the deck also changes.

Pivoting Vang

Bull-Ring Vang

c. The bull-ring vang, mounted a short distance aft on the boom with a corresponding track across the width of the hull, allows the trim angle to be changed without a change in vang tension. The vang slides along the track as the trim angle is adjusted. It offers much more leverage than the pivoting vang in (b), because the pressure exerted by the vang is straight down at every point and at all times.

distance (Fig. 92). After that, you have to ease the sheet to get the boom out, which decreases leech tension. With this rig, or whenever a traveler is not allowed, the vang is the only thing that will maintain leech tension

Fig. 92
Crosby Rig

The Crosby rig offers minimal athwartship control; the boom has to be pushed manually to change the athwartship position and the maximum change you can achieve without changing sheet tension is only a foot or so.

Boom is manually pushed to leeward without change in sheet tension. Sheet goes under tiller when rudder is outboard.

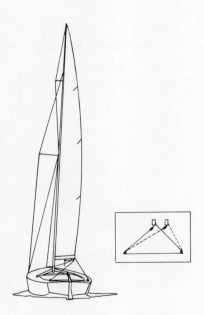

A modified four-part Crosby Rig

when the sheet is eased. However, the tension of the vang is a lot greater than the mainsheet tension because of its disadvantageous leverage. A bendy boom in this case would be a disadvantage, as the vang would bend the boom at the connecting point instead of transferring total downward tension to the boom end.

The athwartship trim of jibs and genoas usually is more complicated than the mainsail. The exception to this is the jib that does not overlap the mast; then the arrangement is much the same as the mainsail traveler. Actually, simple jib travelers have been used as a cruising rig on day sailers for many years but have recently been refined to include the traveler track and sliding carriage with athwartship control (Fig. 93). Again the sail's angle of attack to the apparent wind can be changed without altering the tension on the sheet.

Fig. 93

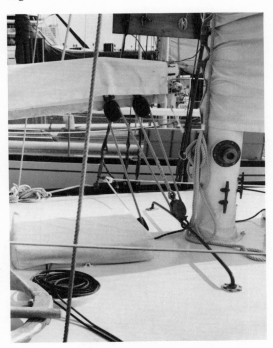

a. The traditional jib traveler is generally used with a club-foot jib on cruising boats.

b. The modern ball-bearing jib traveler can be used for non-overlapping jibs without a club-foot. The athwartship position can be controlled, as with a mainsheet traveler.

Genoas that overlap the mast and/or shrouds present more complicated problems. Here, the sheet has to be released when tacking so that the clew can pass around the mast and be trimmed on the opposite side; you are no longer dealing with fixed sheet traveler-type devices. One designs have developed a variety of other devices to control the angle of attack for both overlapping and non-overlapping jibs. One system requiring a physical repositioning of the carriage is the "H" or "L" tracks, and similar arrangements, which allows both athwartship and fore and aft adjustment (Fig. 94). A relatively new device that is much easier to use and which allows adjustment under load is the Barber haul (Fig. 95). These devices are not easily installed on cruiser-racers because of the number of different-size genoas, requiring great flexibility in the adjustment of leads; fixed arrangements are almost impossible. However, the result is being accomplished by auxiliary rigs.

Fig. 94
One-Design Jib Trim Devices

a. The "H" Track System—this system of tracks allows both athwartship control and fore and aft positioning of the sheet lead. The sheet lead slides from side to side on the connecting bar; the connecting bar slides forward and aft on the two parallel tracks. This is not used for the bigger one designs or for most cruising boats because a system with a strong-enough connecting bar is not yet available. The sheet block and carriage can be moved anywhere within the confines of the two parallel tracks. Two styles are shown.

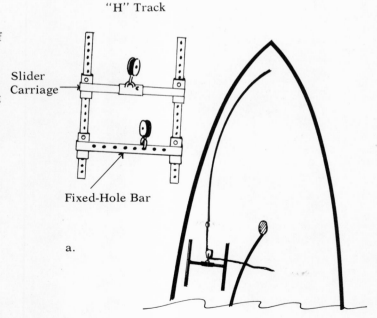

"H" Track

Slider
Carriage

Fixed-Hole Bar

a.

b. "L" Track—the "L" track system is used for larger jibs, which require more trim tension and, therefore, need a double lead. However, this system provides only half the scope of the "H" track.

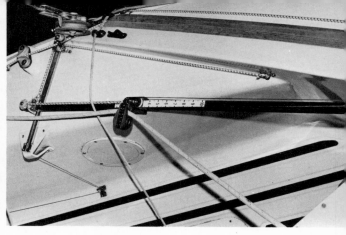

c. "T" Track—the "T" Track provides a long fore-and-aft movement and less lateral scope.

Fig. 95
The Barber Haul and Inhaul

b. Inhaul—most cruising boats are using a genoa-sheet inhaul to bring the clew inboard to a narrower sheeting angle. These are usually jury rigs comprised of a second short sheet tied into the clew and then led to a windward point on the cabinhouse and then to a winch. The sail is thus trimmed toward the centerline in an opposite but similar way to the Barber haul.

Barber Haul Control Line

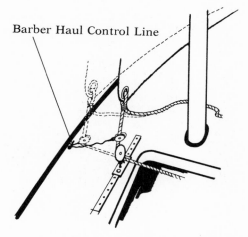

a. The Barber haul is a block riding on the jibsheet. Its control line leads to the outboard rail of the boat and goes through the deck and to the cockpit, where it is secured. Tensioning the Barber haul block moves the jib lead outboard, changing the athwartship angle of trim.

One alternative is to have two genoa tracks, one at the rail and the other at a spot as far inboard as is practical (Fig. 96). By bridling the genoa clew with an auxiliary sheet, you can trim the clew to various angles between the two tracks. This enables you to make some athwartship adjustment of the genoa, varying its angle of attack without too much effect on its shape. The reason that athwartship trim tracks—which bridge the inboard and outboard tracks and allow you to move the athwartship track fore and aft on the one device—have not been used until recently is that it is difficult to design a device strong enough to bridge two tracks under the high loadings exerted by a genoa.

Fig. 96
Inboard and Outboard Genoa
Tracks.   One sheet is permanently
attached and the other is an auxiliary
lead, which is removed when tacking. By
tensioning one more than the other, the
clew can be trimmed anywhere from the
inboard to the outboard position.

FINDING THE CRITICAL ANGLE OF ATTACK

All these devices enable you to aim the sail at the wind so that it is at the proper angle of attack. Remember, the leading edge of the sail cannot exceed the apparent wind or it will luff, nor can the leading edge be inside the apparent-wind angle without stalling. The margin of good performance between these extremes is only 2 to 3 degrees, and this is true for any point of sailing that depends on aerodynamic forces—that is, all but very broad reaching or running.

How do you find this critical angle of attack? The shroud telltale, or masthead fly, which indicates the direction of the apparent wind, will give you a rough guide. However, the luff of the sail is the best indication because you can view it at various heights, whereas the masthead or shroud flies are at only one height. Racing sailors often set up complicated wind-indicator systems; these are discussed later in the chapter. For the average sailor, the easiest way to find this exact angle is to trim in the sail or head the boat off the wind until the sail barely stops luffing. In fact, there should still be the slightest quiver along the leading edge. The reason for this is that luffing is your *only* visual clue to whether or not you are at the proper angle of attack: you cannot see a stall, but you can see a luff. *The moment you no longer see the suggestion of a luff, you have no way of knowing how overtrimmed you are, or how far off you might be sailing.* The top sailor will continually alter course or fiddle with the trim of the sail so that the leading edge plane of the sail is always on the "edge" of the wind—that fine point between the luff and the stall. This is called sailing to the luff.

A subtle phenomenon that seems not to be generally known but which can be critical in maintaining the best possible aerodynamic forces is the development of a local apparent wind. As a low-pressure area develops on the lee side of the sail near the luff, and more and more air is attracted to that side, the flow lines near the leading edge gradually change direction (Fig. 9), veering toward the lee side to form a greater angle to the sail than the apparent wind farther in front of the sail. In other words, as the decreased pressure area on the lee side of the leading edge is reinforced, the angle of the local apparent wind relative to the sail is increased. This is a real, yet local, wind shift that allows you to point higher and requires an adjustment in the angle of attack to keep the leading edge parallel to the local flow lines. If the adjustment is not made, the flow lines will detach or separate from the lee side of the sail, disrupt the smooth flow, and thus cause the aerodynamic forces to break down. To avoid this, the sail should be angled more to the wind. Using the luff as a guide, this can be accomplished by pointing the boat higher, by adjusting the sail so that it is fuller forward, or by easing the sail outboard on the traveler. You might have to try all three before you find out which solution or combination of solutions works best for you.

An important thing to remember is that the apparent-wind direction over the sails will be changing continually: as boat speed changes, as the pointing angle changes, and as the sails are trimmed. If the jib needs to be trimmed because of changing wind conditions, the main will probably also need to be trimmed, both because of the wind shift and because the deflection of wind off the newly trimmed jib will be different. Changing the trim angle of either sail will slightly change the hull speed, in turn necessitating a trim change for the sails. These are usually only very minor adjustments. Nevertheless, the process is endlessly circular because one change affects everything else. Again, the experienced sailor will find he is constantly adjusting his sails, traveler settings, and lead positions in addition to his helm when going to windward to maintain his best angle of attack.

We have been talking as if the sail had only one angle of attack; remember, however, that the wind-gradient factor increases the angle of the apparent wind aloft by as much as 7 or 8 degrees; thus, the angle of attack will be quite different aloft. The sail must be trimmed accordingly. This is accomplished, as we have seen, through leech twist, which is controlled by sheet tension. Easing the sheet allows the leech to twist more and more, so that the chords of the sail are more and more outboard in relation to the centerline. The amount of twist will depend on the wind and sea: the wind gradient is more pronounced in open water and, on smaller boats, in light air, so that twist should be greater in these conditions. The way to determine whether or not you have the right amount of twist is to get the sail to luff up and down the forward edge simultaneously. If it luffs up high first, you have too much twist. If it luffs down low first, you do not have enough.

TRIMMING PROCEDURE

Since the headsail is operating in free air, it should be trimmed first. After you have the proper shape in the headsail, put the boat on the course on which you are going to sail; if it is to windward, head the boat on its usual pointing angle (the angle at which it does best to windward). Then, as a starting point, fix the sail to the trim point specified by the sail designer. Next, experiment with the trim, moving it inboard or outboard until you have the sail on the edge of the luff. Make sure that the twist is right: the sail should luff from top to bottom simultaneously.

Once the jib is trimmed properly, you can turn to the mainsail. After the shape is set, start with the designed trim point and angle the sail to the wind just as you did with the jib. Make sure it luffs simultaneously from top to bottom; if it does not, adjust the twist.

Now, head the boat toward the wind: does one sail luff before the other? Most boats sail best when the jib and main break simultaneously, although with some keel boats it seems preferable to have the main backwind slightly before the jib luffs. With one designs, it will depend on the overlap and rig configuration. You will have to experiment to discover what is right for your boat.

If the sails are trimmed correctly, the slot should be right—not too open or too closed. Generally, the jib or genoa leech curve should follow the curvature of the main directly opposite the jib leech (Fig. 97). This gives a good slot all the way up. If the slot is too wide, when you head up the jib will break first; if the slot is too narrow, the main will backwind first.

If the sails are trimmed correctly and the slot looks right, but the boat still is not going, you might try trimming the jib so that it luffs up high first, and the main so that it luffs down low first. This will ensure proper twist and a good slot. Or, it may be that the jib is trimmed too far inboard. This causes the main to be trimmed in too far as well. First try easing the jib to a more outboard position. If you have a genoa, move the trim point inboard and forward so that when you ease the sheet you get more twist. The twist will open up the slot; you will also get more draft, which will give you more driving power. The main can then be trimmed farther outboard. This situation is a particular problem with small deck-sweeper working jibs which have inboard leads and a large amount of twist. Too much sheet tension will take the twist out of the jib and close the slot, giving the main excessive backwind or choking the slot. With these sails, it is imperative not to sheet them as tight as the normal jib with outboard leads.

The main should not backwind as you are sailing if you have trimmed it to the jib: that is, if you have adjusted it after the jib has been trimmed properly. If it is backwinding (which looks like a luff), the first place to check, as always, is the jib. Is the jib too far inboard? Is there enough twist? Is there a hook in the jib leech? Any of these factors could be causing the problem—or it may be that the main is trimmed too far outboard or is too full.

To summarize, when you are checking your sail trim, it is important to look at the following: (1) the athwartship trim—are your sails on the edge of the luff? (2) the vertical trim—do you have enough twist? (3) the slot—is it neither too wide nor too narrow? Attention to these points will pay off handsomely in boat speed.

Once you have your major trim problems under control, try experimenting with finer adjustments. In light air, try trimming the sails closer to the centerline with the sheet eased slightly. The main traveler sometimes can even be to windward of center, and the jib or genoa at or near the inboard lead spot. Also, in light air, you can increase the flow velocity in the slot by bringing the jib and mainsail closer together—up to the point where the main is on the edge of luffing. Do this by bringing the jib lead inboard toward the lee side of the main or by easing the main out by an outboard adjustment. (See Fig. 58.)

One trim tactic used on one designs with tall, narrow jibs is to place the jib lead quite far inboard—perhaps as little as 6 degrees from the centerline; then the jib is trimmed in until its leech flows into a vertical curvature that comes closest to paralleling the vertical curvature of the main adjacent to the jib leech. This creates a good, even slot all the way up between the two sails. This is basically a light-air or choppy-water tactic.

Sail Trim and the Direction of Sail Forces

So far, we have talked only about trimming the sail in relation to finding the critical angle of attack. However, there is another important aspect of trim that involves the direction of the forces generated by the sail.

Again, imagine that your sails are properly shaped rigid foils. They are suspended in mid-air and fixed at the critical angle of attack to the wind. The wind is flowing over them, and they are generating a force that is slightly forward of the perpendicular to the sail's chord or boom. Now, put the hull underneath them. If you point the boat at a 90-degree angle

Fig. 97
Light-Air Setting.   The jib leech parallels
the curvature of the main, forming an
ideal slot.

Fig. 98
As the hull moves more and more on a
downwind angle, the force remains in the
same direction but the relative amounts
of forward drive and heeling force will
change, depending on the hull's direction.

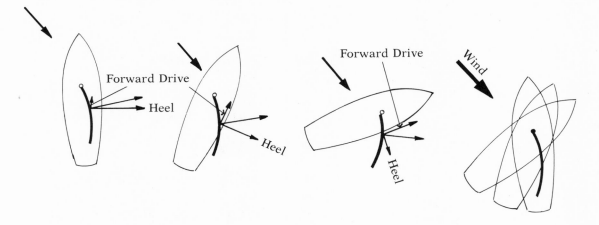

to the wind, you are on a beam reach; if you point the boat higher into the
wind, you are beating to windward. But the sails have changed very little.
They are still at approximately the same angle to the (apparent) wind. It
is the boat that pivots under them (Fig. 98).

As you can see, the force remains in a constant direction. What changes is the boat's relation to the force. Thus, the more the boat heads off toward the direction of the force, the greater the percentage of force used to drive the boat ahead, and the smaller the force to the side. This, along with the change in apparent-wind velocity, is what accounts for the difference in boat speed on different headings (except downwind, where aerodynamic forces no longer operate).

This concept, discussed in detail in Chapter 2, is important to understand in relation to windward work in particular, because it is behind the sailor's constant dilemma of whether to pinch or to foot—that is, whether it is better to point the boat up high and go slower (pinch), or bear off and go faster (foot) but cover a longer distance. When you point up high, what you are doing in effect is bringing the centerline of the boat closer to the boom or chord, which is at a fixed angle to the wind; thus, a great proportion of the force will be to the side, and very little will be forward. Hence, the boat goes slower. If you bear off, you are moving the centerline away from the chord and more of the force will be forward—that is, in the direction in which you are headed. You do not point as well, but you go faster (Fig. 99).

Fig. 99

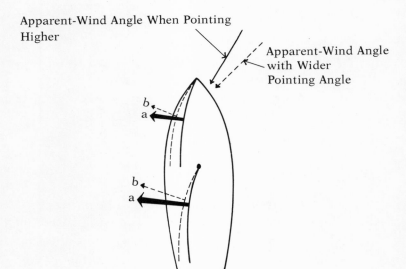

Apparent-Wind Angle When Pointing Higher

Apparent-Wind Angle with Wider Pointing Angle

a. Boat points higher
b. Boat bears off.

And so, when you are depending on aerodynamic forces, the sail's position is a constant and so is the direction of the sail force. What changes is the boat's course in relation to the direction of the force. Therefore, as you change the boat's course, you adjust the sail so that it keeps the same relative angle of attack. This is exactly what the traveler and other athwartship devices are for.

Now, how do you decide whether to point or to foot when tacking to windward? Which will get you to the mark (or your destination) faster?* Each boat will have its own approach, depending on its pointing ability, which in turn depends largely on its hull characteristics. A wide, beamy boat will not point as well and so should not be pinched, while a narrow, easily driven deep hull can usually point quite high and still move reasonably well through the water. Another important consideration is the steering ability of the sailor; someone who can concentrate so intently that he is always "on the edge" will be able to trim the sail in flatter and point higher, without the sail stalling out, as it probably would in the hands of a less skillful sailor.

Wind conditions will also have a big effect on your decision to foot or pinch. In strong winds, sails in an inboard position create too much side force or heeling movement, so that you *have* to trim the sails more outboard. Because of excessive aerodynamic forces, you may have to let the main luff a little and reduce the draft a bit, but the total force on the sails is in a more forward direction, and that is why you heel less. Conversely, in medium air you cannot point well with the sails too far outboard.

Sea conditions, too, have to be considered. A heavy sea not only slows the boat down but also varies its course so that the angle of attack varies as well: the seaway makes you sail a snaking course, first up a little too high and then off too much. As a result, the sail alternates between luffing and stalling, and drive forces are considerably reduced. Stalling, which occurs when the sail is trimmed too inboard of the apparent-wind direction, will do more harm than luffing because it is more difficult to spot. Thus, it is better to trim the sail more outboard in heavy seas. Since the boat is slower and, therefore, the apparent-wind angle is wider, you can trim the sail outboard without sacrificing draft; for the same reason, you can usually add more draft to the sail as well. Anything you can do to get more forward

*The answer is the one that produces the greatest net gain against the wind, which is called speed made good to windward and is discussed in detail in Chapter 20.

drive will help you in this situation; it is probably best to try a combination of easing the sail outboard (to get the forces in a more forward direction) and adding curvature (to build up aerodynamic forces). The motion of a larger boat will be less affected by the same sea, and so again it is a question of knowing your boat and its capabilities.

When analyzing his victory over *Dame Pattie* in the 1967 America's Cup races, Bus Mosbacher attributed it in part to the Australians' tendency to pinch their boat:

Dame Pattie seemed to have her traveler trimmed amidships and her mainsail strapped in very flat. I think the boat was overtrimmed, pointed very high and sailed very close [Fig. 100]. I would have thought when she seemed to tender in the wind and seas we had that they would have set her traveler out to its maximum limits. That's what we did with *Weatherly* in '62 because she was so very tender and needed the traveler out so she could stand up and go.*

The choice of whether to pinch or to foot is obviously an intricate question that depends largely on your knowing your boat and what it can do in different conditions. There are ways to calculate the advantages of one over the other on paper in much the same way that downwind tacking can be plotted (see Chapter 20). But, since the advantage gained from either choice or the other is sometimes only a matter of a boat length, it is much more difficult to plot successfully. The surest way to know which works for you is to watch your performance in comparison with similar boats in competition. Or you can measure your performance against another boat, as top racing sailors do in a procedure called brushing, described in Chapter 8. For most sailors, though, time and experience are enough to give them a gut feeling as to what is right for their boat—and their abilities.

WIND-DIRECTION INDICATORS

Boat speed depends on your ability constantly to keep the ideal angle of attack. To do this, a veteran helmsman uses experience, feel, ESP, and any visual aids that will show whether or not the sails are at their best trim angle. These aids should indicate: (1) the angle between the apparent wind and the centerline of the hull (shroud flies, masthead pennants, electronic

Defending the America's Cup, edited by Robert W. Carrick and Stanley Z. Rosenfield (New York, 1969), p. 183.

Fig. 100
These two pictures show how differences
in trim affect a boat's ability to stand up
and to point. *Dame Pattie* has her
mainsheet trimmed much too close to the
centerline and as a result is heeling way
over, while *Intrepid* is trimmed correctly,
thus keeping on her feet and making good
headway.

wind indicators), and (2) the relative velocity of the flow over either side of
the sail to indicate whether lee flow is strong (yarn, streamers, pressure
gauges).

Shroud flies, masthead pennants, and electronic wind indicators
will help you see the apparent wind direction and give you a general idea of
where the critical angle of attack will be. Yarn or streamers on the sail will
help you get the angle of attack exact: if the local air flow is not parallel to
the leading edge, eddies will occur; if you have yarn attached to the sail
near the luff, you will see these eddies right away.

To make streamers, cloth about the weight of ¾- or ½-ounce spinnaker material works very well. Cut it into strips about ³⁄₁₆ inch wide and

6 inches long. (Edges should be sealed with a hot knife.) The streamers can be neatly attached on both sides of the luff and at three or four heights with small squares of white plastic tape (Fig. 101a). They should be about 4 to 8 inches back from the luff on a small boat and 12 to 18 inches on a larger boat (Fig. 101b). The proper angle of attack will be indicated when the leeward streamers flow strongly aft and the weather streamers float rather lazily aft and slightly upward (Fig. 101c). When sailing too high, even before the luff breaks, the weather-side streamers will flutter, indicating an eddy, and fly straight up. Sailing too low will cause the lee flow to separate; the lee streamers, which usually can be seen through the sail, will flutter and gyrate in the stall zone eddies. Since separation starts aft and works forward, the only way you can see if the whole sail is operating efficiently is to have yarns in the forward, middle, and aft portions of the sail — and at three different heights, roughly one quarter, one half, and three-quarters of the way up the sail. On a reach, however, the middle and lower after streamers are better indicators as to whether the main is overtrimmed and stalled.

You can check the sail shape as well: adjust the shape until all the leeside streamers are flowing aft strongly; the windward streamers will have a lazier motion. When all the streamers are flowing correctly, the shape and trim should be just right.

Streamers have not been used with as much success on the luff of the main as on the jib because the mast itself creates so much turbulence that the streamers continually flutter and are not sensitive to small changes in trim. However, if streamers are placed on the middle and on the leech areas of both the main and jib, they can be used to detect separated flow and stalling. These can be particularly helpful in setting the right trim and shape of new sails.

When racing, too many streamers will distract a skipper, and so it is wise to limit them; two or three yarns on each sail should be sufficient. They should generally be placed at different heights, where they can indicate whether the sail has the correct amount of twist. On jibs, the fore and aft fairlead position which gives the right twist can be set very accurately by having the top and bottom streamers flying identically. (This is more accurate and more sensitive than having the luff break simultaneously.) This same technique, when applied to the main on a reach, can be used to adjust the vang, which also controls twist. If the top and the bottom streamers are not flying identically, the vang needs adjustment.

Fig. 101

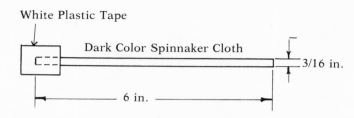

White Plastic Tape

Dark Color Spinnaker Cloth

3/16 in.

6 in.

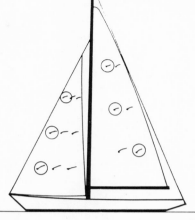

b. The streamers should be attached at different heights and in different fore and aft locations as indicated in the drawing. Only the circled streamers should be left on for racing.

c.

Proper Angle of Attack

(Dashed streamers indicate lee side.)

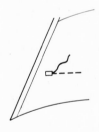

Too High

d. A window in the sail allows you to see the leeward streamer.

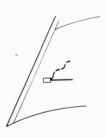

Too Low

Pressure gauges on the sail serve the same function as the streamers by indicating the pressure on the surface of the sail. They are connected to a cockpit dial. Pressure gauges are rather rare, because they are complicated, expensive, and difficult to install. However, because they give you the actual pressure on the sail, and this is the sail force, they are by far the best indicators of how efficient your trim and shape are.

Electronic apparent-wind angle indicators are great assets for offshore racers. (Most one designs have outlawed them.) A cockpit dial is connected to the masthead fly, making the instrument particularly valuable at night. Shining a flashlight on the sails will allow the initial adjustments of shape and trim to be made, after which the helmsman uses the cockpit dial to steer a constant angle of attack. It is most difficult to steer correctly at night without instruments—particularly off the wind.

Many companies make an additional unit known as a close-hauled indicator, which allows you, through an expanded scale, to see small changes in apparent-wind angle. Instead of a 360-degree dial, it goes only up to a 40- or 50-degree apparent-wind angle in the same circumferential sweep as the 360-degree indicator.

Wind indicators, as we have seen, serve as another tool to help you achieve the proper shape and trim of your sails and to help you perfect the adjustment of your athwartship controls.

Chapter 7

Tuning

With so many different modern hull and rigging styles in vogue, specific rules for tuning cannot be made. Some boats have movable masts, some have flexible masts, and some have telephone poles. Some go best with slack shrouds, while others need to have the rigging set up tight. But there are basic adjustments affecting a boat's performance which can be applied to a particular style rig according to its needs.

The basic consideration in tuning is the location of the mast. This has been calculated as closely as possible by the boat's designer, and the sailor must start tuning it from this designed location. It must be centered and plumb in the athwartship plane (from side to side), so that the rig, like the hull, will have lateral symmetry. An unsymmetrical rig will cause different sail shapes and different trim angles for starboard and port tacks. The boat will perform differently on each tack, and the adjustments made on one tack will not give the same results on the other tack.

The fore and aft position of the mast is also extremely important because this sets up the relationship between the total sail force at the center of effort (the calculated location where the one total force from all the sails is exerted) and the center of lateral resistance provided by the hull (the calculated point where the one total hydrodynamic force is exerted on the keel or centerboard and rudder) (Fig. 102).

To find the center of effort, a line is drawn from each corner of the mainsail and foretriangle to the center of the opposite edge. At the intersection of the lines is the center of effort (Fig 103a). This is calculated for each sail on the boat and then the center of effort for the sail plan is calculated by weighting each sail in proportion to its area (Fig 103b). The center of effort will not be the same as the center of pressure on the sail, which depends on the size of the sail, the shape of the draft, and the way the sail is set (Fig. 103c).

If the center of effort of the sail is aligned forward of the center

Fig. 102
In calculating the balancing of center of
effort vs. center of lateral resistance, some
"lead" is given to the center of effort
because it moves aft as the wind increases.

CE = center of effort
CLR = center of lateral resistance

Center of Effort
for Jib

CE

Center of Effort
for Main

CLR

Lead

Fig. 103
a. Plotting the Center of Effort of the Sail
Plan—most cruising-boat sail plans show
separate centers of effort for the main and
the foretriangle. (The foretriangle is used
because there are generally a number of
different headsails.) The center of effort
normally used is at the center of the area,
and can be determined by drawing lines
from each corner to the mid-point of the
opposite side. The point of intersection
will be the center and, for convenience, is
called the CE. The two centers are then
weighted according to the proportionate
size of the sails, and one total center of
effort is found along the line connecting
the two separate centers. For example, if
the foretriangle is two times the area of
the main, the total center of area would be
two-thirds of the distance between the
foretriangle center and main center,
forward of the main center.

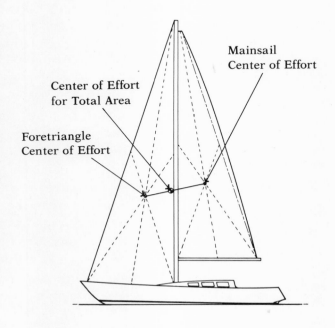

Center of Effort
for Total Area

Foretriangle
Center of Effort

Mainsail
Center of Effort

b. Center of Effort Using Actual Sails—when the center of effort is plotted with actual genoas instead of simply with the foretriangle, the genoa CE moves quite a bit aft as, therefore, does the total CE. The total CE varies with the size of the genoa. In (b), two genoa sizes are shown with the CE for each and the total CE's when each is combined with the mainsail.

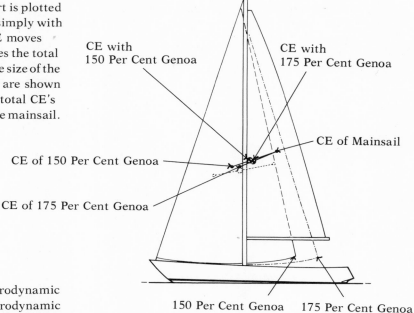

CE with 150 Per Cent Genoa

CE with 175 Per Cent Genoa

CE of Mainsail

CE of 150 Per Cent Genoa

CE of 175 Per Cent Genoa

150 Per Cent Genoa   175 Per Cent Genoa

c. Variables in Location of Aerodynamic Center of Effort—the actual aerodynamic center of pressure, the true center of effort, will usually be different from the plotted center of effort as determined in (b) because it depends on sail shape and trim. Therefore, it changes as sail shape and trim change. The relative efficiency of each sail is also important. In some cases, a main can have as little as 33 per cent of the genoa's pressure per square foot. This is a constantly changing relationship. A number of things will cause the total aerodynamic center to move aft, as shown in (c), including: an amount of draft in the sail, draft moving aft, an increase in leech twist, a wider slot, or the actual addition of sail area to the leech.

Conversely, the total aerodynamic center moves forward when the opposite situations occur; *i.e.*, when the sail is flatter, the draft is farther forward, leech twist is increased, the slot is narrowed, or leech area is decreased.

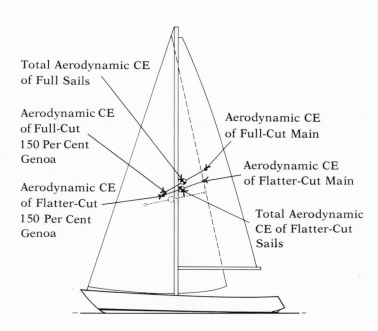

Total Aerodynamic CE of Full Sails

Aerodynamic CE of Full-Cut 150 Per Cent Genoa

Aerodynamic CE of Flatter-Cut 150 Per Cent Genoa

Aerodynamic CE of Full-Cut Main

Aerodynamic CE of Flatter-Cut Main

Total Aerodynamic CE of Flatter-Cut Sails

of lateral resistance, the sail forces will push the bow to leeward, causing lee helm. If the center of effort is aft of the center of lateral resistance, the sail forces will swing the stern to leeward, which means the bow swings to windward; this is called windward or weather helm. Under normal sailing conditions, the primary objective is to have the center of effort and the center of lateral resistance perfectly aligned to produce a balanced helm (Fig. 104).

The balance of a boat can be observed by how she steers. If the boat continues on a straight course when the tiller is held on the centerline, she is balanced. If the boat swings into the wind, she has weather or windward helm and the helm must be held to windward to keep the boat on a straight course. If the bow tends to swing away from the wind, the boat has a lee helm and the helm must be held to leeward to maintain a straight course.

A balanced helm is important because otherwise you get drag forces caused when you have to oversteer the rudder to correct for the imbalance. A lee helm is especially bad because the bow will tend to fall off. Since the rudder helps push the boat to leeward, increasing leeway and greatly increasing drag, the boat will not point well. Most people prefer a slight windward helm because the boat continually tries to point higher and the helmsman need apply only a light pressure on the helm to keep the proper sailing angle.

A boat can be built exactly according to her designed lines, but the kind of helm she has can only be approximated on the drawing board. Consequently, when she gets under sail, some adjustment may be needed to balance the boat or attain the desired amount of helm. (See Fig. 103 on calculation of center of effort of sail plan.)

The balance of a hull can be changed in two ways: (1) by moving the center of effort fore or aft or (2) by moving the center of lateral resistance fore or aft. The adjustment can be made by: (1) moving the whole rig, as in Figure 104; (2) moving just the mast; (3) changing the rake in the mast; (4) changing headsail-mainsail area ratio; or (5) moving underwater surfaces, such as the centerboard.

You seldom have to make such a drastic change as moving the whole rig—that is the spars, shrouds, and stays—but if you do, the same principles as moving the mast alone apply. If the mast is moved aft, weather helm will increase because the center of effort is moved aft. Moving the mast forward decreases weather helm. If the boat has lee helm, the mast should

Fig. 104
Helm Balance.   The balance of the helm
is changed in each drawing by changing
the location of the entire rig, thus
changing the center of effort. The center of
lateral resistance remains the same in
each case.

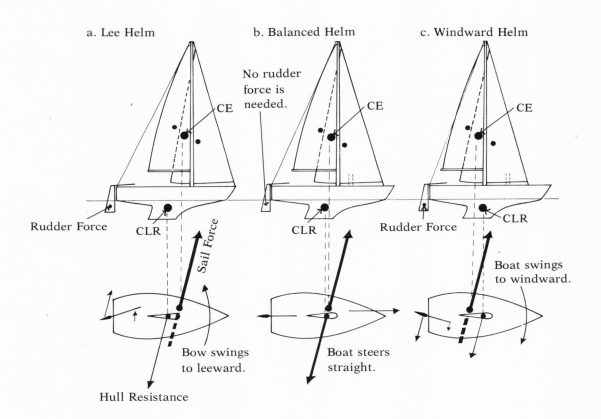

a. Lee Helm   b. Balanced Helm   c. Windward Helm

be moved aft to regain balance and give the desired amount of weather
helm. Some large boats have hydraulic devices at the heel of the mast to
make fore and aft adjustments. On small boats the mast position can frequently be adjusted with cranks or wedges at the partners (where the mast
goes through the deck) and at the step.

On pivoting centerboard boats, minor adjustments to the helm can be
made during a race by raising or lowering the centerboard, which changes

the fore and aft position of the center of lateral resistance. Raising the board decreases weather helm because it moves the center of lateral resistance aft; conversely, lowering it increases weather helm. In some boats, this can be accomplished by changing the fore and aft location of the entire centerboard by moving the pivoting pin position (Fig. 105).

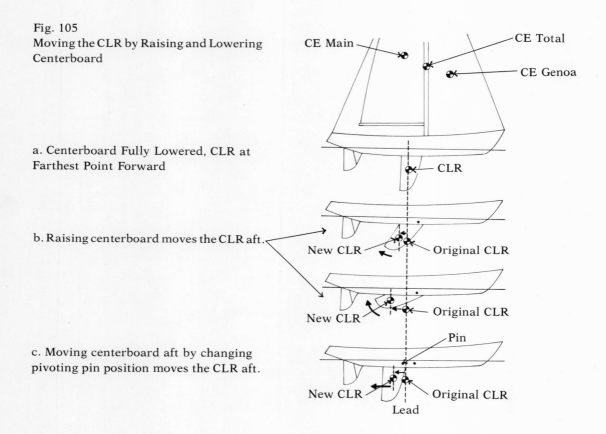

Fig. 105
Moving the CLR by Raising and Lowering Centerboard

a. Centerboard Fully Lowered, CLR at Farthest Point Forward

b. Raising centerboard moves the CLR aft.

c. Moving centerboard aft by changing pivoting pin position moves the CLR aft.

Mast rake (Fig. 106) can also be used to make fine balance adjustments. If the headstay is eased and the backstay taken up, the mast rakes aft and increases weather helm. Slacking the backstay and taking up on the headstay reduces the amount of weather helm. Care should be taken to distinguish between raking the mast for helm control and bending the mast for draft control and leech control (Chapter 5). When you bend the

Fig. 106
The three different rig positions produce three separate centers of effort: (a), (b), and (c). The plumb rake, (b), produces the right lead of center of effort in front of the center of lateral resistance. The aft-raked mast, (a), moves the center of effort back too far, producing windward helm, and the forward rake, (c), moves the center of effort too far forward, producing lee helm.

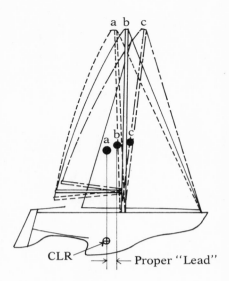

a = aft mast rake
b = plumb mast
c = forward mast rake

mast, the top goes aft while the bottom stays close to the original position. In raking, the whole mast is canted. Normally, you should make adjustments to balance the helm early in the season and apply mast bend corrections on a daily basis to suit the sails and wind conditions.

The pros and cons of mast rake have been discussed among sailors for a long time, but few definitive answers and little scientific data have been developed. Many one-design classes use aft rake with beneficial results going to windward. This can probably be attributed to the increase in the decksweeper effect gained by getting the aft end of the clews closer to the deck. Most cruising boats do not have mast rake; they sail to windward with a plumb mast. In almost all cases, forward rake seems to improve performance when running before the wind. This is probably because the forward angle of the mast tends to keep the air flowing over the rig instead of piling up on the windward side. On a run in light air, forward rake also allows gravity to assist in keeping the proper shape.

FORE AND AFT RIGGING ADJUSTMENT

The sailmaker makes a theoretically ideally shaped sail for your hull design and rig, presupposing the mast is in its optimum designed configuration.

This supposition is not always correct because masts frequently assume some abnormal configurations. Figure 107 shows some common examples of distorted masts and the improper rigging tensions that cause the distortions. If you have this kind of problem, the rigging should be adjusted accordingly. Otherwise, spar bend will disrupt the shape of the sail.

Fig. 107
Fore and Aft Adjustment.

The rig descriptions refer to the height of the forestay

Masthead Rig

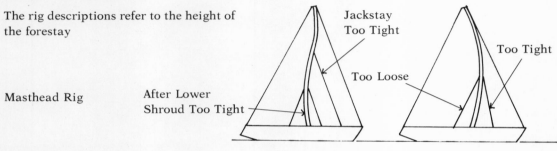

7/8 Rig
With Jumper Strut

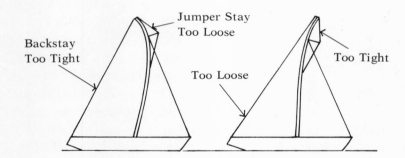

3/4 Rig
with Jumper Strut
and Double Running
Backstays

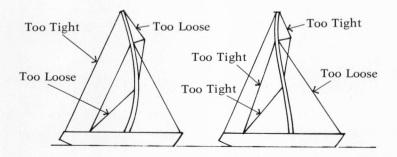

ATHWARTSHIP TUNING OF THE RIG

Stand on the transom of the boat and check the mast for athwartship curvature. Athwartship bend can also be spotted by sighting up the back of the mast from the gooseneck fitting. First, check the spar at the dock. If the mast bows out to one side, adjust the shrouds until it is straight. It is important to eliminate this kind of curvature because it destroys the uniform angle of attack of the leading edge of the sail and makes it impossible to trim the forward area of the sail evenly from head to foot. Now take the boat out and sail it on both tacks to see if the mast remains straight. Adjustments can be made on the leeward shrouds while under way, but remember, not all the correction should be made by tightening. Most good sailors keep their shrouds with just sufficient tension to hold the mast straight, since any excess tension will put excessive loads on the rig and hull.

Here are illustrations that indicate what happens to the mast in actual sailing conditions (Fig. 108). They represent four different rigging systems, some common athwartship distortions in mast shape, and the improper shroud tensions that cause them.

A straight mast is a good all-around configuration for going to windward; when reaching it can cause a tight leech in the mainsail which is helpful. If the head of the mast falls off to leeward, it is helpful going to windward in heavy weather, since it opens the slot between the jib and mainsail and lowers the center of effort, which reduces heeling. On one designs, the fall-off usually produces a better sail shape, which is good on a reach. If the mid-section of the mast falls off to leeward, it closes the slot; this is generally a bad configuration because a tight slot will stop the boat from pointing well and cause excessive backwind in the main that will ruin the effective drive in the main and increase drag forces.

FLEXIBLE THREE-STAY RIG

Most modern small boats have flexible three-stay rigs, but there are large variations in the way they are set up: some have a pivoting mast stepped on deck; others have a mast going through the deck which can be adjusted

Fig. 108
Shroud Adjustment for Athwartship
Mast Bend Under Sail

a. Masthead Rig
Single Spreader

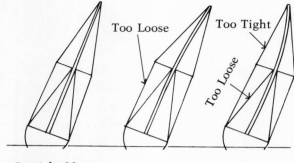

Straight Mast

b. ¾ Rig
Single Spreader

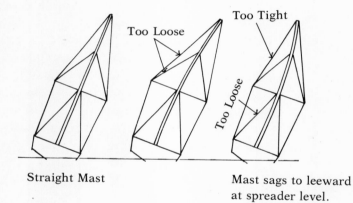

Straight Mast

Mast sags to leeward
at spreader level.

c. Double Spreader Rig

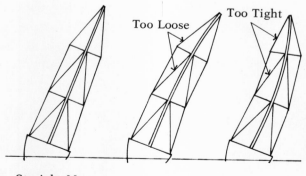

Straight Mast

d. ⅞ Rig
Single Spreader
45-Degree Jumper Strut

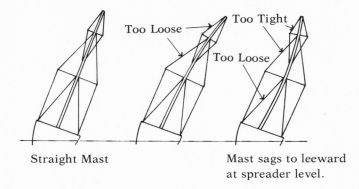

Straight Mast   Mast sags to leeward
                                 at spreader level.

at the partners and at the step. Some masts have no spreaders, some have fixed spreaders, and others have swinging spreaders with stops that control the swing aft. Controlling these masts, thereby obtaining the desired bend, is a controversial subject; there are numerous systems that depend on the type of rig and the rules of the one-design class involved. Ideally, the rigs will be self-tending and will automatically adjust themselves to the desired bend for different winds.

The primary factors involved in this automatic mast bend are spreader length and the angle at which the spreader stops its swing (preload); mast stiffness, which is controlled by cross-sectional dimensions and taper; crew weight, especially with a trapeze; and type and shape of mainsail.

Spreader Length

If spreaders are too long and push the shroud too far outboard, they will, in turn, create a reciprocal thrust on the mast as the shroud tries to straighten out under tension. This may cause an excessive amount of middlemast bend (Fig. 109). If the spreaders are too short, they will not allow enough low fore and aft bend; this will tend to keep the mast straight in the middle instead of assuming the desired bend.

Spreader Stops

With this type of rig, spreaders usually are free to swing forward, so that they are out of the way of the luff of the sail on a run. However, if stops are provided that limit the aft swing of the spreader, they can also be adjusted to keep the middle of the mast from overbending. This is called preloading. The spreader is pinned forward of the normal stay alignment from the mast to the deck. In addition to the athwartship angle that a shroud normally turns at the spreader tip, in preloading, the shroud goes from the mast

Fig. 109
Flexible Three-Stay Rig
Fore-and-Aft Bend

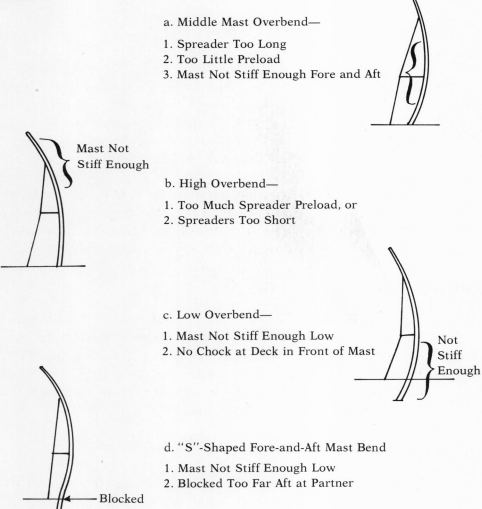

a. Middle Mast Overbend—

1. Spreader Too Long
2. Too Little Preload
3. Mast Not Stiff Enough Fore and Aft

Mast Not
Stiff Enough

b. High Overbend—

1. Too Much Spreader Preload, or
2. Spreaders Too Short

c. Low Overbend—

1. Mast Not Stiff Enough Low
2. No Chock at Deck in Front of Mast

Not
Stiff
Enough

d. "S"-Shaped Fore-and-Aft Mast Bend

1. Mast Not Stiff Enough Low
2. Blocked Too Far Aft at Partner

Blocked

Fig. 110
Flexible Three-Stay Rig Athwartship
Bend

a. Proper Athwartship Bend—

1. Bottom Straight
2. Tip Bent Off Slightly

b. Excess Athwartship Bend—

1. Spreader Too Short, or
2. Not Enough Preload
3. Mast Not Stiff Enough in Lower
Two-Thirds

c. Reversing Athwartship Bend—

1. Mast Not Stiff Enough
2. Too Much Preload, or
3. Spreader Too Long

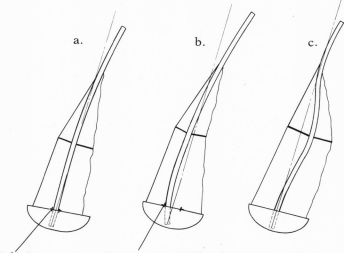

Tight Partners   Partners Too Wide Athwartship, Allowing
                        Mast to Move to Windward

to the spreader tip and then *aft* to the deck, thus pulling the spreader aft. The spreader then pulls the mast aft with it, preventing excess bend. By adjusting the stop angle, the spreader can be used to stiffen a "soft" mast.

Mast Stiffness

Since this rig configuration lends itself to a flexible mast, it is important to have the mast tapered properly so that, like the unstayed mast on a Finn, it tries to assume the proper bend without excessive rigging control. With design emphasis on low weight, very light masts are extremely limber and are not controllable in all weather conditions. This, of course, leads to collapsed rigs.

Crew Weight

Since the bend in the mast is controlled by the forces in the sails, heavy crew weight, which makes the boat stand up straighter, allows the sail to have a higher aerodynamic loading, giving higher rigging forces and making the mast bend more than normally. In other words, the boat heels less than it would with a lighter crew, and the mast bends more. Therefore, stiffer and stronger rigs are needed for heavier crew weights.

Trapezes impose an interesting problem on the three-stay rig. That is, the weight and leverage exerted by the trapeze tends to unload the windward shroud and thus reduce the controlling effect achieved by spreader length and preloaded stops. This allows the mast to overbend.

Mainsails

The draft and leech of the main will affect the bend in the mast. If the sail has a tight leech and is very full, it will cause higher loading on the masthead, thus producing greater bend in the middle of the spar. If the leech is loose and the sail is flat, then the loadings will be more evenly distributed and not so high, causing less mast bend. Unfortunately, the mainsail is not enough by itself to give you the mast bend you need. Therefore, the mast will have to be forced to bend more with very full sails and limited to bend less with very flat sails. Figures 109 and 110 show different mast-bend problems for the flexible three-stay rig, and the causes for each one.

MARK THE RIGGING

Once the rigging is properly set, tape the cotter pins that keep the turnbuckles or adjustment devices locked in position. Experiment with adjustable stays to determine the proper tension. Then, mark them so that there is no doubt about which position they should be set in. Also note that the spreaders usually should be cocked up at an angle from the horizontal, so that the upper and lower sections of the shroud are bisected.

There are hundreds of systems for tuning the standing rigging, but they vary from boat to boat and skipper to skipper. If you are just starting out, find out how boats similar to yours are set up. There is nothing wrong with copying a hot sailor, but you must understand his ideas and check them out through trial and error on your own boat.

Chapter 8

Sail Handling

To the new sailor the myriad adjustments, wind conditions, and sea conditions form a seemingly infinite number of possible combinations with the odds stacked against his ever finding the correct combination of adjustments. Surprisingly, the problem is simpler than it seems, because there are general guidelines for different wind conditions that are universal, with few exceptions. These guidelines reduce the number of combinations to only a few and work for a cruising boat or a one design with only a difference in the degree of trim.

First, a review of general sailing techniques and considerations is in order. Proper upwind steering technique is essential to attain good boat speed. The normal starting point for the beginner is to set the trim angle of the sails and steer the boat to the edge of the luff. Slight wind variations will cause the angle of attack to change. You must steer to these changes—that is, steer to keep the angle of attack constant. One way to learn how to do this is to steer a long scalloping course with the sails luffing slightly at the peaks of the scallops (Fig. 111). When the sails just break (luff), steer the boat gently away until the sails fill; gradually head up the boat until the luff just breaks, and again head away. With experience, the steering corrections used in this technique can be refined until they are barely perceptible and allow the boat to be continually sailed within the 2- to 3-degree range of the best angle of attack. The best skippers can steer to the edge without breaking a luff for long periods of time, but it takes the utmost concentration.

You also have to know how to deal with heeling. Sometimes, if you have a flat-bottomed or shallow-draft hull, you can use heeling to your advantage. In lighter air, you can reduce wetted surface and, therefore, hull drag by inducing a slight heel. This also helps the sails to fill out by gravity.

But your main concern with heeling will be in heavier airs, and to deal with it, you have to understand it. A boat, like a pendulum, has a cer-

Fig. 111
Windward Steering Technique

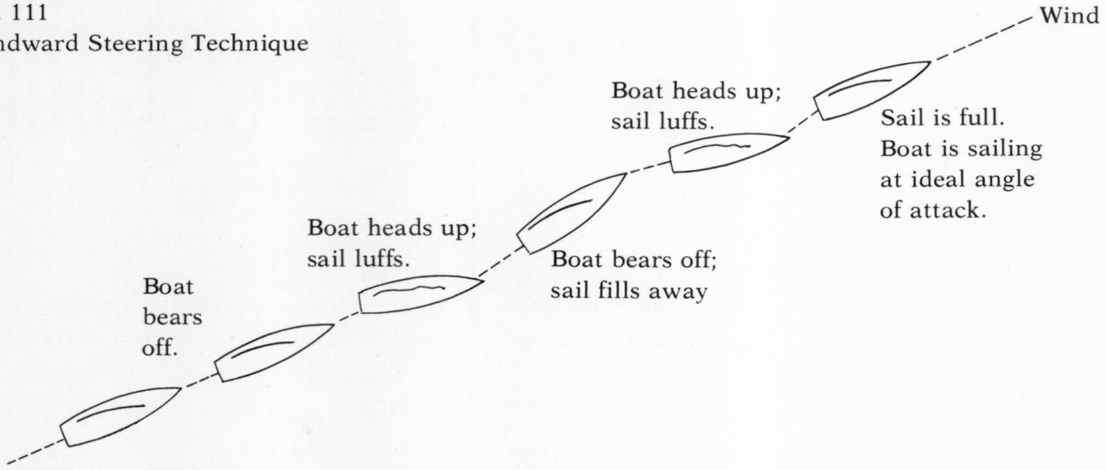

Wind

Boat heads up;
sail luffs.

Sail is full.
Boat is sailing
at ideal angle
of attack.

Boat heads up;
sail luffs.

Boat bears off;
sail fills away

Boat
bears
off.

tain amount of righting ability. A keel boat will always right itself; a centerboarder will, but only up to a certain point. The boat will fight to right itself, but when a critical point of heel is reached, everything changes. This usually occurs at an angle of from 25 to 30 degrees. The efficiency of the hull underbody deteriorates rapidly. The boat's righting force is decreased, and it becomes difficult to steer. The steeper angle of heel causes the sail to luff; the luffing increases drag, slows the boat down further, and you will heel even more.

Here are the ways heel can be countered:

1. Get your crew hiking as far to windward as allowed. The bigger your crew, the more power you can have in your sails.
2. Ease the traveler to get more of the force in a forward direction.
3. Ease the sheet to allow more twist in the leech. With less leech control the leech falls off to leeward; the sail is then a straighter line from luff to leech. This flattens the sail aloft, which is desirable: any side forces on the sail up high are going to have a proportionately greater heeling effect because of the leverage they will have from height. Use mast bend up high if you have a flexible mast.
4. Reef the sail (this again principally removes the side forces from the upper part of the rig).
5. Change to a smaller sail.

As a boat heels, there can be a major change in the balance of the helm. The increased wind velocity, which causes the heel, will force the draft farther aft in the sail, thus moving the center of effort aft, increasing the windward helm. You should look to draft controls to balance the helm as wind changes. Sail trim affects helm as well. Weather helm will decrease as the sails are trimmed out and increase when they are trimmed in. In pivoting centerboarders, lowering centerboard position will increase weather helm and raising it will decrease weather helm.

SPECIFIC WIND RANGES

For each wind speed we will discuss the proper adjustments to be made when sailing to windward. As the true-wind velocity increases, there are changes in the boat's performance. The amount of adjustment necessary to maintain optimum performance will vary from boat to boat, so only general guidelines will be discussed.

Drifter: 0–2 Knots

Very low wind velocities are not steady but usually come in puffs. Because of this, the hull will have very low forward speed. When a zephyr hits, the sail forces will be much greater than the lateral resistance of the hull (because it has no speed), and the hull will slide sideways. In this unsteady condition, it is important to have the boom trimmed well out until the boat gains speed. After attaining this initial momentum, you can sheet the boom nearer the centerline. You should have a medium amount of draft in the sails and keep a slight twist in the leech. Most boats have lee helm in these circumstances, and so if you have a centerboard, put it far forward. Try to induce a heel both to decrease wetted surface and keep the shape in the sails through gravity. Do not let the sails slat. Minimum hull resistance, medium-to-full, loosely sheeted sails, and a good telltale are most important in a drifter.

Light Wind: 2–5 Knots

Generally in these conditions boat speed is quite high compared to wind speed. Since the boat speed is faster, leeway will be less (boat speed increases lateral resistance) and the boat can support all the side force that can be created with the sails. With this little wind, it is important to develop all the power you can; so the boom should be trimmed to the farthest inboard point (the centerline) and the leech should be relatively tight. (Midships travelers will need to be pulled to weather until the end of the boom is centerlined.) Jib fairleads should be at their farthest point inboard, but the sheet should be free and the leech and foot should form easy curves. Maximum draft should be used. In this condition you may even be able to get the draft as full as 18 per cent. Be sure draft is at least 40 per cent aft in the jib and about halfway back in the main. The heads of the sails should be quite full; ease the outhaul and trim the sheet slightly to get the smoothest possible shape. Again, lee helm may be a problem. If it is, induce a slight heel, reduce wetted surface and hull resistance, and put the centerboard forward to get proper helm balance. Excessive helm in these conditions will cause a great deal of drag. Finally, in order to obtain maximum sail forces, the boat should be sailed below the luff—that is, close to the stalling point for the sails.

Light-to-Moderate Wind: 5–9 Knots

These conditions are very similar to the conditions described above, except that sail forces will get rather large and the boat will begin to heel. Crew weight will be needed to balance the boat. Most boats will reach maximum efficiency in this range, and boat speed will be very high in relation to true-wind speed, narrowing the apparent-wind angle. The sails should be flatter and twist reduced. The main traveler should remain close to centerline until the boat has reached maximum heel and the crew is fully hiking; at this point the traveler should be eased if necessary to keep the boat on its feet. The jib athwartship trim should correspondingly be eased and the jib sheet tightened to reduce twist and draft. Moderate draft, about 15 per cent, should be used, and since weather helm begins to increase, the centerboard should be moved slightly aft to balance the helm. Finally, the boat should be sailed to the luff and feathered through heavier puffs: that is, when a puff hits, head the boat higher into the wind, so that the sail is on the verge of a luff. This will prevent excess heeling. This technique can be combined with the scallop steering technique illustrated in Figure 111, so that the peak of the scallops corresponds to the wind gusts.

Moderate Wind: 9–13 Knots

For most boats, this is a very critical range, where you reach and go beyond the heeling angle at which the boat sails well. The maximum heeling angle to maintain optimum performance on most cruising boats is recommended by the yacht designer, and varies from 18 to 32 degrees. Most lightweight centerboard one designs should be sailed relatively flat at all times; 2 to 12 degrees being the maximum heel angle allowed. In the lower wind speeds (9–10 knots) a boat will not heel excessively, but in the upper range a smaller boat might be overpowered. Maximum crew weight and hiking ability are needed to hold centerboarders flat.

At the bottom of this range, begin to let the main twist by loosening the leech and easing the traveler. Draft should be reduced slightly. You will have to exert moderate luff tension to keep draft at the proper place. The jib draft should be reduced slightly, but the slot should remain narrow and the jib twisted. This can be done by moving the fairlead outboard and slightly aft and trimming the sheet tighter.

Once heel affects speed, do everything you can to reduce side force and improve forward drive. The traveler should be eased and the twist increased (by easing mainsheet tension) until the boat can be sailed on an even keel. Mainsail draft should be reduced. The draft should be kept from moving aft.

At this time the slot should be opened to relieve backwind on the main by moving the jib or genoa fairlead outboard. Jibsheet tension should be increased to keep twist constant. The draft in the jib should be kept forward through luff tension. The helm should be carefully balanced: move the centerboard slightly aft to decrease the rising weather helm.

In this wind condition the boat should be feathered through the puffs on the edge of a luff. With proper trimming the boat will point very high and the main will break into a luff slightly before the jib. However, only in the stronger puff should the sails be allowed to luff.

Moderate-to-Heavy: 13–18 Knots

Excessive heeling is the biggest problem. In this wind range the boat should be kept on her feet and driving by easing the traveler and opening the slot.

The best way to reduce heeling force is to reduce the side force up high by increasing twist. The amount of twist will depend on the sea condition. The traveler and jib fairlead should be moved outboard. Jib draft should be reduced by increasing sheet tension. Weather helm will get worse, and so the centerboard should be moved farther aft; make every attempt to reduce the helm, especially in a cruising boat.

Finally, point high, carry more luff than before, but try to drive the boat whenever possible. Again, the main should break first, but probably it will be necessary to carry a constant backwind. If pointing ability is bad, increase twist by easing the mainsheet and pulling the traveler slightly inboard to compensate, thus keeping the same trim angle (Fig. 112).

Heavy Wind: 18–25 Knots

Windward ability is greatly decreased on most boats. This is the point at which larger boats begin reefing. Any sail force in the top of the sails is useless. Since no more side force can be used, every attempt should be made to reduce rig drag by snugging extra lines close to the mast and doing anything else you can to get rid of extra windage aloft. Maximizing the forward driving components is your main concern. Most travelers are eased to their outboard limits in these conditions. Usually a moderate amount of twist in the main and especially the jib will be helpful. Even more luff tension is needed to keep the draft from moving aft. The jib should always be kept driving. The main may become almost useless, but try to keep it trimmed so that the batten area is just firm enough so that it doesn't flog. Weather helm will progressively increase, and every step should be made to reduce it. Steer the boat to keep it upright. Some sailors suggest that you steer to a constant angle of heel. Try to anticipate the puffs by heading up slightly as they hit so that you won't be knocked down. On the new IOR cruisers (with small mains and large genoas) the correct procedure is to let the mainsail luff in strong gusts, so that the boat will remain on her feet and the helm will remain balanced.

Very Heavy Wind: Over 25 Knots

At some point, however, the side force will overwhelm the righting force of the hull, and it will become very difficult to sail any boat upright. Alleviating

Fig. 112
Relationship of Mainsheet Tension and
Traveler Position to Leech Twist

a. Tight Leech—the traveler is outboard
and the sheet tight; there is very little
twist.

b. Loose Leech—the traveler is moved
toward center and the mainsheet eased;
there is increased twist.
Note that the leech setting is almost
identical in the upper half of both mains,
but from the mid-leech down (b) curves
inboard to the center traveler setting,
while (a) goes down straighter to the
outboard point.

these problems on a keel boat is the fundamental reason behind reefing (see Chapter 14). This is the best solution, since the well-shaped smaller sail can be used at maximum power without overpowering the hull and causing excessive heeling.

On most one designs, reefing is not allowed. The only alternative is to reduce draft to a minimum (using the flattest mainsail available), and ease the traveler, to maintain helm control. Open the slot and try to keep the jib full and driving. It is important to carry a lot of twist since excess twist allows the sail to luff high, which is, in effect, a form of reefing. With a flexible mast, make the top of the main a flat board by having the mast bend high. All the problems discussed in the previous wind range are magnified. Again, the boat should be steered to stay on her feet, using every lull to drive her to the highest possible forward speed.

CHOP AND WAVES

Most sailors find that racing in light air with chop is the most difficult condition in which to do well. First, boat speed is greatly reduced due to the added resistance to the hull's movement created by chop and waves. Second, the fore and aft pitching motion caused by the waves, called hobbyhorsing, causes the apparent wind at the top of the mast to continually change direction, first luffing and then stalling the sail. When boat speed is reduced, the entire vertical apparent-wind structure is changed; it is important to correlate sail twist to sea conditions.

In light air it is best to ease the traveler somewhat, open the slot, and ease the sheets. Try to keep the draft full in the top of the sail without causing a tight leech. If the chop conditions are severe, trim the traveler more to the centerline and ease the sheet a good bit to compensate and keep the right angle of trim. A large amount of twist in severe chop will often significantly increase speed and pointing ability. Finally, it is most important to drive a boat through chop and to steer to miss the bigger waves.

In heavy air, waves slow the boat considerably. To gain speed, the most immediate answer to the problem is to ease the traveler, increase twist, and drive the boat through the seaway. This usually works in moderate conditions, but with increasing wind velocity the traveler will be eased so far that adequate pointing ability is lost.   When this occurs in heavy seas, each wave will knock the bow farther to leeward, making it difficult to steer or keep the boat pointing. Many times this condition can be corrected by tightening the sheet, decreasing twist, and moving the traveler outboard to give the boat a better windward helm. Keep the slot open and the jib full. It is important in these conditions to sail the waves: point the boat up in the troughs (where it is a little calmer) and off on the crests. This technique is important for one designs, but is less effective and harder to accomplish as a boat gets larger.

OFFWIND SAIL HANDLING

Sail handling and sailing techniques on a reach or run are entirely different from those used for upwind sailing. Not only is there more variance between the direction of the true wind and the direction of the apparent wind, but offwind sail control is handled by different equipment from that used for upwind trim. Since the traveler width is limited to the beam of the boat, the vang and the sheet have to be used to control sail trim angle. On a one design, unless the vang is secured first, when the sheet is released the boom will lift, the leech will fall off, and twist will increase. The boom vang must be used to keep the boom down and control sail twist (Fig. 113).

Fig. 113
Boom Vang Plus Sheet Control Twist and
Angle of Attack

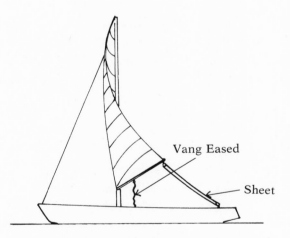

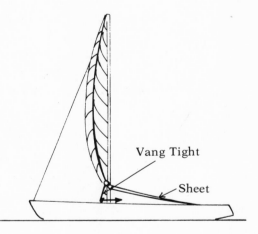

a. With the vang eased, the sheet has to hold the boom both aft and down. Since the angle of downward pull the sheet can exert is small, the boom can lift easily, producing excess twist. Without a vang, the boom has to be overtrimmed to keep the head of the sail full, but the bottom of the sail is then stalled.

b. With the vang secured, the upper portion of the sail will be at the same angle of attack, as in (a), but the lower portion will be fuller and not stalled, as in (a). The vang controls the entire leech; the sheet only controls the fore and aft position of the boom.

The correct angle of attack for upwind sailing is maintained by steering to the luff; when reaching, it is normal to steer to the course and play the sheet to the luff to keep the sail at the proper angle of attack. Jam cleats should not be used offwind on small boats, since you should be constantly trimming the sails.

Sail trim techniques differ radically for close reaching, reaching, and running.

CLOSE REACHING

For a cruising boat, close reaching creates a special problem and requires specific sail combinations; these problems will be discussed further in Chapters 9, 10, and 11. One designs, because of the types of courses used in racing, rarely encounter close reaching, but in most cases combining upwind and reaching techniques by using the vang, sheet, and traveler produces good results. Generally, it is necessary to steer to the luff (holding the proper angle of attack) in the minor wind shifts, changing sail trim in the larger shifts to obtain best performance. The amount of twist will depend on the wind speed, and it will be controlled by the vang. Get the vang set first. Then play the sheet to keep the boat flat and the sail trimmed to the proper angle.

REACHING

On a broader reach, the sails should be trimmed to get maximum driving force: the angle should be such that the sails are always trimmed closer to a stall than to a luff. Use maximum draft. The main outhaul should be eased; there should be no mast bend; the Cunningham should be released. The amount of twist, set by the vang, is critical: one technique is to apply the vang to reduce the twist until the sail luffs evenly from top to bottom, like a jib.

In planing conditions, constant trimming of the sail is necessary to keep sail forces at a maximum. Acceleration and deceleration of the boat as it goes on and off a plane causes the apparent wind to change direction radically: the increasing boat speed in relation to the true wind causes the apparent wind to move forward suddenly; therefore, it is important to trim in the sails as the boat accelerates onto a plane. When you come off the plane, the situation is reversed, and the sails should be slowly eased.

Fore and aft hull trim on smaller boats is very important on reaches. At slow speeds crew weight should be forward to reduce wetted surface; when planing, the hull should be balanced farther aft. At all times, the hull should be kept flat and not be allowed to heel, except in light air. Weather helm will be a problem and can be relieved by raising the center-board until excess side-slipping occurs. This also reduces wetted surface.

With one designs that rely solely on working jibs when reaching, it is important to move the jib fairlead to the rail in order to reduce excessive twist and form a better jib shape.

BROACHING

Broaching occurs when a sudden strong puff adds excess side forces to the sails that were properly trimmed for the pre-puff velocity. Keeping the boat "on its feet" is most important, and the quickest solution is to ease the vang and mainsheet immediately to reduce the sudden side force. This is mostly a problem with a spinnaker and is covered in Chapter 9.

RUNNING

When running, the main is stalled and nothing can normally be done to improve the situation. In most cases, maximum projected sail area, not draft, should be sought; but some curvature is needed to keep the leech firm and avoid an "S"-shaped sail, which occurs when the leech lays off to leeward. No twist should be allowed, since it reduces projected area: tighten the leech with the vang. In one designs, it is advisable to get the crew weight forward, pushing the bow down and so reducing wetted surface. Also, pull the centerboard all the way up. Last, in big and small boats alike, an old trick and a good one is to heel the boat to weather, thereby balancing the helm, getting the main higher up in the wind, and, sometimes, greatly increasing boat speed downwind. This also allows you to sail by the lee (Fig. 114).

Fig. 114
Heeling the boat to windward downwind
lifts the spinnaker out from behind the
main into clear air. It also gets the main
higher up into stronger wind. The
windward heel also balances the helm
and sometimes increases boat speed
significantly.

IMPROVING YOUR SAIL HANDLING

In the end, optimal sail handling can be arrived at only through trial and error. It is everyone's problem, and no one is going to give you the answer in a book—just some guidelines. The final answers come only from testing on the race course. One designs are easier to test than ocean racers because boats in the same class are basically equal, except for the difference in sail shape and trim. These minor differences can be observed by comparing boat speeds and pointing angles with the boats nearby.

The effect of tuning and trim adjustments can also be observed over the period of a race or a season by assuming your competitors are a constant. However, the time-consuming, arduous process of getting your boat going its best in all conditions can well be accomplished by practicing in pairs and keeping one boat a constant. This technique is called *brushing*. Both boats should start on the same tack, a few boat lengths from each other, and sail until it is obvious that one boat is not performing; stop and adjust that boat and start again. New sails and equipment should be tested by brushing against a known constant: a boat of well-proven competitive performance.

Brushing, when combined with practice, will noticeably improve performance and reduce confusion. Start by holding a steady course parallel to the other boat (be sure you are in clear air and in the safe-leeward position). First trim both sails (headsail first) until they are just barely on the edge of luffing. Concentrate on steering fast while the boat settles down, and then decide whether or not the other boat is faster. Study the sail shapes and note how the boat "feels"; do the sails appear in accordance with general concepts, are they trimmed too tight, or does the boat have excessive weather helm? Try easing the main traveler so that there is a little difference in trim between main and jib or vice versa; trim the jib by changing athwartship fairlead position or by changing the sheet tension. Does the boat sail better by carrying a slight luff in the main or jib? Look behind at the wake; is the boat sailing a straight or snaky course? Is the boat heeled over too far, can it be sailed flatter, or is it too flat? Keep fussing and eventually your partner, the constant boat, will lose consistently and it will be your turn to be the constant.

ADJUSTMENTS ON THE RACE COURSE

On the race course, adjustments must be made to an ailing performer as fast as possible; time lost in diddling with adjustments and arbitrarily pulling on strings can never be recovered against top competitors. Brushing is a valuable tool and builds practical experience in proper "gut feel" diagnosis of ailing boat speed; but what if you don't know why the boat is not going? What string should you pull first? As with a color television set on the blink: which of the many knobs should be turned first? Standard practice indicates that main and jib twist are slightly more important than trim angle. Twist should be adjusted first. Balance comes next: does the boat have a noticeably bad helm? Last, the amount of draft and its position in the sails should be checked and adjusted. It is important to go around this cycle quickly, improving each major item and repeating the entire cycle until desired performance is obtained (Fig. 115).

The following chart lists the major items of concern upwind and the primary and secondary adjustments which affect these items; coupled with Figure 115, a logical order of adjustment can be derived for most boats.

"UPWIND" SAIL-HANDLING CHART

A	B	C	D
Major sail-handling categories	*(breakdown)*	*Primary adjustments*	*Secondary adjustments*
I. TWIST	Headsail	1) Jib-sheet tension 2) Fairlead position (fore and aft)	1) Mast rake 2) Genoa-halyard tension (rope-luff genoa) 3) Cunningham tension (jerk string, OD)
	(SLOT) Mainsail	Mainsheet tension	1) High mast bend 2) Cunningham tension
II. TRIM ANGLE	Headsail	Fairlead position (athwartships)	Jibsheet tension
	(SLOT) Mainsail	Traveler	Mainsheet tension
III. HELM BALANCE	Centerboard boat	CB position (fore and aft) a. angle downward b. pin position	1) Mast rake 2) Fore-aft rig position 3) Twist of sails
	Keel boat	Trim-tab angle	4) Draft amount and position 5) Trim angle of sails
	Headsail — Amount high	Jibsheet tension	1) Jibstay sag 2) Fairlead position (fore and aft) 3) Luff tension
	Headsail — Amount low	Fairlead position (fore and aft)	1) Jibsheet tension 2) Jibstay sag 3) Luff tension

IV. DRAFT	Fore-aft maximum position	Luff tension a) genoa-halyard tension b) Cunningham tension c) jerk-string tension	1) Jibsheet tension 2) Fairlead position 3) Jibstay sag
	Amount high	Mast bend (high)	1) Mainsheet tension (leech twist) 2) Cunningham tension
Mainsail	Amount low	Outhaul	1) Mast bend (low 2) Cunningham tension
	Fore-aft maximum position	Cunningham	1) Mainsheet tension (leech tension) 2) Mast bend (high and low)

Fig. 115
Retrimming Cycle

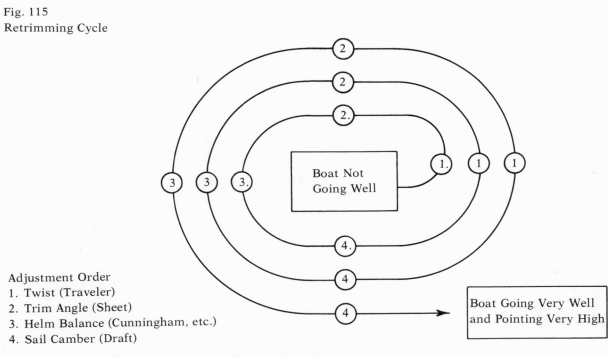

Adjustment Order
1. Twist (Traveler)
2. Trim Angle (Sheet)
3. Helm Balance (Cunningham, etc.)
4. Sail Camber (Draft)

The above chart provides a logical means for deciding which of the myriad adjustments must be made to control the four major categories in sail handling: twist, trim angle, helm balance, and draft control. Using the chart, select the major category to be changed (column A) for either the mainsail or the jib or genoa (column B). Under the heading Primary adjustments (column C) is a listing of the adjustments which most directly control the major category. Secondary adjustments which may be necessary to get the ideal shape and trim are listed in column D.

Example: the trim angle for the mainsail is thought to be incorrect, too far inboard. To adjust this, look down column A to trim angle; then go across to B, the mainsail; continue across to C, for the primary adjustment: Traveler. When this is eased, the main will have a wider trim angle. This may be sufficient, or you may have to go to column D for a further, secondary adjustment to mainsheet tension because the* slot relationship may also have changed and may require different mainsail twist. Therefore, you may have to make the secondary adjustment to mainsheet tension to get the shape and trim right.

Any adjustment may also have side effects which may not be desirable, and which will have to be countered by further adjustments. Once you have made your primary and secondary adjustments, to find out what damage you've done elsewhere check through columns C and D for the adjustment in other categories. For instance, mainsheet tension appears in column D under category 4—Draft—indicating that draft has been affected, and possibly has to be adjusted. Mainsheet tension also appears in category CQ1—Twist. Twist in the mainsail has been examined already, but twist in the headsail has not, and must be, because the slot relationship has changed. Thus, it is a cyclical process as shown in Figure 115.

This chart is laid out for sail control on one designs and cruising boats. Of course, some areas will not apply to both. Those adjustments which are only for one designs have been indicated by the initials OD. Avid sailors will find that the construction of a chart for their own boat is not only good winter homework, but could also reveal weaknesses in their sail-adjustments systems.

Figure 116 shows how different conditions require different settings, as outlined in the chart. On the opposite end of the spectrum, off-wind, there are similar adjustments to be made to produce ideal shape and trim (Fig. 117).

Fig. 116
Upwind Trim Comparisons.   The three
Solings in Figure 120 were photographed
at practically the same angle, allowing a
comparison of sail shape and trim. The
wind varies from light air in (a) to
medium-to-light in (b) to medium air in
(c). Notice that as the wind increases, the
wind force drives the mainsail leech in
each successive picture farther to leeward
into more twist; the jib leech, however, is
doing the opposite. There, the leech is
cupping around more to windward,
creating a fuller shape. The negative leech
can drive air onto the main, causing it to
luff. A more outboard setting of the jib
would help, but luff tension pulling the
draft forward would be the most
important correction. Note that as the
wind increases, the mainsail traveler has
been eased from windward of center in (a)
to quite a bit off to leeward in (c) to reduce
side force or heel. It is interesting to see
how much more of the upper part of the
mast is visible in each successive picture
as mainsail twist increases.

a.

c.

b.

Fig. 117

Downwind Trim Comparisons.   These
two pictures show a striking contrast in
twist control for both main and
spinnaker. In (a) the main boom has no
vang and the sheet does not have enough
downward movement to control leech.
The spinnaker has the pole too low, with
the result that there is too little luff twist.
The sheet is too far aft and, therefore,
there is too much leech twist. In (b) the
correct setting for main and spinnaker is
shown. Note how the vang has made the
main leech almost straight for reaching.
The spinnaker pole is raised to the top of
the track on the mast and the clew is set to
the same height.

a.

b.

Many top sailors keep notebooks recording the adjustments for each improvement in performance during brushing, later to be cataloged for each wind and water condition. Like any cataloging system, later duplication of the adjustments made is only possible if the recording and filing system is good. Start by marking all adjustable controls: sheet lines, travelers, and so on; also mark the halyards, shrouds, and mast position. Add marks to the fore and aft jib and genoa deck-carriage positions, luff tension controls, foot tension controls (outhaul), and traveler controls (Fig. 118), so that when the boat gets moving really well in particular conditions, you can

Fig. 118
All draft control and trim points should be marked with numbered reference points, so that a fast setting can be recorded and duplicated.

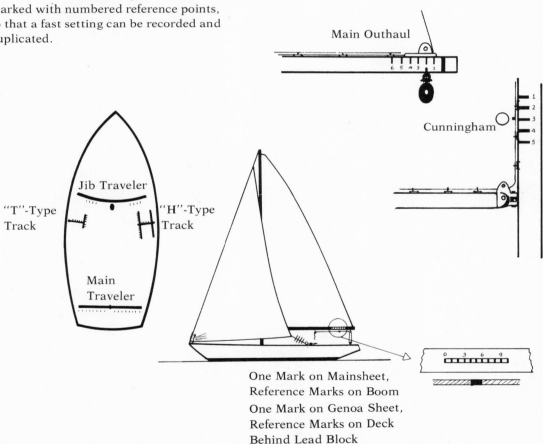

Main Outhaul

Cunningham

Jib Traveler

"T"-Type Track

"H"-Type Track

Main Traveler

One Mark on Mainsheet,
Reference Marks on Boom
One Mark on Genoa Sheet,
Reference Marks on Deck
Behind Lead Block

record the trim positions and duplicate them next time you are in that situation (Fig. 119). Any number of marking methods can be used — for example, plastic tape or a magic marker — but do not get overly complicated, and remember that most rope stretches more when it is wet. A good system will eliminate guesswork after the start of a race, when concentration on steering and tactics is far more important. Always try to get to the starting area well before the warning gun, so that the boat can be preset to the expected conditions; also try brushing with a friend for a short period to assure that nothing is wrong. Most races are won through detailed preparation.

Fig. 119

| | Main and Genoa | | | | Cruising Boat | |
| | | Smooth Sea | | | | |
Wind Speed in Knots	0-3	4-7	8-10	11-14	15-18	19-24
Main						
Traveler		On Centerline				
Sheet		At #8				
Outhaul		At #4				
Cunningham		Mark#6				
Genoa						
Halyard		9 in. Below Maximum				
Cunningham		Slack				
Fore and Aft Sheet Block		Hole #7				
Sheet Tension		Sheet Mark 2 in. Out of Block				
Inhaul		3 in. Inboard				

Part Three

AUXILIARY SAILS:
Which Ones You Need,
How to Use Them

Chapter 9

Spinnakers

DESIGN

There have been innumerable theories about what constitutes the ideal shape for a spinnaker, and this subject continues to provoke heated debates.

Perhaps one of the reasons for the controversy is that few people realize that the spinnaker does not work simply by blocking the wind, but also develops aerodynamic forces in varying degrees in all situations, from running to reaching. The reason for the confusion may be that the spinnaker on a broad reach or run, in effect, attacks the wind backward; the wind comes from behind, yet the luff of the spinnaker meets it at what is, nevertheless, a precise angle of attack (Fig. 120). This is possible because the spinnaker is a free-floating sail and can be rotated around the boat from side to side without a mast interfering. As we have seen, when the wind moves aft from a beat to a reach to a run, the mainsail can maintain the proper angle of attack until the wind is well aft of the beam and the shrouds prevent it from being angled any farther; the mainsail is then stalled. The spinnaker, being attached outside all lines and spars on the boat, does not have this limitation.

Not only can the spinnaker be angled to the wind at the proper angle of attack (which is every bit as exact an angle as upwind, with a margin of only 3 to 5 degrees between luffing and stalling), but the spinnaker develops aerodynamic flow and strong leeward forces up to the point where the curvature is so deep that the flow detaches.

When the spinnaker is thought of as an aerodynamic foil, just as a genoa or main, it is easier to understand the basic principles behind the design of spinnaker shape. First of all, when running dead downwind, the apparent wind angle is at its widest and the sail can be the fullest shape possible. The farther upwind you go, the narrower the angle of apparent wind and the flatter the sail has to be. Thus, for aerodynamic reasons, the running spinnaker can be very full (which is desirable for drag and stability reasons as well) while the reaching spinnaker has to be flatter (Fig. 121).

Fig. 120

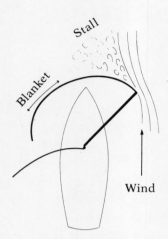

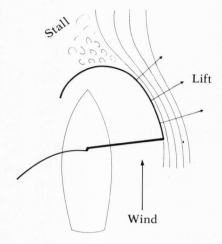

a. Since the spinnaker develops aerodynamic forces, it must be trimmed at the proper angle of attack. If the pole is too far forward, as in (a), the leading edge will be at too great an angle to the wind, the luff area will stall, and lift will not develop. The spinnaker may be blanketed by the mainsail as well. The net result is that the spinnaker will sag somewhat.

b. When the pole is squared to the apparent wind, aerodynamic flow develops and the whole spinnaker will then fill out or "lift."

Fig. 121
The apparent-wind angle determines the trim angle and shape of the spinnaker. As the apparent wind goes forward, the spinnaker should be flatter.

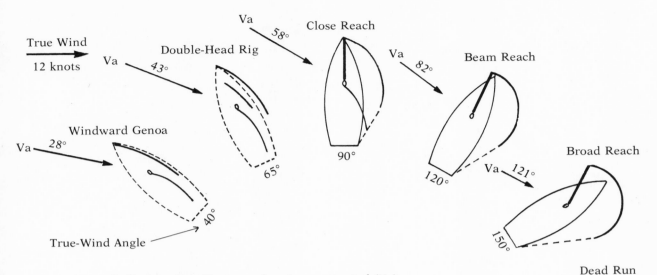

True Wind
12 knots

Double-Head Rig

Close Reach

Beam Reach

Broad Reach

Windward Genoa

True-Wind Angle

Sailing Angle	Boat speed	Apparent-wind (Va)	
		speed:	angle:
40°	5.5 knots	16.6 knots	28°
65°	6.8 knots	16.1 knots	43°
90°	7.5 knots	14.1 knots	58°
120°	7.5 knots	10.4 knots	82°
150°	6.8 knots	7.0 knots	121°
180°	6.0 knots	6.0 knots	180°
210°	5.5 knots	7.8 knots	231°

Dead Run

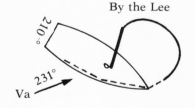

By the Lee

NOTE: apparent-wind angles from the boat centerline at the bow. The length of the arrow represents apparent-wind velocity and the angle of the arrow indicates apparent-wind direction. As the boat more and more approaches a windward angle, the sail, whether a genoa or spinnaker, has to be flattened increasingly to accommodate the narrower apparent-wind angle. As the boat heads closer to the wind direction, the apparent wind over the boat and sail increases, requiring a stronger and heavier sail. As the boat moves away from the wind (downwind), the velocity over the boat and sail decreases, decreasing wind force, so a lighter weight sail can be used. As wind velocity decreases downwind, added fullness is also needed for the spinnaker's stability.

Years of testing on parachutes, which work on exactly the same principles as spinnakers, have shown that stability and fullness are directly related: the fuller the chute, the more stable it is. The flatter it is, the more it oscillates. With a free-floating sail like a spinnaker, this is an important consideration. However, on a reach, fullness adds to the already considerable side-loading because of the strong heeling component of the sail's forces and the increase in apparent wind velocity on this point of sailing; thus, even if you could carry a fuller spinnaker on a reach, it would be counterproductive and cause excess heel. For reaching, therefore, you need a flatter spinnaker that is, in effect, a compromise between the full, running spinnaker and the genoa.

Another important consideration in spinnaker shape is the condition in which the sail is to be used. In average winds, the running spinnaker should be maximum size, but in very light airs or very heavy airs, it should be smaller although still full in shape. In lighter air, boat movement and gravity won't allow a huge sail to fill out; in heavy air, the boat can't support the force of a huge sail. For reaching in light to medium air, spinnakers should be built to the maximum girth* allowed in the center of the sail, but be narrower toward the head or "shoulders" of the spinnaker. The reason for this is, again, to avoid creating stronger negative or heeling forces aloft. For the same reason, reachers for heavier air are often built to only 80 to 90 per cent of maximum girth in the center of the sail (if there is no minimum girth rule forbidding it) and are even narrower in the shoulders.

Also, the cross-sectional shape or draft of the spinnaker should be fairly uniform from the top to bottom of the sail; any bulges or flat spots will decrease the sail's stability (by decreasing fullness) and will also vary the sail's angle of attack and the development of aerodynamic flow. Similarly, the luff and the leech of the spinnaker should be matched in a smooth uniform curve from head to foot; the luff so the angle of attack will be uniform, and the leech so that the air will exit smoothly off the sail.

It's important to keep in mind when talking about spinnakers that the leech and luff of the sail are interchangeable, depending on the boat's tack, and therefore have to be made identical in length and shape. This

*Girth does not refer to the fullness of the sail but to the measurement of the amount of cloth from leech to leech; thus, two sails with the same girth measurement could have different fullnesses: one could be a flatter, wider sail, as in a reacher; and the other, a narrower but fuller sail, as in a cruising-boat spinnaker.

presents a problem of terminology: when under sail, one edge becomes the luff (the edge attached to the pole) and the other edge becomes the leech. But when the sail is off the boat and not related to the wind, the words "luff" or "leech" could be applied to either edge. For the sake of clarity, when the sail is off the boat, we will describe these edges of the sail as leeches. The third edge is always called the foot.

These are the basic aerodynamic considerations to take into account when designing a spinnaker; in addition, however, the size and shape of the spinnaker for many one designs are often limited by class rules, while those for racing-cruising boats are limited by various handicap rules such as the International Offshore Rule. These measurement rules specify maximum and sometimes minimum dimensions for the spinnaker and thus restrict the amount of possible variations in shape (Figs. 122 and 123). In many one-design classes, to prevent the boatowner's having to purchase extra sails and to keep the class spinnaker uniform, only one spinnaker is allowed. This usually means that you cannot have a smaller, flatter sail for reaching, and the result is that you have to compromise by getting a sail that is neither ideal for running nor for reaching.

Also, in one-design classes, a minimum girth dimension is sometimes stipulated, and this, too, can have the effect of preventing the use of a smaller, flatter reaching spinnaker. This can present a problem because many classes today are sailing olympic courses with two tight reaches and a run, as well as three windward legs. The reaches have to be sailed with a spinnaker that is too wide and thus too full, creating tough problems in sail handling for everyone but the real experts.

Cruising-boat spinnakers under most rules have a maximum girth dimension that governs not only the foot but the rest of the sail all the way up to the head (Fig. 122a). This maximum girth dimension is usually about 60 to 65 per cent of the luff dimension and consequently provides a sail of a size that is usually good for reaching but small for running.

Twelve-Meters, 5.5-Meters, and several other open classes have luff restrictions but no girth restrictions (except on the foot in some cases), and the maximum practical dimensions are usually developed through experimentation in each class (Fig. 122c). The 12-Meters, however, with high boat speeds that bring the apparent wind forward quickly as they head up from a dead run to even a slight reaching angle, have found that there are few times when a maximum girth spinnaker will work even when running.

Fig. 122
Examples of Girth Restrictions for
Spinnakers.   Luff lengths are limited in
all cases.

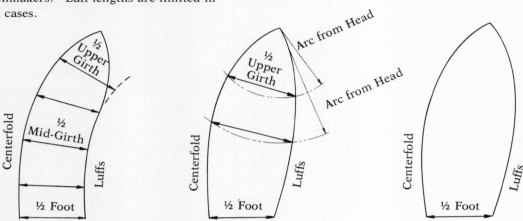

a. The cruising rule specifies one
maximum girth, which may not be
exceeded without penalty anywhere,
including the foot.
b. With the average one-design rule, upper
girth, mid-girth, and foot all have
separate maximum—and usually
minimum—dimensions.
c. Meter rule: 5.5 Meters have a foot
restriction. The 12-Meter rule has no girth
restriction.

Rules governing girth dimensions obviously affect the shape of the
leeches of the spinnaker. The cruising-boat rules provide for just the one
maximum girth dimension, and, as a consequence, the leeches develop an
"S" shape, which is less efficient than the uniformly curved leech (Fig.
123a). This happens because of the desire to get the maximum allowable
area in the sail and because of the way the sail is built. The spinnaker is a
sail with a great deal of curvature, which has to be built by curving the individual panels of the sail. The panels are then sewn together, but the
leeches are left unfinished (they are unsewn and unshaped). The sail is
folded in half at the centerline from top to bottom, so that the raw leeches

Fig. 123

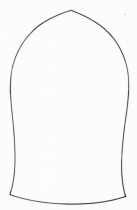

a. Typical Cruising-Rule
Spinnaker

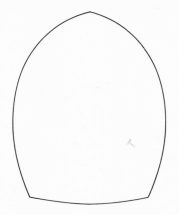

b. One-Design Shape

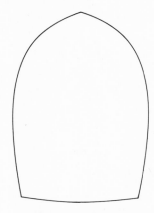

c. Meter or Open Rule
with Only Luff and
Foot Restrictions or
No Restrictions at All

**Effects of Different Rules on Spinnaker
Shape.**   The cruising rules produce the
bell-shaped sail, (a). The open rule
produces the well-rounded and balanced
shape, (c). One-design shapes, (b), are
usually close to the open rule, because of
well-thought-out rules. They can vary
from fairly narrow (Dragons) to very wide
(Lightnings). There may be one or two
girth restrictions in addition to the foot,
but the mid-girth is generally larger than
the foot, allowing a more rounded shape.
The girthpoints are usually found at
specific distances described in arcs from
the head of the sail.

d. Comparison of the Three Shapes

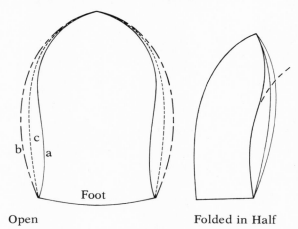

Open

Folded in Half

(Most spinnakers are
measured while
folded in half.)

meet. Then the maximum girth (divided in half because the sail is in half) set by the rule is struck off every 2 to 3 feet from the foot on up. This produces a leech curve parallel to the centerfold curve. However, since the head of the sail comes to a point, at a certain point the leeches have to depart from the maximum girth dimension in order to meet at the head. The leech curve, therefore, starts out being concave as it follows the centerfold curve and then becomes convex as it goes toward the head, producing the "S"-shaped leech (Fig. 124).

Fig. 124
In cruising-boat spinnakers, the one constant girth dimension specified by the rules causes an "S"-shaped leech, (a). "S"-shaped leeches are decreased by cutting the foot smaller than the maximum allowed, (b).

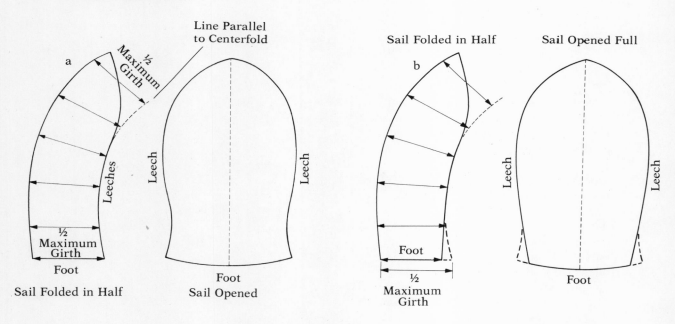

There is a way to avoid this. Since there is no minimum foot measurement for the cruising boat (only a minimum girth in relation to the foot dimension), the leech curve can be drawn in to cut off the lower corners at the tack and the clew, reducing the "S" shaping (Fig. 124b). Admittedly, there is some loss in sail area, but there are some benefits. With the corners of the sail cut off, the new tack moves out toward the end of the spinnaker pole and the entire sail moves out also. This gets the luff of the sail farther away from the boat and into clear air and, when used, farther away from the disturbing effects of the genoa or staysail.

One-design class rules generally circumvent this shape problem by using one measurement for the foot and one or more girth restrictions. The mid-girth is usually wider than the foot and provides a smooth, positive leech curve, which is more ideal (Fig. 123b). Spinnakers with no restrictions can have many different shapes.

Spinnaker Construction

The spinnaker presents a number of special problems in construction. First of all, it is a free-floating sail, unsupported along any edge. For the sail to overcome gravity and stay aloft, the cloth has to be lighter than in most sails; and, therefore, will have more stretch.

Spinnakers are made of nylon because of its light weight and great strength, even though it stretches considerably. Dacron, although it has less stretch, cannot be woven in the light weights required for downwind spinnakers. Moreover, ounce for ounce, nylon is stronger than Dacron. In some instances, nylon's stretch can even be an asset; downwind in light air, for example, when the free-flying spinnaker is often bounced around by boat movement, stretch gives resiliency to the sail and absorbs the shock. However, stretch becomes a real problem the moment the loading on the sail increases, either on a run through heavier air or by the increased forces developed on a reach. It is particularly troublesome on a reach because this is just when you don't want fullness. So, now some of the highly loaded, close-reaching, star-cut spinnakers are being made from 2-ounce Dacron, which is the lightest Dacron available.

One way to lessen the problem of stretch is to use a heavier weight nylon. There are six weights available: ½-ounce, ¾-ounce, 1.2-ounce, 1½-ounce, 2½-ounce, and 4-ounce, and the weight selected depends on the loadings involved, which in turn depend on whether the sail is to be used for running or reaching, in what wind conditions, and on what size boat. For instance, in very light air and for running and broad reaching, where the loads are minimal and gravity is a major factor, ½-ounce would be the ideal weight for almost any size boat. However, even in light air the loads build rapidly on a reach and a ½-ounce sail would quickly stretch out of shape; ¾-ounce material would be required. In fact, the ¾-ounce spinnaker has become the universal weight for all-purpose spinnakers on most boats. A reaching spinnaker for medium-to-light airs on up is generally made from 1½-ounce cloth, while for larger boats, a 2½-ounce or 4-ounce reaching spinnaker might be needed.

Since the spinnaker is attached only at its three corners, the strains radiating from these corners are severe, and there is nothing but the sailcloth itself to counter them (Fig. 125). Since nylon stretches, different panel layouts are used to minimize the stretch in order to maintain the properly designed shape of the spinnaker under load. Some layout systems have the cloths perpendicular to the leeches; others have the cloths perpendicular to the centerline of the sail (Fig. 126). With these two design systems, there is only one load line parallel to the thread line. All other lines of stress are on the bias angle of the cloth, and this can cause stretch and distortion. However, with small spinnakers, loadings are frequently low enough so that stretch is not a prime consideration. These two cloth layouts, therefore, can be used for one-design spinnakers without much problem.

Fig. 125
Strains radiate from all three corners of
the spinnaker.

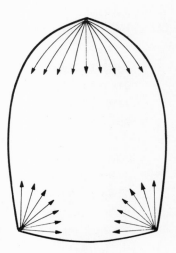

Fig. 126

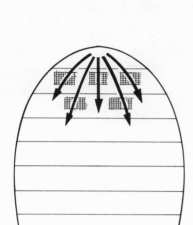

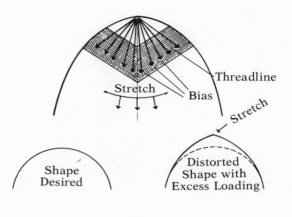

a. Spherical Spinnaker

b. Sunburst Spinnaker

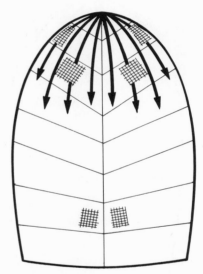

For medium loading conditions in cruising boats, the compound curvature in the head needs more stability. Since the strains radiate out of the head, to reduce stretch all the cloths should radiate from the head as well, so that the loading will be in the same direction as the thread line of the cloths, with no bias strain. This construction produces a "radial head" configuration (Fig. 127).

Fig. 127
Radial-Head Spinnaker.   All stress
loading in the head is parallel to the
threadline.

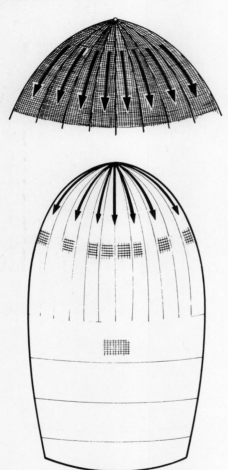

    With larger sails that are used for reaching and have to carry high
loadings, some spinnakers are made with panels radiating out of all three
corners. This tri-radial system, known as a star-cut, is very expensive but
very effective. It produces a spinnaker that can be carried much closer to
the wind than conventional designs because it is a flatter sail to start with,
and under load the cloth layout keeps stretch to a minimum (Fig. 128).

Fig. 128
Star-Cut Spinnaker. Stress loading in
all corners is parallel to the threadline.

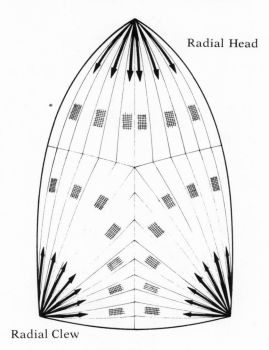

Radial Head

Radial Clew

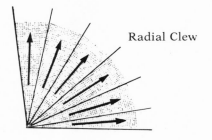

Radial Clew

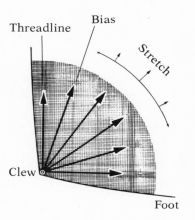

Threadline

Bias

Stretch

Clew

Foot

Radial Clew of Star-Cut—on the clews of
most spinnakers the cloths are generally
laid out perpendicular to the luff, so that
the leech and foot are on or close to the
threadline but the stress lines radiating
toward the central areas are all on the bias.
In the star-cut, the principle of the radial
head is applied to the clews: the lines of
stress are parallel to the threadline.

From time to time, the subject of holes in spinnakers is raised, and sailmakers have actually produced spinnakers containing 6- to 12-inch holes as well as slits and other forms of ventilation. Holes are just an expanded form of porosity, and studies have long shown that increasing porosity decreases the spinnaker's efficiency. Actually, decreasing porosity, by coating the sail, has produced the fastest spinnaker cloth yet.

SPINNAKER CONTROLS

There are more attachments to a spinnaker than to any other sail on your boat. Figure 129 shows a typical rig for the spinnaker control lines, and here is an explanation of what they are and do.

1. The *halyard*, of course, raises and lowers the sail. The fastest way to hoist is hand over hand from a standing position forward. On a large boat this can be hazardous if the spinnaker breaks out prematurely. On some one designs, you cannot stand on deck forward, and so frequently the halyard leads aft and is pulled up by the skipper.

For fast hoisting, you need low-friction blocks yet you also need holding capability in case the sail breaks out while being hoisted. Most cruising boats have a handy winch on the mast or deck to take the load. You should also have a fast-acting halyard cleat for quick engagement and

Fig. 129
Typical Rig for Spinnaker Control Lines

a. There are only slight differences between one designs and cruising-boat rigs: the location of the foreguy and lift differs because of the different jibing systems used. Cruising boats use a dip pole jibe because the pole is too heavy to manage an end-for-end one-design jibe. The foreguy and lift in a cruising boat, therefore, have to be fastened to the pole in the far forward position. On a one design, the foreguy and lift or bridle both go to the middle of the pole. (See Fig. 147 for illustrations of the different types of jibes.)

b. The termination points of lines will be different in one designs and cruising boats; on a one design, the lift and foreguy terminate on the forward edge of the cockpit and the sheet and afterguy in the midcockpit area. On a cruiser-racer, the lift and foreguy terminate on the aft edge of the cabin house and the afterguy and sheet at cockpit winches.

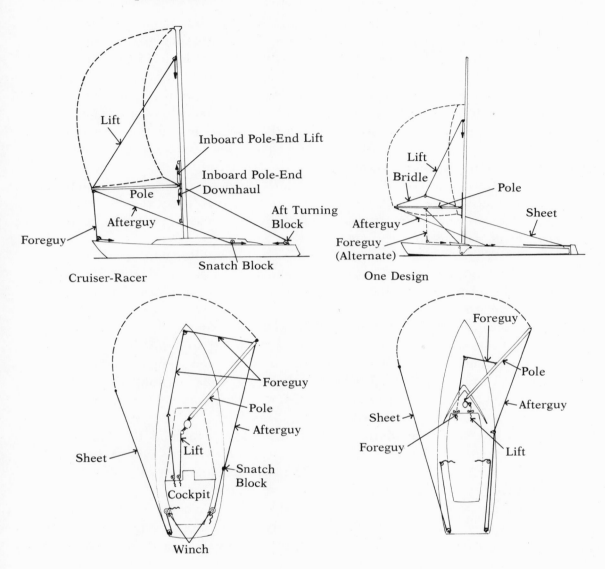

Cruiser-Racer

One Design

positive hold. Make sure the halyard is always free to run—in case you have to drop the sail in a hurry.

2. The *spinnaker pole* is, in effect, a boom used to hold the tack of the spinnaker at the desired location. It should always be kept perpendicular to the mast by means of the pole lift and the foreguy or downhaul.

The pole's purpose is to keep the sail (in most cases) as far from the boat as possible, and so, in order to use the pole's maximum length, you must have it extended straight out, not dipped low or cocked high. Ideally, spinnaker poles should have a one-handed or trigger method to open any fitting on them that is going to be engaged or disengaged while the spinnaker is working. In other words, you should be able to hold the pole with one hand and simultaneously depress a trigger with the other. The situation to avoid is where you need three hands to fasten the pole: one hand to hold the pole end, one hand to open the trigger mechanism, and a third to place the guy or sheet into the fitting. Some newer pole-end fittings have a locking mechanism so that when you pull the pin back, it stays there until the clew ring is in place, at which time the pin automatically releases and locks. This also solves the problem.

3. The *afterguy* or *poleguy* is run to or through the end of the spinnaker pole and controls the fore and aft angle of the pole in relation to the pole and the centerline of the boat. The afterguy is led aft to a fitting along the windward rail.

Because of its very acute trim angle and heavy load, the afterguy usually bears more strain than any line on the boat; so a winch or winch block is needed on small boats in strong airs and on cruising boats under almost all conditions. Cruising boats usually have the winches aft, while one designs, if they use them, locate them amidships on either side. Many larger boats are equipped with multiturn cleats that take a long time to secure and cast off. Loads from a winch are not great and the "quick" cleats used by many small craft are more efficient and can be used on larger craft, up to 35 or 40 feet. Of course, the quick cleats are not as strong and are difficult to disengage if they get in a highly loaded situation.

On a close reach, when the spinnaker pole is against the headstay, the angle of the afterguy from the pole end to the shrouds might be only 15 degrees. This creates a critical trim problem. For example: if the afterguy is trimmed at a 75-degree angle to the pole, it has a loading of 500 pounds; when it is trimmed at a 15-degree angle, the loading will be over *three* times that amount or 1,860 pounds. Then the guy would have 1,860 pounds loading coming to the turning block and 1,860 pounds going forward from the turning block, so that the block itself would have to carry a load of 3,720 pounds.

To reduce this loading, you can rig a strut from the mast that extends through the shrouds to windward. The afterguy passes through a fitting at the end of the strut, creating a wider trimming angle and giving you more leverage. If the angle was opened to, say 22½ degrees, the load on the afterguy would be 1,260 pounds; so the loading is reduced to 1,260 pounds on the afterguy, with a total load of 2,520 instead of 3,720 pounds on the turning block (Fig. 130).

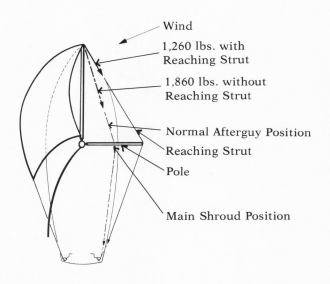

Fig. 130
The farther forward the pole is trimmed, the more acute the trim angle, and the more the pressure on the afterguy is resolved into compression loading and less into turning moment as shown in (a). To relieve the compression and make it easier to trim, increase the trim angle by adding a reaching strut, (b).

Wind
1,260 lbs. with Reaching Strut
1,860 lbs. without Reaching Strut
Normal Afterguy Position
Reaching Strut
Pole
Main Shroud Position

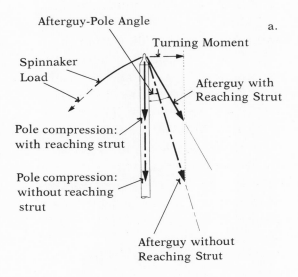

Afterguy-Pole Angle
a.
Turning Moment
Spinnaker Load
Afterguy with Reaching Strut
Pole compression: with reaching strut
Pole compression: without reaching strut
Afterguy without Reaching Strut

b. Reaching Strut in Use

On most cruising boats the afterguy then leads from the turning block forward to a winch. One designs often have a ratchet turning block and no winch; the lead runs from the turning block, which has some holding action, forward to amidships where the crew can adjust it quickly, without having to use a winch.

4. The *spinnaker sheet* trims the clew of the sail like a genoa or jib sheet, and should be led aft at the proper angle; the lead should be located so that the tension on the leech and foot is balanced and the draft is uniform throughout the sail (see page 205).

5. The *pole* (or *topping*) *lift*, attached to a bridle on the pole or to the pole end, is used to adjust the height of the outboard end of the pole (to which the spinnaker is attached) to suit the sailing angle and wind velocity. It is important that this always be under control.

6. The *foreguy*, a counterpart of the lift, holds the spinnaker pole down. When the lift is raised, the foreguy is eased the same amount, so that the pole is always held in a controlled position (Fig. 131). When adjusting the height of the pole in stronger airs, when pressures on the spinnaker are increased, these two lines, the lift and the foreguy, should be kept under control around a cleat or winch at all times.

Remember, there is tremendous aft compression loading on the pole, pushing it directly back into the mast, and if either end of the pole is raised or lowered out of alignment, the pressure will be at an angle and will cause the pole end to flip up or down violently, depending on the direction in which you've moved it (Fig. 131b). The only preventers you have are the topping lift or foreguy, whichever is applicable. For example, as the pole end is raised with the topping lift, until the inboard end of the pole can be adjusted to match, the foreguy is the only control holding the pole down. If it is too slack, the pole will lift up and get out of control very quickly. Care should be taken to avoid this dangerous situation by always having both topping lift and foreguy secured by a couple of turns around the winch, as you adjust one or the other.

On one designs and small cruising boats, the foreguy is attached to the center of a bridle under the pole, just as the lift is attached above the pole. On larger boats, the foreguy is attached to the end of the pole, and, like the lift, works easily in a dip-pole jibe. It usually is trimmed forward on one designs and in the cockpit on cruising boats.

7. The *mast track* and *slide* enable you to adjust the height of the

Fig. 131
Spinnaker Pole Controls

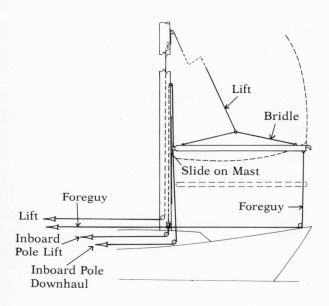

a. The spinnaker pole is raised and lowered by a lift and downhaul at either end. The pole should always be kept square to the mast so; as one end is lifted or lowered, the opposite end should be adjusted the same amount. Thus, the foreguy and lift need side-by-side controls in the cockpit area so that as one is eased, the other can be tensioned. The eased control should be kept around a winch, or one turn around a cleat should be taken to keep the pole manageable.

b. Dangerous situations: when the outboard end of the pole is raised, if the foreguy is not under control the pole can snap up suddenly because of the tremendous loading on the afterguy (see photograph). Conversely, if the outboard end is lowered, the topping lift has to be controlled or the pole can snap down into the water.

In both cases, the pole will form an acute angle to the mast, driving the inboard end up or down if not fully secured.

inboard end of the pole to changes in height made at the outboard end, thereby keeping the entire pole perpendicular to the mast, so that if you ease the foreguy and take up on the lift, thereby lifting the pole end, you can square the pole by sliding the inboard end up the track.

Small boats have a snap-lock pin on the slide, somewhat larger ones have control lines, and the big boats use bicycle chains to regulate the slide (Fig. 132) because the top of the spinnaker pole track is out of reach. Raising and lowering a pole along the slide requires quick, easy, but controlled movement. Positive control is vital because of the great strains involved if the pole is not square.

If rules, such as those in some one-design classes, do not permit the mast track, then two or more eyes are fastened to the mast at different levels.

Fig. 132
Inboard Pole Controls.   Devices
controlling the inboard end of the
spinnaker pole vary from fixed eyes to
slides with different controls, depending
on size.

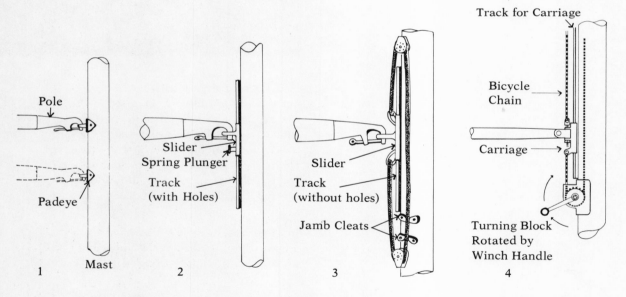

1. One or More Fixed Eyes
2. Sliding Eye on Track with
Spring-Loaded Plunger

3. Sliding Eye on Carriage with Control
Lines Running Continuously on Mast
with Cleats, or Running to Jambs on Deck
4. Large Boat Rig for Adjusting
Spinnaker-Pole Height at Mast

By snapping the pole in one eye or another, the inboard end of the pole can be kept close to the same height as the outboard end. The height above deck of the inboard end of the pole is usually limited by rule, but even when this height is reached, the outboard end of the pole can be canted up if more height is desired. Just keep a tight hold on the foreguy and lift.

SETTING A SPINNAKER

Preparations prior to setting a spinnaker vary with the size of the boat. Small boats use buckets, cloth turtles, spinnaker holes in the deck, and other devices which serve to compact and stuff the sail in a small area until it is ready to be set. Turtles have the advantage of allowing you to move the whole spinnaker from one place to another prior to hookup. They also provide compact stowage (Fig. 133).

Fig. 133
With halyard hooked to the head of the spinnaker, hoop turtle can be clipped to the shrouds, bow pulpit, lifeline, stanchion, or forward area of the cockpit.

a. Turtle on Shrouds and Fully Rigged

Spinnaker Halyard

b. Close-Up of Turtle

Except for ½-ounce spinnakers, larger boats sometimes use a zipper turtle, so that the spinnaker can be raised in a sleeve before the boat reaches the weather mark (Fig. 134). Then, on rounding, the sleeve is released at the bottom, and the spinnaker breaks out. This naturally makes an easier set, but the rig is not appropriate for the smaller one-design boats. The zipper would be too heavy relative to the small spinnaker. In any case, the spinnaker is small enough so that the crew can cope with halyard, guy, or sheet if the sail breaks out prematurely.

Regardless of what packaging system you use, the first thing is to determine the side on which the spinnaker is to be set. Then you have two jobs: (1) attach the halyard, sheet, and afterguy to the spinnaker; (2) attach the pole to the mast and get the foreguy and pole lift in place.

Many people are apprehensive about these jobs and develop a complex about hooking up a spinnaker. Actually, if you know precisely what is involved, it is not a complicated process. A spinnaker can be taken from the bilge in its turtle and hooked up completely with pole in place in less than a minute by a step-by-step routine—which is the only way to do it.

Generally, in a race, it is a mistake to delay hooking up until the boat is approaching the weather mark on its final tack, ordinarily the one it will hold after rounding. Usually races are run so that the second leg of the course is a starboard tack. This means the spinnaker would be set from the port side with the pole to starboard. But the tendency is to wait until the boat is on the final starboard tack to get the spinnaker in place. Then the crew must go to the lee side to set up the turtle at the shrouds. This is awkward and inefficient. It is easier to set the turtle on the shrouds while you are on port tack, which at that moment is the windward side. Then when you go over onto starboard tack, you set up the pole on the windward side. You are thus hooked up and ready to go as you round the mark (Fig. 135).

The biggest problem with the spinnaker is to hook up the afterguy, sheet, and halyard so that they do not become entangled with genoa sheets, shrouds, or spreaders. If done wrong, it can create an unholy mess, as even the best of sailors have found out.

The way to prevent this snafu is to visualize the lines when the spinnaker is flying out in front or to the side of the boat, completely outside of any other sail. The halyard leads directly from the top of the foretriangle to the head of the spinnaker. The sheet runs from the quarter block near

Fig. 134
Zipper Turtle System for Large
Boats.   Two light nylon zip fasteners are
sewn onto spinnaker, which is then rolled
up into a sausage from each side. It is
zipped up with special pliers; a light
stopping holds it at the bottom and, at the
top, the zipper is folded back and tucked
into the tube formed by the spinnaker.
When the spinnaker is being set, the
trimming of the sheet breaks the stopping
and allows the sail to start to fill from the
bottom upward, the zipper being opened
rapidly by the wind.

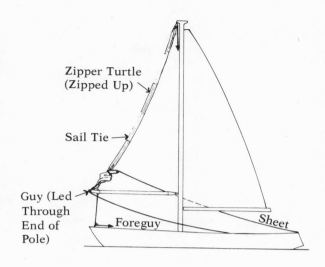

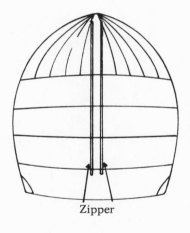

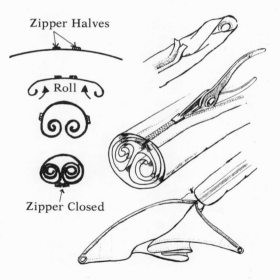

the stern straight out to the clew of the sail. The afterguy runs from the
windward rail right to the tack of the sail at the end of the spinnaker pole.
Now in your imagination take down the spinnaker and bring all the lines
to a point where the deck turtle is placed. This is like doing a reverse set—

Fig. 135
All spinnaker lines are secured and in
place, ready for hoisting as the mark is
rounded.

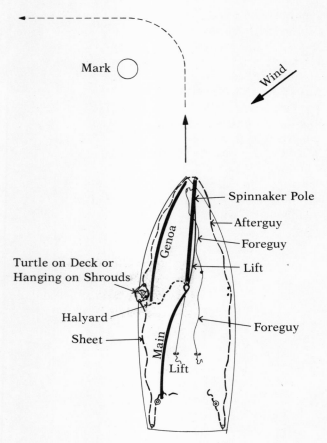

One Design or Small Cruiser

as if you ran a movie camera backward. But as a result, the halyard, sheet,
and guy will be outside of every other line or fitting on the boat and in the
right position for attachment. (The large-boat zipper turtle system avoids
many of these problems because it can be raised in place before it is broken
out.)

One hookup system used by many boats today is to run the afterguy
through the spinnaker pole fitting, then around the headstay, and aft to
the tack of the spinnaker in its turtle on the lee side of the boat. Then, when
the spinnaker is hoisted, the afterguy should be trimmed in quickly, so that
the pole end is close to the tack of the sail. This system enables you to set

up everything in advance. Usually the halyard is attached at the last minute to avoid the possibility of prematurely pulling the sail out of the turtle.

With a nonoverlapping jib, the spinnaker pole and lift can be hooked up early and the boat can be tacked with the pole in place (Fig. 136). If the pole is set to starboard and the boat goes over onto port tack, the pole is simply brought back to its squared position, where it can clear the leech of the sail. If you have an overlapping genoa, the pole cannot be raised until you are on your final tack for the weather mark. If you have a track and slide on the forward side of the mast, the pole can be hooked into the slide fitting in a lower position. The foreguy can be hooked up, but you cannot set the lift until you get on the final tack.

There are times when you have the turtle set in place, the lines made fast to the spinnaker, and the pole all rigged — and you find a wind shift has ruined your calculations. The spinnaker should have been set on the other side. What to do?

First of all, if the next leg is almost a run, you might be better off rounding the mark, setting your spinnaker, and then jibing it. This is usually a faster procedure than trying to switch everything around.

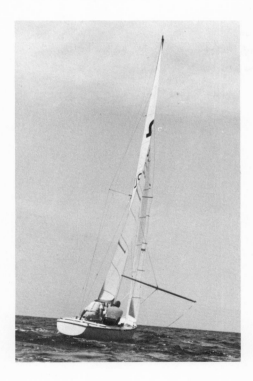

Fig. 136
Presetting the Spinnaker Pole, So the Boat Can Be Tacked.   The pole is set square to the hull, so that when the boat is on port tack the pole will be behind the leech of the jib. On the final starboard tack to the mark, the pole is pushed forward to headstay. (Presetting is only possible with a working jib.)

If you really have to move the whole rig to the other side of the boat, take in the pole, lift, and foreguy. Then detach afterguy, sheet, and halyard from the spinnaker and hook or tie all three together. By pulling in the afterguy and easing the sheet, you move the ends of all three lines around the forestay to the new turtle location on the opposite side. This can be done by a man in the cockpit.*

Check to make sure the halyard does not get twisted and that it is still outside everything. Then hook up the spinnaker again and set up the pole, lift, and foreguy on the new side. If you have your afterguy lead through the spinnaker pole fitting, you will have to disconnect on one side and hook up on the other when you shift the pole.

Incidentally, if you make a practice of running the afterguy through the pole fitting, remember that it is illegal in most classes to fly a spinnaker without a pole, and the tack has to be within a reasonable distance of the pole end. Therefore, you have to get that afterguy in quickly.

Hoisting

In the actual hoisting procedure, first raise the pole to a predetermined height. If there are boats ahead of you with spinnakers set, see what height looks best. If you have no one to check with, you decide from experience at what height the pole would work most effectively.

Take a good look at the next course to determine how far aft the pole should be. This should be decided ahead of time, so that as the spinnaker is raised, the pole is squared to its proper position. If the pole is too far forward, the spinnaker could be blanketed by a headsail or the mainsail and not fill. As soon as you round the mark and are on course, pick your position and hoist. Get the pole perpendicular to the apparent wind (a fly on the main shroud is a good guide). Then trim or ease the sheet until the leading edge or luff of the spinnaker is parallel to the wind flow and at more or less the same angle of attack from top to bottom. If these rules are followed and everything is done quickly, the spinnaker should fill quickly. Then fine adjustments in trim and in height of pole and clew can be made.

The spinnaker may get twisted around itself or the headstay as

*If the boat can stand temporary weight in the bow, you can also take the spinnaker with guy and sheet attached and physically run it around the headstay. Sometimes the halyard can remain attached also. This depends on the freedom of the block aloft.

Fig. 137
Spinnaker Twist.   The spinnaker usually twists because the tack and clew have not been trimmed fast enough while hoisting. This causes the top of the sail to rotate, forming a small twist; it is often very difficult to undo without dropping the spinnaker. A spinnaker net made with several horizontal tapes is sometimes hoisted to prevent twist.

it is hoisted (Fig. 137). There is a way to avoid this: when you start to hoist the sail, the afterguy and sheet are right next to each other in the turtle. As the sail is being raised, the faster you trim both the sheet and afterguy and the quicker you separate them and spread the spinnaker, the less chance there is that twisting will occur. If you do get a twist, try pulling the center of the foot down hard so that the spinnaker is more of a vertical column and is under tension. This will make it easier for the spinnaker to unwind itself. If it does not come untwisted within a few seconds, it is probably wisest to take it down. The twist can be removed on deck and the spinnaker can be quickly raised again. This can save you precious time in the long run.

Takedowns

Experience is a quick teacher about spinnaker takedowns. You will understand the problem at hand if you visualize two men pulling a net through the water, one man on one side and one man on the other. As they both pull, the central areas of the net create a lot of resistance. If one man lets go of his side, it immediately goes downstream, the resistance is greatly reduced, and it goes through the water with ease. The same is true of taking down a spinnaker. You want to put tension on one side only, generally the leech, and let the rest of the sail go downstream or flutter like a flag in the wind (Fig. 138). In this way it will offer least resistance. Often someone starts to do this properly and an eager beaver spoils it by grabbing any piece of the spinnaker he can find. Sometimes this will be the other leech, and as soon as he puts tension on it the sail may fill away, and both people pull even harder, working against themselves. You can prevent this by good communication and good instruction beforehand as to how and why the spinnaker is to come down and who is to do what job.

To take in the spinnaker requires two fairly quick and almost simultaneous acts. One is to release the tack from the end of the pole so that the luff of the sail swings off to leeward and becomes the trailing edge of the fluttering spinnaker. The tack can be released in two ways: (1) let the guy run right through the pole; or (2) if you have a top action snap shackle on the guy which will cast free without hanging up in the spinnaker tack eye, you can just pull the shackle pin and set the tack free. The other action involves the leech: before the tack is cast free, one or more men, depending on the size boat, should have the clew in hand or even hold onto part of the leech of the sail. As soon as the tack is released, a strong downward pull should be exerted on the leech so that it is tensioned vertically. In this way the entire leech, which has now become the leading edge of the spinnaker, is close in under the mainsail. If you do not tension the leech, it might flow out into a great arc and catch some wind and offer more resistance.

At this point, the spinnaker is ready to be lowered. It takes teamwork and practice between the man lowering the halyard and the crew taking in the spinnaker. The halyard has to be lowered at about the same speed that the crew is able to take in the sail. Sometimes a spinnaker man is a little overexuberant and lets the halyard down so fast that the spinnaker goes in the water, which creates the fishnet situation described above. If the spinnaker is pulled on two or three sides while it is being dragged through the water, you can imagine the resistance that will build up. The first thing you should do, as quickly as possible, is to determine which side can be released to flow downstream through the water and which side can be pulled toward the boat. Do not pull two sides toward the boat at once. Hoisting the spinnaker quickly out of the water before it begins to drag can also be tried. Once the sail is under control again, lower away properly.

Fig. 138
Steps in Lowering the Spinnaker

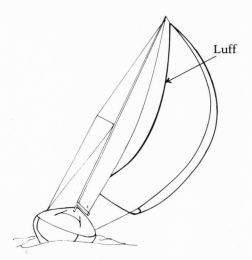

a. Spinnaker is flying in normal position.

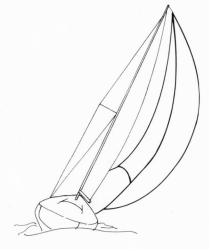

b. For lowering, first pull clew into boat, where eventually it will be gathered in.

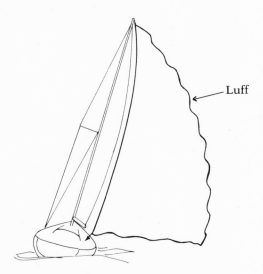

c. Release spinnaker tack at pole end. Pull down hard on leech, so that it becomes leading edge, like the front edge of a flag.

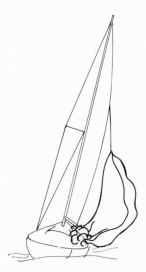

d. Lower halyard and gather in spinnaker, keeping leech tight. Let luff flutter downwind as sail is lowered.

SPINNAKER TRIM

Because the spinnaker is free-floating and attached only at its corners, it is somewhat trickier than other sails to control. It can be rotated from windward to leeward and fore and aft, moved higher or lower, and in toward the boat or farther out—all by manipulating the lines attached to these corners. And these same lines control draft as well. It all seems quite complicated at first, but if you remember that, with only a few exceptions, the principles of sail handling apply to the spinnaker in the same way that they apply to all other sails, the mysteries of the spinnaker should quickly fade away.

Just like the mainsail, jib, or genoa, the leading edge of the spinnaker should be at the correct angle of attack. Just like the working sails, if the spinnaker is overtrimmed, it stalls, and if it is undertrimmed, it luffs or collapses.

To find the correct angle of attack, the spinnaker is rotated horizontally by manipulating the tack and clew, the ends attached respectively to the pole and the sheet. By easing one and tightening the other, you move the sail horizontally. (Remember that the leading edge or luff is always attached to the pole.) The luff is at the correct angle of attack when it is just at the breaking point—that is, when it has a slight curl (2 to 5 inches on a small boat and up to 1 to 1½ feet on a large boat) in its upper part or shoulder (Fig. 139).

If the spinnaker starts to luff or "break" low because the pole is set too low, as in Figure 139b, the whole sail is liable to collapse, whereas with a shoulder break the sail is still fairly stable, and there is time to make quick trim adjustments. The reason for this is that if the upper part of the spinnaker starts to collapse, it still has the support of the lower part of the sail; while if the lower part collapses, there's nothing to support it and the whole sail "wipes out."

Because the leading edge of the sail is at the pole, in adjusting trim you can use the afterguy first instead of the sheet. Many people seem to use the sheet, although this is often the more difficult method because of the trim distance and load involved. If the apparent wind suddenly moves ahead and puts a luff in the spinnaker, it is much simpler to quickly ease the guy forward until the luff disappears, unless the pole is already on the

Fig. 139

a. A high break usually indicates that the spinnaker is on edge. The spinnaker will tolerate 1 or 2 feet of "fold-back" before a collapse will occur.

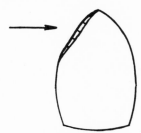

b. A low break is very dangerous. As soon as the break reaches the shoulder, the whole sail will wipe out and collapse.

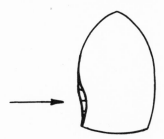

c. The ideal break is at the shoulder level.

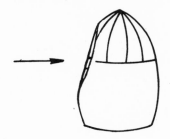

An Example of Low Break

Well-Set Spinnaker Just Before Breaking Point

headstay. In this case, you have to use the sheet. Another quick remedy for a header is to bring the boat off the wind with the helm. It is a lot easier to change course slightly or ease the guy a foot than it is to trim the sheet

2 or 3 feet. Trimming the sheet also brings the spinnaker inboard behind the staysail or mainsail, which may partially blanket it. On the other hand, easing the pole lets the sail out into freer air. If the wind moves aft, the spinnaker pole is moved aft to keep its perpendicular alignment to the apparent wind. Otherwise, the sail will stall and sag downwind.

Star-cut spinnakers have to be handled somewhat differently, since they have much smaller girth aloft and therefore appear not to have any shoulders. With star-cuts, the pole height should be set so that the spinnaker luff breaks at the junction seam at the base of the radial head panels. If the luff breaks low, the pole is too high; if the luff breaks high on the shoulders, the pole is too low. Once the pole is at the right height, set the clew to match by moving the lead forward or aft.

Generally, with narrow and, therefore, flatter spinnakers, more luff tension is required to control the set at the junction seams. A wide spinnaker has to be made fuller and, as such, requires less luff tension to have it break properly at the junction seam. Therefore, on the flatter sail the pole end is set lower and the sheet is set farther forward for leech support; on a fuller sail, the leads are set farther aft and the pole is set higher.

The vertical position of the spinnaker and its closeness to the top half of the boat are controlled by the halyard. Ideally, the spinnaker should be as far out from the boat as possible—away from the disturbances caused by the main, and this is accomplished by easing the halyard. However, in light airs with the attendant reduction of forces, if the halyard is eased off, the spinnaker will hang down. Since it is important in light airs to get the sail as high as possible to take advantage of the stronger wind flow aloft, it is usual to raise the halyard to its fullest height. In heavier airs, the force of the wind is strong enough to keep the sail aloft, so the halyard can be eased somewhat to allow the head of the sail to move out from the boat.

SPINNAKER DRAFT CONTROL

Although you cannot control the location of draft in a spinnaker, you can control the proportionate amount of draft from top to bottom. Many of the same principles of draft control for working sails apply: tensioning the foot removes draft from the spinnaker, and easing the foot adds draft, while tensioning the leeches adds draft, and easing them decreases draft.

First, the foot: by pulling the tack and clew farther apart, you flatten the lower portion of the spinnaker; by moving them closer together, you add fullness to the sail, just as in a main or jib. In a sense, this draft control is automatic. On a run, when you want as much fullness as possible, the tack and clew are much closer together than on a reach because they can only be trimmed from the pole end to the lee side, so that the maximum spread of the sail is the pole length plus one half the beam. The tack and clew cannot assume their maximum distance apart. On a reach, however, the spinnaker is brought around to the leeward side of the boat and the two corners can be trimmed from points as far apart as the length of the boat. Thus, the two corners are quite separated on a reach and quite close together on a run—just the way they should be (Fig. 140).

Leech control works the same as in a working sail. Imagine you are at the clew of a genoa looking up the leech. If you trim the sheet in, some twist is removed and the leech will curve to windward, making the sail fuller, while if you ease the sheet, the leech will fall off, flattening the sail aloft. This is exactly what happens to the spinnaker when you tension or ease the leech; the only difference is that on the spinnaker you have, in effect, two leeches. If you allow both tack and clew of a spinnaker to rise, you can see the leeches falling off to leeward as twist increases, flattening the sail aloft. As the tack and clew are lowered, the leeches are tensioned, causing the edges of the sail to roll around into more curvature, thus creating a fuller sail. On a run, in actual fact you have little control over the leeches because the clew is a long way from the block and tends to float freely, adjusting itself to a height dependent on its lift forces. With a reaching or star-cut spinnaker, you have much more control over the leech.

Tension on the leeches of a spinnaker is applied to the pole end by the afterguy and to the clew by the sheet. (The halyard, as we have seen, is not generally used as a draft-control mechanism; it controls the height of the sail and its relation to the boat and should not be used to tension the edges.)

Sheet trim and the position of the sheet lead control the amount of twist in the edge that, under sail, becomes the leech (Fig. 141). It is important that the spinnaker sheet lead be located to balance the tensions on the leech and foot, just as in a working jib or genoa. Moving the lead forward

Fig. 140   a. Run   b. Beam Reach

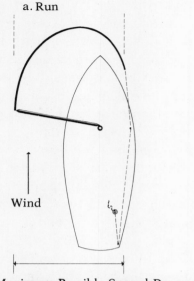

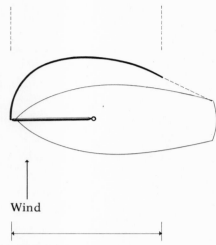

Maximum Possible Spread Downwind   Longer Spread Possible on Reach
Restricted by Beam of Boat and Pole End   Utilizing Fore and Aft Length of the Boat

Fig. 141

a. The differences in design and concept between the conventional all-purpose spinnaker cut and the star-cut (right) are graphically shown here. The conventional shape has a fuller head, while the star-cut is very flat aloft. As you can see, the draft of the star-cut approaches the flatter shape of a genoa. It is used for close-reaching angles when neither the genoa nor all-purpose spinnaker is the ideal sail—the genoa because it is smaller and the all-purpose spinnaker because it is too full. The star-cut is ideal because it is both large and flat.

a.

accentuates the tension on the leech; if the lead is too far forward, the leech will be too tight, causing the trailing edge to curve inward in a negative angle and adding too much fullness to the sail aloft. On the other hand, moving the sheet lead aft accentuates the tension on the foot. If the lead is too far aft, the foot will be overtensioned, and the spinnaker will

b. On a spinnaker reach, particularly with the flatter star-cut, the sheet lead is as sensitive as the genoa lead position. If the lead is too far forward, the leech will be tight. If the lead is too far aft, the leech will be fair but the foot will be overtensioned and curve inward, causing the cross-sections to be very different from bottom to top.

When reaching, both the luff and leech are treated individually. The pole height determines the proper luff twist to get the initial "break" at shoulder height, and the clew lead balances the tensions on the leech and foot.

c. & d. Initially (c) and (d) look identical. Notice, however, that the lead on the clew of (d) has been moved aft, so that the clew has been raised about 1 foot. The foot is slightly flatter, but the leech has been eased, so there is less negative angle aft. As a result, the spinnaker is wider and flatter in the shoulder area.

b.

c.

d.

be too flat and low, causing the cross-sectional shapes of the sail to be very different from top to bottom. Either condition is, as we have seen, aerodynamically undesirable.

On a run, the most difficult part of trimming the spinnaker is getting the correct tension on the sheet and leech, and should be done first; once this is done, you can adjust the pole so that it is the same height as the clew. This is a different procedure from the one outlined for a star-cut spinnaker. This procedure should be followed for both running and reaching.

The height of the pole controls the amount of twist in the luff or leading edge of the sail (Fig. 142). Since the purpose of the pole is primarily to hold the sail away from the turbulence around the boat, it should virtually always be perpendicular to the mast, so that its maximum length is being utilized; that is, it should not be cocked up or down. The only exceptions to this rule are in heavier air or very light air.*

Some sailors believe that the pole should be lowered on a reach and raised on a run. But this is true only with a star-cut spinnaker; with the average spinnaker, it would be completely wrong. On a reach, the pole should be raised to increase luff twist and, thus, flatten the sail. If the luff is put under tension by lowering the pole, the edge will curl inward, creating a tendency for the leading edge to collapse. The pole is also raised as the wind velocity increases, and for the same reason: to flatten the sail by causing luff twist. (This question would never arise if the rule that the tack height should match the clew were followed.)

In light air, the luff may sag below the pole level, making it much harder for the spinnaker to fill away. To avoid this, lower the pole end until there is a very slight amount of tension on the luff. This will remove some of the negative sag, and the tack will probably match the clew. As the wind freshens, the spinnaker will lift, raising the luff. If the pole height is not changed, the luff will be overtensioned, straining against the fixed pole, and curling around into negative curvature. Raising the pole will ease the luff tension and allow the upper portion of the spinnaker to flow into a wider, flatter section that will project more surface to resist the wind. (See Fig. 142.)

When adjusting the fullness of the spinnaker, remember the basic

---

*In very light air, the maximum outboard pole position may create an angular slope to the luff that will cause it to collapse by gravity. Shortening the pole by an angular set allows the luff to develop a more vertical position.

Fig. 142
Luff twist is controlled by raising or
lowering the pole end.

a. Lowering the outboard pole end
tensions the luff, which curls back to
windward.

b. Raising the outboard pole end releases
luff tension; the luff falls to leeward.
With a properly shaped and well-set
spinnaker, the clew and tack should be
approximately the same height, but the
clew cannot be arbitrarily set to the pole
height or vice versa—they both are set so
that the luff and leech are at the best twist
condition.

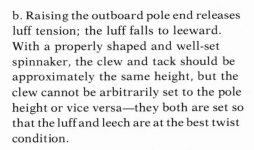

c. Three different spinnakers show the
differences in sail trim. The star-cut on the
lead boat is trimmed correctly. The pole
and clew are fairly low to tension the
flatter sail. The fuller spinnaker on the
second boat has the same low setting on
the tack and clew, but the corners are
obviously strained and the luff is curving
more to windward. The third boat has a
good setting.

principle that the spinnaker should be fuller for running and flatter for reaching. However, it is important to bear in mind that too much curvature, even when running, may be more of a hindrance than a help. This is because the spinnaker works not only as an aerodynamic foil, creating aerodynamic forces, but also derives some force from the sheer resistance of the sail to the wind. If the spinnaker has too much curvature, not only will the aerodynamic flow detach from the sail before it normally would but you may be cutting down too much on the sail area that is actually exposed to and resisting the force of the wind. Thus, even downwind, only a moderate amount of downward tension on poleguy and sheet should be used. There should be just enough pressure to stiffen the luff and leech so the overall shape of the spinnaker is held firm while allowing the sail to fly as high as possible. The following table of shapes (Fig. 143), with the corresponding coefficients representing the amount of drag or resistance each one causes, will give you a good way of computing the most effective shape downwind for a spinnaker or mainsail.

Fig. 143
Drag Coefficients of Downwind Shapes

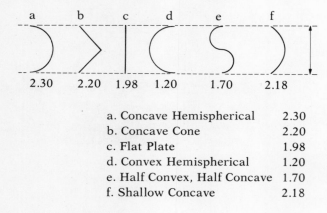

a   b   c   d   e   f

2.30   2.20   1.98   1.20   1.70   2.18

	Shape	Coefficient
a.	Concave Hemispherical	2.30
b.	Concave Cone	2.20
c.	Flat Plate	1.98
d.	Convex Hemispherical	1.20
e.	Half Convex, Half Concave	1.70
f.	Shallow Concave	2.18

These shapes are also applicable to mainsail shapes downwind. As shape changes downwind, where drag is the key factor, a fuller shape creates more drag but has narrower girth and less exposure to the wind. You can figure the most effective resistance by multiplying the chord by the drag coefficient. The most resistance is created by the combination of shape and projection.

COORDINATING HELM AND TRIM

Maintaining the proper angle of attack to the apparent wind when sailing downwind with the spinnaker set requires precise trim and helmsmanship, just as it does on the wind. If you vary your course more than a few degrees, you begin to stall or luff. This is a pretty narrow margin, but it is what you have to work within to get optimum results.

If you are sailing in clear air and have no fleet-maneuvering problems, use the helm to adjust for small wind shifts. This requires strict concentration and skill. Change the helm slowly and stop turning the instant the spinnaker is at the proper angle of attack (that is, when the luff is carrying a slight break or curl in the upper part or shoulder of the sail). Larger wind shifts in a fairing direction should be handled by the sheet, since the spinnaker will have to be squared to the new wind angle. Quick heading shifts should be counteracted by easing the guy. These are immediate reactions. Then, as soon as possible, guy and sheet should be reset to the proper configuration. In other words, first make a fast move to adjust the sail to keep it pulling, and then follow immediately with fine tuning.

On a smaller boat and cruisers up to 35 to 40 feet, the helmsman should try to keep his eyes on the luff at all times to see that it has just the right amount of curl in it. If the curl increases, it indicates he is too high; if the curl disappears and the spinnaker starts to sag, a stall is indicated. The helm should be adjusted accordingly, *without overcorrection*. All too frequently helmsmen change course 5 or 10 degrees, going past the correction and sailing from a luff to a stall condition or vice versa. Avoid this by using a light touch on the helm; as soon as the sail lifts and the edge of a luff appears, hold that exact sailing angle. If a correction takes you off course, gradually and slowly come down to course as you adjust sheet and guy. Then resume steering by the luff.

The helmsman has to know when a shift is too great for a helm adjustment. If it is, the pole has to be quickly squared to the wind and the sheet tension changed so the luff is "on edge" again. A spinnaker thus becomes a matter of precise teamwork, and this can only come through practice. One important rule is that the crews on guy and sheet must watch the spinnaker at all times. The sheet and guy should never be cleated but should be led around a winch (on larger boats) and held by hand, so that instant changes can be made.

Take the case of a sudden header (when the wind comes from a more forward direction). The luff starts to collapse very quickly because the pole is no longer square to the wind and the sheet is undertrimmed; the leading edge is not at the correct angle of attack. The helmsman can try to bear off somewhat, but the fastest remedy is to ease the pole forward. This will stop the collapse of the sail, giving you time to trim the sheet, which takes longer. Then the fine adjustments can be made for the new apparent-wind angle.

As the boat size gets larger, it becomes increasingly difficult to steer it quickly under the spinnaker in a sudden shift. Therefore, on larger cruiser-racers the boat is held to course and the spinnaker is trimmed. Of course, any sudden wind shift requires that guy, sheet, and helm all be quickly changed to prevent the spinnaker's collapse.

A good technique to use when you are sailing dead downwind is heeling the boat to windward. (See Fig. 114.) This swings the spinnaker to the weather side of the boat. Then the pole can be squared and the clew eased until it is almost on the headstay. In this position, the entire spinnaker is exposed to the clear air stream, and the leading edge is more easily trimmed parallel to the wind flow. You get more drive this way than you do when the sail is in disturbed air and partially blanketed by the mainsail.

This technique also offsets some of the pull of gravity on the sail. With the boat heeled to windward slightly, the luff of the spinnaker becomes more vertical and less susceptible to gravitational forces, particularly in very light airs. Hence, there is more chance for the sail to lift in whatever breeze there is.

Spectators were amazed in the 1967 America's Cup series when, in the last race, *Dame Pattie* took almost 3 minutes from *Intrepid* on the last downwind leg. In the second race of the 1970 series, *Gretel* went through *Intrepid* on the run. In both instances, the Australians had their crew on the weather rail, apparently trying to heel their boat slightly to windward. Aussies do not admit this, but it was fairly obvious.

BROACHING

Besides knowing how to get more drive out of your spinnaker under normal conditions, you should learn how to cope with emergency situations, such as broaching. A broach can occur to windward or to leeward, with the latter being the most common. It can happen on any downward angle but more often on a close reach or beam reach. It is caused by excessive side loading on the spinnaker in heavy air and usually in a rough seaway.

Here is what happens. A strong puff hits the boat, heeling it over at a critical angle. The helmsman tries to head off in a downwind direction, but the boat does not respond to the helm, which is sometimes partially out of the water. Instead, the boat keeps rounding up to windward. The spinnaker does not collapse, in spite of the fact that the boat has rounded up well into the wind. This phenomenon at first is hard to understand. Actually, once the boat heels over beyond 45 or 50 degrees, it not only loses steering capabilities but the air flow enters the sail at the foot of the spinnaker as well as along the luff. The foot acts as a wind scoop, and that is why the sail does not collapse (Fig. 144).

The initial reaction of most crews is to hike out to flatten the boat and produce enough steerage to bear off with the puff. This is only effective on a small boat when crew weight can sometimes balance heeling force. On a larger boat, however, the side force vastly overpowers any counteraction of crew weight.

But concentrating crew weight in the windward quarter of the stern keeps the bow up and the stern down for better steerage; this will prevent a broach more than will keeping weight to weather amidships.

To control a broach, you quickly ease the mainsheet to reduce side loading and counteract the spinning effect of the main, which tends to round up the boat. If easing is not enough, you will have to let the spinnaker sheet run until the spinnaker collapses and the boat regains its normal posture. The most important thing to do is anticipate the puff before it heels the boat excessively, and bear off before it hits. You can also reduce the size or the effectiveness of your sail. In the case of a spinnaker in heavy air, you could lower the pole and overtrim the sheet. This results in a reduction of the forces acting on the sail and also reduces both drive and heeling forces.

In heavy seas, the boat on a dead downwind run can be subject to a windward broach. (See Fig. 144c.) What happens is that, due to severe rolling, the spinnaker can lurch around too far to windward and, with the rocking motion of the hull exaggerating the windward heel, the large side force of the spinnaker can pull the boat over to weather, causing a jibe. Usually a vang is on, causing further problems. Before this happens, and

Fig. 144

a. This boat is out of control on a leeward broach. The large spinnaker area has moved aft, so that its total force is almost entirely to the side, moving the center of effort considerably aft and causing the boat to round up to windward. Even though it is pointing at a very narrow angle of attack, the sail remains full because, at that severe an angle of heel, the wind flow enters onto the sail from the foot. Excess heeling caused by the spinnaker results in a loss of steering capability. Easing the main will generally help at the beginning of a broach, but easing the main in the middle of a broach while the spinnaker remains full will not stand the boat upright any appreciable amount. The only solution at this point is to let the spinnaker sheet run.

b. In a seaway, the spinnaker can yaw from side to side. As it swings to leeward, the boat heels to leeward; as it swings to windward, the boat heels to windward. If the spinnaker has excessive side-to-side movement, the boat will roll excessively.

c. Sailing by the lee can sometimes cause a windward broach. Again, helm control may be lost; the boat rounds up in reverse by going more and more by the lee. The biggest danger is that during this round-up the main may jibe with the vang on tight. In this case, the main would be fully aback, with the vang still secured and holding the boom perpendicular and skyward at a steep angle because the spinnaker would still be heeling the boat excessively. With a jibe like this, the boat will stop dead in the water. To prevent a windward broach, first try to head downwind, away from the by-the-lee course. Next, try to swing the spinnaker around in front of the boat to eliminate the excess side-loading. If this does not work, you may have to let the guy run to its extreme end, rather than the sheet (the guy is in the by-the-lee position, similar to the sheet position in [a]).

if the spinnaker seems to be swinging too far to windward, ease the pole forward immediately and trim the sheet as fast as possible.

If you do broach to windward, you have, in essence, jibed. Since you can't steer, you can't jibe back. The main is aback with the vang, holding it to windward. The spinnaker pole is probably abeam and now on the lee side, so it will more than likely be dragging in the water. Your boat speed is nil. In this situation, you must jibe both the main and spinnaker pole. Work on the main first to reduce heel. If you can't release the vang, cut it. The boat will straighten up enough to get the pole end out of the water. Now you must jibe the spinnaker pole. On a large boat if you are rigged for a dip-pole jibe, you can probably get the pole over. An end-for-end jibe is impossible on a large boat and very difficult on a small boat in the heavy air but is perhaps the only method available. Remember that all this time the spinnaker is still flying and although the helmsman/skipper is probably trying to direct operations, he has a full-time job just steering the free-flying spinnaker, which will be oscillating back and forth, rolling the boat badly.

A slight reaching angle is best to minimize rolling. Set the windward sheet (guy) so that the spinnaker tack is just in front of the headstay. Trim the sheet until the sail sets properly. Then jibe the pole.

If this is too difficult, lower the spinnaker, raise a maximum-luff and small-girth genoa, and wing it out to windward with the pole. Auxiliary staysails may be set also, and with this rig you will not lose a great amount of speed until you can reset the spinnaker. On a larger boat, a main, genoa, banana staysail, and big boy or blooper (see Chapter 12, on proper sail inventory) can generate substantial speed without the risk of broaching.

RACING TACTICS

When the breeze is light, it is doubly important to keep in clear air. Visualize yourself sailing downwind in a large fleet. You have a small hole in the pack where you are getting free wind. You have to concentrate on the spinnaker, but you also have to keep track of your position relative to the other boats. The best thing to do is watch the leading edge of your chute and have a crew member watch your competitors and your course, or vice versa, whichever works best for you. Again, teamwork is vital. Once someone climbs on your wind and blankets you, the whole fleet could sail past.

It is even more difficult to keep your air clear when rounding a reaching mark. If there is a jam at the buoy, sailing around the fleet is usually disastrous unless the other boats are virtually stalled. Rounding on the outside puts you in a leeward position for the next leg and leaves you behind the eightball. It is generally better to stay slightly behind and wait until a hole appears (Fig. 145). Then jibe into the hole and round the mark a little later than you might have otherwise. Then you will come out on the windward side of the fleet and, most likely, will have no one on your wind. This maneuver, which is strictly a matter of timing, can be learned only through experience. As you round a weather mark, you should know the location and course to the next mark. This gives you a guideline to steer by as you try to avoid being luffed by leeward boats or blanketed by windward boats. If you can make a rough calculation of what the apparent wind will be on the new leg, you will have some idea of how your spinnaker should be trimmed.

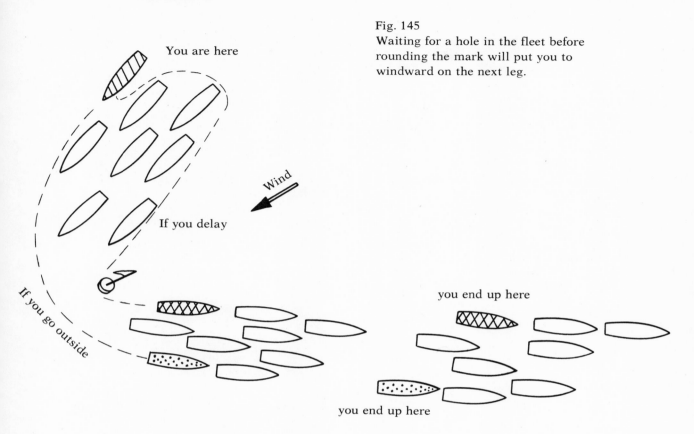

Fig. 145
Waiting for a hole in the fleet before rounding the mark will put you to windward on the next leg.

WHEN TO SET A SPINNAKER

Too much emphasis has been put on fast spinnaker sets. Often on one of these rush jobs the jib is not trimmed and the boat is working only under mainsail. Sometimes even the main is not drawing properly because of the preoccupation with the spinnaker. Consequently, there is a loss of boat speed, which the helmsman sorely needs if he's going to work into a desired position. In addition, if all hands are concentrating on the chute, some boats can round the mark, hold high, and be on your wind by the time you have squared away. So when you are coming onto a reaching leg, see if it is better to work out to windward a little and then set your spinnaker smartly when you are in clear air (Fig. 146).

Fig. 146
On a reach, it is better to work out to
windward before setting your spinnaker.

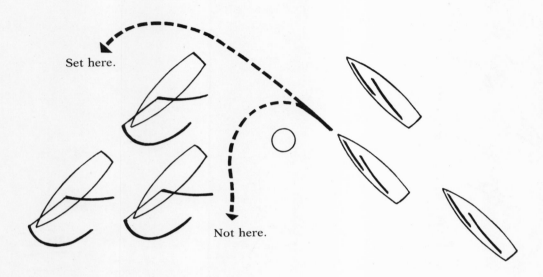

Set here.

Not here.

In discussing spinnaker sets, the inevitable question arises: when do you set the spinnaker on a reach? As a general rule, when the true wind is abeam, a genoa will do as well as a spinnaker. The sensible thing to do is check out your own boat, especially if it is a one design and you have identical boats around you. You can readily see if your spinnaker is doing you any good or not. If you are debating, make sure the sail is properly trimmed before you decide to take it down. For the ardent racer the polar plots detailing sail selection at all sailing angles, covered in Chapter 20, will be invaluable.

You will also have to determine when the wind is too light to set a spinnaker. Usually, if the sail hangs limp and does not fill at all, it is not doing much good. When the sail droops from the head and swings up in a big arc to the end of the spinnaker pole, even a slight pull will not lift the sail. In that situation, try this: lower the pole, raise the halyard all the way, and keep a slight tension on the luff. You want the spinnaker to fill with a minimum of movement. This is as much as you can do to trap cat's-paws.

In light air, when the breeze is minimal, the angle of attack is more important than ever. You will find that if you bring the boat up slightly, the spinnaker may fill, and if you go off, it will collapse. And so you have a very fine line to steer by downwind. It is better to sail a little above the fleet and keep your chute drawing than it is to stay on course with a collapsed sail. You have to decide how long you can sail high of the course. It is not wise to sail too far away from the fleet. When you come around, sail a little high of the course on the other jibe. "Tacking downwind" pays off, as long as you do not overdo it.

In extremely light conditions you have to fight the laws of gravity to get your spinnaker to fill. The more the fittings and sheets weigh, the more resistance there will be to the sail lifting to its proper set. Cloth weight, obviously, is a vital consideration; in light air you would fly the minimum weight cloth allowed under class rules.

On many large boats the spinnaker halyard has a heavy swivel, to which is attached a swivel snap shackle. This is undesirable weight at a very high point. A light, abrasion-resistant eye in the head of the sail would be sufficient. Excess weight is not so prevalent on smaller boats, where Brummel hooks and other simple fastening devices reduce weight aloft.

The tack area of the sail is supported by the pole. The clew, however, has a sheet that runs all the way back to the trimming block, and this line represents a considerable amount of weight. As soon as the clew begins to droop from the sheer weight of the sheet, you should change to lighter gear. Fish string or ⅛-inch line is often used.

JIBING

Jibing a spinnaker is not easy for anyone. It involves perhaps more crew members and more steps than any other maneuver in sailing. Many people have a fear of jibing. The only way this can be overcome is by practice, which builds confidence in your ability to do the job right. It helps if you think in terms of jibing the boat and not the spinnaker. The chute stays at the correct angle of attack to the wind while the boat changes course beneath it and reciprocal adjustments are made to the sheet and guy. This requires coordinated action by line tenders and again is a matter of experience.

There are several methods of jibing. In the end-for-end jibe (Fig. 147A) the pole is first detached from the mast and the detached end is crossed over and connected to what has been the clew or sheet end of the spinnaker. While this is being done, the boat is in the process of coming around. What has been the tack end of the spinnaker is detached from the pole, and this end of the pole is attached to the mast. Actually, you have done a crossover with the pole and substituted the sheet for the guy. Now you are ready to trim on the new tack. This system is used by many one-design and small cruising boats. The two-pole jibe consists of securing a second pole on the opposite (leeward) side of the boat. Then, when the boat is jibed, it becomes the new windward pole and the old pole is re-moved (Fig. 147B).

The dip-pole jibe, which was developed from the *Vim* jibe (Fig. 147C), keeps the inboard end of the pole on the mast and lowers the outer end at an angle, so that it can swing through the foretriangle and over to the other side of the boat. This means detaching the pole from one side of the spin-naker and fastening it to the other side. The guy becomes the sheet and vice versa. During this switch, the mainsail comes over and the boat changes to its new course.

The patented *Windigo* system of jibing (Fig. 147D) is perhaps the easiest system of all for a larger boat, but requires special equipment to make it work properly. The system consists of normal guy and sheet running aft, and also two lengths of wire running through the spinnaker pole to the tack and clew of the spinnaker. These lines are anchored on the inboard edge of the pole. They exit through the pole on the inboard edge and then turn down through a locking mechanism. The use of wire is necessary because rope will stretch, allowing the tack to move away from the end of the pole. But rope is necessary to lock the poleguy through the locking mechanism, and so a rope-to-wire splice is required. Then the inboard end will already have its rope for cleating.

To jibe this mechanism you simply release the poleguy (on the windward side) that is holding the end of the pole to the tack of the spin-naker. As the pole is released, the pole lift is eased so that the pole swings down through the foretriangle, leaving the spinnaker tack in its outboard, raised position. The old afterguy is paid out as the pole end gets farther and farther away from the old tack. Then the new poleguy is pulled in, bringing the end of the pole up to where the clew was, and is locked into position. As the boat jibes, the pole is in place and the old clew becomes the new tack.

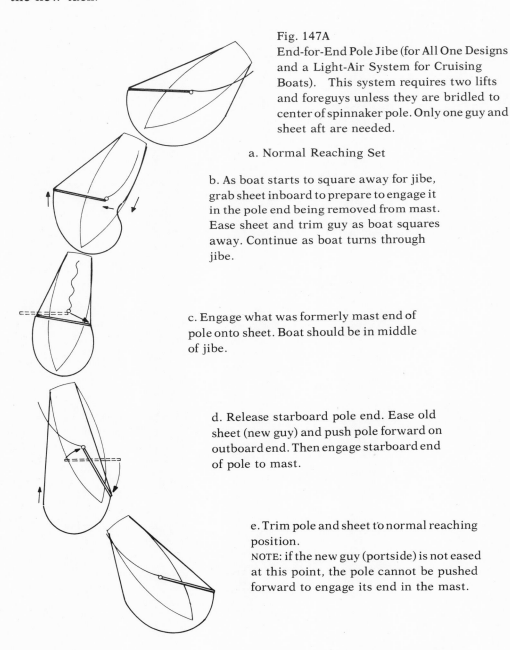

Fig. 147A
End-for-End Pole Jibe (for All One Designs and a Light-Air System for Cruising Boats). This system requires two lifts and foreguys unless they are bridled to center of spinnaker pole. Only one guy and sheet aft are needed.

a. Normal Reaching Set

b. As boat starts to square away for jibe, grab sheet inboard to prepare to engage it in the pole end being removed from mast. Ease sheet and trim guy as boat squares away. Continue as boat turns through jibe.

c. Engage what was formerly mast end of pole onto sheet. Boat should be in middle of jibe.

d. Release starboard pole end. Ease old sheet (new guy) and push pole forward on outboard end. Then engage starboard end of pole to mast.

e. Trim pole and sheet to normal reaching position.
NOTE: if the new guy (portside) is not eased at this point, the pole cannot be pushed forward to engage its end in the mast.

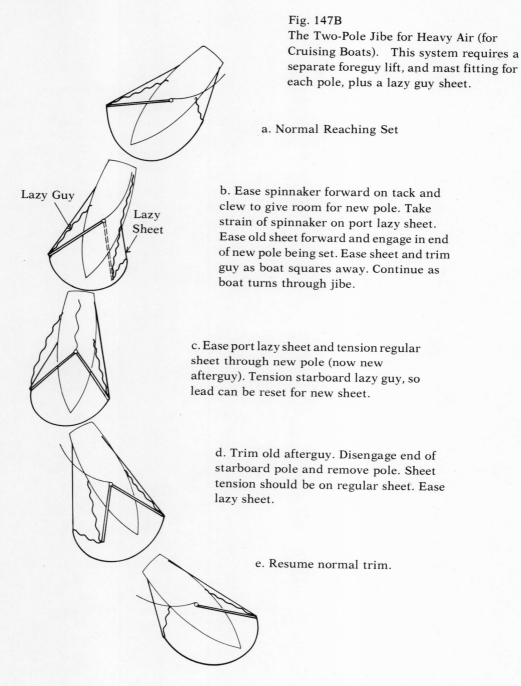

Fig. 147B
The Two-Pole Jibe for Heavy Air (for Cruising Boats).   This system requires a separate foreguy lift, and mast fitting for each pole, plus a lazy guy sheet.

a. Normal Reaching Set

Lazy Guy

Lazy Sheet

b. Ease spinnaker forward on tack and clew to give room for new pole. Take strain of spinnaker on port lazy sheet. Ease old sheet forward and engage in end of new pole being set. Ease sheet and trim guy as boat squares away. Continue as boat turns through jibe.

c. Ease port lazy sheet and tension regular sheet through new pole (now new afterguy). Tension starboard lazy guy, so lead can be reset for new sheet.

d. Trim old afterguy. Disengage end of starboard pole and remove pole. Sheet tension should be on regular sheet. Ease lazy sheet.

e. Resume normal trim.

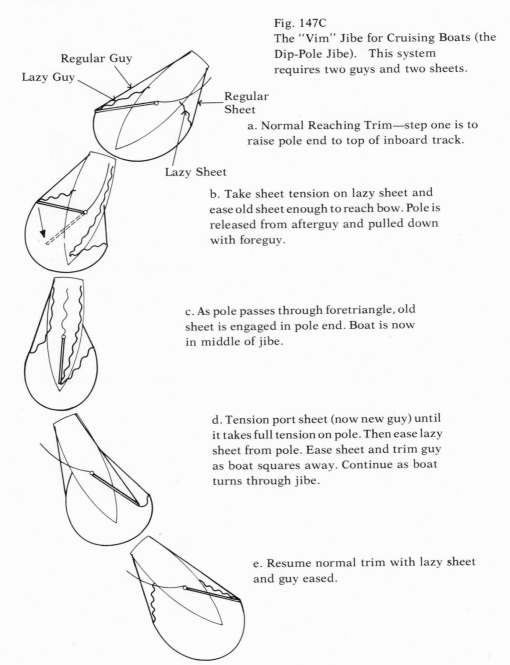

Regular Guy

Lazy Guy

Regular Sheet

Lazy Sheet

Fig. 147C
The "Vim" Jibe for Cruising Boats (the Dip-Pole Jibe). This system requires two guys and two sheets.

a. Normal Reaching Trim—step one is to raise pole end to top of inboard track.

b. Take sheet tension on lazy sheet and ease old sheet enough to reach bow. Pole is released from afterguy and pulled down with foreguy.

c. As pole passes through foretriangle, old sheet is engaged in pole end. Boat is now in middle of jibe.

d. Tension port sheet (now new guy) until it takes full tension on pole. Then ease lazy sheet from pole. Ease sheet and trim guy as boat squares away. Continue as boat turns through jibe.

e. Resume normal trim with lazy sheet and guy eased.

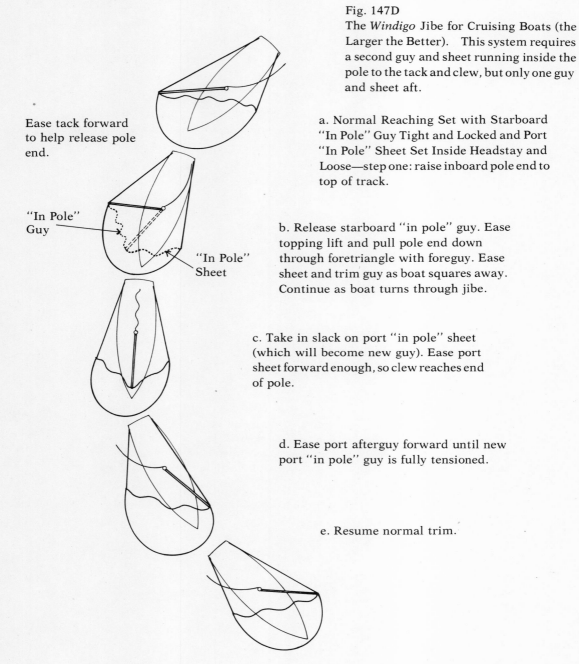

Fig. 147D
The *Windigo* Jibe for Cruising Boats (the Larger the Better).   This system requires a second guy and sheet running inside the pole to the tack and clew, but only one guy and sheet aft.

a. Normal Reaching Set with Starboard "In Pole" Guy Tight and Locked and Port "In Pole" Sheet Set Inside Headstay and Loose—step one: raise inboard pole end to top of track.

b. Release starboard "in pole" guy. Ease topping lift and pull pole end down through foretriangle with foreguy. Ease sheet and trim guy as boat squares away. Continue as boat turns through jibe.

c. Take in slack on port "in pole" sheet (which will become new guy). Ease port sheet forward enough, so clew reaches end of pole.

d. Ease port afterguy forward until new port "in pole" guy is fully tensioned.

e. Resume normal trim.

Ease tack forward to help release pole end.

"In Pole" Guy

"In Pole" Sheet

Chapter 10

Headsails

The headsail alone is a unit of propulsion, but it also has an interaction with the mainsail. It closes the air passage from the large opening between the mast and headsail luff and changes the rate of air flow through the narrow slot between the leech of the headsail and the lee side of the mainsail.

Modern aerodynamicists look at the main and jib or genoa as a total entity. The wind-flow pattern extends from in front of the headsail to behind the main or mizzen. The slot is a localized condition within this larger aerodynamic picture, and the flow velocity within the slot varies with the size of the headsail in relation to the main. This can be helpful or not, as detailed in Figure 148.

The air flow through the slot also disperses the eddies created by the mast around the leading edge of the mainsail and helps maintain the laminar or smooth flow which otherwise would be disturbed, or "bad," air.

Most of what has been written concerns the positive effects of the headsail, but it also has bad effects. If the flow in the slot is so much faster, it means that this same faster flow is also passing over the *windward* side of the headsail in the overlap area. The faster slot flow can reduce the strength of the forces on the after portions of the genoa. This is called the "venetian blind" effect, and describes the conditions where, if several headsails are in an overlap condition, each one affects the other to reduce total efficiency.

Theoretical data indicate that the relative position of the two sails is of primary importance. Highest efficiency for large overlapping headsails, for example, requires enough separation between the sails so that the apparent wind angle on the main will not be too narrow and thus prevent the main from having any draft. (See Fig. 149a.) Jibs with very small overlaps, on the other hand, do not redirect the air at so acute an angle over the main, so the slot can be narrower and the jib trimmed more inboard (Fig. 149).

Today, one-design headsails are being trimmed farther and farther inboard, but not without some drawbacks; the newest configurations are

Fig. 148

In the flow pattern shown
in (a) the streamlines are in an
uplift over the bow area because of the
main, so the genoa region would be in a
wider local apparent-wind flow.
Conversely, in (b) the genoa deflects air
flow in a more aft direction, so the
mainsail region has a narrower local
apparent-wind flow. When the main and
headsail are of different sizes, this
relationship is magnified for the larger
sail and diminished for the smaller sail. In
(c) a smaller working jib is combined with
a larger main. The larger main has a
stronger flow field and causes streamlines
to have more uplift over the main. The
result is that the flow lines converge when
approaching the slot area. They further
converge within the slot, increasing the
flow velocity over the lee surface of the
larger mainsail. Thus, more air goes
through the slot because of the mainsail's
effect of "lifting" air up into the slot area.
In (d), the opposite occurs: the genoa is the
larger sail and the streamlines lift up at a
sharper angle as they approach the genoa
luff and travel around the lee side. Thus,
the larger and more powerful genoa is
attracting air flow up and around its lee
side, which normally enters the slot area.
In effect, the genoa is "robbing" air flow
from the slot area. This causes the flow
approaching the slot to diverge and
consequently to slow down. Once it is well
within the area where the two sails are
closest together it converges and speeds
up.

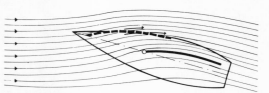

a. Main Only—without the genoa, the
main has a standard aerodynamic flow
pattern.

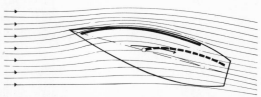

b. Genoa Only—without the main, the
genoa has a similar pattern.

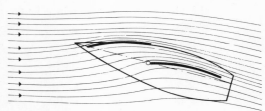

c. Main with Working Jib

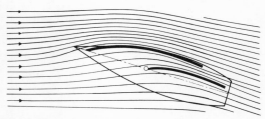

d. Main with Genoa—the modern sloop
has a genoa that is 2 to 2½ times the area
of the main. It is the major aerodynamic
sail-force generator.

Fig. 149

a. The average cruising boat has a genoa with considerable overlap that automatically creates a narrow slot, partly because it overlaps to the region of maximum draft in the main, and partly because, on cruising boats, the average hull is quite narrow compared to a one design.

b. As overlap decreases and as the beam of the boat increases, the trim position of the jib or genoa must be moved inboard, so that the leech will not be too far away from the main—thus reducing the slot effect.

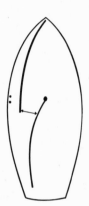

c. When there is no overlap, the jib leech has to be moved even farther inboard to produce a slot effect.

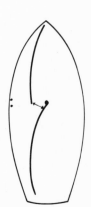

extremely sensitive to proper trimming and sheet tension and are unforgiving to mistakes.*

The critical aerodynamic relationship between the headsail and main leads to two questions concerning the design and trim of the jib or genoa: what happens when the slot is closed, and what happens when it is open?

If the headsail leech area is too close to the main, it will reduce the opening in the slot and "choke" the air flow (Fig. 150a), sometimes causing backwinding. On the other hand, if the headsail is trimmed too far outboard, or the upper leech falls off to leeward, opening the slot, the necessary squeezing effect will not be provided (Fig. 150b). Either condition reduces the strength of the combined driving force. With the slot working at maximum efficiency, a more inboard trim is needed on the main, since the direction of the apparent wind is altered to a more acute angle by the jib as it passes through the slot. (See *Windigo*, Fig. 163.)

Since the relative velocities in the slot vary as the strength of the wind varies, the leech of the headsail should be adjusted either farther away from or closer to the main with changes in wind conditions, in order to create the optimum acceleration of air in the slot. Sometimes, in light air, the leech of the headsail can be closer to the main, when the air flow is proportionately slower and therefore the volume of air is less. Conversely, in heavy air, the genoa leech should be trimmed outboard to open the slot and let the greater volume of air through. Also, in light air, the mainsail is moved toward the centerline by the traveler, opening up the slot. In these conditions, the headsail lead should be brought farther inboard to narrow the slot.

*Chapter 5 covers fore and aft lead position, and Chapter 6 covers athwartship trim.

Fig. 150

Apparent Wind

a. "Choked Slot"—apparent-wind slot too narrow; air flow is restricted, air slows down; half the main is not working.

Apparent Wind

b. Open Slot—slot too big, no squeezing; air slows down; flow on the lee side of the main is greatly reduced and boat probably cannot point.

THE DECKSWEEPER

The decksweeper jib or genoa is just what its name indicates: a sail with a foot so low that it sweeps the deck (Fig. 151). The low-profile genoa is more effective than a regular sail of the same area because of end-plate effect, which can best be explained as follows: an ordinary jib or genoa has positive forces on the windward side trying to join the negative forces on the leeward side, and the sail acts as a separator. However, at the foot of the sail,

Fig. 151

a. Typical One-Design Decksweeper Jib

b. One-Design Decksweeper Genoa

c. Decksweeper Genoa for a Cruiser-Racer

the pressures join by flowing around underneath the foot, from the positive side to the negative side (Fig. 152). Moving from the center of the sail, where the force is strongest, toward the foot, the pressure differential on the surface gradually decreases until it reaches zero at the bottom. The flow lines form a *tip vortex*, a corkscrewlike air flow that travels down the weather side (Fig. 153), around the bottom, and up the leeward side, separating at the leech. The result is called *induced drag*.

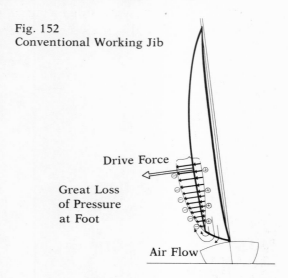

Fig. 152
Conventional Working Jib

Drive Force

Great Loss
of Pressure
at Foot

Air Flow

Fig. 153
Air Flow and the
Conventional Working Jib

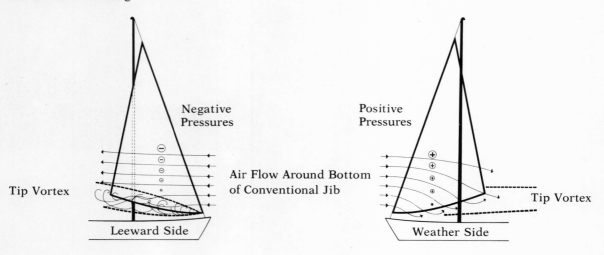

Negative
Pressures

Positive
Pressures

Air Flow Around Bottom
of Conventional Jib

Tip Vortex

Tip Vortex

Leeward Side

Weather Side

Since the bottom third of vertical height of the sail contains just about half of the total sail area, you can see how the inefficiency of induced drag results in a great loss of total force. However, if the foot of the sail touches the deck (Fig. 154), it blocks off the air flow around the foot, stops the neutralization of forces, and maintains near-maximum pressure on the sail (Fig. 155). The center of pressure is lowered, which helps reduce heeling forces. And so a major improvement in the driving power of a jib can be

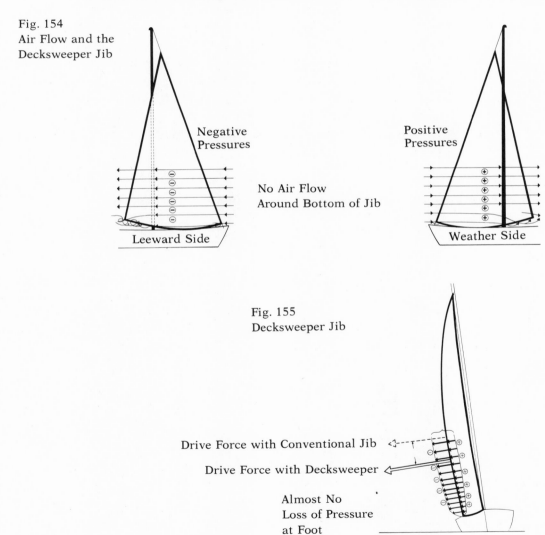

Fig. 154
Air Flow and the
Docksweeper Jib

Negative
Pressures

Positive
Pressures

No Air Flow
Around Bottom of Jib

Leeward Side

Weather Side

Fig. 155
Docksweeper Jib

Drive Force with Conventional Jib

Drive Force with Docksweeper

Almost No
Loss of Pressure
at Foot

achieved by cutting the sail with a large enough foot-skirt to touch the deck (Fig. 156). Even if the foot of the sail does not touch the deck, reducing the gap under the sail helps. If the air passage is narrower, the flow around the foot is reduced and a greater percentage of forces is maintained over the lower areas of the sail. On an overlapping genoa, the skirt does not have to touch the deck all the way but should make contact at least from the bow to past the shrouds.

There is an additional advantage from the decksweeper on a one design. If the decksweeper has the same area as an ordinary jib, the girth of the sail (a line perpendicular to the luff and intersecting the clew) remains the same. But the decksweeper clew is lower, since it moves downward in a forward-sloping line parallel to the headstay (Fig. 157) and the leech moves forward with it, reducing the overlap and allowing a fuller, more powerful mainsail. In addition, the wider slot allows the jib leads to be moved farther inboard, so that the fuller headsail adds power and the inboard lead adds pointing ability.

Fig. 156
Foot Skirt.   On a decksweeper jib, the foot roach or skirt will lay on the deck and in some cases even curl up, thus ensuring deck contact.

Fig. 157
Comparison of Conventional Working Jib and the Decksweeper

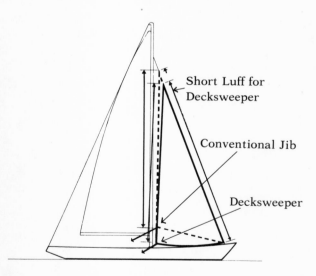

Short Luff for Decksweeper

Conventional Jib

Decksweeper

The leech and foot are the same length in both jibs. Only the luff varies.

Fig. 158

a. In recent years one-design working jibs have been made fuller; they are sheeted farther inboard. On cruiser-racers with smaller mains, the larger genoas are being made very full and powerful. They require more inboard trim positions with inboard track or inhauls. (See Figure 95 b.)

b. The quarter-ton world champion demonstrates the fuller genoa trimmed more inboard. Note how much to windward the main has to be trimmed in order to match the genoa.

Now a further development has taken place. The jibs are made much fuller, with the leads moved even farther inboard, but are not sheeted so tight. The leech therefore has more twist or curvature and is more parallel to the vertical curvature of the lee side of the fuller main when sighted from astern. These jibs have enormous drive, and they allow slot width to be changed simply by changing sheet tension (Fig. 158). This trim is now being duplicated in genoas on larger boats.

Genoas

There are some important factors to be considered when choosing the best usable genoa overlap. The total length of the foot of the genoa depends largely on hull shape, overlap rating penalty, shroud position, and deck shape and rig.

There is, normally, limited athwartship adjustment for the genoa sheet, and it has to trim at the rail or on an inboard track near the rail. When it is desirable to trim the genoa at the rail, such as in heavy air, its trim angle, in relation to the centerline of the boat, is dependent on the boat's beam and the shroud position. If the maximum beam of a boat is carried well aft, the trim point of the genoa can be farther outboard than it would be on a hull whose beam is narrow aft.

A genoa will have a forward driving force from the luff to the shrouds, but the direction of the driving force aft of the shrouds will be determined by the relative angle of the sail from the shrouds aft. If the clew point is trimmed at the same distance from the centerline as the shrouds, there will be no negative angle in the after portion of the sail. But if the clew of a genoa trims to a point farther inboard than the shrouds, the sail area from the shrouds to the clew will drive in a negative direction (Fig. 159). However, where fullness is very important, moving the clew point inboard will produce a fuller sail at a slight sacrifice in angle.

Nevertheless, the maximum overlap point is only at the clew. The area is relatively small—just one corner of a triangle. As we have already discussed, however, it can pull the leech section of the genoa into a negative angle (cupped leech), and this could be detrimental. Although, because of leech twist, the negative angle would only be at the foot level, thus reducing the detrimental effects (Fig. 160).

Recently one hears quite a bit about jibs and genoas being trimmed more inboard so that the after portion of the sail is at a negative angle down low. (The sheet is eased to get more fullness and allow more than normal twist to get the middle of the leech in about the same position as with the outboard lead.) The success of the inboard lead depends almost solely on whether or not the flow remains attached to the increased curvature of the sail. If it does, the deeper draft creates more lift and causes the flow to change out in front of the sail. The air will split more to windward (stagnation point moves to windward) so more air volume flows over the lee side and travels faster. Hence the local apparent-wind direction changes to a wider angle allowing the boat to point higher. (See Chapter 2, Fig. 9.)

If the flow does not remain attached with the inboard lead, the sail will stall more than normally and the lead then could do more harm than good. This could happen in very light air, when in essence the inboard lead might constitute overtrimming, and in stronger air, when the outboard lead reduces heel. Therefore, the inboard lead is a medium-to-light air technique.

Easing genoa sheets from the normal lead position allows the center of the genoa to move farther away from the shrouds. Since the sheeting

Fig. 159
Hull Width and Genoa Trim

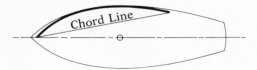

B =Width at shroud
T = trim width

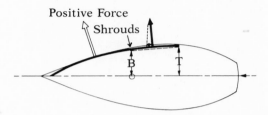

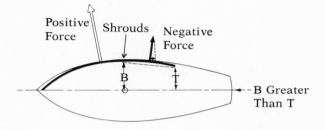

a. Maximum Beam Well Aft—trim point is farther outboard than shroud position; no negative forces are developed.

b. Maximum Beam Well Forward—trim point is inboard of shroud position, causing negative forces aft.

Fig. 160
Overlap Efficiency

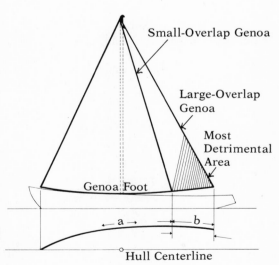

From the tack through (a), the overlap is beneficial; in area (b) it is detrimental.

point remains in the same location, farther outboard, the draft will be increased. This causes the magnitude of both the positive and negative forces to be increased. And so, if more total force can be developed in the right direction, slacking the sheet is worthwhile. However, this is usually not the case.

When easing the genoa sheets for reaching, the sail bulges out aft, and flow separation may occur (Fig. 161). The leeward side air flow leaves the sail before it reaches the leech, creates a stalled area, and reduces lift forces. When this happens, the extra overlap is inefficient. In such conditions, a smaller overlap genoa may be more effective.

Fig. 161
Easing the genoa sheet on a reach causes excessive curvature aft in the lower leech because the clew hooks back into the sheet lead. This causes negative forces aft, as well as separation.

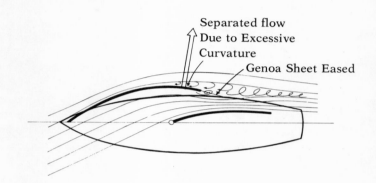

Separated flow
Due to Excessive
Curvature
Genoa Sheet Eased

Genoas and the IOR

Thus far genoas have been discussed largely in terms of physical performance and how the sails function. The question of overlap has been related to trim and the genoa's interaction with the mainsail. Determining the right size is a matter of competitive performance. Each boat needs a certain amount of area to produce adequate speed. But the whole subject of overlap and its effect on your boat's rating or racing handicap should be examined (see Chapter 9, The International Offshore Rule).

For rating measurement purposes, overlap is designated as LP— the length of a perpendicular drawn from the luff and intersecting the clew. However, LP is expressed as a percentage of the base of the foretriangle (Fig. 162). If the base of the foretriangle is 20 feet and the LP is 30 feet, the overlap is 150 per cent. Consequently, the size of a sail is designated by its

Fig. 162
International Offshore Rule Overlap
Definition

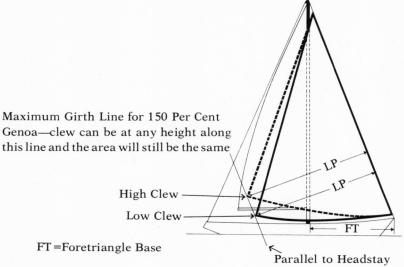

Maximum Girth Line for 150 Per Cent
Genoa—clew can be at any height along
this line and the area will still be the same

High Clew

Low Clew

FT =Foretriangle Base

Parallel to Headstay

overlap, or LP, and we speak in terms of a 150 per cent genoa or a 170 per cent genoa, etc.

Cruising boats engaged in racing are subject to certain measurement rules. The most universally used rule is the International Offshore Rule (IOR). This rule applies a penalty to genoas with greater than 150 per cent LP. (There is no penalty under 150 per cent.) The penalty increases your rating, which gives you a less favorable time allowance or handicap in relation to other racing boats.

Up until a few years ago, sailors were clinging to the idea of keeping their rating down by having a minimum genoa overlap. Recently there has been a trend in the other direction. Yacht designers in particular are saying, "Never mind the rating; let's go for performance, because that more than offsets the rating increase." Employing a taller rig is another way of increasing sail area.

The best way to evaluate overlaps is to recognize that most boats will perform adequately with a minimum-size genoa (150 per cent LP) in winds over the 12-to-15-knot range. Therefore, if you sail in an area that normally has medium-to-heavy air, there is no sense in carrying a penalty by having a genoa larger than 150 per cent LP. If you sail in an area of generally light airs, which seems to be the case for a large part of the country, then you have to consider what size genoa is best for the average wind condition of your area.

Each size genoa will effectively drive a boat at a specific minimum wind velocity. Below that velocity, the boat will not perform competitively with that particular sail. If a boat has a 150 per cent genoa that performs well in winds over 12 knots, the boat's performance may be hurt in lighter air. The amount you get hurt could be far worse than the seconds-per-mile penalty you would get with a larger genoa. An actual example is as follows: a 39-footer tested the speed difference between a 150 and 170 per cent genoa and found that the speed increased from 5.8 to 6 knots in 10 knots of apparent-wind velocity. This was a 3.4 per cent increase in speed. This increase in sail area created a rating change of .3 feet—that is, the rating was changed from 32.4 to 32.7 (final ratings are resolved to the nearest tenth) or an increase in rating of one per cent. At this rating range, a tenth of a foot in rating is equal to 1.74 seconds per mile, so that in a race such as the 186-mile Miami–Nassau race, for which the boat was being tested, it produced a handicap difference of 5 minutes 24 seconds. However, if the race was to windward all the way in conditions close to the 10 knots at which the boat was tested, the boat would sail the course approximately 74 minutes faster. These are the kind of measures you have to consider in deciding the amount of overlap you want to carry.

The average wind velocity on Long Island Sound is estimated at approximately 6 knots. Consider a situation in which one boat, having a 150 per cent genoa, enters an overnight race against a boat with a 180 per cent genoa. At the start of the race with the winds at 12 to 14 knots both boats will be approximately equal. As evening approaches, the winds die to around 2 to 4 knots. The boat with the 150 per cent genoa does not have enough power to keep moving through the water. The competing boat with a 180 per cent genoa will be able to sail much faster and may work out a very large lead over the boat that is underpowered. The increase in performance of the 180 per cent genoa far exceeds the rating penalty under these conditions. Most long-distance races are won or lost at night, when the wind is frequently light. It is essential to determine how much light weather there is in the racing you do and how much night racing you do.

Some people think the IOR overlap penalty applies to genoas starting at the minimum of 150 per cent LP and going to a maximum of 180 per cent

LP. Actually, you may set as large a genoa as you want on a boat, but your penalty is increased in proportion to the size of the sail.

An extreme example of overlap was demonstrated in 1956 by *Windigo* (Fig. 163), which carried a 3-ounce, 264 per cent genoa. At the time there were no restrictions on overlap. The sail had a luff of 80 feet and an LP of 64 feet. The clew of the genoa overlapped the mizzenmast, and the sail had so much area that *Windigo* was considerably faster in light air. The next year, overlap restrictions were written into the measurement rule and *Windigo*'s sail had to be recut and, in light air, her speed was considerably slower—a graphic demonstration of what one big sail can do. In the photograph, the winds were blowing about 5 to 6 knots, and the boat was going 4 to 5 knots through the water, as you can see from the bow wave.

In addition, there has been another significant change in attitude toward sails. Most new boats designed under the IOR are made with taller rigs with larger foretriangles, which means higher aspect-ratio genoas and mainsails. One reason for this is that the IOR has less aspect-ratio penalty than the Cruising Club of America (CCA) rule (see Chapter 19). Therefore, the more efficient, higher rigs have become increasingly popular. In a taller rig, less overlap is required to have the same amount of total area in the genoa.

Fig. 163
Windigo with Her 264 Per Cent Genoa

Genoas and Reaching

The main is trimmed to its most inboard position only when sailing close-hauled; hence maximum genoa overlap is practical only when hard on the wind. As we have seen in Figure 161, a genoa with a large overlap is not a good sail for most reaching conditions when the genoa sheet is eased out. The low clew of the average genoa has no outboard trim point, it curves into the mainsail, and it has an inefficient area aft (Fig. 164). On a beam reach, just before the point where a spinnaker can be set, a full-hoist genoa with 150 per cent overlap might perform just as well as a full-hoist genoa with 170 per cent overlap. However, there is an alternative. Since the main boom is already outboard for reaching, the genoa sheet can be trimmed to the end of the boom, providing a much more favorable angle of trim (Fig. 165). This cannot be done using a low-clewed genoa, but a high-clewed reacher or a ballooner will work. This sail is designed with a high-cut clew so that it can be trimmed to the end of the main boom. However, extra-long footed bal-looners, trimmed to the end of the boom, may end up clew-to-clew in a less efficient setup.

This boils down to the fact that your best sail for reaching should have a high clew, a maximum luff, and an LP between 150 and 160 per cent.

Fig. 164
Effects of Reaching with a Standard
Genoa Trimmed to Deck

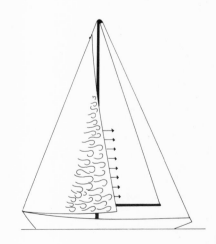

Sail is stalled.
(Separation)

←Trim
Point

Apparent
Wind

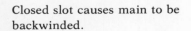

Closed slot causes main to be
backwinded.

Fig. 165
Sheeting to the End of the Boom

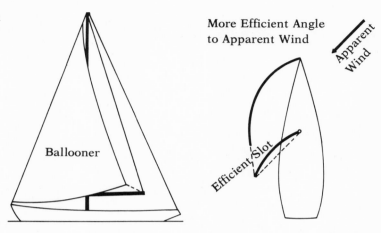

Fig. 166
Staysails Added to Reaching
Combination

The dotted line on (b) represents the jib
topsail sheet, which goes to the end of the
boom and then forward along the boom,
so the boom is free to be trimmed at the
widest possible angle.

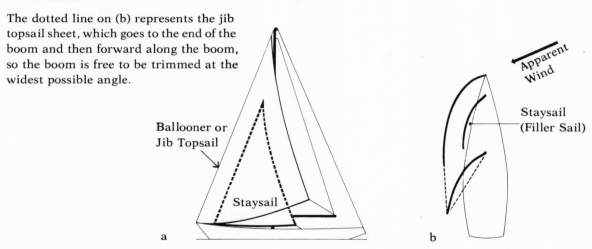

Since the high-clewed genoa has some empty space underneath the
high foot, a staysail can be added with the lowest clew possible to fill in the
gap (Fig. 166). The staysail has the advantage of adding free area; it also adds
greatly to the forward drive of the total sail plan. Usually it has almost the

same area as the main and hence makes the boat go faster. The high-clewed genoa with staysail added is commonly called a double headsail rig; it has proved highly successful in close reaching and on many boats has worked well going to windward in light air. A fuller explanation of staysail rigs can be found in Chapter 11.

The ultimate decision on the right amount of overlap for your boat depends on hull design or trimming platform (deck shape), the kind of rig you have, the average wind conditions you sail in, and the amount of competitive racing you do.

Foretriangle Staysails and Double-Head Rigs

The staysail is largely an auxiliary or "filler" sail used to provide more sail on specific points of sailing. There is no International Offshore Rule at present governing the size of a staysail, except the overlap restriction which prohibits trimming the staysail clew farther aft than the overlap of the No. 1 genoa. As a result, staysails are being made in a great variety of shapes, sizes, and sailcloth weights for running, reaching, and going to windward (Fig. 167). (See Chapter 12 for a discussion of cloth weights.) In actual use, they are subject to the following restrictions: (1) they should not blanket any adjacent sail; and (2) they can only be used when the added sail area will not overpower the boat.

The most familiar and most traditional staysail is the standard spinnaker staysail (Fig. 167a) that is used for reaching when the apparent wind is coming anywhere from a little aft of abeam to fairly far forward of abeam. The tack of the sail is set at a point about one quarter of the way back in the base of the foretriangle and at the centerline on a close reach or on the windward rail on a broader reach. It can be set without interfering appreciably with the spinnaker.

For years the field of staysails was very unsophisticated; the one standard spinnaker staysail could only be practically used in reaching conditions, and when the wind went aft of the beam no staysail was flown efficiently. To design new staysails for other purposes, the following problems had to be surmounted:

1. If the staysail area was increased, the luff came forward and, on a reach, closed the slot between the staysail and the spinnaker to such a degree that the spinnaker tended to collapse prematurely.
2. Although blanketing is not much of a problem when the apparent wind is forward (since the flow is from fore to aft), as the wind goes aft, a

Fig. 167
Staysails Used with a Spinnaker

a. Standard Spinnaker Staysail

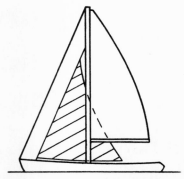

b. Genoa Staysail (Part of the
Double-Head Rig)

c. Super Staysail

d. No. 1 Genoa

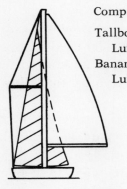

Comparison of Tallboy and Banana:

Tallboy foot = 80 per cent of beam
Luff = 80 per cent of genoa luff
Banana foot = 120 per cent of beam
Luff = 90 per cent of genoa luff

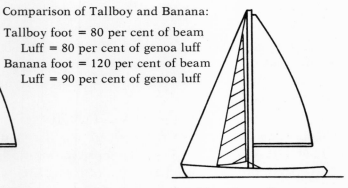

e. Banana Staysail

f. Tallboy Staysail

No. 1 Genoa

Banana

The banana staysail is very full compared to the flat tallboy.

Blooper

large staysail set to windward of the spinnaker can be in a blanketing position. Since the foot of the spinnaker is fairly high above the deck, any width low in the staysail would be all right, but girth up high could be dangerous.

3. Since a boat is long and narrow, even a low, wide staysail cannot be set at the proper angle of attack off the wind. For the proper setting, the clew would have to be trimmed at a point well outboard of the leeward rail — out over the water. (This is the same reason excessive genoa overlap does not generally increase boat speed on a reach as compared to normal overlap.)

Only recently have these problems been circumvented. The results have been a variety of highly specialized new staysails. As with most specialized sails, however, they are really effective only over a narrow range of apparent wind angles and, too, they require a lot of practice to handle effectively. One result of this new direction is the bigger genoa staysail now used as the standard staysail. (See Fig. 167b.) This is actually an enlargement of the standard spinnaker staysail. The "super" staysail carries this to the extreme but loses range in the process. (See Fig. 167c.) The luff is about 90 per cent of the maximum genoa luff length, and the foot extends a few feet behind the mast. So long as the apparent wind is forward of abeam and the wind is moderate, this sail can be used under the spinnaker, if handled carefully. However, the fact that it is set so close to the headstay closes the slot between the staysail and spinnaker to such a degree that there is much less tolerance before the spinnaker will collapse, and once collapsed, the spinnaker is extremely difficult to refill. If the wind goes aft of the beam, because of its size the sail will blanket the spinnaker. Therefore, it has to be lowered sooner than the standard staysail.

The ultimate in maximum close-reaching staysail area and, at the same time, the most critical to set effectively is the No. 1 genoa used under the spinnaker. (See Fig. 167d.) Here the luff is very close to the spinnaker, and the overlap is maximum. An expert crew can use the genoa as a staysail on a close reach in moderate air by raising the spinnaker pole as high as possible and lifting the outboard end above square to get the spinnaker luff farther out in front of the headstay, thus opening up the slot between the spinnaker and the staysail (Fig. 168). However, without an expert crew, this rig may not be worth using. One or two collapses, along with the in-

Fig. 168
Lifting the spinnaker pole moves the
spinnaker luff farther out in front of the
headstay, allowing the experienced sailor
to use the No. 1 genoa as a staysail on a
close reach in moderate air.

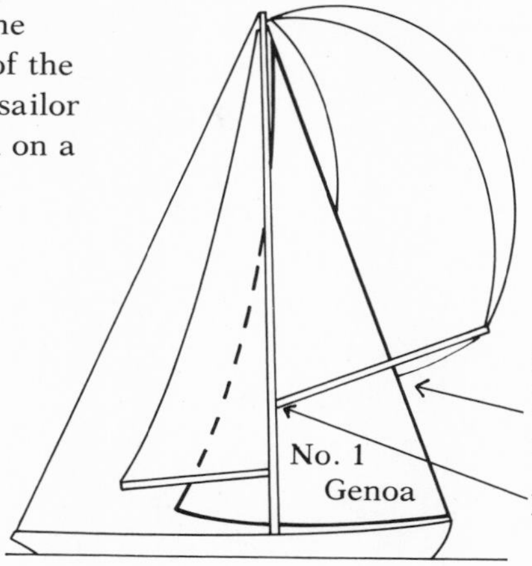

No. 1
Genoa

Pole is perpendicular to
headstay, so end is
farther in front of stay.

Pole at Top of Track

creased difficulty in getting the spinnaker refilled, can more than offset
any speed increase.

Prior to 1968 there was no effective filler sail used in the foretriangle
for broad reaching or dead downwind sailing. If the standard spinnaker
staysail was set on a broad reach, its luff was trimmed to the windward
rail but its clew, because of its width, would stretch well to leeward behind
the mainsail. As a result, the major portion of the sail was in the blanket
zone with only the luff area doing some good. The natural solution to this
problem was to make a sail that trimmed to the windward rail but had
minimal area behind the mainsail in the blanket zone, and maximum luff
length in the exposed area. This thin, lofty sail is called the "banana" and,
in effect, extends the area of mainsail to the windward rail downwind. The
banana staysail is very full, has a long luff (almost to the masthead), and
is made of ¾-ounce nylon. (See Fig. 167e.) Since the spinnaker on a run is
squared to windward, and therefore has its luff quite far away from the
luff of the staysail, the staysail does not interfere with the spinnaker.

This banana staysail proved to be very effective. In wind ranges from
0 to 12 knots, there was less improvement in performance. But as the wind
became stronger, this staysail added as much as a knot to downwind speed.
This was demonstrated by early tests in 1967–68 on Jack Price's *Comanche*.
Here, however, the increase in speed could not be attributed to added sail

area alone. The only logical conclusion was that the staysail created a slot effect. The relatively slow flow lines on the lee side of the mainsail in this downwind position were strengthened to a greater flow velocity, adding more drive to that sail. Thus, the staysail contributed its own driving forces and added to the overall forces on the mainsail (Fig. 169).

Fig. 169

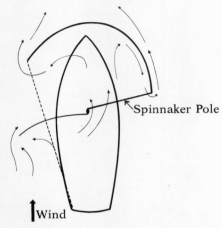

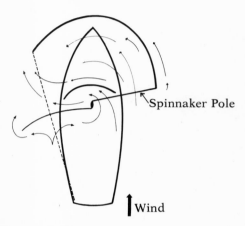

a. No Staysail
Without the banana staysail, the entire main is stalled out, which results in a stronger lee distance at the leech and luff.

b. Banana in Place
The staysail creates a flow over the luff of the main, which results in a stronger leeside force, in addition to the drag forces—so the total force of the main is stronger.

Track layout on the foredeck allows fore and aft adjustment for close-reaching spinnaker staysails and more athwartship trim for the banana or tallboy as the wind goes aft.

In the 1968 Bermuda race, the "tallboy" (see Fig. 167f) was developed. This was a high, narrow, much flatter sail, smaller than the banana staysail, and made of medium-weight Dacron (4 or 5 ounces). It was first designed as a reaching staysail to be used inside the conventional low-clewed genoa on a close reach.

The tallboy has been used as an all-purpose sail on many boats when other specialized staysails are not carried. Since it is tall and narrow, it can be set as a downwind staysail in place of the banana, although not quite as effectively because it is smaller, flatter, and heavier. It could be used for broad reaching because, being narrow aloft, it would not blanket the spinnaker. Originally designed for close reaching with the genoa, it can also be used with the spinnaker, although it does not have the area the specialized reaching staysails have.

One different kind of staysail gaining in popularity is the "big boy" or "blooper" (see Fig. 167), photograph, a lightweight, very full, high-clewed genoa tacked near the bow and trimmed opposite the spinnaker on the leeward side behind the main. Its area is appreciably larger than the main, and to get it drawing better, some boats may take one or two reefs in the main to get air to the blooper. This sail is only used dead downwind in true winds over 10 or 12 knots.

THE MODERN DOUBLE-HEAD RIG

Another major development in recent years has been sails for close reaching, up to the point where a spinnaker can be used. This has been done through a modernization of the old double-head rig, producing maximum possible area under the handicap rule.

In the first America's Cup race, over 100 years ago, two and three sails were set in the foretriangle. The J-boats in the Cup competition of the 1930s made extensive use of this rig (Fig. 170a). These sails were designed for going to windward in a strong breeze. They were relatively flat, barely overlapped each other, and did not overlap the mainsail. In those days the theory was to use a genoa jib in light-to-moderate air and shift to the double-head rig when the wind freshened. In effect, this was a way of shortening sail. The modern double-head rig is quite different. For reaching, when the spinnaker cannot be used, maximum sail area is important, and

Fig. 170

a. J-Boat with the Heavy-Air
Double-Head Rig

b. Heavy-Air Double-Head Rig on a
Cruiser-Racer

the new double-head rig provides a way of doing this without increasing a boat's rating, as using a bigger genoa overlap would do. The double-head rig allows two sails to be set to the restricting genoa overlap point, one with a high clew and one with a low clew (Fig. 171). The high clew of the reacher genoa increases the leech overlap and the low-clewed genoa staysail fills in underneath the reacher to produce a decksweeper effect. Yet if the leech of the reacher and the foot of the staysail were projected, they would come to a hypothetical point well aft of the restriction line for the No. 1 genoa. Thus, together, they have the profile of a much larger genoa than is allowed, with only the negative clew area missing (Fig. 172). However, since the sails are used on a close reach where, because of the fore and aft flow, narrower slots can be utilized, all the area of both sails is used efficiently. This produces an actual area increase of more than 50 per cent over the No. 1 genoa, without an increase in penalty.

Fig. 171
The Modern Double-Head Rig

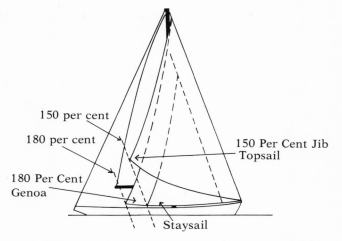

150 per cent

180 per cent

180 Per Cent
Genoa

150 Per Cent Jib
Topsail

Staysail

The double-head rig with the smaller
rated overlap at 150 per cent has 36 per
cent more actual area than the single
genoa rated at 180 per cent.

Fig. 172
With a 150 per cent double-head rig, if the
leech of the jibtop and the foot of the
staysail were each projected, they would
join at a hypothetical clew at the 190-200
per cent LP line. The actual area of the
double-head rig is equal to about a 235 per
cent genoa.

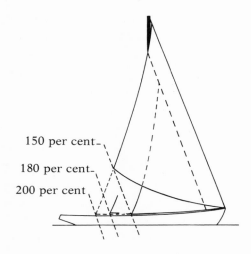

150 per cent

180 per cent

200 per cent

The genoa staysail used with a double-head rig is a 4- or 5-ounce Dacron sail. The luff is parallel to the jibtop or reacher but is set about one quarter of the way aft from the bow to the mast; the halyard reaches about three-quarters of the way up the mast. It goes inside the reacher, as shown in Figure 171. The clew generally goes back to the restriction point of the No. 1 genoa.

The reacher or jibtop is nothing more than a high-clewed No. 1 genoa, with the same area. It is the staysail that provides the bonus area.

Basically the modern double-head rig was designed as a close reaching combination and works well on all boats. However, some boats have used them successfully to windward. The concept was to try and hold the rating penalty for genoa overlap to a minimum and gain better light-air windward performance through the extra area of the double-head rig. This was a good idea, but there were problems. The rig, as originally designed, worked fairly well on a relatively slow boat, particularly one that was underpowered and one that did not point well because of excess beam. It did not work well on the more modern, more sophisticated hulls until some years later when smaller staysails set farther back in the foretriangle and utilizing less overlap were developed (Fig. 173). These perform well. However, they are still restricted in their use to windward because of their great sensitivity compared to the standard No. 1 genoa. These sails can only be used well to windward by the most experienced helmsmen and crews. Most sailors will have a great deal of trouble with them because the slots are extremely narrow and the range of efficiency has very little tolerance.

With the double-head rig, you are dealing with two slot effects (Fig. 174), one between the staysail and jib topsail and one between the staysail and the mainsail. These two slots are narrower than the mainsail-genoa slot, and thus a small amount of trim has a greater effect. The staysail acts as a flow straightener because the air flow through the slot on its windward side decreases the eddies caused by the mast.

Another difficulty to windward is that the helmsman cannot see the reacher luff and cannot "read" the sail. Since this rig is much more sensitive to trim and helm than ordinary staysail combinations, it lost much of its initial popularity as a windward rig, although it has held its own for reaching. (On close reaches, when a spinnaker is not efficient, there is no faster rig.)

However, with the advent of the One Ton boats, where the boats are

Fig. 173
Different Double-Head Rig Staysails to Be
Used with the Same Jib top

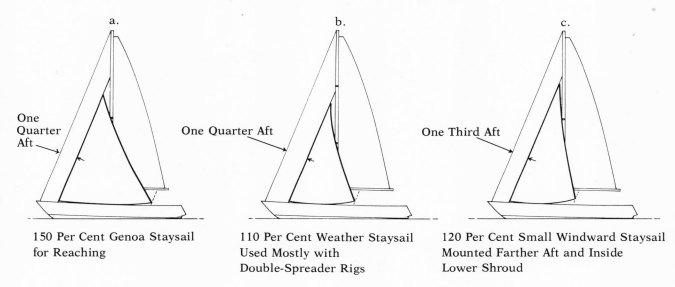

a.

One
Quarter
Aft

150 Per Cent Genoa Staysail
for Reaching

b.

One Quarter Aft

110 Per Cent Weather Staysail
Used Mostly with
Double-Spreader Rigs

c.

One Third Aft

120 Per Cent Small Windward Staysail
Mounted Farther Aft and Inside
Lower Shroud

Fig. 174
With the double-head rig, there are two
sails in the foretriangle instead of the
single genoa. Thus, there are two slots and
they are narrower than the
mainsail-genoa slot and require precise
trim. With the double-head rig, the main
is trimmed more toward the
centerline in order to open up the slot.

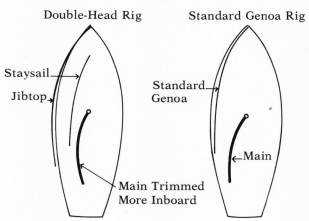

Double-Head Rig

Standard Genoa Rig

Staysail

Jibtop

Standard
Genoa

←Main

Main Trimmed
More Inboard

built to a formula like the 12-Meters and are not handicapped but race boat
for boat, small changes in boat speed could be measured—just as they
could be in one designs. Since the double-head rig clearly added speed to

windward, it has made a comeback as a windward combination, although usually with a much smaller staysail, in some cases extending only to the after lower shrouds. This is called a windward staysail. The longer genoa staysail, however, is still used for reaching.

The "Ton" boats have brought many one-design characteristics with them. One major change is that since "level" racing means no handicap, the onus is entirely on hull design, sails, sail handling, and helm. It is tough competition, and these crews practice a great deal compared to an average offshore racer but similar to the one-design practice routine. Therefore, for the first time, really significant testing can be accomplished, and the value of certain sails or sail combinations can really be assessed. This will surely mean more refinement and development in the area of staysails, and possibly in all areas of sailing. However, don't forget that these specialized rigs take a great deal of practice, and the average skipper and crew will not be able to use them effectively, unless they're willing to devote an enormous amount of time to practice.

Handling the Double-Head Rig

The large genoa staysail goes inside the upper shrouds on a very close reach and outside on a wider reach. On the wind, the genoa staysail will be set between the upper shroud and the lower shroud (Fig. 175). The smaller or windward staysail is used mostly on the wind, and the clew should be in one of two places: when the luff is well forward, the clew should be between the outer and lower shrouds; when the luff is farther aft, the clew should be inside the lower shrouds. In this case the leech has to be cut with an appreciable negative curve to miss the spreader.

With the double-head rig, sail handling is not as complicated as you might expect. Both the jib topsail and staysail sheets can be led to the cockpit. Sail-trim problems are minimal while reaching, and since to windward you are generally using the rig only in light weather, any tacking can be done by three men. The jib topsail requires the same trim procedures as the No. 1 genoa; a minimum of winch work is required. The jib topsail sheet has to be led forward of the staysail luff, since the jib topsail has to tack between the headstay and the staysail. A man can be stationed to help the jib topsail through this slot, but usually the sail will blow through easily if you let it, especially if the staysail is momentarily held in a backed po-

Fig. 175
On the wind, the large genoa staysail in a double-head rig trims between the outer and lower shrouds.

Fig. 176
Tacking a Double-Head Rig

Jibtop sheets are led around luff of staysail because jibtop has to tack in front of staysail. Jibtop slides forward along backed staysail.
Staysail is released and tacked when clew of jibtop passes in front of staysail luff.

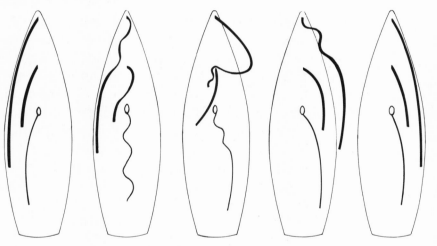

sition (Fig. 176). Be sure that your sheets are long enough, much longer than regular genoa sheets.

For a windward rig, the staysail is cut flatter than the jib topsail because it is trimmed at a more acute angle and can be sheeted in more than the jib topsail. The topsail (which has a high clew) trims outside the spreaders to the transom, while the staysail is trimmed between the outer and lower shrouds or inside the lower shrouds, thus providing some separation between the sails going to windward. When reaching, they both can be trimmed outside, as eased sheets allow the sails to move farther apart.

If you are setting up the double-head rig for the first time to try it to windward, here is a good system to follow. First, strap the mainsail in fairly tight so that the leech has an 8- to 10-inch fall-off about two-thirds of the way up. Move the traveler to windward, so that the end of the boom is over the centerline of the boat.

Second, trim the staysail until it is fairly flat but still retains some aerodynamic curvature and does not backwind the main. Some skippers report a very flat staysail works well; others say it is better to ease the sheet to get some draft. This trim will vary from boat to boat.

Third, trim the jib topsail until it backwinds the staysail. Then ease it until the staysail just stops luffing. Be sure the jib topsail lead is far enough forward so that the foot is free and has the same curvature as the mid-section of the sail. With the lead too far aft, the foot will be pulled flatter and in toward the staysail, backwinding it prematurely. Moving the lead forward frees the foot and allows air to flow in the slot between the sails. The right lead is vital to the function of the double-head rig, and the best way to get it is to set the jib topsail without the staysail. Move the lead forward and aft until the entire leading edge luffs at the same time. When you have the staysail in place, you can see only the upper third; when this luffs, you will know the entire jib topsail is luffing.

You must watch that upper third. It is important to keep the jib topsail full all the time. Boat speed will drop rapidly if this sail is partially aback. Also remember that a boat with a double-head rig will not point well until speed is built up; you may have to sail at a slightly wider angle to achieve this speed.

Changing from the double-head rig to a No. 1 genoa is a relatively painless process. You just swap the topsail for the genoa and leave the staysail standing. This sail is large enough so that boat speed will drop only slightly. Once the genoa is up, you lower the staysail.

Even though sail handling is not difficult once the crew has practiced, there still is a strong feeling that the double-head rig is not practical for round-the-buoys racing because of the added sail handling needed. This is a decision to be made by each owner, but you should bear in mind that while its use to windward has many pros and cons, the rig is unquestionably faster for any close-reaching situation up to the point where a spinnaker can be used and up to at least 18–22 knots of true-wind velocity.*

*The star-cut, used for close reaching, has a limit of 18–20 knots of apparent wind (12–15 true). The choice in the increased wind velocity is between a double-head and a smaller, super star-cut which can be used in 18–25 knots of apparent wind. The double-head will work well in the marginal areas of either size star-cut. If the boat has one or two broaches under the spinnaker, the distance lost may be greater than the slight gain in speed, and thus less advantageous than using a double-head rig, which may offer 10 per cent less speed, but no loss through broaching.

Chapter 12

Sail Inventory

If you are a one-design racer, you are lucky, because your sail inventory is generally limited by class rules to one or two mainsails, one or two jibs, and, if used, one or two spinnakers. Many class rules allow you to purchase only one suit of sails a year, which simplifies the economics of the situation but puts prime importance on sail handling to make one suit of sails cover a wide range of weather conditions.

In some cases, sails for an entire fleet are purchased by the one-design association and distributed to the boatowners. So the question of "What sails should you have?" is academic as far as most one-design racers are concerned. However, the material that follows should prove helpful to any sailor.

CRUISING-BOAT SAILS

Cruising-boat owners generally fall into three general categories, and their sail inventories should be chosen accordingly. There is the cruising sailor who wants just the minimum of sails needed to get from one place to another in a reasonable length of time; the part-time racer who wants to cruise and race with the minimum of sails required to be competitive in average conditions (he will have his problems in special conditions—very light air and very heavy air); and the serious racer who needs a complete racing inventory.

Building Your Sail Inventory

If you wanted to consider every possible sail you might use on your boat, you would find that there are about thirty-five different sails for a sloop and over forty for a yawl or ketch. The following sail inventory and accompanying figures show virtually all the existing possibilities—without duplication. A review of this list will give you an idea of the great variety of sails that are available and can serve as a point of departure in building your own inventory.

Bear in mind that the sails listed here are generic types that vary from boat to boat.

MAXIMUM SAIL INVENTORY WITHOUT DUPLICATION

Genoas

Sail	Weight (ounces)
Small ghoster (wind finder)	.5 or .75
High-clew drifter and reacher	.75
Low-clew drifter and reacher	2.2–3.0
Light-air No. 1 genoa	4–5
Heavy No. 1 genoa	
No. 2 genoa	
No. 3 genoa	
Mule	
Lapper	
Working jib	
Club-footed jib	
No. 4 genoa	
Storm jib	

Sails set aft of the mainmast

Sail	Weight (ounces)
Main	
Storm trysail	
Mizzen	
Mizzen spinnaker	.75
Large mizzen staysail	1.5
Heavy-air mizzen staysail	2.2
Light-air mizzen staysail	.5
Mizzen genoa	4–5

Headsails and staysails

Sail	Weight (ounces)
High-clew No. 1 jibtop reacher	2–3
High-clew No. 1 jibtop	4–5
Large double-head staysail	4–5
Small double-head staysail (windward)	4–5
No. 2 jibtop	5–6.5
No. 2 staysail	5–6.5

Spinnakers

Sail	Weight (ounces)
Small drifter spinnaker	.5 or less
Light-air runner	.5
All-purpose	.75
No. 5 spinnaker short luff— storm spinnaker	4.0
Star-cut	1.5
Super star-cut	2.2

Headsails and staysails

Sail	Weight (ounces)
No. 3 jibtop	6.5–7
Yankee	6.5–9
Inner staysail—tall	8–12
Super staysail	1.5
Running staysail—banana	.75
Tallboy	4.0
Blooper or big boy	.75

SELECTING SAILS

The chart below lists the recommended sails for three types of boatowners: the cruising sailor, the part-time racer, and the serious racer.

SAIL INVENTORY FOR THREE TYPES OF SAILORS

Cruising	Part-time racer	Complete racer
Main	Main	Main
Working jib or club-footed jib or No. 3 genoa	—	Light genoa
—	No. 1 genoa	No. 1 genoa
No. 2 genoa	—	No. 2 genoa
—	No. 3 genoa	No. 3 genoa
—	—	Reacher (jibtop)*
—	—	Genoa staysail* or tallboy
—	—	Spinnaker staysail, running
—	—	Light spinnaker
—	Medium all-purpose spinnaker	Medium all-purpose spinnaker
Reaching spinnaker	Reaching spinnaker (star-cut)	Reaching spinnaker
		Blooper

*Doubles as double-head rig.

Cruising	_Part-time racer_	_Complete racer_
Reaching spinnaker	Storm jib or heavy-weather job	Storm jib
	Yawl or ketch	
Mizzen	Mizzen	Mizzen
—	Triangular mizzen staysail	Triangular mizzen staysail
—	—	Spinnaker mizzen staysail
		Mizzen genoa

There is a minimum inventory for cruising. Just two sails, the No. 2 genoa and the narrow-shouldered reaching spinnaker, are suggested in addition to the working sails (main and jib). In the foretriangle, either the working jib or club-footed jib can be selected for ease of handling.

For the part-time racer, the first sail in the foretriangle you should get is not a working jib but a No. 3 genoa instead. This is a real racing sail of the same approximate area as a working jib and can be used for cruising with little extra handling. Then if you get a No. 1 genoa, you will have, together with your main, a competitive inventory for windward work for winds from 6 knots up to 30 knots. For offwind work, you need at least two spinnakers. Even if you race only occasionally, spinnakers rip too easily to take a chance on racing with just one. However, the two should be different enough to cover a wide range of weather conditions. First of all, get the all-purpose, ¾-ounce No. 1 spinnaker, which should be the maximum size practical for your boat. Then add the close-reaching star-cut. With these two spinnakers, you are adequately covered for running in 5 knots to at least 25 knots of true wind and for reaching in 3 or 4 knots up to 18 knots of wind. In fact, you are set for most conditions when a spinnaker is used, except for reaching and running in very light air, when the special, ½-ounce chute is needed, and for close reaching over 18 knots. With a yawl or ketch rig, a mizzen staysail will keep you up with the fleet on a reach.

For the serious racer there is an inventory of at least eight to ten sails in addition to the working complement (see the chart above). The light genoa is faster in winds under 6 to 8 knots apparent. The No. 2 and No. 3 genoas enable you to reduce sail according to the strength of wind and still have plenty of drive from the foretriangle going to windward. For close reaching you have the 4- or 5-ounce high-clew jib topsail, which forms part of a double-head rig with a large 3- to 5-ounce staysail. The large staysail can also be used with the spinnaker on a reach. The banana staysail is used with the spinnaker on a run.

There are three spinnakers in the inventory. The No. 1, of ¾-ounce cloth, may be used as an all-around sail in everything except light air, when the ½-ounce light-air runner should be used. The star-cut reacher made of 1½-ounce cloth is highly competitive in close-reaching conditions.

If you have a yawl or ketch, you need a mizzen staysail, mizzen genoa, and a mizzen spinnaker to give you extra drive off the wind.

From this base inventory, each racing skipper then adds additional specialized sails. These may include light-air drifters and ghosters, additional spinnaker staysails, super staysail, tallboy, and heavy-air headsails such as a No. 4 genoa and a heavy-air double-head rig.

WEIGHT OF MAINSAILS

Under International Offshore and many other racing rules, cruising boats are not allowed to use more than one mainsail during a race, except for a storm trysail. So when you are building your sail inventory, you should think in terms of one mainsail. This has to be versatile and of the right weight cloth. An offshore cruising boat that is going to be away from a sailmaker for an extended period of time naturally needs a heavier weight main, one that can take a beating in heavy air and still keep its shape. A boat that stays close to home can use a lighter-weight sail or, perhaps, in this case, two mains: a light and a heavy. The light sail, which is used primarily to save weight aloft, may need recutting from time to time because of its lower strength.

If you have one of the many models of class cruising boats, the experience of other skippers will serve as a guide to the weight of your mainsail. However, this should be modified according to how you intend to use the boat and the weather conditions you will encounter. If you have a custom-built boat, your naval architect can help you select the proper sail. To give some examples, for a 25- to 35-foot boat, a 6-ounce cloth would be a good, substantial weight; for a 31- to 35-foot boat, 6½ ounces would be good; for a 36- to 45-foot boat, 7¼ to 8 ounces; for a 46- to 50-foot boat, 9 ounces; for a 51- to 60-footer, 9 to 10 ounces; for a 61- to 73-footer, 10 to 12 ounces would be suitable.

WEIGHT AND AREA OF HEADSAILS

Before discussing the selection of headsails, which can be of many shapes and weights of cloth, you should understand how wind velocity and the sailing angle of the boat to the wind affect the loading on the sails.

As the point of sailing changes from beating to close reaching, two things happen: (1) the angle of attack to the apparent wind is broader and so the genoa can be fuller; and (2) since the stress on the sailcloth is less, a genoa used for close reaching does not have to be as heavy as the one used for straight windward work.

This can be shown by an example. When hard on the wind, the last 6 to 12 inches of sheet taken in when trimming the genoa can double the load on the corners of the sail. As the sheet is eased for reaching, the loading on the sail decreases rapidly, and the sail can be used when reaching in a higher wind range, or a lighter-weight sail can be used. As a result, for most cruising boats, the maximum-size genoa for windward work in light-to-moderate air has proved to be best in a 4- or 5-ounce weight.

We have seen that, going to windward, the genoa is subjected to maximum loading forces. In addition to a heavy weight sail, you need maximum sail area in winds from 2 to 5 knots to supply essential driving power; the recommended cloth weight is 2 to 4 ounces in this range. These sails are

Fig. 177
Sail Plan Showing Various Headsails

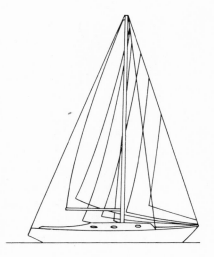

lighter in weight in proportion to the mainsail because, unlike the main, they can be changed for a smaller and heavier weight sail as soon as the wind gets too heavy. Maximum sail area should be used until it becomes too much for the boat to carry. Then you reduce sail. This is the basic rule, except at the bottom of the wind-velocity range: in very light air you start with a small, very light genoa that will fill away in the slightest whisper of wind.

In very light drifting conditions, say from 0 to 2 knots, there is not enough wind to fill maximum area sails. When the big ones will not fill, the only thing that will is a smaller sail made of the lightest possible material. This is because, with little or no wind, steerage way is vital. As soon as a boat generates even slight forward movement, it creates an increased apparent-wind velocity of its own over the sails, and if you then find that very fine angle of attack to this apparent wind, you can sail right through many boats. If you have the wrong sail up, and it won't fill properly, you'll drift with the pack. In order to be effective, your drifting sail not only has to be lightweight material, ½- or ¾-ounce nylon, but must have very light fittings. Obviously, it is not going to have much strength, and as soon as any breeze, say ½ knot, comes in, you probably should change to a slightly heavier sail, say, of 1½-ounce nylon and of near maximum area. If the wind gets over 3 knots, you should shift from a lightweight nylon sail to a 2-ounce Dacron genoa of maximum area. In a still stronger wind, you will probably need a 4-ounce sail, and if it is a large boat, a 5-ounce sail.

This sail is usually classified as the No. 1 genoa, a workhorse of a sail with a wide range of capabilities. Generally, it can be used in winds of 4 knots up to 12 to 15 knots (17 to 22 knots apparent-wind maximum). If you have a stiff boat, and the forces are too much for the No. 1, you can change to a "heavy" No. 1, which is 5 ounces for small boats and 6½ ounces or 7½ ounces on large boats. This heavy No. 1 might be a foot shorter on the hoist and have a foot or two less overlap. You should use this slightly smaller sail only when the true wind is over the 12 to 15 knot range.

When the heavy No.1 proves to be too much sail, go into your normal genoa sequence: a No. 2 genoa has 75 to 80 per cent of the area of the No. 1; the No. 3 is 75 to 80 per cent of the No. 2. A No. 4 might be 42 to 45 per cent of the No. 1.

For cruising, the working jib with a small overlap is easier to handle than a genoa. It has about the same area as a No. 3 genoa.

GENOAS

Cloth weight (ounces)	True-wind (knots)
.5	0–1
.75	1–1.5
1.5	1.5–2
2.2	2–5
4	5–10
5	10–14

The "mule" is a dual-purpose sail, used for cruising and racing. It is slightly larger than the No. 3 genoa. The same is true of the "lapper." These sails are slightly different in configuration from the No. 3 genoa, having a little longer luff and slightly less overlap, but they serve about the same purpose.

The club-footed jib has the foot attached to a boom (club) that can be rigged to a traveler similar to that of the mainsail. It makes a good cruising sail because you can tack the boat without handling any sheets. The storm jib, which is used in very heavy air, and is required in some long-distance ocean races, is a very small sail with a luff 45 to 55 per cent of the maximum and a foot about two-thirds the base of the foretriangle. It will be used in winds over 40–45 knots.

The next group of sails on the list (page 259) contains a wide variety of headsails, most of which are used for reaching conditions. This requires a high-clewed genoa (jib top) that forms the top half of the double-head rig. The lower or inner sail is the genoa staysail, with both sails of 4- or 5-ounce cloth.

DOUBLE-HEAD RIGS

Instead of genoas, some skippers prefer to use the double-head system for the full windward range. Instead of changing from a light-air double-head rig to the No. 1 genoa, these sailors will change to a smaller double-head rig: a No. 2 jibtop and a No. 2 staysail. Both sails will be smaller and heavier than the No. 1. In stronger airs, an even smaller and heavier double-head combination is used. This progression works all the way down to the traditional double-head used by many large ocean racers in the Thirties and Forties in very heavy air. This style jibtop is called the "Yankee" and has a very small overlap sail with its clew well above the deck. The staysail is rigged on a permanent stay and has no overlap.

In any case, the large staysail in this double-head rig combination is a good all-purpose sail. If it is made of 4- or 5-ounce Dacron, it can be used with the jib topsail or as a reaching spinnaker staysail. It can be used until the wind goes abaft the beam and then it will begin to blanket the spinnaker. It also has another valuable attribute: if you don't have one of the new double-slot headstays, it is great when you are changing sails. When you shift from a genoa to a spinnaker or from a jib topsail to a No. 1 genoa, you do not have an appreciable drop in boat speed if the staysail is left up.

SPINNAKER INVENTORY

Spinnakers have been discussed quite thoroughly in Chapter 9, so a brief review covering the key points regarding inventory is all that is necessary here.

Remember that when the boat bears off onto a reach and the sailing angle broadens to the point where you can use a reaching spinnaker, the forces on the sail are reduced substantially and as the apparent wind comes aft of abeam, it is virtually equal to the velocity of the true wind. This further reduces the loading on the sail and explains why you can use a ¾-ounce spinnaker in the same 10-knot wind that requires a 5-ounce genoa to windward.

As the boat broadens its sailing angle to a dead run, the apparent wind is less than the true wind. There are decreased aerodynamic forces on the lee side of the spinnaker, and the apparent-wind velocity becomes less and less as the boat assumes the same course as the true wind. On a dead run, the loading on the cloth is at a minimum.

The list of spinnakers in the maximum sail inventory (page 259) indicates the many types from which you can choose. At the top of the list is a small drifter made of ½-ounce cloth. There is a very good reason for having this sail on board. Visualize a boat in the ocean with a good sea running and less then 2 or 3 knots of wind. The masthead will swing from side to side perhaps 6 to 10 feet at a time, carrying the head of a spinnaker with it. In this light air, a maximum-girth, full-shouldered spinnaker will continually collapse because of the combination of the motion of the boat and the forces of gravity. The only sail that will work under these conditions is a small, minimum-weight spinnaker. It has to be small enough and light enough so that the slightest breeze will fill it; and because it is so light, the problem of gravity is minimized.

The light-air runner is also of ½-ounce cloth and is of near maximum area. It is a relatively large sail. It has some fullness, which is not as good for reaching but which adds a certain amount of stability. This light spinnaker could be used in up to about 7 or 8 knots of apparent wind.

If you want an all-purpose No. 1 spinnaker that is good from 5 knots through 15 knots, get a ¾-ounce sail. Large boats, 65 feet and up, sometimes divide this medium range, using a ¾-ounce for the lower half and a 1½-ounce cloth for up to 18 knots.

While reaching, a boat is overpowered by large sail area, and therefore the size of the spinnaker starts going down while the weight of the cloth goes up. Since wind velocity is stronger aloft, a big-shouldered spinnaker can create a lot of side forces that can lay the boat over on a reach. Consequently, for close reaching over 6 to 8 knots apparent wind use a spinnaker cut with flatter draft and narrow shoulders like a star-cut to reduce the heeling movement and to provide more stability. This sail should be made of at least 1½-ounce cloth (2½ on the big boats). This reaching spinnaker acts somewhat like a genoa; so the shoulders should be cut so that they are halfway between a full-size spinnaker and a genoa.

The regular star-cut spinnaker generally has an efficient pointing angle between 50 degrees and 80 degrees. At 50 degrees, its maximum range is about 18 knots. Over this limit, the smaller, super star-cut is used. The No. 5 storm spinnaker has a minimum girth and a shorter luff than the No. 4 and is made of 4-ounce nylon. It should be moderately full to give stability and reduce oscillation.

To help you choose from this wide variety of spinnakers, here is a list of recommended sails and the order in which they should be purchased. In other words, if you want only one spinnaker, get the first one on the list.

1. The ¾-ounce all-purpose No.1 spinnaker—for winds of 5–15 knots.
2. The narrow-shouldered star-cut reaching spinnaker—used for sail-

ing angles of 50–80 degrees and in winds of 4–5 knots, up to the point where the boat is overpowered, about 18–20 knots apparent winds. The weight should be ¾ ounce for boats under 26 feet, and 1½ ounces for boats over 26 feet, and 2½ ounces for boats over 55 feet.

3. The large light-air runner of ½-ounce cloth, which can be used in apparent winds up to the maximum of 7–8 knots. Do not confuse this with the smaller, ½-ounce sail for extremely light conditions.

4. A 1½- or 2½-ounce nylon storm spinnaker for very heavy weather. This should be short on the luff and narrow on the girth so it can be used for running in true winds of 30–35 knots and for broad reaching in true winds of 20–30 knots.

5. The small, ½-ounce drifter — for extremely light conditions.

SPINNAKERS

(Recommended cloth weights for a 35-foot boat.)

	Maximum apparent-wind velocities (knots)	
Cloth weight (ounces)	Reaching	Running
.5	6–8	8
.75	9–18	9–20
1.5	19–25	21–30
2.5	25*	35–40
4.0	25*	Over 40

*Should not be used for close reaching.

The weights of cloth used in staysails are determined in the same way as those of other sails. If the sail is used with the apparent wind forward, it should be of heavier weight cloth than a sail that is used when the apparent wind is aft. The farther aft the wind goes, the lighter a sail can be. Therefore, a staysail used for windward work will be relatively heavy, whereas a running staysail will be made of lightweight cloth.

For many years the traditional spinnaker staysail was made in 1½-ounce nylon. More recently this sail has been made in 2.2-ounce Dacron when the value of developing more stable shape in close-reaching staysails became recognized.

The genoa staysail which replaces the standard spinnaker staysail is made in 4- or 5-ounce Dacron. It is therefore heavier than the older staysail, but the heavier weight does not appear to be detrimental in lighter airs.

One exception is the super staysail, which is made of anywhere from 1½-ounce nylon to 4-ounce Dacron. The heavier, 4-ounce weight would be used in medium airs on a very stable boat.

Downwind, the banana is quite light, usually ¾ ounce. This sail is built to design principles more akin to the spinnaker and is too full to be used for reaching, so the ¾-ounce is adequate. The tallboy has to be heavier because it is used for both running and reaching and is a sail carried into a higher wind range than any other sail except the genoa staysail (when used with the jibtop).

MIZZEN STAYSAILS

If you have a yawl or ketch, considerable thought should be given the sails set from the mizzenmast. The mizzen itself can vary in cloth weight, depending on the use of the boat. If the emphasis is on cruising or on long-distance ocean racing, you will want a heavier-than-average mizzen because in strong winds you might sail with just the jib and mizzen. A lighter-weight sail could be used by the racing sailor, since he drops his mizzen going to windward in a strong breeze.

Other sails set from the mizzenmast are generally used for racing (Fig. 178a). The maximum-area reaching mizzen staysail is set from the top of the mizzenmast to a point on deck just aft of the mainmast. The tack can be anywhere from the centerline to the windward rail. The sail is shaped like a light-air genoa and is made of 1½-ounce nylon or 2-ounce Dacron. Since it is a reaching sail, it can be used when the apparent wind comes from the forward quadrant and exerts heavy loading on the sail. Once the wind moves aft to a broad reach, the mizzen staysail, like the genoa, is relatively ineffective.

With the wind aft, you use a mizzen spinnaker. This sail, which flies from the top of the mizzenmast, should not be set directly on top of the mainsail but off the leech of that sail, if possible. This is done by letting off the halyard, sheet, and guy until the sail is in a position trailing off behind and somewhat to leeward of the main. It is not easy to accomplish this,

Fig. 178

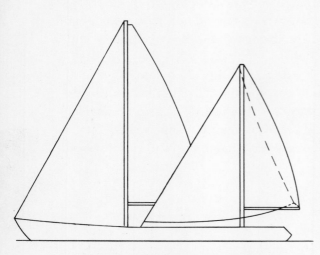

a. Large Triangular Mizzen Staysail—the large mizzen staysail is used for spinnaker reaches.

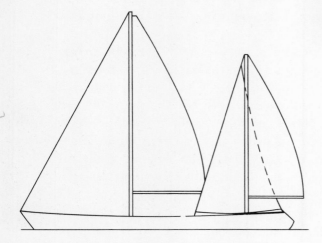

b. Mizzen Genoa (Close-Reaching Mizzen Staysail)—the mizzen genoa is used on a very close reach, generally where the spinnaker cannot be used.

and the sail requires constant attention, but if you can keep the sail full, it is well worth it.

Other sails in this group include a mizzen genoa staysail that is used for close reaching (Fig. 178b). This sail is smaller and of heavier-weight cloth than a regular mizzen staysail. For near drifting conditions, there is a fairly large mizzen staysail made of ½-ounce cloth. This sail should be used at the same time as the very light genoa.

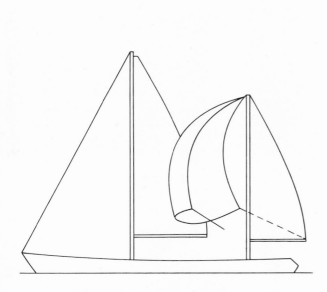

c. Mizzen Spinnaker—the mizzen spinnaker is used for broad reaching and downwind. It flies freely from the mizzen masthead without a pole.

Chapter 13

How to
Shorten Sail

There are many great old tales of the sea that tell of fearless skippers who drove their vessels through violent storms without taking in an inch of sail. Of course, you hear only about those who made record passages from port to port — not about those who did not make it at all. The commercial sea captains were sailing for money. Today you sail for fun, and there is no reason for taking hazardous chances.

A gale at sea, in a bay, or even on a lake is not something you can ignore. A good sailor has a healthy respect for the weather and knows there is more boat control by shortening sail when the going gets rough. In fact, the wise skipper with an eye on the sky and horizon will have his vessel under reduced sail before the bad weather hits.

The manner and amount of sail reduction depends on your boat and the force of the wind and the sea. If it is blowing a full gale, you generally have no choice but to take off all sail and ride it out under bare poles. Or, if you have one, you might set a storm trysail. (See Fig. 186 for instructions on setting this sail.) This small sail of heavyweight cloth steadies the boat and gives you enough steerage way to heave to and head into the seas. These are emergency measures for extreme conditions with peak velocity winds, which you probably will not encounter very often.

In strong but not overpowering winds, you can change to a smaller headsail or reduce the number of sails. On a sloop, take down the main and sail under jib; on a yawl or ketch, take down the main and sail with jib and mizzen. Of course, every boat is different and the sail or sails you take off depend on the handling characteristics of the vessel, which you can learn only by experience.

Another method of shortening sail, which usually applies to the mainsail, is reefing. When the breeze is not so strong that you have to reduce the number of sails, but is still heavy enough to heel the boat beyond its efficient sailing angle, then you must cut down on the area of the mainsail. You do this by lowering the halyard 10 to 20 per cent of the hoist (depending on the boat and the wind) and gathering in the slack sailcloth along the boom. This reduces the side-loading forces, the boat straightens up, and boat speed is maintained or even increased.

There are various methods of reefing. Roller reefing rolls the sail around the boom, which is rotated by a special crank and gear system. Or you can tie in a reef using lines attached to the sail at reef point. Another system, slab reefing, is also an effective means of quickly reducing sail area.

ROLLER REEFING

This system became popular with both ocean-racing and cruising sailors because it was an easy way of controlling mainsail area.

The roller reefing mechanism is a housing or socket. On the forward side of the socket is a gooseneck fitting, which is attached to a slide on the sail track. The socket has a worm gear that engages a gear on the forward end of the boom; as you turn the worm crank, the boom rotates with the socket (Fig. 179).

To roll in a reef, first ease the mainsheet while maintaining way. This takes part of the wind load off the sail, so that it can be rolled up evenly. Slack the downhaul if you have a gooseneck slide. Then crank away, rolling the sail around the boom, until you have taken up all the downhaul slack. Next, ease the main halyard until the slide reaches the bottom of the track. Start cranking again and repeat the process until the desired reef is rolled in. The reason for this seemingly slow procedure is to use the weight of the boom to keep a strain on the sail while cranking so that it will roll smoothly.

With roller reefing, the mainsheet is attached to the end of the boom by a fitting which allows the boom to rotate. Small boats use a simple sheet tang, while cruising boats have a well-engineered swivel fitting for the sheet attachment (Fig. 180). On large and small boats, when the mainsheet leads from the end of the boom, there is a great strain on the mid-section of the spar, and it has to be designed to take this load.

During roller reefing, the sail has a tendency to work forward; so it is usually advisable to pull it out at the leech as the turns are cranked in. An-

Fig. 179
Roller Reefing.

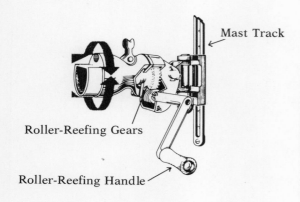

Mast Track

Roller-Reefing Gears

Roller-Reefing Handle

a. A handle is inserted into a worm gear below the main roller-reefing gear unit at the forward end of the boom.

b. By rotating the handle, the worm gear rotates the main gear, which rotates the boom, causing the sail to wrap around it. The gear structure requires the tack pin to be mounted farther aft. The sail must be cut back to match.

c. A Roller-Reefed Main

Fig. 180
With roller reefing for cruising boats,
mainsheet leads are attached to a special
fitting at the end of the boom that allows
the boom to rotate.

other important thing to remember: always crank from the windward side, so that you have good footing and can see what you're doing. Unless you can operate your crank from either side of the boom, you have to be on the right tack to reef.

A difficulty with some roller-reefing booms is the adjustment of outhaul tension—these booms have a worm and crank system at the aft end to adjust the tension. The trouble is that you cannot get at it when you are off the wind and want to ease the outhaul to add a little draft in the sail. To make the adjustment, you have to trim the sail.

There is a handier arrangement whereby the outhaul is led over a sheave at the aft end and forward through the boom to a worm-geared winch inside the forward end of the spar (Fig. 181). This enables you to regulate foot tension at any time, using the same handle that operates the reefing gear.

Fig. 181
This system for adjusting foot tension has the outhaul led through a sheave at the end of the boom and forward through the boom to a worm-geared winch near the tack. This permits outhaul adjustment when reaching or running.

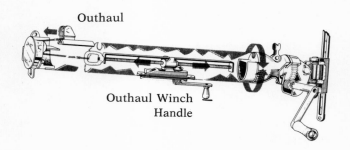

Outhaul

Outhaul Winch
Handle

Mainsails have to be specially cut to accommodate roller reefing. The luff at the tack has to be cut back along the foot as in Figure 179 to allow for the gooseneck fitting and socket and to permit the bolt rope to roll in contiguous turns instead of piling up on itself. This means that the sail leaves its straight-line direction along the mast and moves aft to the roller-reefing tack location. To accommodate the cutback, there is a jackline that runs from eyes on the sail to the three or four lower slides on the track. This line keeps an even tension on the sail as it moves back from the mast. Unfortunately, when you roll the sail up to the point where there is no more cutback, you pull the straight-cut luff aft to a position behind the tack and thus distort the lower part of the sail somewhat.

There is another roller-reefing system (Fig. 182), the proponents of which claim it works extremely well. This consists of gearing inside the mast, which turns the boom. The winch handle is inserted in front of the mast. The gooseneck cannot be raised or lowered, but since modern rigs use the Cunningham hole for mainsail luff tensioning this is not a problem. Of course, with the Cunningham-hole method of tensioning, there is less need to have a sliding gooseneck. In fact, the sliding gooseneck is not really functional anymore, although it probably will not disappear from the scene for many years. Its main purpose nowadays is to allow the boom to be raised or lowered when the sail is hoisted or taken down.

If you want to change your existing rig to roller reefing, you will have to make a number of adjustments, such as moving the mainsheet lead to the end of the boom. The mainsail foot rope or tape will have to be cut back at the tack and reroped. You will not be able to use your old boom if it is not round. The sail track on the mast, if you have it, will need to be rein-

Fig. 182
A system used in Europe places the reef crank handle in front of the mast with the gearing inside the mast. A minimal fitting is thus required on the forward part of the boom.

forced. It is probably already beefed up at the top, where the headboard exerts a heavy strain, as well as down the mast at the point where the headboard would be if you tied in a reef. With roller reefing, however, the track should be reinforced all the way down to the point where the headboard would be located with a maximum rolled-in reef.

Roller reefing is recommended for several reasons: for safety, primarily, but also as a practical means of shortening sail when racing. However, when you are not racing but are faced with a reefing breeze, you have to start with your sail fully hoisted before you roll in a reef.

TYING IN A REEF

Older boats without roller reefing usually have a mainsail with one or more rows of reef points that run horizontally from luff to leech (Fig. 183). At the luff end of the reef line there is a grommet that becomes the tack fitting of the reefed sail. Similarly, there is an eye that serves as the clew of the reefed sail. To tie in a reef, lower the main halyard so that you can secure the new tack fitting right at the gooseneck. A preset line from the end of the boom to the reefing clew serves as an outhaul. Pull out this line until there is normal foot tension along the row of reef points, stretching them out on the boom.

Now gather the folds of the sail along the foot into a tight furl, bunching the excess cloth in an orderly manner along the boom. Tie the reef points

Fig. 183
To tie a reef in the mainsail, the halyard is
lowered and the worked hole at the luff is
secured at the tack. The hole at the leech is
secured to the outhaul and the sail is
furled and tied with reef points.

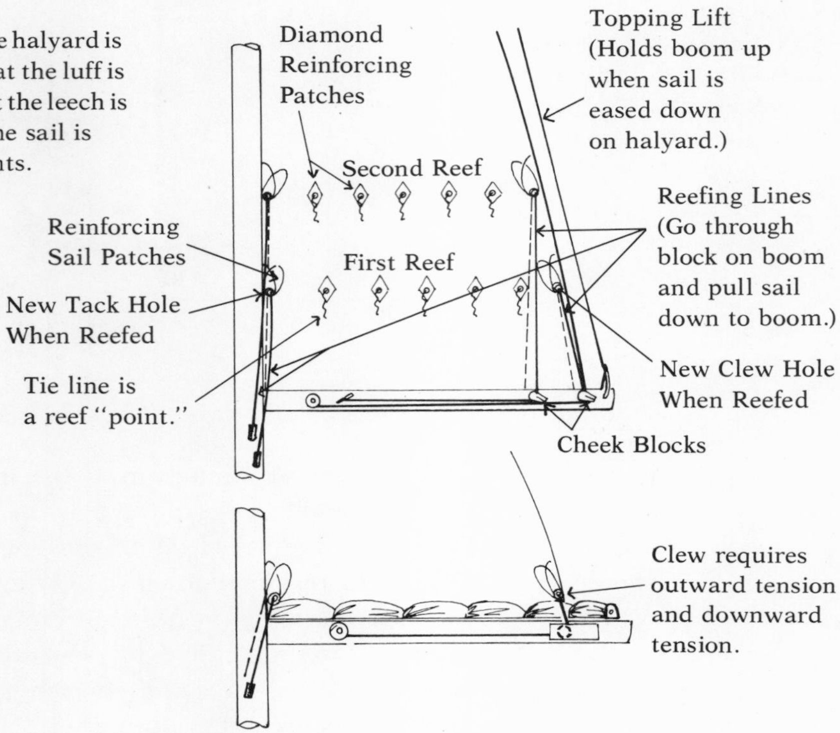

Diamond
Reinforcing
Patches

Second Reef

First Reef

Reinforcing
Sail Patches

New Tack Hole
When Reefed

Tie line is
a reef "point."

Topping Lift
(Holds boom up
when sail is
eased down
on halyard.)

Reefing Lines
(Go through
block on boom
and pull sail
down to boom.)

New Clew Hole
When Reefed

Cheek Blocks

Clew requires
outward tension
and downward
tension.

around the furl, making sure they are tied around the sail itself and not
around the boom or adjacent lines. Then put good strain on the halyard
to take the wrinkles out of the sail and allow it to assume its new shape.

If you elect to put in a second reef, tie it on top of the first, using the
same system and the next row of reef points. As the wind moderates, you
can shake out one reef at a time. This is done by loosening the reef points,
freeing the tack and clew, and hoisting away on the halyard.

SLAB REEFING

A system of shortening sail known as "jiffy reefing" or "slab reefing" is
becoming increasingly popular on racing boats. Many sailors prefer it to
roller reefing because it is a faster way to reduce mainsail area.

Fig. 184
The General Set-up for the Jiffy or Slab
Reefing System

The main difference between standard
reefing and jiffy reefing is the lack of reef
points and the increased speed of reefing
with the jiffy system in boats under 35 to
40 feet.

The flattening reef (Fig. 185a) is done in
the same way as a jiffy reef, but only a
small amount of sail above the boom is
taken in. The aim is to remove excess draft
in the foot area. The leech cringle is placed
at about the same height as the
Cunningham hole, which is used as the
luff end of the flattening reef.

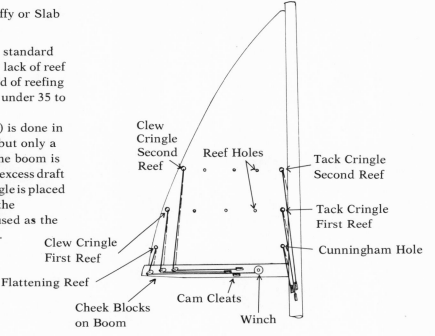

Clew
Cringle
Second
Reef

Reef Holes

Tack Cringle
Second Reef

Tack Cringle
First Reef

Clew Cringle
First Reef

Cunningham Hole

Flattening Reef

Cam Cleats

Cheek Blocks
on Boom

Winch

With this method, the main halyard is dropped to a predetermined
reef level, and the excess sail is gathered in by trimming lines at the tack
and clew points. The boat is set up so that a line is run from the gooseneck
through the reef cringle at the luff down to a sheave and to a winch or jam
cleat on the boom. Similarly, a line is run from the end of the boom through
a reef cringle on the leech and then through a block to a winch on the boom
(Fig. 184).

When you are ready to reef, the sequence on a smaller cruiser (see
Fig. 185b) is to cast off the mainsheet, which releases the downward tension
on the boom. (Be sure to keep the boat underway with the jib or genoa.)
Then, pull the boom up to the leech cringle level and drop the main to the predetermined point so the luff can be tensioned. Excess sail between the luff
and the leech can be secured once the basic reef is tied in (Fig. 185c). It is
important to use the reef points so that the central portion of the sail takes
some of the loading, not just the clew and tack. All this can be done in a
matter of seconds, even in a good breeze. On a larger boat the boom cannot

be raised with the leech reef line. The reef is secured by holding the boom end in position by the topping lift and then dropping the halyard while the leech and luff lines are tensioned (see Fig. 185c).

Fig. 185

a. The steps in securing the flattening reef are:

1. Ease mainsheet;

2. Pull clew-flattening reef line until boom is pulled up to hole; and

3. Pull Cunningham until draft looks correct.

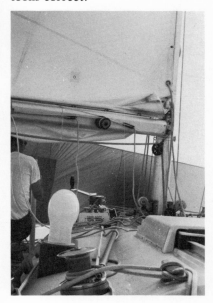

b. The steps in securing the jiffy reef are similar to those for the flattening reef, only the luff (Cunningham) and leech lines are led through the next-higher holes:

1. Ease mainsheet;
2. Pull clew reef line until boom is raised to reef-hole level.
3. Lower main halyard to predetermined point; and tighten luff reefing line.

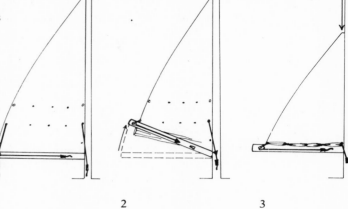

1   2   3

c. The steps in securing the jiffy reef on a larger boat are different because the boom is heavy and cannot be raised:

1. Secure topping lift;
2. Lower main halyard to predetermined point;
3. Tighten both luff and leech reefing lines; secure intermediate reef points in sail, if necessary.

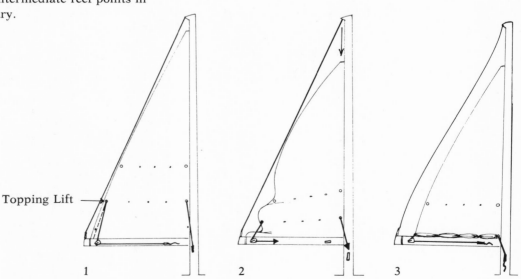

Topping Lift

1   2   3

One of the key factors in this "instant" reefing system is the location of the leech reefing block on the boom. This should be mounted on the boom so that the leech cringle is definitely pulled aft as well as down. This pulls the reefed sail out on the foot and is essential for proper foot tension. However, these blocks are not easy to locate and almost impossible to install before the main has been fitted on and set. Rod Stevens has recommended a method of tying the reef eye to the boom and running the other end to the boom end, thus placing a downward and outboard tension automatically.

The location of the winches on the boom indicates the most convenient tack on which to reef. If the winches are on the starboard side of the boom, it is best to put in your reef on the starboard tack when the gear is to windward.

Remember, if you do not have a topping lift the only thing that keeps the end of the boom from falling on your head is the sailcloth between the head and the clew. Normally, the corners of the sail are built up with reinforcing patches to disseminate the point loading strains from the corners into the body of the sail. However, the leech-reefing cringle and the reef points will get an even higher loading because the sail is only shortened down to this point in heavier airs, and the greater wind force exerts more leech pressure. Therefore, reinforcing patches are sewn on the leech at several points above the boom to absorb the loading. However, it is advisable to have the topping lift in place so that if there are any mistakes in reefing procedure or if the sail tears, the boom will not drop on your head.

THE STORM TRYSAIL

If your boat is overpowered under full-reefed main, you should set a storm trysail, the small triangular sail mentioned above. This sail usually is set on a track that parallels the mainsail luff track in the gooseneck area. The trysail track extends from 3 to 5 feet up the mast to where there is a gate like a railroad track switch. The storm trysail slides are fed onto its track and then the mainsail is lowered on its track so that its slides are below the gate. The storm trysail is hoisted and switches over onto the mainsail track (Fig. 186).

Since the storm trysail has a short luff, it has a pennant or extra line running from the head of the sail to the halyard and another pennant from

Fig. 186
The slides of the storm trysail are first fed onto a separate auxiliary track, and after the mainsail is lowered they are switched over to the mainsail track and the small sail is hoisted. Notice the cutback of the sail to the roller-reefing tack pin.

Track Switch or Gate

Auxiliary Track for Loading Slides of Storm Trysail

Regular Mainsail Track

the tack to the gooseneck. The clew of the sail is trimmed to the end of the boom or on the quarter.

Although this sail is seldom, if ever, used, you would be wise to practice setting it so that you could rig the sail in a hurry if you had to.

ROLLER-FURLING GENOAS

Roller furling, where the genoa rolls up around its luff wire, is, in a sense, related to roller reefing. Roller furling operates somewhat like a window shade, except that you have a furling line which turns a drum at the tack and rolls the sail up as the sheet is played out.

In equipping your boat with roller furling, be sure to get a large enough drum so that you will have the power to roll up your sail all the way in an overpowering breeze. The larger drum will give you more leverage in winding in the sail with the furling line. When you install the drum, make sure it is slightly aft of the headstay, which sometimes can get fouled in the

Fig. 187
The roller-furling system for a jib has a drum at the tack and a swivel at the head of the sail. Reeling up a furling wire on the drum rotates the halyard and rolls in the sail.

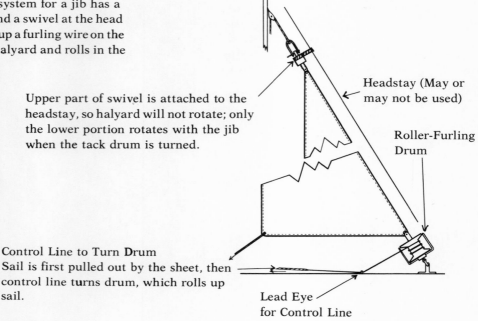

Upper part of swivel is attached to the headstay, so halyard will not rotate; only the lower portion rotates with the jib when the tack drum is turned.

Headstay (May or may not be used)

Roller-Furling Drum

Control Line to Turn Drum
Sail is first pulled out by the sheet, then control line turns drum, which rolls up sail.

Lead Eye
for Control Line

rolling process (unless the roller-reefing rig replaces the headstay) (Fig. 187).

To convert an existing genoa to roller furling, you have to remove the snap hooks, patch the holes, and put on a new luff wire. Usually the luff of the sail will also have to be recut since it is no longer hooked to the headstay for support; the luff will set in a more negative arc.

Roller furling, where the genoa rolls up on its own luff wire, is debatable as a form of reefing and is used strictly as a cruising, not a racing rig. The reason is that the rolling mechanism, a drum, is operated only at the bottom of the sail, so that when normal heavier loadings are placed on the sail itself in a partly wound condition, the upper portion of the sail will tend to unwind. Therefore, roller furling can be used for reaching conditions only when the loads are low. If partially reefed, it would never produce the most efficient racing sail. As a result, it is strictly for a cruising rig and not a racing rig. To minimize this unwinding aloft, a special luff wire that is heavier and more rigid—sometimes even a solid rod—can be installed in the luff of the roller-furling jib. (This creates a problem in stowing the sail below decks, however, as this low-twist wire is very stiff and can only be rolled into a 4- or 5-foot-diameter loop.)

Nevertheless, when used by the cruising sailor, roller furling is a very convenient method of utilizing one sail over many conditions. If you are sailing single-handed, the jib is already in place and it can be unrolled without leaving the cockpit, a good safety feature. Conversely, when you finish sailing, it can be rolled up and left in place indefinitely. Although deterioration caused by sunlight is an important factor, roller-furling jibs are made so that the last 10 or 12 inches of exposed sail around the furl have a covering piece, which acts like a sail cover, to protect against the sun. For either cruising or racing sails, once the wind is overpowering, a storm jib should be used.

Part Four

HARDWARE
AND DECK LAYOUT

Chapter 14

Hardware: Mechanics, Materials, and Properties

The sails of a boat are controlled by various devices, some complex, some simple. The principles on which you should base your choice of these devices, however, are the same. First, the equipment should give you enough mechanical advantage (power) to perform the job with relative ease. Second, the fittings should be strong enough to accept any possible loads, durable enough to withstand normal wear and tear, yet compact and reasonably light in weight. In this chapter, we will first look at the simple mechanical principles on which these devices operate and then discuss what materials are available and desirable, and finally the causes of equipment failure.

MECHANICAL ADVANTAGE

All of the various sail-handling systems have a common problem: they are powered by human muscles. For example, the Cunningham hole on a small one design in a 5-knot breeze can be adjusted with 10 pounds of tension, while in 25 knots of wind it may require 50 pounds of tension. The genoa of a 70-foot sloop may require 5,000 pounds of trimming force in a blow, but regardless of the size, the trimming engine is the same: a human being. Today, with advanced materials, the loads that fittings can handle are rapidly increasing, but large crews of paid hands have all but disappeared. Therefore, efficient use of manpower for the trimming and adjustment of all devices on a boat is imperative.

What is the maximum force a typical crew member is able to provide under normal racing conditions?

A. If a man is pulling on a sheet he can:
   1. Pull directly downward from above with a force equivalent to his weight.
   2. Pull horizontally, standing up with feet braced, approximately 75 pounds with both hands and 50 pounds with one hand.
   3. Pull horizontally, in a hiking position, approximately 100 pounds.
   4. Pull horizontally, while suspended from a trapeze, approximately 150 pounds by using his legs against the boat.
B. If he is pulling adjustment control lines (such as a Cunningham or traveler control) he can comfortably deal with loads of 25 to 35 pounds.

And so, since human force is limited to rather small pulling power, and the tensions the sails require are enormous, some sort of mechanical advantage must be applied through winches, block systems, and other devices if the yachtsman is to keep his boat in proper trim and adjustment in all weather conditions. Since so many women are sailing these days, it is even more important to figure the mechanical advantage needed very carefully.

Once you know the maximum force that a crew member can apply to a particular adjustment, you must then find the maximum force that will be required to make the adjustment in an extreme situation, in order to determine how much mechanical advantage is needed. The best way to find out how much force is required is to rig a temporary lead from the device or sail to be adjusted to a winch, insert a load dynamometer on the line so that it is between the winch and the device, and pull to the amount of maximum adjustment that may possibly be required (Fig. 188). It is best to use only a single line when gauging this, so that *all* the load is measured. If two lines are used, the amount shown on the strain gauge has to be doubled. To measure loads up to 500 pounds, you can buy a hanging tension gauge in a hardware store. To measure the larger loads on genoa halyards, spinnaker pole guys, etc., you need a dynamometer. Naval architects usually have these on hand and some boatyards have them too.

This simple procedure can tell you not only the mechanical advantage needed, but will enable you to determine what the strength of the block or fitting should be.

Mechanical advantage (or power ratio) can be defined as the ratio

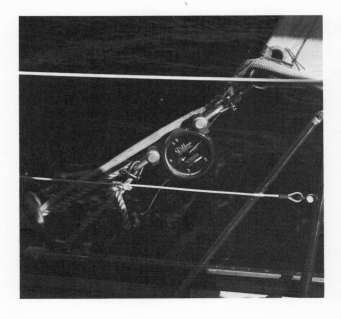

Fig. 188
Strain Gauge.   The loads on a sheet can be measured by a dynamometer mounted before a turning block and secured so that the meter takes the entire strain. The mainsheet load is best measured by a specially rigged single-part sheet with the dynamometer between the boom and sheet end.

of the power that goes into a device to the power that comes out. For example, a mechanical advantage of 4:1 means for every one pound of force applied, 4 pounds of usable force are derived from the device. Thus, you are getting four times the force out that you put in.

The usefulness of mechanical advantage depends on the ratio of power input to output, but as with any device, there are drawbacks to be considered. These are the amounts of relative movement needed to work the device and the amount of friction generated, both of which increase as the mechanical advantage increases.

For example, consider a downhaul that requires 100 pounds of tension to adjust in a certain condition. A crew member has a pulling power of 50 pounds. If a block and tackle rig that has a mechanical advantage of 4:1 is used, he only needs to apply 25 pounds of tension, plus a little extra (5 or 10 per cent) to overcome friction. If the downhaul is to be adjusted 6 inches, then the input line (the line on which the tension is applied) must be moved four times 6 inches, or 2 feet. If the loading on the Cunningham increases to 250 pounds, the crew member who can pull 50 pounds will be unable to adjust it with a 4:1 block and tackle rig but, if the mechanical advantage is increased to 6:1, the crew member will be able to pull a maximum of 300 pounds. At the same time, he will have to take in 6 inches of line on the running end for each inch of adjustment, which could be more unwieldy to handle. An alternative would be to take the 4:1 block and tackle and lead the running end to a winch which supplies additional mechanical advantage. However, this requires additional power input because, besides pulling the line 4 inches for each inch of adjustment, the winch handle is being turned. You have to balance out the advantages and disadvantages for each situation, until you have a system that works easily and gives you the power you need with as little extra effort as possible.

Obviously, efficient operation of a sailboat requires the use of mechanical advantage, and it can be applied by five simple devices: the crank and lever, the gear unit, the drum, the screw, and the block and fall. Common commercial items utilizing the principles of mechanical advantage are the turnbuckle (screw), roller furling (drum), mainsheets and boom vangs (block and tackle), winch handle (crank), and the hyfield lever used for stays and wire control adjustments (lever). Combinations of these principles go into a whole host of items such as winches (drum, gears, and crank) and roller reefing (gears, drum, and crank). We will show how to find the mechanical advantage of each.

Crank and Lever

The mechanical advantage of the lever results from the proportion of the length of the lever arm to the length of the resistance arm. If the lever arm is 3 feet and the resistance arm is 1 foot, the mechanical advantage will be 3:1.

The mechanical advantage of the crank is determined by the proportion of the length of the lever arm to the radius of the drum or gear being turned, which is, in effect, the resistance arm: thus, the crank is very much like a continuous lever.

Both the lever and the crank have high mechanical advantage, low friction, and are simple and able to accommodate high loads. The crank is compact and can handle continuous adjustment but the lever is not compact and can only be used for short-distance adjustments (Fig. 189).

The way in which we have described the crank exactly follows the principle of the single-action winch (non-geared). The winch handle provides the input and the drum the mechanical advantage of the unit. If you have a winch with a 1½-inch-radius drum and a 12-inch-long handle, then

Fig. 189

a. Lever   3:1 MA

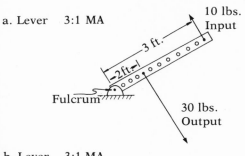

10 lbs.
Input

3 ft.

2 ft.

Fulcrum

30 lbs.
Output

b. Lever   3:1 MA

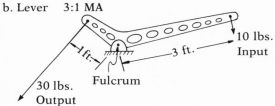

1 ft.

Fulcrum

3 ft.

10 lbs.
Input

30 lbs.
Output

c. Hyfield Lever
5:1 MA to Infinite MA

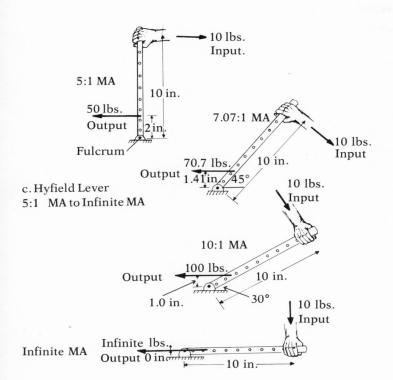

10 lbs.
Input.

5:1 MA

10 in.

50 lbs.
Output

2 in.

Fulcrum

7.07:1 MA

10 lbs.
Input

70.7 lbs.
Output

10 in.

1.41 in.

45°

10 lbs.
Input

10:1 MA

100 lbs.
Output

10 in.

1.0 in.

30°

10 lbs.
Input

Infinite MA

Infinite lbs.
Output 0 in

10 in.

d. Crank   10:1   MA

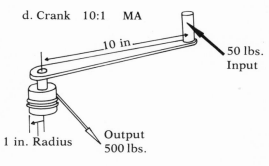

10 in.

50 lbs.
Input

1 in. Radius

Output
500 lbs.

the rope the winch is pulling is being pulled with eight times the force applied to the winch handle, i.e., a winch with these dimensions has a mechanical advantage of 8:1 (Fig. 190).

Fig. 190
Crank as a Winch

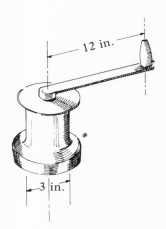

Handle radius = 12 in.
Drum diameter = 3 in.
Drum radius = 1.5 in.
MA = 12/1.5 or 8:1

Drum

The drum is a device similar to the lever and crank or winch. It actually consists of two drums: the inner drum (corresponding to a drum connected to a crank) and the outer drum (which corresponds to the arc of the crank handle). It is used mostly for raising and lowering the centerboard and sometimes for one-design vangs. A line raising or lowering the centerboard is wound around a small drum, to which it is permanently attached. It is married to the larger drum, which is controlled by another line led back to the cockpit area where it is operated. The mechanical advantage is found in the same way as the crank and winch above: it results from the proportion of the radius of the large drum to the radius of the small drum. The bigger the drum, the easier it is to adjust. However, you have to consider the bulk of the drum and also the amount of line you are going to reel off.

The drum utilizes the crank principle but it is more compact and accommodates long adjustment lengths. It is sometimes hard to mount and will break if misused. Using a rope or wire or both, the drum has a high mechanical advantage and low friction (Fig. 191).

The crank, the drum, and the winch work on the similar principle of turning a larger radius (input) to produce a greater output on the smaller radius (drum or spindle).

Gear Unit

Gear units are used to transfer power and force in the form of twisting motion called torque. Crank handles produce torque, defined as force times the length of the arm from shaft to force. In the case of Figure 189, the crank handle is producing 50 pounds times 10 inches or 500 lb.-in. of torque. The drum to which the crank is attached is experiencing 500 lb.-in. of torque, and since its arm is 1 inch, the force being exerted on the surface of the drum is 500 pounds.

Gear units transfer torque from one shaft to another; by the use of different-size gears, cogged together, the torque can be changed by the mechanical advantage of the gear unit. The mechanical advantage is calculated by the proportion of the output gear diameter divided by the input gear diameter (Fig. 191a).

This unit has the advantage of being compact, fast, and continuous in operation. But it has medium to low mechanical advantage and also requires lubrication and high precision in manufacturing.

Fig. 191

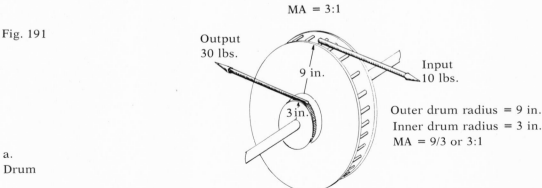

MA = 3:1

Output
30 lbs.

9 in.

Input
10 lbs.

3 in.

Outer drum radius = 9 in.
Inner drum radius = 3 in.
MA = 9/3 or 3:1

a.
Drum

b. The gear unit has the advantage of being compact and fast in operation, but it has low mechanical advantage and also requires lubrication.

In a winch, two or more gears may be used to produce the MA required.

Gears

$$MA = \frac{\text{Diameter Output}}{\text{Diameter Input}} = \frac{6}{3} = 2:1$$

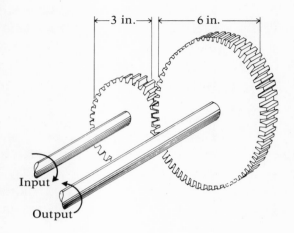

c. Gear Chain
Multiply for mechanical advantage.
$MA = 3 \times 2 = 6:1$

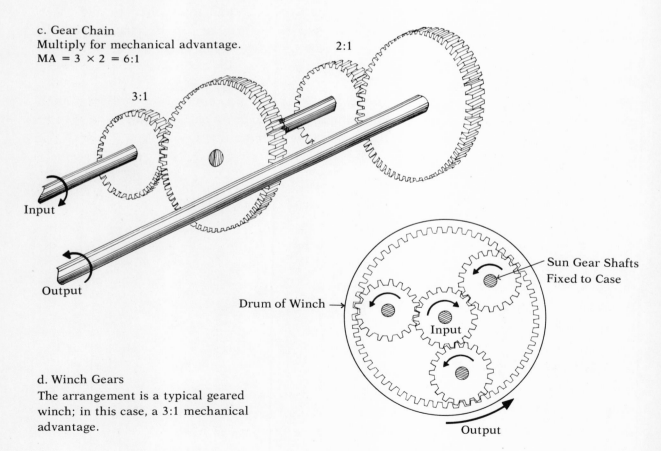

d. Winch Gears
The arrangement is a typical geared winch; in this case, a 3:1 mechanical advantage.

With a geared winch in which one gear is set inside, the mechanical advantage is simply the multiple of the mechanical advantage of the crank and drum unit times the mechanical advantage of the gear unit. If we take the single-action winch with a mechanical advantage of 8:1 in Figure 190 and put a set of 3:1 gears inside, the total mechanical advantage of the winch will be $3:1 \times 8:1 = 3 \times 8 = 24:1$.

In geared winches, the clusters of gears increase the mechanical advantage by a multiple equal to the size and number of gears used. The gears multiply the mechanical advantage of the simple single-action winch previously described.

Screw

The screw is a threaded shaft: when the screw is turned, it moves in the body or housing into which it fits. The mechanical advantage derived from the inclined plane of the screw threads is figured by the number of threads per inch. If you have too few threads per inch, you cannot handle heavy loads because the inclined plane of the thread will be too steep. In general, the greater the load, the finer the thread should be. On the other hand, the threads have to be deep enough to catch hold, and the threads' angle of pitch low enough so that the screw can be turned under a fairly high load. The more the angle of pitch, the greater the friction when turning. Generally, turnbuckles will need an auxiliary turning device such as a screwdriver, crank handle, or wrench. This gives you an additional mechanical advantage of a difference in lever arm length. To insure that the screw will not snap at maximum loads, the shaft diameter should be roughly one and a half times that of the wire used in stays and shrouds. Aside from turnbuckles, the screw is used in nut and bolt fastenings on a boat.

The screw has high mechanical advantage and low friction. It is compact and provides precise self-locking adjustment. However, it is slow to operate and requires lubrication (Fig. 192).

Block and Tackle

The mechanical advantage of the block and tackle can be figured by counting the tensioned strands pulling on the turning block or moving end of the system: the more strands, the more mechanical advantage. This is caused

Fig. 192
Screw (Crank Turnbuckle)

MA = 6(Crank-Arm Length) (Number of
Threads Per Inch)
Example: MA = 6 × 3 × 10 = 180:1

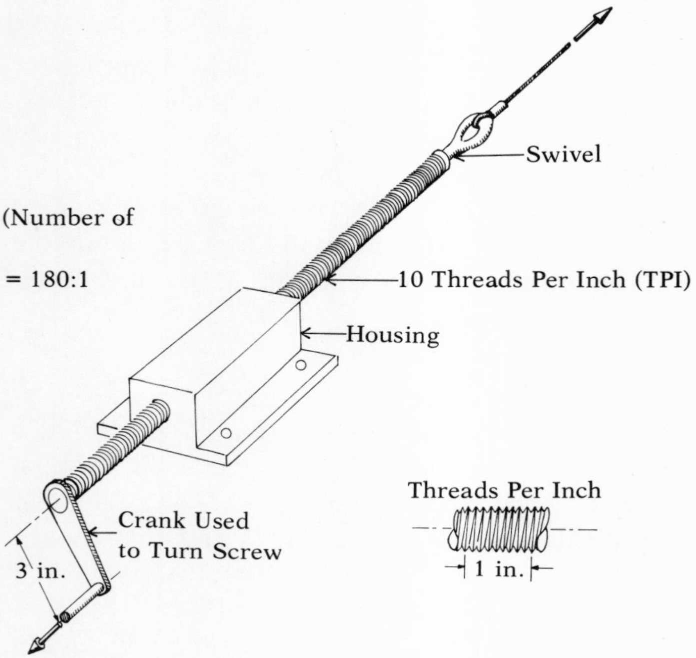

Swivel

10 Threads Per Inch (TPI)

Housing

Crank Used
to Turn Screw

3 in.

Threads Per Inch

1 in.

by the fact that tension seeks an equilibrium; the tension applied to one strand will be duplicated on each of the other strands. For example, if you run a line through a block and hold both ends—one in each hand—and exert a pull of 10 pounds on each, the load on the turning block is 20 pounds. However, by tying one end and pulling only on the other you get the same effect, but the mechanical advantage is 2:1 (Fig. 193a). The rope seeks a constant tension throughout, so that both strands will still have 10 pounds of tension and the turning block therefore has 20 pounds of load exerted on it. The fixed point, however, will only have 10 pounds of force working on it (Fig. 193b).

The total force generated by the block and tackle system is found by multiplying the number of strands from the particular block that is being moved by the force on the running or free end (Fig 193c).

A block-and-tackle system can have its mechanical advantage changed, depending on the way it is set up. For example, when used as a

Fig. 193

a. If each strand of the line is held, one in each hand, at a load of 10 pounds per strand, the load on the block will be the total of the two strands or 20 pounds.

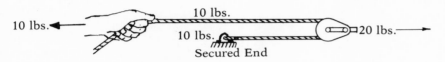

b. Even if one end is fastened, if a load of 10 pounds is applied to the other end each line will have 10 pounds of loading, so both strands are still totaled to get the same 20 pounds on the block.

c. Total loading on a block can be found by multiplying the loading on a strand times the number of strands.

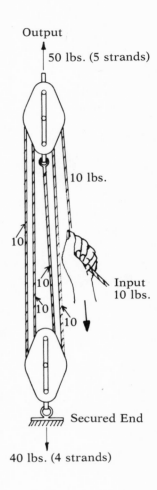

vang with the running end coming downward from the boom (the moving part), you get an additional strand of pulling power on the boom (Fig. 194a). By having the running end come up from the deck, you waste the additional strand because it is not exerting any downward pull on the boom block (Fig. 194b). Just by rearranging the system to shift the cleating position of the running end, you gain mechanical advantage without any increase in friction or length of line.

To figure the strength of the fittings needed for the block and tackle system, you first count the strands coming from the particular block that is

Fig. 194
The mechanical advantage of the block
and tackle is changed by the terminal
cleat position of the running end.

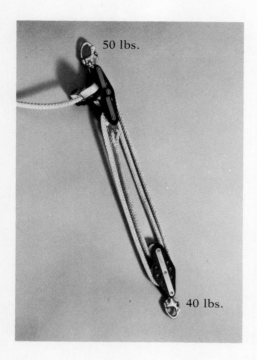

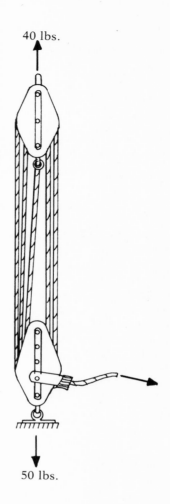

being moved. Then, you multiply the force exerted on the free end by the
number of strands. Theoretically, this would give you the total force. However, there is another factor involved in block loading. This is the turning
angle—the angle between the straight-line projection of the line's entering
direction and the line's departing direction, after turning the sheave (Fig.
195a). Once the line starts to bend around the sheave, the loads on the
sheave increase until at 180 degrees they reach the maximum sheave loading of twice the line tension. If the block and tackle has only 180-degree-
turns—that is, if there is a complete reversal of direction of the rope when
turning the sheave—the equilibrium of the strands produces a tension of 10

pounds in each strand (Fig. 195b). The sheave around which the strand turns will bear the total load of both strands or 20 pounds. Conversely, if a line is tensioned in a straight line through a block, the turning angle is zero, the line still has 10 pounds of tension, and the load on the block will be zero (Fig. 195c).

Fig. 195
The sheave load varies with the turning angle. The direction of the load bisects the angle.

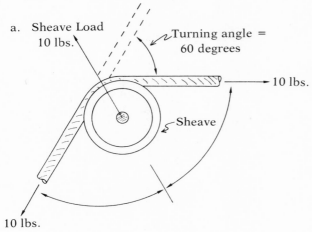

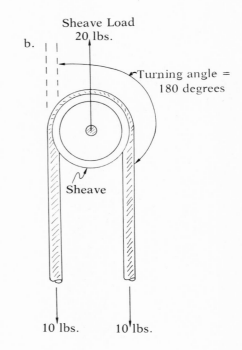

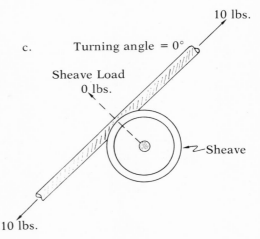

Thus, knowing the line tension and knowing the block loading factor for a specific angle (see Fig. 196 and the chart below) will allow you to calculate the maximum loading on the block, which in turn determines block strength required.

If the turning angle is:	The block loading factor is:	If line tension is 100 lbs., it will exert loading on block of:
0°	0	0 lbs.
30° line tension x	.518	51.8 lbs.
45° line tension x	.767	76.7 lbs.
60° line tension x	1.00	100 lbs.
90° line tension x	1.414	141.4 lbs.
120° line tension x	1.732	173.2 lbs.
135° line tension x	1.846	184.6 lbs.
150° line tension x	1.931	193.1 lbs.
180° line tension x	2.0	200 lbs.

Fig. 196
The sheave load varies with the turning angle.
Sheave load = turning-angle factor × line load.

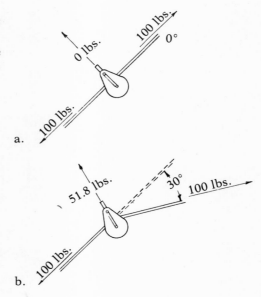

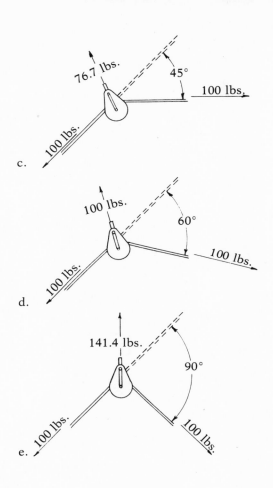

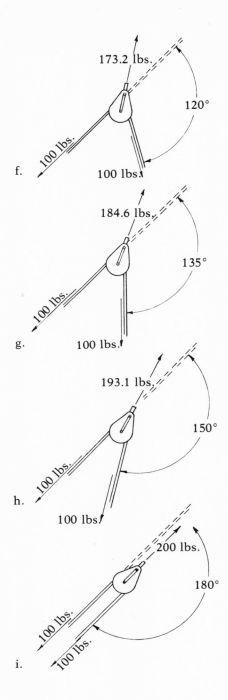

Therefore, the same line tension will produce different loads on various turning blocks, depending on the angle of the turn (Fig. 197).

Fig. 197
Here is a breakdown of the major components of the rig of a sloop to show how you would determine the loads that they undergo. (Loads and angles are approximate.)

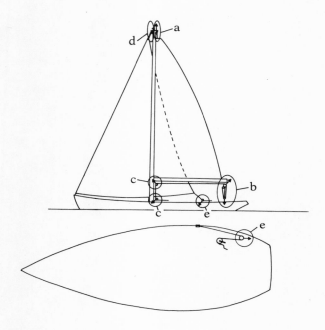

a. Main halyard sheave has a 180-degree turning angle.

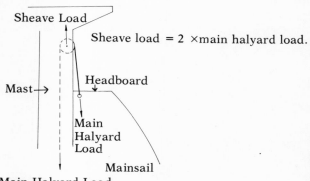

Sheave load = 2 ×main halyard load.

Example: if main halyard load = 300 lbs., then sheave load = 2 × 300 = 600 lbs.

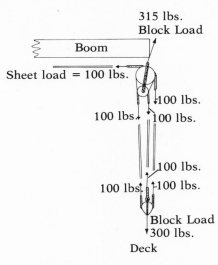

315 lbs.
Block Load

Boom

Sheet load = 100 lbs.

100 lbs.

100 lbs. | 100 lbs.

100 lbs.

100 lbs. | 100 lbs.

Block Load
300 lbs.

Deck

b. Mainsheet Loads
Two sheaves on one block require
calculation of combined sheet loads and
angles of two sheaves by plotting.

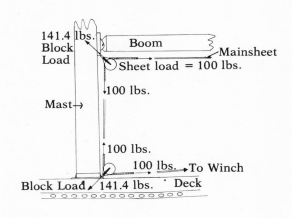

141.4 lbs.
Block
Load

Boom

Mainsheet

Sheet load = 100 lbs.

100 lbs.

Mast→

100 lbs.

100 lbs. →To Winch

Block Load 141.4 lbs.   Deck

c. Mainsheet Loads

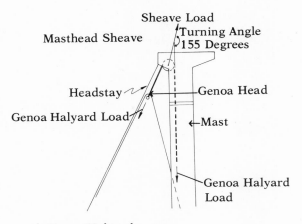

Sheave Load

Masthead Sheave

Turning Angle
155 Degrees

Headstay

Genoa Head

Genoa Halyard Load

←Mast

Genoa Halyard
Load

d. Genoa Halyard
Sheave Load = 1.95 × genoa halyard load.
genoa halyard load
Example: if Genoa halyard load = 100
lbs., sheave load = 1.95 ×
1,000 lbs. = 1,950 lbs.

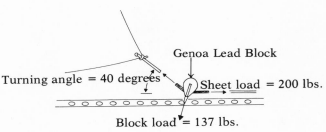

Turning angle = 40 degrees

Genoa Lead Block

Sheet load = 200 lbs.

Block load = 137 lbs.

e. Genoa Sheet Blocks

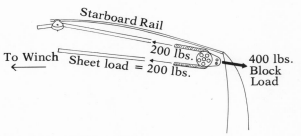

Starboard Rail

200 lbs.

To Winch   Sheet load = 200 lbs.

400 lbs.
Block
Load

e. Genoa Turning Block

A main halyard generally turns about 180 degrees, so the load on the sheave is double the halyard load. The mainsheet can have several different turning angles on various blocks, including some blocks, such as double or fiddle blocks, that have two separate loading conditions on the same fitting.

On the other hand, the genoa halyard block or staysail blocks turn less than 180 degrees—usually 140–160 degrees—so the loading on the block is slightly less than double. However, the halyard itself is usually under much higher tension than the main halyard; therefore the sheave (and particularly the axle pin) has to be considerably stronger.

Thus, the same line tension will require different strength blocks in different turning positions. A halyard turn is close to 150 degrees, and so the load on the block is 1.91 times the halyard tension. If the halyard turns a block at deck level at 90 degrees, the load would be 1.4 times the line tension.

Genoa blocks have a large variance in this loading. If the genoa sheet is led from the clew through a deck block and then directly to a winch, the line angle change might be only 20 or 30 degrees, producing a low block loading. However, if the sheet is led aft to a turning block and then forward to the winch, the sheet will make a 180-degree turn and the block loading will be double the line load.

Bear in mind that if the sheet were tied aft so that the cleat replaced the turning block, the load on the cleat would be half of the load on the turning block! This principle is also true of halyard locks. Generally, if the halyard is locked aloft, the downward compression force exerted on the mast is reduced by half.

Friction

Any device utilizing mechanical advantage has the mathematical ratio reduced by friction. Under load, one surface bears against and moves against another: i.e., sheave = axle against the bushing or spindle; gear = gear tooth vs. gear tooth; screw = screw vs. housing; etc.

Although friction is generally regarded as a deterrent it can be an asset also. For example, when a sheet or halyard is motionless but hand-held, friction helps take some of the loading. While pulling in friction requires more input and increases the load on the input block by 10 to 20 per cent, once the pulling is over and the line is secure, friction may contribute to holding power and decrease loading on the line.

When several blocks are involved in a mainsheet system, one block can be a friction block which absorbs much of the load on the running end while all the others are ball-bearing blocks. Friction is thus purposely used as an asset, just like the drag control on a fishing reel—the sheave turns easily one way but not the other.

The extreme of this action is a ratchet block or a winch. When loads are too high for the friction principle, the sheave or winch drum is retarded from turning backward by a pawl which catches in "V"-shaped notches around the edge of the sheave or drum and stops the reverse action completely, much like a window shade.

When an extreme load is applied to bearings, axles, and other frictioned surfaces, if the materials are different, one material—usually the harder—will wear away the other, so the device is only as strong as the softer material.

If the materials are identical and the loads are heavy enough, the two materials will imbed into one another. In metals, this is called galling and causes two moving parts such as a turnbuckle to lock up and not function. A stainless slider under load will not work on a stainless track, but it will slide on a bronze track. (Certain metals cannot, however, be used together, as a galvanic reaction occurs and causes severe erosion. See below, p. 323.)

Therefore, when high-friction loads are unavoidable, dissimilar metals, or a metal and a plastic or metal coated with a plastic lubricator, are used to prevent galling. (Oils and greases are, of course, used to counter friction, and help to prevent galling at high loads.)

So the real solution, when applicable, is the use of ball or roller bearings to cut down the friction. Consequently, ball bearings are used in blocks, travelers, and winches. Ball bearings have the lowest friction of all types of bearings, roller bearings are next, then specially lubricated bearings.

FITTING PROPERTIES

With information about the loads generated on fittings in various applications, one can choose the right fitting made of the proper metals and/or plastics.

Here are some of the areas for consideration:

1. Fittings should be as light as possible and yet strong enough to avoid distortion or breaking. Thus, you have to consider:
   a. The strength-to-weight ratio of the materials used.
   b. The definition of a safe working load, the load at which the fitting will work plus a large safety margin for extraordinary load situations.
2. All metals have the following strength characteristics to consider (all of which apply to plastics also):
   a. Shear—resistance to transverse cut.
   b. Tensile—resistance to pulling apart.
   c. Compressive—resistance to crushing.
   d. Yield—strength before permanent deformation.
   e. Elongation—amount of stretch under tension.
   f. Creep—prolonged stress producing, over a period of time, gradual and continuous elongation.
   g. Fatigue—resistance to repeated large loadings, particularly to repeated stress reversals (bending back and forth under load).
   h. Hardness—obtained by temperature control in metals to produce higher yield strength; this can make the material more brittle.
   i. Stress—load in pounds per square inch.
   j. Strain—elongation as a per cent of initial length.
   k. Stress corrosion—stress due to processing or endurance of high loads.

Strength Characteristics

A. Shear Strength

Shear strength, simply, is a metal's resistance to transverse rupture. It is not related to tensile strength, which is the resistance to longitudinal pull. Shear is a cleavage load caused by combined pushing or pulling loads 90 degrees from the axis. An everyday example of shear would be the breaking of a dowl rod which protruded above a table top and was broken off as the table top was being planed—the plane, in hitting the peg, caused rupture at the planing surface. This is exactly the way a bolt or rivet is sheared (Fig. 198). Another example would be a bolt used as a pulley axle, which shears as the load on the pulley exceeds the shear value of the bolt. For bolts and

Fig. 198
Shear.

Shear is a transverse loading
that is perpendicular to the axis of the bolt
or screw.

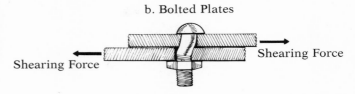

b. Bolted Plates

Shearing Force   Shearing Force

a. Shear

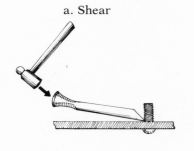

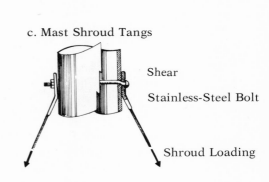

c. Mast Shroud Tangs

Shear

Stainless-Steel Bolt

Shroud Loading

screws, shear can be calculated, on a rule of thumb basis, to be two-thirds of the working tensile strength of a given material for normal metals, one half for brittle metals, and one tenth for most wood.

B. Tensile Strength

Tensile strength, a metal's resistance to being pulled apart longitudinally, is its most important characteristic. Tensile strength figures (pounds per square inch) are used as a common standard in comparing different materials. There is, further, a relationship between the hardness and the tensile strength of a given alloy. The harder it is, the more tensile strength it has. Tensile strength is important to watch in connection with "inline" or longitudinal loading, such as on shroud material, turnbuckle ends, and all bolting requirements.

C. Compressive Strength

This is a material's resistance to being deformed or crushed. A prime example is the sheave in a block. The rope or wire turning the top of the sheave compresses the sheave against the axle. Under enough stress, the sheave may crack or disintegrate.

D. Yield Strength

Yield strength is a measure of resistance to permanent deformation of material subjected to longitudinal loading. It is the point at which the material exhibits a very small specified permanent deformation. This occurs in blocks where the pin exerts so much pressure on the cheek of the block that the hole in the cheek yields and grows larger. The original shape has been deformed (Fig. 199). Thus, when selecting a block, for example, you have to check to see that the cheek is thick enough so it will not distort from the shear loading of the pin.

E. Elongation

Generally, the extension of a material in a tension test at any specified load is considered elongation (Fig. 200). Specifically, the extension of a material at the rupture load is the *stretch* span involved. It is an indicator of ductility in various alloys. Shroud stretch is an example of elongation; it is important that you get a shroud that is large enough in diameter to minimize elongation and keep your rig constant. The manufacturers can supply the elongation figures.

F. Creep

Creep is the slow elongation of a material under a constant large load over a period of time. It is important that a material's resistance to creep be low, especially if it is going to be under tension for a long period of time, such as shrouds in a long-distance race. Creep can just keep on to the point where it breaks under the loading. So many parts of a boat are under sustained loading that creep strength is a key consideration for safety. Plastics—and to a smaller degree, some exotic, lightweight alloys—are particularly susceptible to creep while most metals are not.

G. Fatigue

Fatigue is the failure of a metal due to repeated loads, first in one direction and then another. The simplest form of fatigue is that which occurs when thin metal is bent back and forth and finally breaks (Fig. 201). (The up and down motion of an airplane wing is a classic example.)

Fig. 199
Yield.   Yield is the first sign of
permanent deformation of the material
under stress.

Fig. 200
Elongation.   As a metal elongates under
load, its cross-section gets thinner and
weaker and could eventually break.

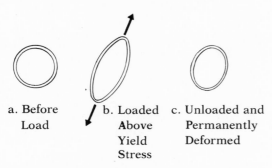

a. Before
   Load

b. Loaded
   Above
   Yield
   Stress

c. Unloaded and
   Permanently
   Deformed

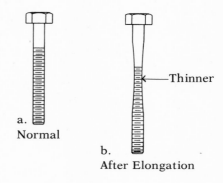

a. Normal

b. After Elongation

—Thinner

Example: the stainless strap on the cheek
of the block undergoes yield when the
sheave axle hole elongates permanently.

Permanent Deformation

Fig. 201
Metal fatigue is most likely to occur when
there are continual and repeated stress
reversals in bending loads: for example, a
metal tang flexed back and forth for a
sustained period can be weakened and
eventually broken through fatigue.

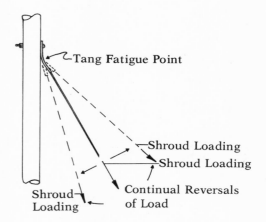

Tang Fatigue Point

Shroud Loading

Shroud Loading

Continual Reversals
of Load

Shroud
Loading

H. Hardness

Many of the above strength characteristics are enhanced by temperature
control or heat treatment during the manufacture of fittings. The proper
temperature in the arc furnace, the extrusion process of the material about
to be forged, and the final heat treatment may all affect the finished product.

Proper temperature control at the arc furnace assures that the ingot will meet specifications. Temperature control of the extrusion process makes the difference in surface finish and inside molecular grain, and allows the metal to be extruded. Controlled annealing is another heat control process used on the finished product. All of these processes make a stronger, more durable fitting.

I. Stress

Stress is load measured in pounds per square inch. A rod that is one inch square in cross-section has stress equal to the load. The stress on a rod ¼ inch square in cross-section is four times the load. Conversely, the stress on a 2-inch-square section is one quarter of the load.

J. Strain

Strain is the amount of deformation resulting from the stress demonstrated in elongation, compression, or shear. It is measured in decimal inches of change per inch of length. If a rod 10 inches long elongates under stress to 10.01 inches strain, its strain is indexed as .001.

Thus, the stress/strain relationship, a phrase commonly used by engineers, is the modules of elasticity of a material measured by the amount of deformation (strain) from various stresses (load in pounds per square inch).

Stress Corrosion

Stress corrosion concerns the behavior of metal under the combined action of internal stresses due to cold working* or fatigue and external stresses due to enduring high loads (Fig. 202). Some metals may show a greater acceleration of corrosion than others under the combination of internal stresses and external loads. This has no relation to their tensile strength. Some of the strongest metals in the world suffer stress corrosion. Thus, depending upon circumstances, the selection of the proper alloy should include consideration of the environment, the external loads to which the alloy will be subject, and the manner of manufacture of the alloy.

*A method of shaping metal through compression that adds considerably to its hardness and strength.

Fig. 202
Stress Corrosion.   Certain metals under
permanently high loading can develop
microscopic stress cracks that corrode
and grow larger, eventually forming a pit
and weakening the local area.

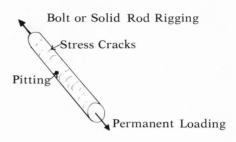

Bolt or Solid Rod Rigging

Stress Cracks

Pitting

Permanent Loading

STRENGTH-TO-WEIGHT ASPECTS

Strength-to-weight ratio is one of the most important things to consider when choosing a fitting. It refers to the ratio between the tensile strength and the weight of the item. Some metals are very light, yet very strong, giving them a high strength-to-weight ratio. The titanium alloys can produce equal tensile strength to some of the carbon steel alloys, but the titanium alloys weigh 58 per cent less. Aluminum is two-thirds the weight of titanium but only one fifth the strength.* Because of its light weight and high strength, titanium is the most desirable metal to use aloft. However, it is so expensive that it is not in common use.

On smaller boats, the strength of the fitting, like that of sailcloth, is much greater in proportion to the hull weight and the fitting loads. Also, because of sheer numbers, far more is known about the performance of small-boat fittings than about those made for larger boats. Testing of the larger fittings needed for the greater loads of big boats is very expensive, and consequently advances in materials and design are not as rapid as they are in small boats. Many fittings for a large boat could be made better, stronger, more functional, and at one third to half the weight, but the more sophisticated metals and methods used for relatively small production runs make these fittings quite expensive. Custom fittings are designed for the 12-Meter Cup defenders and there is some spinoff from this. However, a 72-foot ocean racer, which may weigh 95,000 pounds and sail in gale-force winds, probably has two to three times the loading of a Twelve, which is

*These relationships change as the aluminum or titanium alloys vary.

approximately 65 feet long but weighs only about 60,000 pounds and is never started in over 25 knots of wind. Thus, this research is only part of the answer.

Engineering terminology is best used to describe a fitting's strength properties: *ultimate strength* is the breaking point of a fitting, while *working strength* is the maximum usable strength of the fitting and is always lower than ultimate strength. What separates these two values is an area where the fitting may be permanently harmed but not break. To take a common example: if a rubber band is stretched and when unloaded returns to its original length, then its working strength has not been exceeded. But, if it is stretched and when unloaded is longer than before, its working strength has been exceeded, and the extra length is called permanent distortion. If the rubber band breaks, then its ultimate strength has been exceeded. The difference between the working strength and the ultimate strength is very important and gives a material a built-in *factor of safety*. Brittle materials, china and tool steels, etc., have a working strength and ultimate strength that are the same. When these materials are overloaded they give no warning and fail catastrophically. Mild structural steel, such as the wire in a coat hanger, fails somewhat less dramatically, and there is enough time to correct the overload.

With fittings, this factor of safety is particularly important because of the surge loads that can develop as a boat is pounded in a seaway or the shock loading that occurs when a sail suddenly fills away and snaps smartly on the sheet. Foul leads, as well, put an abnormal stress on the fitting.

The easiest way to evaluate a material is by comparison of its strength-to-weight ratio, while taking into account both ultimate strength and safe working load. Since fittings are fabricated from a variety of materials, here is a comparison of the most popular fitting materials showing weight, maximum working strength, and strength-to-weight ratio. The higher the number of the strength-to-weight ratio, the better the material.

MATERIALS

Stainless steel and plastics generally are used for small-boat fittings because they are the easiest lightweight fittings to make and they are strong enough for small-boat loadings. Stainless in thin, flat sheet configurations and plastics in molded configurations, however, do not have the strength needed for large boats. For these boats, thicker stainless stampings and aluminum are now being used in place of the heavy bronze fittings formerly used. Compared to bronze, stainless steel and the 17/4 pH stainless alloy have the great advantage of good strength when cast. Although it cannot be classified as a true stainless steel because it is magnetic, 17/4 pH is a precipitated hardened steel and nevertheless has fair salt-water resistance. Stainless steel and 17/4 pH cast or forged fittings are expensive to make and difficult to machine.

Aluminum fittings are used extensively in medium- to low-loading situations. Although it has a medium strength-to-weight ratio, aluminum is the easiest metal to fabricate, particularly by casting or stamping. On the other hand, aluminum can be one of the most sophisticated metals to deal with: there are many alloys which vary in strength, finish, and salt-water resistance. Cast aluminum is the weakest; forged aluminum is stronger; and aluminum fittings made by extrusion or machined from solid bars have almost double the strength of cast fittings. Fittings for low-loading situations, such as cleats and chocks, are made from cast aluminum; masts are made from extruded aluminum. Cam cleats are made from forged or extruded aluminum. When you have an intricate shape that must be cast or forged, such as a cam, cleat, or chock, the cost is usually most reasonable if aluminum is used.

Like iron, aluminum will oxidize and corrode unless the outer surface is protected by either paint or a process called anodizing, in which a hard, inert coating is applied to the outer surface. Titanium requires the same treatment.

Titanium fittings parts are made mostly from sheet stamping, since casting and forging are quite difficult. Some extrusions are made for traveler tracks and mast sections. Titanium tangs and fabricated masthead configurations are used to minimize weight aloft.

Carbon fiber, which rivals titanium in its high strength-to-weight ratio, is difficult to work with. It is becoming available but is very expensive. Berylium copper is very strong but is also very hard to manufacture and is not in extensive use.

Magnesium is not used much because of its very high corrosiveness in salt water. It is also very bulky.

Plastics

Plastics such as nylon, Delrin, and fiberglass have their own special properties and are usually quite different from metals. The thermoplastics such as nylon and Delrin have low wear-resistance, low elasticity, and relatively high yield but are cheap and easy to manufacture by molding. They are very low in friction and can be used as a lubricant between metals.

Plastics are light and, therefore, can be used in bulky applications—such as a thick cheek of a block. Blocks made with plastic walls are usually reinforced with stainless straps from pin to pin.

Fiberglass is stronger under tension than thermoplastics but more brittle. A fiberglass fitting is not easy or cheap to manufacture. However, glass fibers can be used with nylon or Delrin to add significant strength to the plastic, while retaining the easy and low-cost molding process.

Plastics have a fair compression resistance and, therefore, are widely used for sheaves. The low friction also allows the sheaves to turn readily under moderate loads.

Often a fitting is made by mixing materials, each of which will be chosen according to the strength requirements of that part of the fitting. A simple block, for example, may be composed of four different materials. In Figure 203, the holding strap, the cheek straps, and the sheave pin, which are the main strength members of the fitting, are all stainless. The connector between the holding strap and the cheeks should also be stainless but, to save expense, can be made of bronze. The cheek can be nylon for a small boat fitting or aluminum for a medium boat because all the cheek has to do is hold the rope on the sheave. This is not a high-load situation, but the cheek should not bend. The sheave can be nylon for fairly high loads. Thus, each part of the block is made of a material suited to its function.

WHY FITTINGS FAIL

In thinking about the strength of deck hardware, it is important to consider the system as well as the individual piece of equipment. Too often you will find a high-strength masthead halyard block attached to a tang with half the strength of the block or a high-strength block connected to a deck pad

Fig. 203
Mixing Materials in a Block.   Metals sometimes have to be mixed, so that the strongest metals are used at the highest stressed points.

a. Stainless Holding Strap—needs high tensile load
b. Bronze Connector—needs high tensile load
c. Nylon Cheek—needs rigidity and low yield
d. Stainless Cheek Strap—needs high tensile and low yield
e. Stainless Bushing
f. Nylon Sheave—needs high crush resistance
g. Stainless Axle or Pin—needs high shear resistance and low elasticity

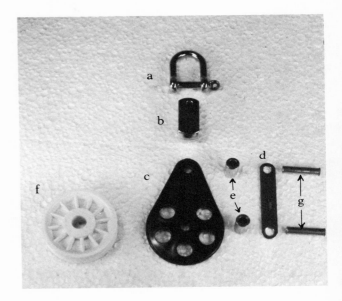

with a shackle that has half the strength of the block. This is a common error, and unless you think of the whole strength system — the fitting, the device to which it is attached, and the unit that makes the attachment — you have the classic situation of the weakest link in the chain causing a failure.

This strength problem does not apply just to fittings. A certain place in the deck might not be strong enough to hold a fitting, and the deck could pull up. A mast section to which a high-strength unit is attached might not have enough strength to hold two or three bolts. You should examine areas of greatest loadings, such as halyard blocks or turning blocks where lines have a 180-degree or even a 90-degree turn. At these points, you have to watch the components for their individual strengths and also watch for misleads. For instance, a fitting that is anchored by a ball and socket might have a scope of 30 degrees in a side-to-side motion. If this block is pulled sideways at a 40-degree angle, high leverage loading might break the ball and socket. Blocks anchored to deck fittings have a tendency to flop over when not in use and when raised again might hang up at an angle that could put too great a leverage on the attachment devices.

Equipment failure on all sizes of boats usually occurs because of loading other than the direct loading for which the fitting was designed. This is particularly true of most sheet blocks, lead blocks, travelers, and turning blocks, including not only stern turning blocks for genoa sheets and spinnaker guys but also genoa and spinnaker halyard blocks.

It is safe to estimate that a great majority of fitting failure is caused by misuse. Most manufacturers test their fittings and publish the results. Testing is usually done with the fitting at the alignment in which it was designed and is to be used, and in this situation it usually has a wide safety margin. However, nonalignment places a large load in an untested direction which the fitting was not designed or constructed to handle. Here are some examples:

A. A snatch block is usually led from an eye or bale, allowing it to swing in a full scope. However, if the shackle is put into a deck rail and used as a turning block, the misuse causes two extra-ordinary loads: (1) side loading on the shackle at a high leverage angle instead of the normal inline direction, which could break the shackle; (2) the line is pulled into the side wall of the block instead of directly on the sheave. With enough load the sheet can be wedged between the sheave and the wall, making it inoperative and ruining the block (Fig. 204). Recently a new hinged snatch block has been introduced to relieve this problem.

Fig. 204

a. When a snatch block is used as a turning block, it should lie flat against the deck. If the snap shackle is secured into a rail hole, however, it cannot lie flat. Thus, high-torque loadings are created, which are one of the main causes of breakage, damage, or jumped sheaves.

b. This can be avoided by using a lead shackle from the rail hole to the top of the rail track. The snap shackle is then attached to that.

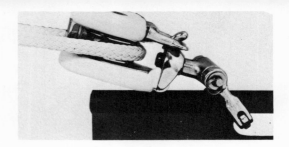

c. A new design has a swivel in the snap shackle to lower torque loading.

B. A flush-mounted halyard sheave set into the mast is used for a hankless genoa or staysail. The side loading of the sail causes the wire halyard to bear toward the side of the sheave box, and if there is any space between the sheave and the side wall, the wire could "jump the sheave" (Fig. 205). An external hanging block would be best or, as illustrated, a guide below the sheave.

Fig. 205
The staysail and any other free-flying hankless sails will have a side loading when full, causing the halyard to push against the side of the sheave box. Besides causing friction, this can cause the wire to wedge between the sheave and the side wall of the box. This does not occur with an external hanging block and could also be prevented by an external halyard-straightening guide just below the sheave.

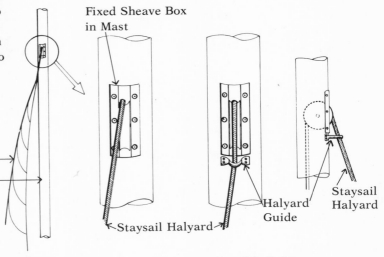

Staysail

Mast

Fixed Sheave Box in Mast

Staysail Halyard

Halyard Guide

Staysail Halyard

a. Without Guide

b. With Guide

C. Fittings can "hang up" accidentally at unplanned angles, placing leverage or torque on the fitting well beyond the normal stress loading, and can thus cause deformation or breakage (Fig. 206).

Fig. 206
Fitting Hangups. Fittings are sometimes loaded while misaligned, placing high-torque loadings that cause breakage.

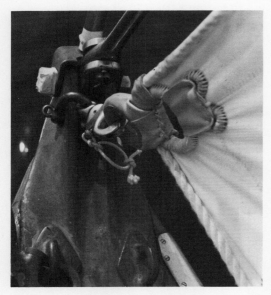

a. This non-aligned snapshackle supports a halyard tension of over 3,000 pounds and could distort or break.

b. The jaw connection of a fitting may have a restricted swing, depending on the sail or style of eye to which it is connected.

D. A traveler is mounted vertically, but the sheet lead is 30 or 40 degrees forward, placing heavy torque loading on the track. Even a ball-bearing traveler will not be friction free under the heavy load caused by such a torque angle (Fig. 207a). Canting the track forward will help relieve the condition (Fig. 207b; also see Fig. 229).

Fig. 207
Mounting the Traveler Track.   Traveler track should be mounted so that its vertical axis points toward the boom blocks to which the sheet runs.
PROBLEM: if the traveler carriage is not under the point of attachment, it will put a torque loading on the track.
SOLUTION: (1) Try to move the track forward until it is under boom block. (2) If track cannot be moved, angle track forward until it lines up with stress direction.

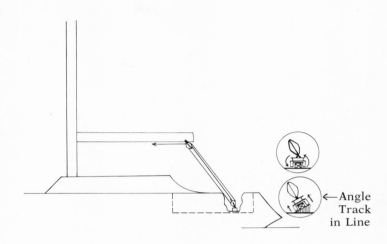

←Angle
Track
in Line

Corrosion

Another cause of failure is corrosion, a term that is widely discussed but not widely understood. Corrosion is the wearing away or alteration of a metal or alloy either by direct chemical attack or by electrochemical reaction. There are several basic types which may occur singly or in combination.

1. Atmospheric Corrosion

This refers to the effect of corrosive agents present in the atmosphere, such as oxygen, carbon dioxide, water vapor, and sulfur and chlorine compounds. The severity of this type of attack is directly related to the amount of water vapor and sulfur and chlorine compounds present. This is prevented by anodizing and other coatings.

2. Galvanic Corrosion

This is caused by the coupling of unlike metals in an electrolyte, such as salt water, which results in an electrical transfer of particles from one metal to another. A reference to the Galvanic Series on page 323 will show the relative position of various metals and alloys. In general, depending upon the electrolyte, the farther apart on the list, the greater the degree of attack, with the less noble metal corroding sacrificially and protecting the more noble (Fig. 208).

Fig. 208
Corrosion is caused by the proximity of two metals that are dissimilar on the galvanic scale—the least noble sacrificing particles that pass across and build up on the more noble metal.

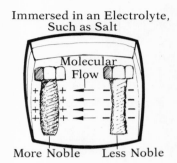

Immersed in an Electrolyte, Such as Salt

Molecular Flow

More Noble   Less Noble

The chart shows a representative sample of metals and alloys arranged in sequence from the most "sacrificial" to the most "noble." In the presence of an electrolyte, any of these metals will have a tendency to corrode when in contact with another metal in a lower position in the series. For example, if you have aluminum 6061 and 316 stainless so close that they are touching or nearly touching, the aluminum will get eaten away and the stainless will receive a build-up of aluminum particles. If the aluminum is heavily anodized, the galvanic reaction is prevented. In addition, if an inert sheet such as nylon is placed between the two metals, it will reduce galvanic potential.

3. Pitting

Even passive or corrosion-resistant metals will corrode in specialized environments. Extreme temperatures or acids will cause a localized breakdown of the material. The weakened area then becomes the anode and loses metal locally to the passive or cathodic area. The result is pitting.

4. Concentration Cell Corrosion

This is sometimes called "deposit attack" or "crevice corrosion." It refers to the tendency of corrosion to build up more rapidly in the cracks and crevices of a fitting.

5. Stress Corrosion

As explained previously, stresses in metal caused either by internal or continual external loads will create paths within the grain of the metal which tend to corrode more readily under certain conditions. Corrosion is accelerated along these paths, resulting in premature failure.

How to Avoid Corrosion

To minimize corrosion in general, you should:

1. Select the material most likely to resist the corrosive environment to which it will be subjected.

2. Avoid irregular stresses and complicated shapes in design.

3. Be sure your corrodible metal fittings are anodized or coated.

Where galvanic corrosion is involved, if possible use the same or similar metals in an assembly. Avoid combinations where the area of the less noble material is relatively small. When dissimilar metals are used together in the presence of an electrolyte, separate them with an inert substance such as plastics, paint, or anodized coating.

Material	Weight*	Maximum working strength	Strength to weight ratio
Titanium	218	110,000 psi**	505
Magnesium***	107	38,000 psi	355
17/4 PH Steel	484	160,000 psi	330
Aluminum 6061	168	35,000 psi	208
Stainless Steel 316	483	90,000 psi	186
Phosphor Bronze	550	90,000 psi	163
Nylon	490	33,000 psi	67
Mild Steel	67	8,500 psi	127

*pounds per cubic foot
**psi=pounds per square inch
***Magnesium is highly corrosive and therefore is not used

Chapter 15

Deck Layout and Fittings

Keener and more competitive racing in both one-design and cruising classes is producing many refinements in hull designs and sail plans. Most of these sophisticated improvements have been developed by naval architects and sailmakers who strive to add a few seconds per mile to boat speed. However, performance also depends on fast and efficient sail handling: this is an area where hardware designers and boatowners can make major improvements.

Today, with everyone trying his own ideas and with so many new fittings to choose from, no one deck plan could be called average. Devising a good deck layout for either one-design boats or cruising boats is an extremely difficult task. The Soling, for example, has become more and more complicated since these boats were named an Olympic class. Great arrays of ball-bearing blocks, ratchet blocks, and cleats have been added so that the cockpit now looks like the console of a master organ and as if it could be operated only by computer.

However, with common sense, a thorough analysis of what is needed, and a few basic principles, a deck layout that is very efficient and workable can be organized.

Since there are so many different sizes and types of boats, it is impossible to make specific recommendations here. Consequently, what follows are general principles which can be adapted to each particular boat.

Before you begin planning a layout, consider what you are primarily going to use your boat for. Are you going to race? Or are you going to use it for pleasure sailing and/or cruising? For cruising and pleasure sailing, a simplified layout is required, one that can be handled by one or two people if necessary. Racing requires fittings for every sail-handling eventuality and, of course, a lot more sails will be used. If you have a cruiser-racer, leave room on the deck to walk around. Try, as well, to leave a clean deck area fore and aft. Remember, you also have to sail at night, and a cleat in the middle of the deck can trip you up. If you have a large boat, you have room for convenient deck storage areas for extra fittings. This is important to plan for, since emergency replacements for fittings are usually needed in heavy air, when going below is difficult and time-consuming.

Before any of the sail-handling devices are laid down, other necessary items must go on the deck in specific places. Nearly every boat will have mooring chocks and mooring cleats. Cruiser-racers, in addition, must have many other safety and utility devices on the deck. These include lifelines, lights, life raft, life rings and man overboard poles, flagpole sockets, vents and dorades, hatch covers, spinnaker pole and strut holders, deck quartz prisms, storage boxes, stove fuel box, antennas, and fuel and water tank caps. Many of these fittings have to be in specific locations. Safety devices and security devices generally have mandatory locations. After they are positioned, then the sail-handling devices should be laid out. If there are any remaining accessory devices, they can be put in place last.

LOCATION OF SAIL-HANDLING CONTROLS

A great deal of thought should be given to the arrangement of the sail-handling devices and to the location of the control lines for these devices, so that maximum crew efficiency is obtained. If a jam cleat is mounted on the mast directly under the Cunningham, or if the winch or cleat for the spinnaker pole topping lift is put on the mast under the pole socket, a crewman has to take a special trip halfway across the boat to make an important and frequently used adjustment. Here are some basic principles to bear in mind to insure the best use of your crew:

1. The layout should be designed so that each job can be accomplished with a minimum of movement and/or loss of concentration.

2. The control lines should be clustered according to whether they are primary or secondary. Crewmen should be stationed near each cluster.

3. The minimum number of fittings needed to do the job adequately should be used. See if you can find fittings that can do more than one job.

4. The equipment must have enough mechanical advantage (power) so that the job function can be performed with relative ease. On one designs, power ratios should be high enough to allow adjustment to be made with one hand without having to move from a hiking position.

5. The comfort and direction of the pull required to perform specified functions should be considered.

6. The location and amount of space allotted to the crewman performing the specified job must be ample enough for him to work easily.

7. Last, and most important, control leads for sail shape adjustment devices should be designed so that the sail can be watched when the adjustment is being made. It does not make any sense to turn one's back to the sail to make an adjustment, because it takes twice as long to get the right shape.

One-Design Deck Layouts

Deck arrangements on one designs depend on the type of cockpit and deck allowed by class rules and on the number of crewmen. Control consoles are used in two ways: center cluster or side deck controls. Since hiking or trapezing is the normal station for most one-design sailors, primary sail controls should be placed on side deck control consoles (Fig. 209). Primary sail controls—that is, mainsheet, main traveler, boom vang, and Cunningham for the skipper; and jib sheet, jib traveler, and hiking straps or trapeze for the crewmen—should be arranged in batteries of jam cleats between the two crewmen. Side deck controls require double-ended leads (Fig. 210) and require careful routing of control lines to work efficiently.

Center clusters, jam cleats at the front of the cockpit for the crewmen (Fig. 211), and the centerboard trunk or barney post for the skipper should have only secondary adjustments (those which are adjusted only once or twice a race—halyards, mast and rigging controls, and so on) (Fig. 212).

The classification of an adjustment as primary or secondary is an important one and can be decided only by practice and experimentation.

Fig. 209
Control Consoles—these controls are
grouped and located in two
areas,depending on the type of boat and
the skipper's preference.
See Figure 212b, c, and d, for examples of
central control clusters. The other
possibility is the sidedeck control cluster.

Sidedeck Control Cluster.   Primary
controls are on the side of the cockpit,
secondary controls on the forward end.

Fig. 210
Double-Ended Adjustments

a.
Systems for Primary Controls.

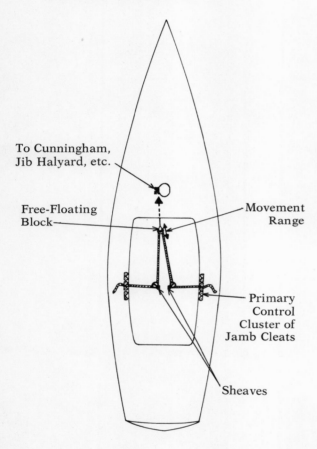

To Cunningham,
Jib Halyard, etc.

Free-Floating
Block

Movement
Range

Primary
Control
Cluster of
Jamb Cleats

Sheaves

b.
Continuous Double-Ended System
A large adjustment scope, such as that of a
mainsheet or jibsheet, necessitates that
the free ends be attached, making the
system continuous.

Fig. 211
Front Cockpit Control Cluster—
Secondary Adjustments

Fig. 212

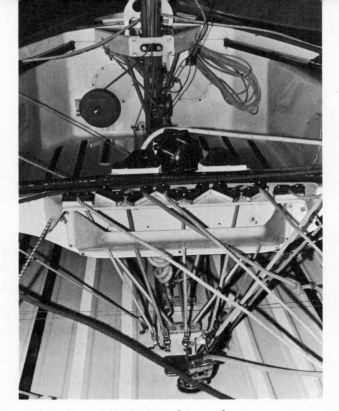

c. Complicated Evolution of Central Control System for a Keel Boat

a. The Barney post was the first central control. It was used on a one-design keel boat to trim the mainsheet.

b. The Barney post then developed into a central control cluster for the skipper.

d. On a centerboarder, the Barney post is not needed for the central controls because the centerboard trunk can be used as a mounting base for some controls.

Cluttering side deck consoles with a dozen jam cleats is a temptation, but it is anything but efficient. Rank the adjustments as to their per cent usage, making the heavily used primary and the lightly used secondary. Each skipper will find some things more important to him than others. Some constantly adjust their centerboard position, while others, such as Starboat sailors, are constantly adjusting their rigging. Also, division of work between skipper and crew depends on the quality and permanence of the crew members. Reliable permanent crewmen should take care of most adjustments, letting the skipper concentrate on steering fast. Remember that trapezing crewmen can do little adjusting and must concentrate on keeping the boat flat, so the skipper ends up with all the adjustments. Clever simplicity is the key to the most efficient sail-control system.

Cruising-Boat Deck Layouts and Winches

Like their smaller brothers just mentioned, cruising boats should have their controls divided into primary and secondary ones. Due to the mobility and larger number of crewmen, controls may be somewhat more spread out and have lower power ratios, but they still should be arranged to produce a minimum of running around. Winches are the usual source of power, so our discussion will be centered around their effective use in the primary or secondary control clusters. Most recently, on larger boats the tendency has been to have primary controls lead to the cockpit and cabin trunk and/or split cockpit area, while secondary controls have been centered around the base of the mast (Fig. 213). On smaller boats, most controls should be led aft to the cockpit (Fig. 214).

The arrangement of controls in the cockpit area of a cruising boat is dependent upon the proper positioning of the large primary and secondary winches. Generally, the largest winches, the primaries, are used to handle the genoa sheets and are placed on both sides near the forward end of the cockpit. The secondaries, slightly smaller in size than the primaries, are used for handling spinnaker and staysail sheets, and are placed behind the primaries on the cockpit coaming. On larger boats, usually over 50 feet, coffee grinders are used as primaries, and they are placed mid-deck (Fig. 215). With some of the newer boats with specialized rigs, such as a double-head rig, the larger winches are put aft and the smaller winches forward.

Fig. 213
On the average medium-size
cruiser-racer, the primary controls are
clustered on the aft end of the cabinhouse
and accessible to the cockpit. The
secondary controls are around the mast
base.

Fig. 214
On smaller cruiser-racers, most controls
are led aft to the cockpit, so that the crew
will not have to go forward to make
changes.

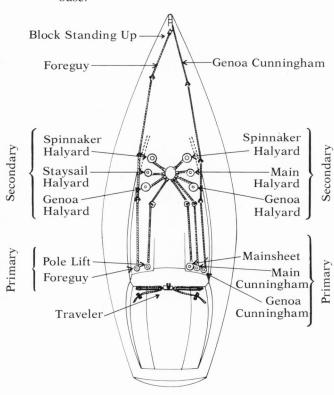

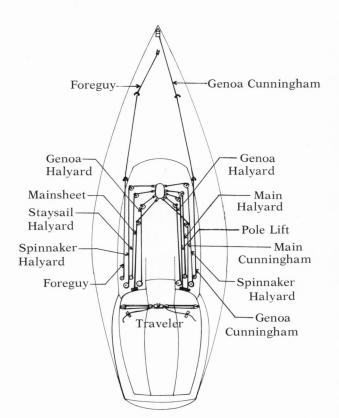

Fig. 215
Sheet Winch Plan for Small, Medium,
and Large Cruisers

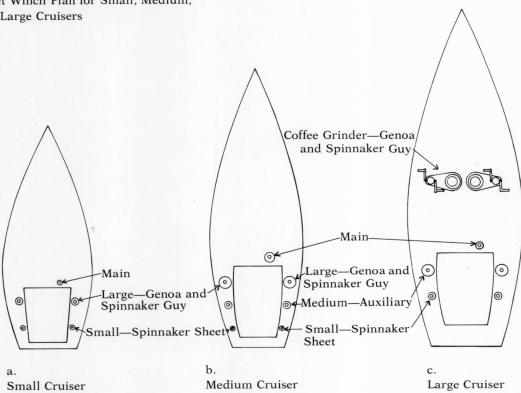

a.
Small Cruiser

b.
Medium Cruiser

c.
Large Cruiser

Some layouts are complicated by the improper location of sheet winches. Winches may be positioned in spots where it is difficult to tail or even more difficult to operate the winch without getting into an awkward stance. A sheet winch should be located so that the crewman can plant both feet at the same level and operate the winch without hitting the helmsman, a lifeline, or some other crew member (Fig. 216). Winches are frequently laid out between the edge of the cockpit and the rail, but they should be brought to the inboard edge of the cockpit; then the grinder can stand in the middle of the cockpit and have a free turn of the winch handle and also be cranking at about waist level, where he can apply maximum leverage to the winch.

Fig. 216
Primary and Secondary Sheet Winch
Placement. Winches are located well
inboard to allow handle to be turned
without interference from lifelines.

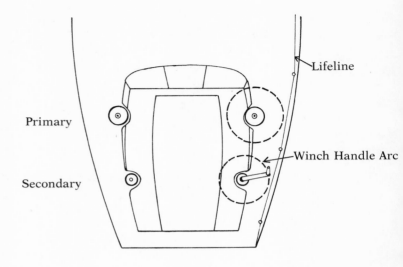

Primary

Secondary

Lifeline

Winch Handle Arc

Tailing a genoa winch takes a lot of room to keep the line being trimmed under tension at all times. Many larger boats have one or two crew members run the clew of the genoa toward the genoa lead block after a tack. It is surprising how fast a jib or genoa can be trimmed when it is manually hauled to the lead block. This operation depends almost entirely on the speed at which the tailer pulls in the slack line. If he can keep a steady tension on the sheet, the run-back crew will have a firm line to hold on to and the clew can be brought to within 2 or 3 feet of the block before it has to be winched; but if the tailer allows any slack in the sheet, the line will flail and the crewmen will have trouble running back the genoa. When attempting this, it is generally best to take only two turns on the winch and pull in the sheet as fast as possible. As the load begins to get higher, put another turn on the winch, pull the sheet in farther, and take another turn; with four turns, put in the winch handle and start cranking. If the handle is put in first together with four turns around the winch, too much friction is built up, and fast tailing is impossible. Also you cannot throw the extra turns around the winch unless the handle is out.

The remaining controls should lead to jam cleats or winches and jam cleats on the cabin top at the front of the cockpit. Special provisions should be made for placing the mainsheet winch and traveler controls in accessible places in the cockpit while Cunninghams, boom vangs, rigging controls, the topping lift, and so on, should be led to the front of the cockpit so that crew members do not have to go forward to make minor adjustments.

The control cluster around the base of the mast should be devised with halyards and fast sail changes in mind. The attachment of winches directly to the side of the mast should be done only with great thought and care. As mentioned previously, spinnaker and genoa halyards should exit from the mast interior 8 to 9 feet above the deck, go through a turning block at the deck, and then to specific multispeed winches in the control cluster, while the rest of the halyards should exit at the base and be led to their respective winches.

Both spinnaker halyards and genoa halyards should be hoisted in a hand-over-hand method from a standing position, so that the full weight of the crewman can be utilized (Fig. 218). A back-up device that can hold the halyard in case the sail fills away prematurely is always advisable; the halyard can be pulled through a light-action cleat or, as is now done on most cruising boats, the halyard can turn a deck block and then be led to a winch. (This line has to be tailed by a second crewman who can take a quick turn around the cleat in an emergency while hoisting.) The spinnaker halyard is generally external because the block aloft is external and describes a 180-degree arc in its free swing. The genoa halyard on the other hand leads to an internal sheave in the mast and can come down inside the mast.

SAIL-HANDLING DEVICES

In planning the layout of sail-handling devices, consider the following:

1. Each sail has to be hoisted, requiring halyards, turning blocks or sheaves, and winches and cleats.
2. The sails have to be trimmed, requiring blocks, sheets, track, travelers, and more winches and cleats.
3. Sails require changes in draft which involve blocks, sheets, winches and cleats, and wire or rope control lines.

These are the main categories (spinnaker equipment which falls under categories 1 and 2 can be added later, since it does not affect the basic deck plan in most cases).

Fig. 217
Halyard Winch Set-Up for Medium
Cruiser
Two spinnaker halyards are in front of
mast.
Two genoas are aft of mast, and the main
and staysail halyards are in the center of
each side. (See Fig. 213.)

Fig. 218
Genoa Halyard Set-Up on Large Boat.
On medium and large cruisers, genoa
halyards should exit 8 or 9 feet above deck
to allow hand-over-hand raising, thus
utilizing the weight of the crew member
to greatest advantage. This system
requires a crewman tailing.
Spinnaker halyards are usually all
external, but if internal they should exit
high also.

Halyards

The main halyard sheave should be positioned at or as near as possible to the headboard at the top of the mast. They should be made of wire because any halyard stretch will affect the luff tension and thus the draft position in the sail. The halyard will stretch even farther when the Cunningham is tensioned.

Jib halyards in small boats, which generally support the mast in lieu of the jibstay, also should be made of wire and can be used to adjust mast rake when connected to a screw crank. In cruising boats the genoa halyard is tensioned to a much higher loading than the mainsail halyard because the sail is so much larger than the mainsail. Therefore, the genoa halyard wire has to be much heavier than the main halyard.

On a small boat the genoa and spinnaker halyards are usually led to deck level or below deck level, turn at a block, and then are led aft to a cam or winch. On a cruising boat the mainsail and staysail that do not need instant raising can exit at the base of the mast and go to deck winches.

SAIL-TRIMMING DEVICES

In Chapter 6, sail-trimming techniques were discussed, but the actual layout of the different mechanical systems that provide the means for easy sail trim has been left until now. Sail-trimming devices have two functions: they set the trim or sheeting angle of the sail and provide the proper amount of leech tension (controlling sail twist). Basically, the mainsail is trimmed by a combination of three devices: the traveler, the mainsheet, and the boom vang. The headsails are trimmed by the sheet tension and fairlead position.

Over the years, many sail-trim arrangements have been conceived, in a slow march toward greater functionality and convenience. Cruising-boat trimming systems have until recently been dictated by demands of deck layout, human comfort, and headroom, while the evolution of one-design deck layouts has been brought about solely by improved concepts of traveler and sheeting arrangements. The underlying ingredient of functional trimming devices is the reduction of interaction. This interaction can be defined as the amount of coupling between the trim angle function and the draft control and leech tension function of a sail-trim device. Coupling can be described as one device controlling two or more functions. In older systems, sail trim was changed by "cracking the sheets"; the result was probably more change in leech tension (increased sail twist) than change of the trim angle of the boom—the boom hardly moved outward. Coupling was very high since both leech tension and trim angle could be controlled only by the sheets. Since the advent of the traveler, it has become possible to change the trim angle by moving the traveler carriage only; twist is controlled by pulling in or letting off the mainsheet. Thus, one device controls sheeting angle and the other controls sail twist, so that the system is not coupled.

The concept of uncoupling is clear for mains, but how about jibs? Most headsails are controlled (draft, foot draft, leech twist, and trim angle) by one sheetline, so that uncoupling of functions appears impossible. However, if the sail clew and fairlead are close together, then athwartship fairlead movement changes trim angle, fore and aft fairlead location changes draft, and changing sheet tension controls leech tension and twist. By use of a well-thought-out adjustable fairlead (see pages 121—4), the trimming functions of a headsail can be uncoupled.

Trimming the sails to make a boat go fast depends upon the ease with which proper adjustment can be made; this in turn depends on the lack of interaction (coupling) of trim adjustments.

Mainsail Trimming

Mainsheet trimming facilities are among those things often overlooked or taken for granted. Actually, the trimming system needs a lot of thought and must be adapted to each type of deck plan for efficient sail handling. Two basic systems for trimming mainsails are in general use today: end-of-boom travelers and mid-boom travelers (Fig. 219). In general, traveler position and trim systems are dictated by cabins, helm position, cockpit size and location, and so on. Basically, to provide a good system for trim angle con-

Fig. 219
Mainsheet and Traveler Systems

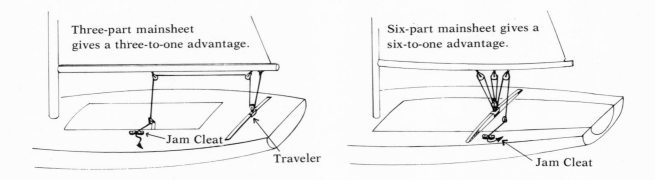

Three-part mainsheet
gives a three-to-one advantage.

Six-part mainsheet gives a
six-to-one advantage.

Jam Cleat

Traveler

Jam Cleat

a. End-of-Boom System

b. Mid-Boom System

trol, the traveler should scribe an arc (Fig. 220) from the mainsail's pivotal center, the mast.

If the traveler is mounted on the deck below the end of the boom, the sheet can be led from the boom to a block fixed to the traveler carriage, back to the boom, and forward to a mid-boom block or a block under the gooseneck. The same system can be used if the traveler is mounted amidships, except that more power will be needed because you have less leverage; this system is sometimes called a mid-horse traveler.

Each system has many advantages and disadvantages (Fig. 220). Geometrically, the mid-boom traveler will allow a greater trimming range before the sheets must be cracked to ease the boom out. If the carriage on

Fig. 220
The Effect of Traveler Positioning on
Sheeting Angles

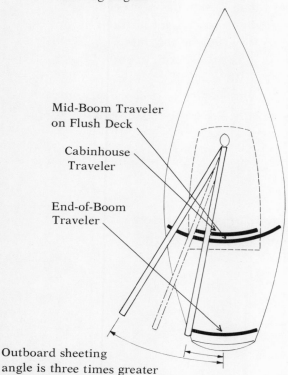

Mid-Boom Traveler
on Flush Deck

Cabinhouse
Traveler

End-of-Boom
Traveler

Outboard sheeting
angle is three times greater
with full-width mid-boom traveler.

a. A relatively narrow mount, such as on a cruising-boat cabinhouse, restricts the athwartship scope of the traveler.

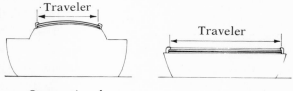

Conventional
Cruising Boat

b. Many one designs can use the full-width mid-boom traveler almost as a vang.

a mid-boom traveler is in the exact center of the boat and is eased off 2 feet from the centerline, it will have the same effect as easing off the carriage on an end-of-boom traveler 4 feet. With the amidships traveler extended to the full beam of the boat, trim can be controlled over a far greater range than with the end-of-boom traveler before the sheet must be cracked and the vang must be employed. From the aspect of loadings, the loads at the end of the boom are only half those exerted on a mid-boom system to maintain the same leech control; that is, the loads on the traveler and sheet blocks are magnified by two because the lever arm is divided in half (Fig. 221). More parts must be put on the mid-boom systems, and the boom must be stiff enough to take the center loading; to reduce stress concentrations on the boom it is better to spread out the blocks, using single sheaves rather than concentrating them in one multisheaved block (Fig. 221c). End-of-boom

Fig. 221

The amount of downward tension on the leech depends on the number of parts in the mainsheet system and the location of the sheet blocks on the boom. The location of the blocks sets up the length of the lever arm; the farther outboard on the boom they are, the more mechanical advantage you get. In addition, the more parts in the sheeting system, the greater the mechanical advantage. In (a), if the sheet loading is 100 pounds and there are four parts in the sheet system, which is located on the end of the boom, the downward loading on the leech will be 400 pounds. If you move the same four-part system to the middle of the boom, as in (b), the lever arm is cut in half and the total load on the leech is 200 pounds. To equal the leech loading obtained by the end-of-boom system, the number of parts must be doubled. However, this places an extremely high loading on the boom at one point, and it is better to spread the sheeting blocks on the boom, as in (c).

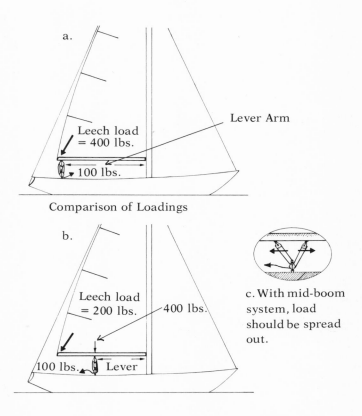

a.

Lever Arm

Leech load = 400 lbs.

100 lbs.

Comparison of Loadings

b.

Leech load = 200 lbs.

400 lbs.

100 lbs.

Lever

c. With mid-boom system, load should be spread out.

sheeting allows roller reefing, while the amidships sheeting does not; however, alternate jiffy or tie-in reefing methods can be used instead (see Chapter 13).

Setting up the traveler and the block and tackle system only partially solves the main trimming problem; leading the trimming end of the sheet in the best way to a cleat or winch is also a troublesome problem. Basically there are three solutions: (1) mount the cleat on the traveler carriage; (2) on a one design, you can lead the sheet to a mid-boom block and downward to a sheave with integral cleat on the cockpit sole (keelson) or up to a cleat on the cockpit coaming; or (3) lead the sheet forward to the gooseneck and down to the deckhouse-mount winch and cleat (Fig. 222).

Fig. 222
Various Mainsheet Lead Systems

a. Jam Cleat on Traveler Carriage

b. Sheave on Cockpit Sole (One Design)

c. Sheet Lead Forward to Mast

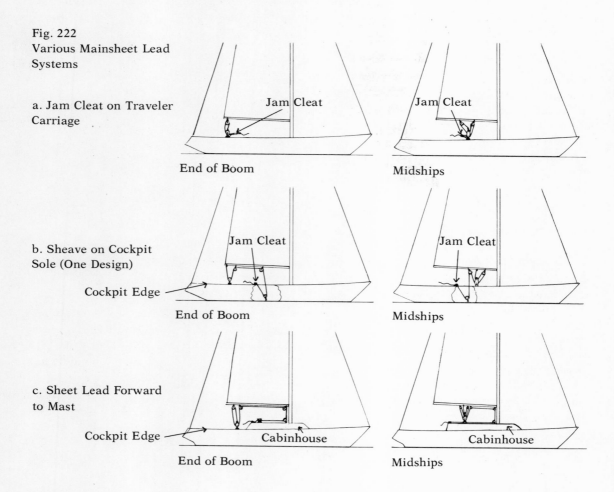

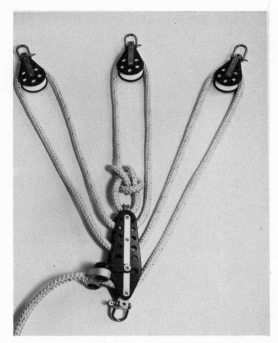

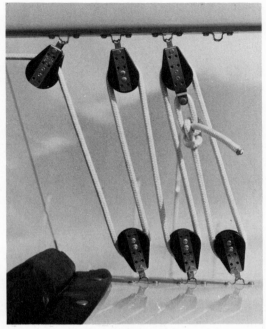

d. Once the number of parts in the system has been decided upon, the mainsheet system can be arranged in different ways; multiple single blocks can be used on either the deck or boom or on both. Two sheeting systems are shown here, the first a mid-boom mainsheet system with single blocks on the boom (see Fig. 221c), and the second an end-of-boom mainsheet system with single blocks on both boom and deck. Both systems have 6:1 MA.

Many cruising boats are now using multiple-sheave lower-mainsheet blocks with integral jam cleats and mounting them directly on the traveler carriage (Fig. 223a). This works well in light air, but in a breeze the running end of the mainsheet must be put on a winch. If the winch is on the weather side of the carriage or on the centerline, it will pull the traveler carriage inboard when you trim in the sheet, thus interfering with proper traveler trim (Fig. 223b). One solution is to anchor the traveler with both windward and leeward control lines. Another solution is to mount open-end deck snatch blocks on both sides of the boat near the ends of the traveler track (Fig. 223c). The mainsheet running end can then be led from the carriage to the leeward deck block and back to the winch, thus pulling the carriage to leeward against the control lines. When the sheet is trimmed as desired, it can be released from the winch, flipped out of the deck block, and it will

Fig. 223

a. Jam Cleat for Mainsheet Mounted on Traveler

b. In heavier air, a winch is usually required to trim the mainsheet. Because the winch must be located in one position (usually in the center of the boat), when the sheet is winched in, it pulls the traveler toward the centerline. This happens because the only thing holding the traveler to leeward is the pressure of the wind, and the winch is strong enough to overcome this. The only way this problem can be countered is to anchor the traveler with both leeward and windward control lines. However, this is quite inconvenient, since it doesn't allow you to adjust the traveler very quickly; each time the windward control line is adjusted, the leeward control has to be adjusted as well. This problem does not arise when the sheet is run forward on the boom, down to the deck, and aft to the winch and cleat.

c. Another solution is to place open deck blocks at either end of the traveler, around which the sheet can be turned and then led back to the winch. Thus, the sheet can be trimmed to a leeward point first, before going to the winch. This too is inconvenient because the sheet has to be re-led each time you tack. Again, the sheet led forward is preferable.

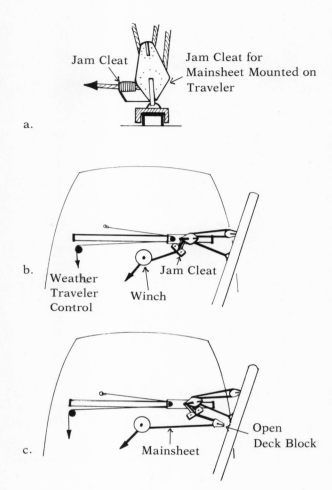

a.

Jam Cleat   Jam Cleat for Mainsheet Mounted on Traveler

b.   Weather Traveler Control   Winch   Jam Cleat

c.   Mainsheet   Open Deck Block

be held securely by the jam cleat on the mainsheet block. Neither of these solutions is completely satisfactory.

Most small boats with either midship or end-of-boom travelers have the mainsheet running from a block at the middle of the boom to a sheave at the cockpit sole with integral cleat, or to a sheave at the cockpit sole and then to jam cleats on the cockpit coaming (Fig. 224). The whole system is then free to swing with the traveler without the hindrance caused by the

Fig. 224
Dinghy Traveler and Mainsheet System

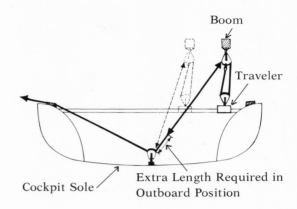

On one designs, the final sheet block should be mounted as low in the cockpit as possible, to give a long length from the boom block. This reduces the amount of extra length required in the mainsheet when the traveler is eased outboard. In most cases, however, because of the system interaction, the traveler cannot be fully eased without also easing the mainsheet. With this system it is important to remember to check the mainsheet tension after adjusting the traveler.

running end of the mainsheet being trimmed to a winch at deck level. On Finns, the interaction of this system is noticeable when easing the traveler to the end of the track, because the mainsheet must also be eased to allow for the change in distance from the boom to the lead sheave at the cockpit sole. To reduce this interaction, the sheave must be mounted as low as possible, preferably on the keelson. Other alternatives are to use a continuous double-ended mainsheet or to curve up the ends of the traveler track to allow for the change in length.

The last system, mainly used on cruising boats but with good possibilities for one designs, is that of taking the running end of the mainsheet forward along the boom to a block under the gooseneck, and then down to the deck and back to a winch and jam cleats, which are generally mounted on the cabin top (Fig. 225). Then the traveler can be trimmed without changing sheet tension, so that there is no coupling in this system.

Problems can arise on small boats when the mainsheet is trimmed to a jam cleat mounted on the centerboard trunk or barney post in the center of the cockpit. Generally, the sheet comes through a block, then up through a leader eye and onto the set of jam cleats (an integral device), as in Figure 226. The jam cleats are engaged by pressing the sheet down through the cams and are released by pulling the line up. In some cases, this creates an effect opposite of that desired. As a boat starts to heel, the skipper and crew hike out, so that if they want to release the mainsheet, they have to sit

Fig. 225
Ideal Mainsheet System If Traveler Is
Used.   When the mainsheet is led
forward to the mast, it does not restrict
the athwartship movement of the
traveler as does the mid-boom system.
(See Fig. 91.) This arrangement also
avoids the problems encountered in
heavy air described in Figures 223 and
224. Whenever it can be used, this is by far
the best mainsheet system.

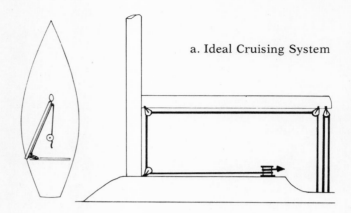

a. Ideal Cruising System

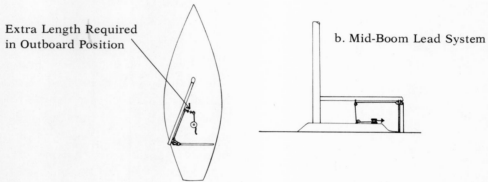

Extra Length Required
in Outboard Position

b. Mid-Boom Lead System

Fig. 226
a. Upright Cam Cleat with Swivel Block.
On a small one design, the mainsheet can
sometimes be released more easily while
hiking if the cams are mounted upside
down.

b.

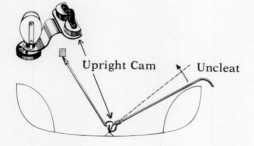

Upright Cam   Uncleat

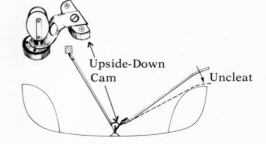

Upside-Down
Cam   Uncleat

up and lift up on the line to release it. To solve the problem, some boats have the jam cleats mounted upside down underneath the mounting platform instead of on top of it (Fig. 226b). Then when the boat heels, the hiking crew or skipper can disengage the sheet simply by pulling on it. From the hiking angle, you exert a downward pull and an extra tug on the sheet, which disengages it from the jams.

Mainsheet leads are often analyzed with the boom over the centerline of the boat, but the problem must be considered when the boom is out in a reaching position because the mainsheet leaves the boom at a different angle. This situation requires a block that can turn, especially the block at the center of the boom. Two common blocks used in end-of-boom sheeting are fiddle blocks (one block with two sheaves vertically mounted) or double blocks (one block with two side-by-side sheaves). However, problems occur with double blocks when going to windward with maximum loading. The fiddle block arrangement (Fig. 227a) puts a 180-degree loading on one sheave and a 90-degree loading on the other, which is not perfect, but is required for end-of-boom sheeting when roller reefing is used. The double block (Fig. 227b) creates a twisted load on the block, so that the lines are binding against both walls of the block, impairing the strength of the fitting. When roller reefing is not used, the best solution is to use two single blocks with separate bails fore and aft on the end of the boom and a becket block (single block with securing eye) on the traveler (Fig. 227c). However, if both blocks are on the same bail (Fig. 227d), the two blocks might collide, causing chafing damage.

Traveler Control

A traveler should be set up so that the carriage can be pulled to windward of the boat's centerline in light air. Many carriage control systems have been devised, but the most popular is a control line for each side. The control line can be dead-ended at the end of the track, and then go through the central sheave on the traveler carriage and back to the windward side. Since most travelers are probably never trimmed more than a foot or two to weather, the running end can terminate 20 inches to windward of the centerline (Fig. 228a) or continue to the end of the traveler track (Fig. 228b), or be routed to a convenient position (most one designs have traveler control-line cleats mounted adjacent to mainsheet cleats). Provision should

Fig. 227
Four Different Ways of Rigging a
Three-Part Aft Traveler Mainsheet
System.   All use a becket block on the
traveler or deck, but vary in arrangement
at the boom end. The end-of-boom
blocks all have one 180-degree turn and
one 90-degree turn, and this creates a
problem. Overloads will result when the
two different directional loadings are
applied to one block. But when the
loadings are applied to two different
blocks, the blocks align themselves to the
loads, and no overload results.

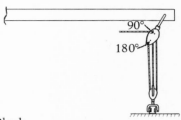

a. Fiddle Block
One sheave is being pulled downward and
one is being pulled forward at a 45-degree
angle. (See Fig. 197b.)

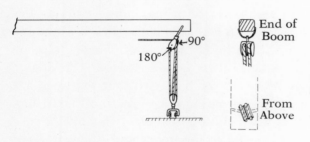

b. Double blocks used on the end of the
boom will have one lead down and one
lead forward, causing the block to twist 20
or 30 degrees. The forward lead turns an
angle around the cheek as it exits. This can
spread the cheek and cause a failure or
jumped sheave.

c. Separate Blocks
on Fore and Aft Bails

e. As traveler is eased outboard, the
double block cannot accommodate two
directions of load, and cheek damage may
result.

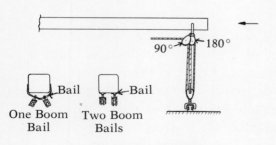

d. Separate Blocks
on Side-by-Side Bails
or on Same Bail

Fig. 228
Typical Traveler Control Line
Arrangement (One Designs).   Control
lines must originate (dead end) far
enough to weather to allow the carriage
to be pulled to weather.

Traveler Trim Control Lines.   The
traveler control lines should be arranged
to allow the quickest and easiest
adjustment. The running end should be in
a position where the best direction of pull
can be utilized. On some boats, it can
terminate a short distance to weather (a),
but usually go to the end of the traveler
track (b).

The most difficult installation to adjust is
on the cockpit seat mount, where the
cockpit wall prohibits a direct outward
pull in line with direction of the traveler's
movement (c). To avoid this you need a
turning block to turn the line to a better
leverage angle, either up (c) or aft (d).
Another solution is a three or four-part
block-and-tackle system (e) with a cleat
on the outboard block (essentially a vang
system turned on its side). This system
allows you to pull the running end in any
direction from the cockpit wall. On larger
cruisers a winch may be needed to trim
the control line (f).

e. Duplicate Vang System

a. Typical Traveler
Control-Line Arrangement

Turning Block
to Change Angle
of Control Line

Traveler Carriage

b. Alternate
Arrangement

Padeye

Jam cleat
mounted on coaming is
better than inside cockpit.

c. Cockpit
Seat Mount

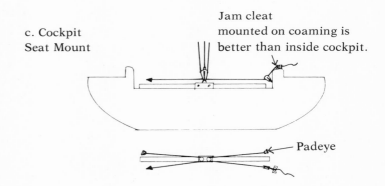

Padeye

d. Aft Turning
Blocks for
Cockpit Mounts

To Cluster Area
(on One Design)

f. Winch-Aided
Control Lines

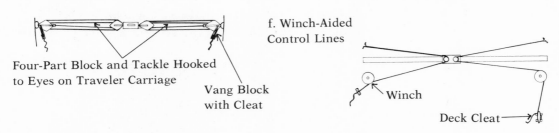

Four-Part Block and Tackle Hooked
to Eyes on Traveler Carriage

Vang Block
with Cleat

Winch

Deck Cleat

be made so that the running end of the control line is not below the cockpit coaming, where a direct pull cannot be exerted (Figs. 228c&d).

The traveler is a major trimming device and usually should be adjusted for each change in weather conditions; therefore, it should be easily controlled in all situations with little loss of concentration. The system mentioned here has only a 2:1 power advantage; on large boats the power should be increased (Fig. 228e), or a winch should be placed in a convenient location to operate both control lines (Fig. 228f).

In recent years, on cruising boats, masts have become taller and booms shorter. Conversion to this type of rig can cause problems. The location of travelers and mainsheet leads is sometimes complicated by the fact that the boats were originally designed with long booms, and the end of the boom was over flat deck area suitable for mounting a traveler. The end of a shorter boom might be awkwardly located between the wheel and the companionway. Consequently, the only place the traveler can be mounted is in this inconvenient area (Fig. 229a). Some skippers, converting to a high-aspect-ratio rig, run their mainsheet to the end of the boom and then aft to the normal traveler position. However, the traveler track has to be angled forward and pointed toward the end of the boom; otherwise, high torque loading is created on one side of the traveler, which would eventually cause damage, as shown in Figure 207.

Other skippers keep their old full-length boom and have their mainsail terminate 2, 3, or 4 feet forward of the end of the boom. This is legal under measurement rules, so long as no sail is trimmed beyond a point 6 inches aft of the black band at the clew of the mainsail.

Some cruising-boat deck layouts are built around a mid-boom "horse," which means the traveler is installed on the cabin top forward of or spanning the companionway. In evaluating this system, there are three things to consider: (1) the scope of the traveler is restricted by the width of the cabin top (see Fig. 90); (2) the loads on the traveler and sheet blocks are larger, causing large loads in the cabin house top; and (3) the traveler may have to bridge the companionway sliding hatch (Fig. 229b).

Fig. 229
Traveler Locations for High-Aspect-Ratio
Mainsail

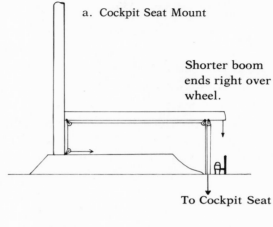

a. Cockpit Seat Mount

Shorter boom
ends right over
wheel.

To Cockpit Seat

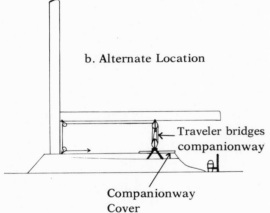

b. Alternate Location

Traveler bridges
companionway

Companionway
Cover

c. Conversion to High-Aspect-
Ratio Mainsail—when the boom is cut
down, the traveler must be moved from
the aft cockpit area to the forward end of
the cockpit. Many times the traveler has
been left in the aft area, and the pull from
the mainsheet twists the carriage and it
binds. If the traveler cannot be moved,
another solution is to angle the traveler
toward the mainsheet load.

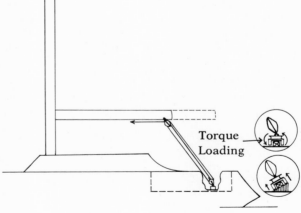

Torque
Loading

Boom Vangs

Vangs have been around for over twenty years. Around 1942, Arthur Deacon of Larchmont, New York, gained some notoriety in the Star Class by hanging a 25-pound anchor off the end of his boom on a downwind leg. In the late forties, Stars and other classes sailed downwind with a man sitting on the boom to provide leech control. This direct downward pressure on the boom provided the needed leech tension to keep the upper part of the sail from falling off to a point where it would be highly ineffective.

In 1948, the Stars started using a block and tackle system to provide the downward load. It was attached to the boom and could be hooked up at various points on the deck, depending on the reaching angle. The first boats to use this vang system could gain as much as 200 or 300 yards on a downwind leg. However, the vang had to be changed with each change in the sail's position. Consequently, skippers had a tendency not to play the main in and out in the shifts. Hence some advantage was lost.

During the past few years, three different systems of vangs have arisen: the standard vang, the bull-ring vang, and the fully articulated vang. These have been discussed in detail in Chapter 6 (see pages 118—20). The most common vang is an auxiliary unit that can be attached by a strop or other device to any part of the boom and can be connected at the other end to various points on the deck. (See Fig. 91.) A number of specialized vangs are used for different circumstances. For instance, many one designs use a permanently installed vang where the lower end of the block and tackle is permanently affixed to the mast just above the deck (Fig. 230a). Since the vang is fixed directly in line with the gooseneck pivot, the boom can swing freely with no interference from the vang. This type of vang does not pull straight down, but pulls at an inward angle to the mast partners; thus, its function can be greatly inhibited if the boom is very close to the deck. A vang mounted roughly a quarter or third of the way aft on the boom has even less leverage than a mid-boom traveler system: that is, if it is mounted one quarter of the way back, it will have four times more downward loading than the leech loading on the end of the boom and will have up to two times more load if the inward angle (due to low boom) is 60 degrees. Figure 230b shows a variation of the standard vang that gives high power by employing a lever arm. When the vang leads below deck, the run-

Fig. 230
Standard Vangs

a. Permanently Mounted
Block-and-Tackle Vang

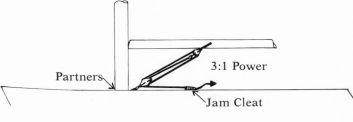

Partners

3:1 Power

Jam Cleat

b. High-Powered Lever Vang
Used with Low Deck Clearance

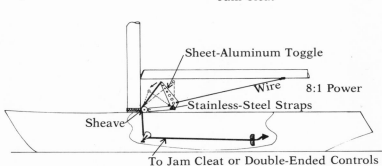

Sheet-Aluminum Toggle

Wire   8:1 Power

Stainless-Steel Straps

Sheave

To Jam Cleat or Double-Ended Controls

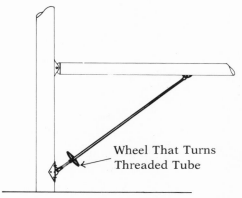

Wheel That Turns
Threaded Tube

c. Solid Vang—this vang is composed of a
tubular rod that is internally threaded; it
works on the screw principle.

d. Conventional Vang Utilizing Block and
Tackle—the deck securing point and
boom location change with the swing of
the boom.

ning end of the vang control line can be fastened to a drum winch for extra power and fast action.

The bull-ring vang, which has been used on boats ranging from International 14 dinghies to Stars to 12-Meters, utilizes a ball-bearing traveler operating on a semicircular track that follows the arc described by the vang attachment point on the boom. As the boom is trimmed in or out by the mainsheet, the vang carriage (at deck level) slides on its ball bearings along the track, keeping alignment at all times (Fig. 231a). It is really an inboard traveler located where the full 180-degree scope of travel of the boom is still over the deck, but at a sacrifice of leverage. The 12-Meters involved in the 1970 America's Cup competition used such a system (Fig. 231b). The defender, *Intrepid*, the French challenger, *France*, and the French trial horse, *Chancegger*, used the new semicircular vang. These

Fig. 231

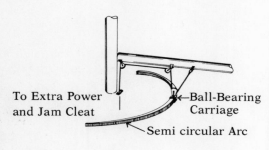

To Extra Power
and Jam Cleat

←Ball-Bearing
Carriage

Semi circular Arc

a.
Bull-Ring Vang
The vang remains permanently attached. The track is installed to a flat deck in an arc described by the boom blocks of the vang.

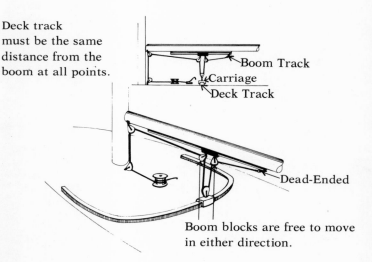

Deck track must be the same distance from the boom at all points.

Boom Track

Carriage

Deck Track

Dead-Ended

Boom blocks are free to move in either direction.

b.
Fully Articulated Vang
When the deck track cannot be semicircular, the boom blocks can be made to follow above the traveler by mounting them on the underside of the boom.

vangs could exert a maximum downwind tension of 8,000 pounds at the clew, and 20,000 pounds at the vang attachment point. They proved quite successful. They can be used only on flush-deck boats because they need a flat mount from rail to rail, parallel to the boom's swing, i.e., the track and the boom must remain at a constant distance from one another.

When you cannot mount track in a perfect semicircle, an articulated vang is used like the bull-ring vang, but it has the vang attached to a slide on a track mounted on the underside of the boom. As the boom swings out, the slide on the boom and the slide on the deck move simultaneously and produce a self-adjusting system (Fig. 231). Therefore, the track on the deck need not be a perfect semicircle but can follow the shear line of the boat. Genoa fairlead tracks can be used, and thus one track serves two functions. The only difficulty with both the bull-ring and the articulated vang is that the boom has to be parallel with the deck at all times if the vang is to work efficiently. In addition, this kind of control should be watched carefully in light air, when the vang friction might overtrim the leech if there is not enough wind to push it out to leeward. Nevertheless, the self-adjusting vang is a step in the right direction.

A new vang, now popular in Europe and in limited use in the United States, is the solid vang.

Jibs and Genoas

The layout and installation of jib and genoa trim controls involve mainly the positioning of deck tracks. These are covered quite thoroughly in Sail Trim (Chapter 6) and Headsails (Chapter 10), and only a few additional comments are necessary here.

For cruising boats, the most common type of genoa lead adjustment is a long fore-aft track from shrouds to transom. The sheet blocks are either shackled through holes in the track (see Fig. 204) or mounted on a slide or carriage that slides on the track. Invariably the fairleads must be changed while the sheet is under load, making the former setup more difficult for ocean racers because it is harder to adjust than a sliding track. The slides can be held in position either by a pull-pin mechanism that fits into vertical holes spaced in the track or by wire fore-and-aft control lines. But sheeting loads are getting higher, making it harder to move the lead under load. The main force is directly upward and bisects the angle that the sheet makes at the turning block; thus, the load on the fairlead slide is in an upward and aft direction, making it very difficult to pull the lead forward under load; this can be done by hand on a smaller boat and by an auxiliary line to a winch on a cruising boat.* To cope with this loading, the sliding and securing mechanisms should have very low friction. The carriage positioning pin should be of the spring-loaded type and not the typical wing nut; even a ratchet-type latch could be used that would move forward when pushed, but not aft unless released.

On one designs, the Barber haul was a major stride in jib adjustment, since it is easily adjustable under sail. (See Fig. 95.) The fore-and-aft jib track is placed farther inboard than usual and the Barber haul, a control line idling on the jib sheet from an outboard point, pulls the sheet to a more outboard position when desired. To do this, the outboard Barber haul control wire terminates at a block which idles on the jib sheet. The running end of the Barber haul goes through the deck at the rail and then connects to an underdeck block and cam for adjustment (Fig. 232). As the Barber haul is tightened, the block idling on the sheet is pulled outboard, taking the sheet with it. The sheet then goes from the jib's clew to the Barber haul block and then to the track block (which can be moved fore and aft by manual track adjustment if necessary). Recently Barber hauls have been turned around and used backward on some classes and in cruising boats. The idling block is pulled inboard to some point on the inboard edge of the cockpit, and the fore and aft fairlead tracks are mounted well outboard. In certain classes where deck width is a problem, the inhauler allows the jib to be trimmed closer than in the past.

The racing jib traveler used on one designs also has the controls under the deck, since it is desirable to keep the deck as clear as possible (Fig. 233). Generally, when allowed, the sheet goes from the clew to a turning block on the traveler carriage and then forward to the jib's pivotal area (the headstay) to a flush-deck turning block and then aft under the deck to a double-ended continuous sheet in the cockpit. The carriage has an athwartship control like the main's, so that the sail's angle to the wind can also be changed without changing trim tension. However, since the fore and aft fairlead position controls leech and foot tension, the fore and aft location

---

*The auxiliary line holds the genoa clew while the regular sheet is eased and the lead moved. Then the sheet is tensioned and the auxiliary line removed.

of the track is critical; but, when rules allow, the jib can have a clewboard (similar to a headboard) mounted on the clew that has several holes to allow the sheet trim point to be raised or lowered.

Of all the sailing subjects, deck layout is one of the most difficult because almost every boat is different. Boatowners spend more time in planning this phase of the boat than almost any other area. Everyone has his own ideas about how things should be done or laid out. Therefore, this chapter has been restricted primarily to principles of deck layout rather than being overly specific. Ideas of deck layout also are continually undergoing change; typical layouts today could be entirely different next year or the year after. So it is important to study every new boat, particularly the top winning boats, to see what is going on.

Fig. 232
Underdeck Block and Tackle for Barber Haul. The Barber haul requires considerable power to adjust, and in some cases you need a three-part block and tackle system under the deck. Two wires are joined, so that reaching pulleys move in unison.

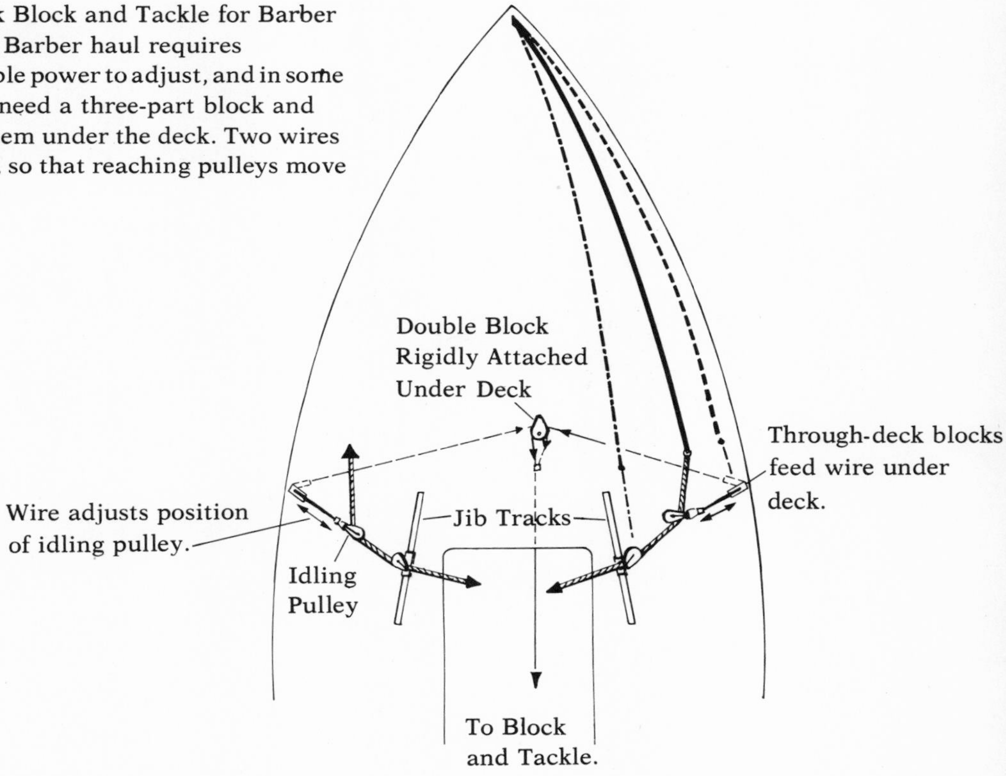

Double Block Rigidly Attached Under Deck

Through-deck blocks feed wire under deck.

Wire adjusts position of idling pulley.

Jib Tracks

Idling Pulley

To Block and Tackle.

Fig. 233
The Racing-Jib Traveler. Both sheet tension and athwartship position can be controlled from the cockpit. Like the mainsheet, the jibsheet is led forward to the jib tack area and then down and through the deck and aft to the winch or cleat, so that the clew is free to swing from side to side with a constant sheet tension. The traveler control restricts the athwartship distance of the swing and is led through the deck at the traveler and back into the cockpit.

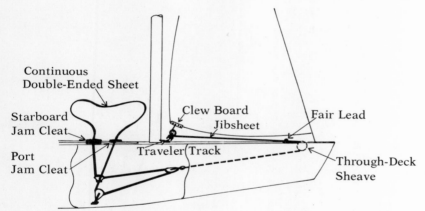

Continuous
Double-Ended Sheet

Starboard
Jam Cleat

Port
Jam Cleat

Clew Board

Jibsheet

Fair Lead

Traveler Track

Through-Deck
Sheave

Chapter 16

Who Does What

When racing, each leg and each turning mark require precise procedures and, hence, precise crew actions. Usually there are too many things to remember at once, and the only remedy is extensive practice with the same crew. It is a safe estimate that much of the frantic commotion during a critical maneuver comes from lack of practice or from having a different crew each race.

Whether you have a two-man crew or a twelve-man crew, there should be specific routines for the execution of all standard maneuvers on your boat. In competitive racing, the skipper has his hands full steering his boat, watching for wind shifts, and matching wits with the fleet in tactical skirmishes. So when it comes time to tack, jibe, or set a spinnaker, the operation should be virtually automatic with little or no coaching from the helmsman. The main exception is on a two-man one-design boat where, of necessity, the skipper has to do a lot, particularly if the crew is on a trapeze.

First, to help you find the correct job breakdown for your boat, here is a review of the devices used in sail handling, followed by a simplified list of job assignments for boats of all sizes. A more detailed analysis that defines supplementary crew assignments during a race follows, for both seven-man and three-man crews.

DEVICE REVIEW

Control	Cruising	One design	Main	Genoa or jib	Function
Outhaul	X	X	X		Controls amount of draft
Cunningham	X	X	X	X	Controls fore and aft location of main or genoa draft
Jerk string		X		X	Controls fore and aft location of jib draft
Stretchy luff	X			X	Controls location of genoa draft
Barber haul	X	X		X	Moves jib lead outboard or inboard
Double tracks	X	X		X	Alternates genoa lead inboard or outboard or points in between
Zipper or roach reef	X		X		Removes draft low in main
Flattening reef	X		X		Removes draft low in main
Bendy mast	X	X	X		Removes forward draft in main
Traveler	X	X	X		Athwartship trim for main
Vang	X	X	X		Leech control offwind
Backstay	X	X	X		Bends mast, tensions headstay, eases mast forward for running
Mainsheet	X	X	X		Controls leech twist
Genoa sheet	X	X	X		Acts as outhaul and twist control

NOTE: For the sake of simplicity, we have had to leave out many other devices such as leech lines, bendy booms, etc. We have also not included who does navigation, cooking, etc., and the assignments on a watch. When watches are set, some jobs can be done slower with fewer crew, while others need the full crew alerted and on deck.

Now, let's start right before the race and go through a typical triangular windward–leeward course to see the order of the jobs. This is more of a one-design course, but will include most of the maneuvers encountered at one time or other in either a one-design or a cruising-boat race. Crew members vary with the size of the boat, from one on a monotype to eighteen or twenty on a 75- or 80-foot ocean racer (Fig. 234). Therefore, an example has been selected—a one design with a three-man crew. (A 36-foot

Fig. 234
Since crew positions vary with different
maneuvers, the approximate positions of
crews, from two-man to twelve-man, are
shown when setting a spinnaker.

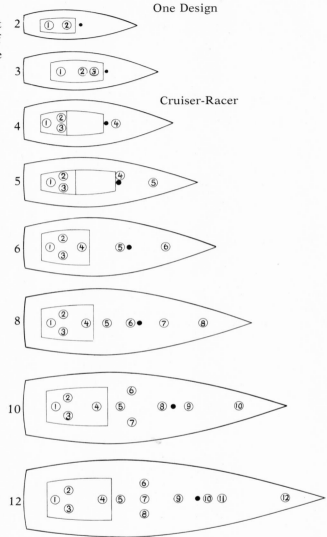

One Design

Cruiser-Racer

ocean racer with a seven-man crew will be discussed later.) These jobs, once
listed, can be modified to suit a larger or smaller crew. On a smaller boat,
with lower loadings and strains, one crew member can do the jobs of two
men on the 36-footer. As the boat gets larger, more mechanical advantage is
required for the greater loads, which means more winches, more fittings,

and more crewmen to operate this gear. However, the job sequence is basically the same.

DETAILED ASSIGNMENT BREAKDOWN
for Three-Man Racing Crew

For the sake of simplicity, the following breakdown is confined to the first four legs of a triangular windward–leeward course. As nearly as possible, job assignments are listed in chronological order. Numerals indicate: 1—skipper; 2—midships crew; 3—foredeck crew.

Before the Race

1 or 2—Determine position of weather mark relative to wind direction. Plan windward tactics. Check current.

1—Determine course for the second leg, on which a spinnaker will be used.

3—Place spinnaker pole on the side of the boat it will be raised on.

—Bring sheet and afterguy to the proper side.

—Clear spinnaker halyard and bring it to the side on which it will be used.

2—Pack spinnaker and place it on the side where it will be hooked on.

1—Check jib and mainsheet leads; prepare for any athwartship changes.

—Check mast bend fore and aft and athwartship.

Just Before the Start

2—Double-check compass or committee boat flags to see if any last-minute wind shifts have taken place.

2—Set downhaul, Cunningham hole, and outhaul* tension to position mainsail draft to suit wind conditions.

3—Adjust jib luff tension for correct draft.

*Outhaul is better set before the race, if possible, as it is difficult to move during the race.

2,3 — Mark above settings, so that they can be preset when approaching the next windward leg.

1 — At the start, move main traveler slightly inboard to get better pointing angle while speed builds up. Then ease traveler to desired setting.

Approaching the Windward Mark

3 — Approaching the windward mark on the port tack, set up spinnaker turtle, if possible (which is now on the windward side). Connect afterguy and sheet. Check halyard.

— Close to the mark on final starboard tack, set spinnaker pole and fasten end to afterguy, if tactics permit.

— Attach pole lift and foreguy.

— Adjust pole on the mast to best estimated height.

2 — Take up on the pole lift and trim the foreguy.

— Preset jib to estimated reaching position.

At the Turning Mark for the Reach (Second Leg)

1 — Steer best course for rounding, relative to other boats.

— Maneuver to best reaching position before ordering spinnaker set.

— Take mainsheet and ease when necessary.

3 — Apply boom vang before rounding.

1 or 3 — Hoist spinnaker quickly.

— Check pole height.

2 — Pull both afterguy and sheet (with turns on winches) so that the spinnaker is spread apart to prevent a twist while being raised.

— Trim afterguy until the pole is at right angles to the masthead fly. Then cleat afterguy and concentrate on sheet to get exact trim.

3 — Check foreguy and counterbalance the tension of the lift.

— Release tension on the Cunningham hole.

— Ease the outhaul.

— Tension vang.

— Ease the traveler.

— Ease jib luff tension and tighten Barber haul to outboard position.

—Ease backstay tension.
—Take turtle in from the shrouds.

Reaching Jibe at the Second Mark (Third Leg)

3—Approaching the second mark, preset the jib (if used) on the opposite tack.
—Release the vang.
2—Stand by afterguy and sheet winches with one line in each hand, ready to square the afterguy and ease the sheet until the clew reaches the headstay as the boat jibes.
1—Handle mainsheet during the jibe.
—Round slowly, if possible, keeping boat momentarily in dead downwind position so that 3 can shift pole easily from one side to the other.
3—Lower spinnaker pole lift if necessary.
—Unsnap pole from the mast and take that end to the new windward side. Snap on the sheet, which becomes the afterguy.
—Disconnect the other end of the pole from what was the afterguy and snap the end onto the mast. Push pole end forward until it is at tack of spinnaker.
2—Trim new afterguy and new sheet to proper adjustment.
3—Set up vang on opposite side.
—Adjust lift and foreguy to keep pole immovable vertically.
—Take afterguy from 2 after all other jobs are done.
2—Concentrate on sheet only.

Approaching the Leeward Mark (Fourth Leg)

2—Reset backstay tension.
3—Trim jib to windward setting and overtrim slightly.
1—Trim mainsheet.
2,3—Set traveler to established setting for going to windward.
—Release Barber hauls.
—Ease vang and tension Cunningham hole. Tighten main outhaul.
—Tension jib luff.
—Reset backstay tension.

—Check all fittings to see that they are readjusted to the settings marked on the first leg.

2—Ease afterguy.

—Take spinnaker sheet in hand.

3—Uncleat spinnaker halyard and let it run at controlled speed.

2—Let afterguy run through pole end.

2—Pull in spinnaker starting with sheet and clew. Get entire sail and lines into cockpit.

1—Set traveler.

2—Trim jib as you round the mark.

1—Trim main while rounding.

After Rounding the Leeward Mark (Onto Fourth Leg)

2—Fine-tune main and jib trim.

3—Secure end of spinnaker halyard.

—Take off vang.

—Uncleat pole lift and remove pole from the mast.

—Disconnect all lines from the pole and stow.

—Secure lift and foreguy.

2—Detach sheet and halyard from the spinnaker.

—Clip afterguy and sheet together and move them to the side of the boat on which they will be used next.

2,3—Pack spinnaker in the turtle and stow it on the side of the boat where it will be used next.

3—Clear spinnaker halyard. Take it around the headstay to the other side of the boat if necessary and secure.

2—Continue to check jib and mainsail set.

3—Clean up cockpit.

Now let's turn to a 36-footer. As the boat gets larger, the jobs become more complicated and time-consuming to do. Two men often must handle what one can manage on a one design. Movement increases because controls are no longer as centralized. There is more sail handling, and more sails must be set. Job assignments are more numerous. For this same reason the figures show crewman 7 out of normal sequence in the deck-assignment diagrams.

The following section shows the job descriptions for a yawl or ketch, chosen because they have the most jobs. For a sloop, the mizzen area can be left out and for a one design the large boat jobs are omitted. In this way one master table can be presented.

The assignments are in the approximate sequence that one might find in a normal race. When a job is duplicated it is listed only once.

BASIC CREW ASSIGNMENTS

(Numerals represent crewmen indicated in Fig. 234.)

Job description	Two-man crew	Three-man crew	Four-man crew	Five-man crew	Six-man crew	Eight-man crew	Ten-man crew	Twelve-man crew
Bend on mainsail	1,2	2,4	2,3	3,4	3,4	4,5	7,8	7,8
Bend on jib or genoa (and attach sheets)	2	2	3,4	4,5	5,6	7,8	9,10	9,10
Bend on mizzen.	. . .	. . .	2	2	3	3	5	3,4
Hoist mainsail.	2	2	3	4	5	6	8	9,10
Hoist jib.	2	3	4	5	5,6	7,8	9,10	10,11
Hoist mizzen.	. . .	. . .	2	2	3	3	5	3,4
Adjust mainsail luff.	2	2	4	4	5	6	8	9
Adjust mainsail foot	2	2	4	4	5	6	8	9
Trim mainsheet.	1	1	3	3	4	4	4	5,4*
Adjust main traveler	1	1	3	3	4	4	4	4
Adjust headsail luff (halyard).	2	3	4	4	5	6	9	9,10
Adjust headsail luff (Cunningham)	2	3	4	4	5˙	6	9	10
Trim headsail sheet	2	2	2	2	2	2	6,7	6,9
Adjust headsail sheet leads. . .	2	2	2,3	2,3	2,3	2,4	5,8	7,8
Adjust mizzen luff.	. . .	. . .	3	3	3	3	5	4
Adjust mizzen foot.	. . .	. . .	3	3	3	3	5	4
Trim mizzensheet	. . .	. . .	3	3	3	3	5	4
Adjust mizzen traveler	. . .	. . .	3	3	3	3	5	4

*Denotes crewman functioning as a tailer.

Set spinnaker pole.........	2	3	4	5	6	7,8	9,10	11,12
Hoist spinnaker pole lift	2	2	3	4	5	6	7	10,3*
Hook up spinnaker	2	3	4	5	6	8	10	12
Hoist spinnaker...........	1	3	4	4	5	7,6*	9,8*	10,11,9*
Trim spinnaker foreguy	2	2	3	3	3	4	4	10,4*
Trim spinnaker afterguy.....	1	2	2	3	3	3,4*	3,5*	8,2*
Trim spinnaker sheet.......	2	2	3	2	2	2,4*	2,4*	2,6*
Lower headsail	2	3	4	5	5,6	7,8	9,10	10,11
Install reaching strut.........	...	...	3,4	4,5	5,6	5,6	7,8	9,10
Hook up staysail...........	...	...	4	5	6	7	7	11
Hoist staysail	...	...	4	5	6	6	6	10,9*
Trim staysail.............	...	...	3	3	4	5	5	7
Hook up mizzen staysail	...	...	3	3	3	3	5	3
Hoist mizzen staysail........	...	...	3	3	3	3	5	2
Trim mizzen staysail	...	...	3	3	3	3	5	3
Hook up boom vang	2**	3	3	4	5	5	6	7
Adjust permanent backstay	2	3	3	3	3	5	5	4
Raise headsail	2	3	4	5	5,6	7,8	9,10	10,11
Ease spinnaker afterguy.....	2	3	3	3	3	3	3	8
Lower staysail halyard			4	5	6	7	8	10
Lower spinnaker pole lift	2	3	3	4	5	6	8	4
Detach spinnaker tack	2	3	4	5	6	8	10	12
Lower spinnaker halyard	1	3	4	4	5	7	9	10
Gather in spinnaker........	2	2	2	2,3	4,5	5,6	5,6,7	6,7,8
Detach spinnaker sheet and halyard and stow sail	2	2	2	2,3	4,5	5,6	5,6	3,8
Clear spinnaker halyard	2	3	4	4	6	8	10	12
Detach pole and stow	2	3	4	5	5,6	7,8	9,10	11,12
Secure foreguy	2	2	3	4	5	7	8	10
Secure spinnaker pole lift....	2	3	4	4	5	6	8	10
Reset spinnaker sheet	2	3	2	4	5	7	8	10
Reset afterguy...........	2	3	2	4	6	6	7	10
Remove boom vang	2	3	2	4	5	5	6	9
Remove reaching strut			3	4	5,6	5,6	5,6	10

**This job is done automatically (without crewman) on high-performance boats such as the Flying Dutchman.

Job description	Two-man crew	Three-man crew	Four-man crew	Five-man crew	Six-man crew	Eight-man crew	Ten-man crew	Twelve-man crew
Pack, zip, or stop spinnaker...	2	2,3	2	3,4	3,5	3,5	3,5	9,10
Gather in staysail, detach and stow			3	4	5,6	5,6	7*	9
Lower mizzen staysail			3	3	3	3	5	3
Gather in, detach, and stow mizzen staysail..........			3	3	3	3	5	3
Overhaul all lines	2	2,3	2	3,4,5	3,4,5	3,8	3,8	6,12

DETAILED ASSIGNMENT BREAKDOWN
for Seven-Man Racing Crew

A 36-footer, which could be a typical One-Tonner, may be sailed with six or seven in crew. Therefore, crewman 7 is given the odd jobs that can be assigned to another crew member if only six are on hand. The numbers in parentheses show which crewman does what. Before you begin the race, there are some jobs to be done for which there do not have to be specific assignments but for which the crew should be ready at any time. The following is a brief list of these procedures to be followed before and at the start.

Before the Race

1. Pack spinnakers.
2. Practice windward tack. Set outhaul, downhaul (backstay to control jib or genoa luff sag), headsail leads. Barber hauls or athwartship jib lead, traveler. Mark main and headsail trim points for later reference.
3. Tack on both port and starboard and note compass angles on each. This should be done as often as possible to record any shifts, so you know angles of lifts and headers in advance of start. Double-check by also going head to wind several times and record true-wind direction.
4. Test starting line to find favored end—double-check again just before final starting maneuvers.

5. Note compass course of each leg and post on traveler bridge, coaming, or other visible area. Wind angle for reaching legs can be estimated.
6. Sight windward mark or compass course to see if mark is dead to windward or off to one side. Can you make it in one tack?
7. Sail close to a buoy and check current. Consult tide tables to see when it will change.

Maneuvering Before the Start

1. Double-check wind now vs. recorded information for shift, know whether you are in uplift or header, and plan position so you are mobile to tack where required.
2. Double-check favored end of line.
3. Overtrim traveler to center to point better at start (unless you are clear and no one is under you).
4. Double-check wind velocity for change—it is too late for test on wind, so adjustments will have to be made as soon as you settle down on course. Do not do too much at the start—just trim and sail. Concentrate on getting the boat moving fast.

Fig. 235
Seven-Man Crew
Going to Windward
(Moderate-to-Heavy Breeze)

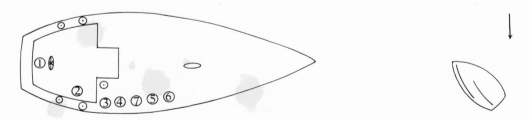

Crew positions will vary with the different maneuvers at or before the start, so no diagrams are shown. Figure 236 shows the boat underway to windward after the start.

Tacking (Fig. 236)

1. Release genoa sheet (2); pull in slack on new sheet (3)
2. Overhaul windward genoa sheet on deck (7)
3. Clear genoa through foredeck (6)
4. Run back genoa clew (5), (6)
5. Tail genoa sheet (3)
6. Grind genoa winch (2); (2) and (3) can interchange for relief
7. Reset main traveler (4)
8. Reserve winch grinder (7)

    As boat tacks, sheet is eased (2); overhauled (7); cleared through fore-triangle and run back (5); (6); with continuous tailing (3); then winched in—all one continuous motion (2). The main traveler is changed simultaneously.

Fig. 236
Seven-Man Crew
Tacking—Windward Leg
(Similar to Positions at Start)

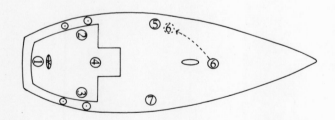
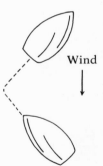

Approaching Windward Mark (Fig. 237)

1. Bring spinnaker on deck together with sheet and guy (5), if not rigged
2. Check spinnaker sheets to see if they are outside everything (7)
3. Hook up sheet and guy, run guy through pole end (6); and ease lines aft (3)

4. Raise pole on mast (trim pole slide downhaul and lift) (5)
5. Hook up pole lift and foreguy (6); raise pole end (6); and help with control lines aft (7)
6. Attach boom vang loosely (4)
7. Sight angle of next leg and estimate how far off stay pole position should be when spinnaker is up (3)
8. Check spinnaker halyard to be sure it is not twisted (5)
9. Attach spinnaker halyard (6)
10. Stand by genoa sheet to ease (2)
11. Stand by mainsheet and traveler (4)
12. Stand by guy to trim (3)
13. Raise pole end (5); and tail (7)

Fig. 237
Seven-Man Crew
Approaching Windward Mark and
Turning

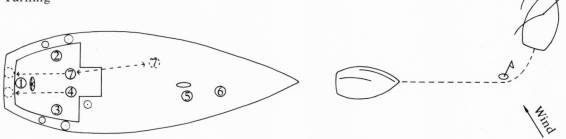

Turning the Windward Mark — To Port — To a Reach (Fig. 237)

1. Ease main traveler (4)
2. Ease mainsheet quite fast while turning and then trim to suit (4)
3. Ease genoa but кeep overtrimmed so spinnaker can go up behind (2)
4. Check boat position. If some maneuver needed under main and genoa, do before raising spinnaker (1)
5. Hoist spinnaker (5); tail (6); trim guy (3) and sheet (2) simultaneously to spread spinnaker while being raised.

6. Quickly, ease sheet (2) and square pole perpendicular to apparent wind (3); fine-trim sheet until luff has slight curl (2)
7. Lower genoa (5), (6)
8. Check pole height (5), (7)
9. Ease main Cunningham (4)
10. Ease main outhaul and check vang tension (4)
11. Staysail on deck (if needed) (5)
12. Hook up staysail (6)
13. Attach staysail sheets (7)
14. Set staysail lead blocks and put sheets through blocks (7)
15. Hoist staysail and tail (5), (6)
16. Trim staysail and tail (7), (4)
17. Rig reaching strut and run guy through (if enough wind to warrant) (5), (6)
18. Ease backstay (4) with help from (7) if needed
19. Remove turtle or sailbag (spin) (6)
20. Pump if necessary (4)
21. Get sheets, if needed at any time, from below (4)

Approaching the Jibe Mark (Fig. 238)

1. Attach lazy sheet (5), (6)
2. Lower staysail (5); and move halyard to mast or bow to clear fore-triangle so pole can swing through (6)
3. Remove vang (7)
4. Select best rounding procedure (1)—try to be inside to mark and in clear air after
5. Take strain on lazy sheet and ease regular sheet to get considerable slack (2)
6. Raise spinnaker pole on mast (5) to allow pole end to get inside headstay; if control line is aft, (7)
7. Remove reaching strut (5)

Dip-Pole Jibe (See Fig. 147c)

1. Try to turn so that you end up inside boat to windward on new tack but do everything you can to avoid a sharp turn (1) (a momentary down-

Fig. 238
Seven-Man Crew
Approaching Jibe Mark and Actual Jibe,
Either Dip Pole or End-for-End

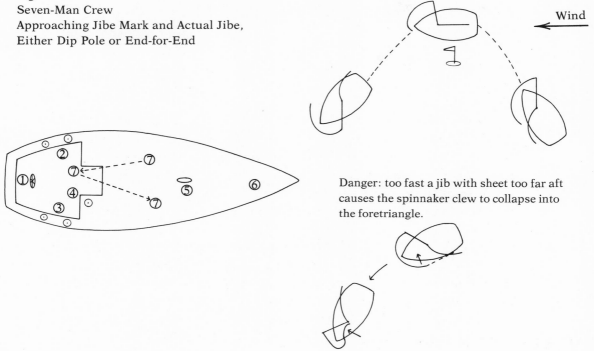

Danger: too fast a jib with sheet too far aft causes the spinnaker clew to collapse into the foretriangle.

    wind run will help the crew in the jibe maneuver when guy and sheet strains are minimal)

2. As boat starts its turn, first trim pole (3); and ease sheet forward (2)
3. Ease foreguy (7)
4. Trim main to centerline and then ease out after jibe (4)
5. Release pole end from spinnaker tack with remote control (5)
6. Lower topping lift (7); tension foreguy (7)
7. Insert slacked spinnaker sheet in pole end (will become new guy) (6)
8. Push pole to new side (6); ease foreguy (7) and trim lift (7)
9. Trim new afterguy (old sheet) (2); and when under tension ease lazy sheet (2)
10. *At all times* keep spinnaker trimmed square to the wind during jibe, then as soon as new guy is tensioned on new jibe, trim pole square to apparent wind, and trim sheet until luff just breaks (both jobs have to be changed quickly whenever boat is swinging underneath spinnaker)

11. Reset vang (7)
12. Reattach staysail halyard (6); hoist (5); tail (6)
13. Trim staysail (4)
14. Double-check set of main (4)
15. Reset reaching strut (5), (6)

End-for-End Pole Jibe (See Fig. 147A)

1. Attach alternate foreguy on inboard end if no bridle (6), (7)
2. As boat starts to swing, trim guy aft (3); and ease sheet (2)
3. Ease old foreguy (7)
4. Trim main toward center and ease out after jibe (4)
5. Detach pole from mast (6)
6. Detach outboard end of pole (5)
7. Engage old mast end in sheet (6)
8. Ease sheet (2); and push pole forward (6) (sheet has to be eased enough to allow inboard end of pole to be pushed forward to fore side of mast)
9. Engage pole in mast slide (6), (5)
10. Trim new guy (old sheet) until pole is square to wind (2)
11. Trim sheet (old guy) until shoulder is "on edge" (3)

NOTE: vang change and staysail lowering and raising after jibe same as dip-pole jibe.

Approaching Home Mark (Fig. 239)

1. Tighten backstay (4)
2. Lower staysail and stow (5), (6)
3. Secure halyard to mast (6)
4. Raise genoa (5), (6)
5. Remove vang (7)
6. Trim and sail-handling controls
   a. Main Cunningham down (4)
   b. Main outhaul out (7)
   c. Main traveler in (4)
   d. Genoa Cunningham down (7)
   e. Stand by genoa, and trim while rounding (3)
   f. Stand by main to trim while rounding (4)
7. Spinnaker takedown

    a. Ease afterguy until pole end against forestay (2)

    b. Lower topping lift and tension foreguy until pole end is about 5 feet above deck (7)

    c. Pull in spinnaker sheet to center of boat on lee side (7)

    d. Release spinnaker tack—by releasing afterguy shackle (6) or letting guy run through pole end (2)

    e. Lower spinnaker halyard at a rate equal to speed of those gathering in sail (5)

    f. Gather in spinnaker (6), (7)

Fig. 239
Seven-Man Crew
Approaching Home Mark and Rounding
to Windward

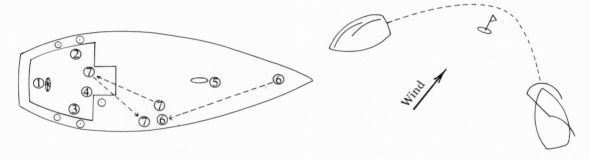

After Rounding and Assuming Windward Tack

1. Concentrate on main (4) and genoa (3) trim; then complete spinnaker gear removal (7), (5), (6)

    a. Detach spinnaker halyard, untwist, and secure to mast (6); take up slack on winch (5)

    b. Lower pole (5) on mast; and lower lift (7); remove pole and set in chocks (5), (6)

    c. Secure foreguy and lift (7)

    d. Stow spinnaker (5)

2. Stuff spinnaker in bag or turtle (5), (6)

3. Clean up all lines (7), (2); and take slack out of all halyards not in use (5)

4. Reset spinnaker sheets to proper side for next reach or run (6), (2)

Obviously, there are a multitude of additional chores to be done when you are racing, but this will give you an idea of how to set up the crew assignments for your boat.

Part Five

MAXIMIZING SAIL POWER

Chapter 17

Sail Care

Since sails today are made of synthetic fibers, they are virtually maintenance-free; with very little care, they will give you years of satisfactory service. Nevertheless, it pays to check them over periodically. Here are the areas you should examine.

In the mainsail, look for wear around the batten pockets. Check over parts of the sail that come in contact with such parts of the rigging as the spreaders and lower shrouds. Look at the headboard and clew areas, which are subjected to the heaviest strains. You should also examine the slides in these areas. Actually, you would be wise to have extra slides installed near the head and clew, where the heavy loadings occur. Take a look at the seams. Unless a thread has let go, it is difficult to tell the condition of a seam without opening it up and examining the condition of the thread.

In a genoa you ordinarily look for wear along the leech tabling area, where the sail chafes against the spreaders. (Do not have a spreader patch installed until you are sure where it should go.) Examine the tack area where it may rub against the pulpit. On large boats you may find signs of wear along the foot of the sail, since it can rub against the lower shroud when sheeted in hard. You can usually spot corner weaknesses by elongation in the cloth where there is a thimble in the sail. All snap hooks should be carefully checked, particularly the top one and the one just above the tack. You may find these fittings bent by strain. The first snap hook above the tack should be carefully lined up by positioning the tack so that the luff wire is parallel to and the same distance from the headstay as the snap hook. If the tack is farther away from the headstay, it places an angular strain on the snap hook (Fig. 240). Remember, if the bottom or top snap hook lets go in a breeze, all the hooks can go; so extra snap hooks in these areas are warranted.

Batten pockets are the most vulnerable spot in a working jib. The batten often breaks from constant flogging; if it does, its rough edges can start a hole in the cloth.

In a roller-furling jib, the part of the sail which is constantly exposed to the sun can deteriorate. This is usually an area 1 foot wide along the leech and 1 foot wide along the foot of the sail. If the sail is more than two years old, you may find the seams deteriorating inside the tabling. Since nylon staysails are not in constant use, their only failures occur through misuse or overloading. Spinnakers should be thoroughly examined for little holes. Two people should hold the sail up to the light and look carefully at every panel of cloth as it is stretched out.

Fig. 240
The tack-pin shackle should be the same distance behind the headstay as the higher portions of the luff, where it is held by snap hooks. Otherwise, the tack will move back, placing an excessive load on the first hook above it, and the hook may break, starting a chain reaction of breakage in the remaining snap hooks.

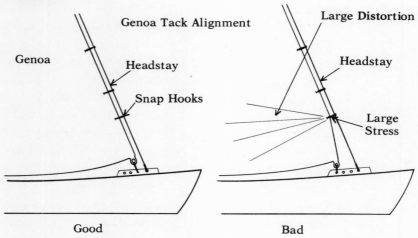

Genoa Tack Alignment

Genoa

Headstay

Snap Hooks

Large Distortion

Headstay

Large Stress

Good

Bad

SAIL REPAIRS

Basically, sail damage involves three things: lost fittings, such as a slide or snap hook, cloth rips, and seam failure.

It is easy to lose a fitting, so you should always have extras on board along with a supply of waxed Dacron or nylon thread. Then it is a simple job to sew the hook or slide to the bolt rope on the sail (Fig. 241).

Fig. 241
Sail Slide Attachment

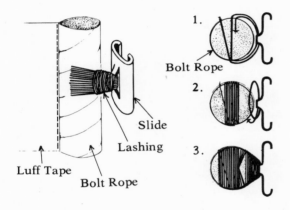

1. Use heavy waxed Dacron or nylon thread. Stitch through the bolt rope and through the eye of the slide.

2. Whip lashing and alternately sew through the bolt rope and slide.

3. Finished Attachment—on larger boats, lashing is secured to an eye in the sail just behind the bolt rope.

4. Genoa snap hooks are attached in the same manner.

In repairing cloth rips, the most difficult problem is dealing with a frayed edge and the threads running parallel to it. If you insert a needle two or three thread rows in from the edge and pull the needle toward the edge, it will pull the threads with it; and you cannot start sewing at the edge of a tear. You have to move ½ inch or more away from the tear before you can get a point that is strong enough to anchor your thread. However, in the case of sails made with synthetic fibers, there is a better solution. Synthetic fibers will melt when they are brought in contact with a hot soldering iron or heated knife; therefore, you can seal the edges of a tear. This stops the fraying and will enable you to sew within ¼ inch of the tear.

A small rip or tear can be repaired by sewing it with the round stitch, which is just an over-and-under lacing that pulls the edges together. An alternative is the herringbone stitch, which will not pucker the fabric (Fig. 242).

Fig. 242
Stitching

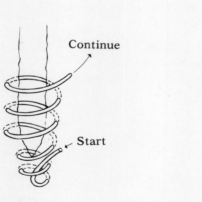
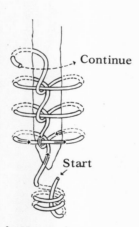

a. Round   b. Herringbone

Large tears should be patched. To make this kind of repair, start by cutting away the torn fabric, leaving a rectangular slot in the sail, and your patch should cover this slot with about a 1½- or 2-inch overlap on all four sides. However, it is often difficult to find good working space for on-board repairs, and it is also hard to keep the patch in line with the ripped area. Therefore, it is wise to use the adhesive-backed patches that are available. Dacron patches come in a number of cloth weights for mainsail, jibs, and genoas; and patches of an adhesive-backed nylon are available for repairing spinnakers. The adhesive backing will hold the patch in place while you sew it. Your patch should be about the same weight cloth as the sail you are repairing. Too heavy a patch, for example, can put excessive strain on the sail area adjacent to the tear. Also, be sure the patch is put on so that its warp coincides with the warp in the sailcloth. In this way, the patched area assumes the same directional strains as the sail.

Cut the patch to the proper dimensions and heat-seal the edges. Place the sail on deck and stick the patch over the tear. Then make a pencil line around the patch about ½ inch away from the edges of the rip and another line about ½ inch away from the outer edge of the patching material (Fig. 243). These will serve as sewing lines. With an awl, punch holes in the material approximately ½ inch apart. This prepunching makes it easier to push the sail needle back and forth, and all you do is go from one side to the other with the needle.

For a fast repair on a heavy sail, it is sometimes easier to hold the ripped area of the sail in a vertical position with a crewman on either side. Then the needle is pushed in from one side and pulled through with pliers on the other. This process is repeated back and forth. By this method a 6- to 8-inch tear can be repaired in 10 or 15 minutes.

Fig. 243
Hand Repair of Small Rip

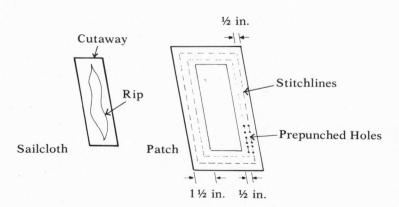

There is another patching system that appears to be practical, although it has not been widely used. It uses rust-free staples, such as those made from Monel, a high-strength stainless-steel alloy. A large number of staples can be used instead of stitches to make a good, fast patch.

However, as with any temporary repair, there is a chance that patches will not hold. Consequently, a professional repair job should be made as soon as possible.

One of the most difficult repair jobs for the inexperienced sailor is a tear that occurs at the edge of a sail next to the tape or bolt rope. It is hard to install a patch close enough to the edge without covering the tape or rope. If you have a tear in this area, wrap the patch around the tape or rope and then sew through from one side of the patch to the other. There is nothing wrong with this method of repairing a tear. The same technique is used if you get a tear near the base of the headboard. In this case, start your patch several inches below the board and extend the patch material up and over both sides of the headboard. Stitch through the headboard holes and sew the two sides of the patch together around the perimeter of the headboard.

A rip along the side of a batten pocket is also difficult. If you lay a patch over any part of the pocket and sew it down, you will sew right through the batten pocket itself. Therefore, if a rip occurs in this area, the proper way to repair it is to lift one edge of the batten pocket by removing the stitches, then install your patch material along the edge of the pocket, and, finally, sew the pocket down. If you have to make a fast repair, you might be able to sew along the edge of the pocket as long as you leave room to insert the batten.

Another difficult repair area is at the corner of a sail, such as at the tack or clew attachment point. On the newer sails, the corner holes are made of two metal rings pressed into the sail and held in place by a stainless-steel liner. Since there is no sewing, if this unit pulls out, generally the entire clew area is damaged and will have to be built up by a sailmaker, and a new unit pressed in place.

The most common practice in the past was to have hand-worked holes. These holes were made by the sailmaker placing a ring within a stamped-out area in the sail and sewing the sailcloth to the ring (Fig. 244). Then a metal liner is inserted inside the ring and the liner sides are flared out to allow the attachment fitting to bear on the liner and not the threads. If the ring tears out of the sail, you can easily solve the problem by installing

Fig. 244

a. Steps in Completing a Handworked
Hole

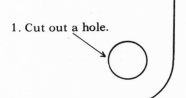

1. Cut out a hole.

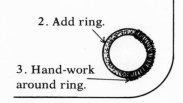

2. Add ring.

3. Hand-work
around ring.

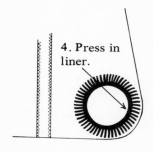

4. Press in
liner.

Handworked Hole with Liner

b. Handworked Hole Compared to
Pressed Ring—the latter can only be done
in the loft.

Pressed Ring

a larger ring, sewing it to the sail and installing a liner. You should keep
on board some rings and liners and a punch to do the job in an emergency.
This type of repair, however, is very sophisticated and in most cases should
be done by a sailmaker.

The most common tearing problem is a rip in the spinnaker cloth.
Nylon cloth is weak enough so that a tear that is not stopped at once can
go completely across the sail, either destroying the sail or requiring a major

repair job. Fortunately, spinnaker repair tape comes in many colors and in long rolls, and if you can spread the sail out on a long flat surface and put a slight tension on it so that the two edges of the tear are parallel and close together, you can seal the tear with the tape. Sometimes, if the sail is dry and relatively salt-free, tape alone (on both sides of the sail) may hold for some time. Usually spinnaker tears are so extensive that hand-sewing is most difficult. However, if a tear occurs near one of the corners of the sail (tack, head, or clew), where the loading is heavy, sewing is mandatory. Use the right weight nylon patch and sew it on as you would other patches.

If a spinnaker tears down the leech, it usually does so just inside the leech reinforcing tape. This is very difficult to fix. The only immediate solution is to join the two sides of the rip together with repair tape. The repair tape should have at least one row of hand stitching on either edge. This is a short-term repair which is not satisfactory because of excess weight along the edge. The proper repair can only be done by the sailmaker. He has to retrim the spinnaker along the torn edge and sew standard leech tape to the new edge.

Finally, a very common repair job is that of mending a seam. The hard part of this is holding the sail panels together while you are sewing, but your sailmaker can supply you with two-sided sticky-back tape that can make this job fairly easy. Pin the panels together or secure them with tape. Then use the flat-seam stitch and sew diagonally across the warp of the sailcloth (Fig. 245). If the seam failure was caused by the thread letting go and if the sailcloth is still perfectly good, you can use the existing ma-

Fig. 245
Flat-Seam Zigzag Stitch

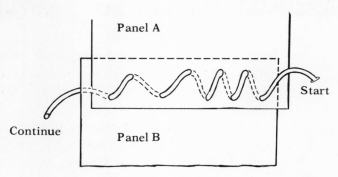

chine-stitch holes to make your repairs. This is a tedious but sometimes necessary task.

CLEANING SAILS

Before you attempt to clean synthetic sails, you should understand their chemical properties. Under normal use, Dacron and nylon are damaged by only two things: severe chafing and exposure to ultraviolet light.

Dacron sailcloth has a silicone coating which accomplishes several things. It helps prevent the fabric from absorbing water and becoming unduly heavy. It acts as a barrier that sheds dirt and also lowers the porosity of the cloth. In addition, silicones are considered helpful in resisting wear and tear caused by chafing and friction. Consequently, if you remove this protective coating, the cloth will deteriorate over a period of time, ruining the sail. Sometimes you have to scrub sails on a concrete base. In this case, take every precaution to avoid chafing, which may remove some of the silicone coating and weaken the threads or roughen the surface of the fabric.

Under normal conditions, sensitivity to ultraviolet light is not an important factor with either Dacron or nylon. The average sail does not get enough exposure to affect its durability. However, the sensitivity to ultraviolet light is materially affected by the alkaline or acid materials which may remain in contact with the fibers after a sail has been cleaned. Dacron's sensitivity to ultraviolet light is greatly increased under alkaline conditions, while nylon, when subjected to acid conditions, will deteriorate rapidly. So nothing of an alkaline nature (such as an alkaline-based detergent) should be allowed to remain in Dacron fabrics and nothing acid should be left in nylon.

The pH, or "potential of hydrogen" scale, used universally in chemistry, provides a measurement of relative alkalinity and acidity. The neutral point on this scale is 7; so pH values from 0 to 7 indicate acidity, and values from 7 to 14 indicate alkalinity. You can get the pH test papers at any drugstore. Moisten a patch of sailcloth and put the test paper against it. If there is alkaline or acid present, the paper will turn color. You then compare the color with a chart that gives the values on the pH scale. If no color appears, neither acid nor alkaline is present.

You can remove surface dirt and soil from sails by washing them with household soap or detergent and water. Usually soaps and detergents are alkaline; so after washing, sails should be rinsed four or five times in clear, fresh water to remove the cleaning agent from the cloth completely.

Petroleum products, such as oils, greases, and tar, are difficult to remove from sails, but they will come off if you treat the cloth properly. Oily stains or deposits may be safely dissolved by dipping the sailcloth in a good solvent such as mineral spirits. This is a combination of high-flash solvents which will not harm the surface of Dacron sails. You should be careful in selecting solvents to take into consideration the flash point or temperature at which vapors will ignite when used in a confined space. Benzene has a flash point of 12 degrees, Xylol's is 85 degrees, while that of mineral spirits is 104 degrees. This is a high flash point and therefore does not constitute a fire hazard.

The cleaning process can be helped along by agitating the cloth in the solvent. If yellowish stains remain after the oil and grease are dissolved, you can remove them by bleaching only the area of the stain with oxalic acid. Afterward, the sail should have a thorough rinsing with fresh water, then a wash with mild soap or detergent, and finally, a good freshwater rinse.

Salt will cake on Dacron sails, making them stiffer and thus not as easy to handle. Washing the salt off by hosing them down will keep them pliable.

Nylon has the same problem, but as mentioned, dampness elongates nylon. Also, since salt retains water, a salty sail might measure larger than a washed-down dry sail.

Both nylon and Dacron sails are, of course, increased in weight by the salt deposits. The moisture retained by the salt, except on an extremely dry day, will make the sails heavier. Since there is so much concern about weight aloft, this is an important fact to remember. A wet spinnaker particularly can have a significant increase in weight and, therefore, a significant decrease in performance. You can usually remove salt by hosing sails frequently with fresh water. If salt has been on a sail for some time, you may have to give the cloth a light brushing. Use clear water only and a soft brush, preferably with nylon bristles. If you have a large tank or large container available, soak the entire sail in lukewarm water; most of the salt will dissolve without scrubbing.

How to Fold a Sail (Fig. 246)

Fig. 246
How to Fold a Sail

1. Spread the sail out flat with the foot toward the wind.

2. Start at the foot and fold the sail in panels like a roadmap. (If the sail has a window, fold the foot over the window first.)

3. The secret of a smooth fold is to keep tension on the fold (between both sets of hands).

4. Make the width of each fold slightly shorter than the length of the sail bag.

5. Continue folding until the entire sail is flaked down.

6. The bolt rope lies flat as the size of the folds decreases.

7. Fold both ends toward the middle of the sail.

8. Roll or fold the sail into a rectangular shape.

9. Slide the compact package into the sail bag horizontally, so that the folds don't telescope out by gravity, as they will if the sail is inserted vertically.

NOTE: if the folds are properly arranged, the head, clew, and tack patches will never be folded.

Chapter 18

Measuring Sails

Ideally, one-design measurement rules put the burden for winning or losing a race on the skipper by ruling out as many variables in the boats, sails, and equipment as possible. The boatbuilder, working with modern materials such as fiberglass, is able to turn out similar hulls time after time. Unfortunately, the sailmaker has a tougher job because he works with a flexible material, the properties of which are not always constant.

Despite close controls maintained by most mills, sailcloth varies slightly from lot to lot. Cloth manufacturers are continuously trying to improve their product; therefore, a recently received shipment of cloth may have different characteristics compared to a shipment of the same cloth received six months before. When cloth characteristics change, the design and cut of the sail have to be adjusted, and this makes production of duplicate sails much more difficult. Besides, there is a certain amount of variation due to the human element involved in making the sail. Providing identical sails for a single class requires high technical ability, the same run of cloth, and using the same people on each job. However, in most cases, sails are made by a number of different sailmakers from all kinds of cloth and with all different cuts. Therefore, when identical sails are not purchased by a class, a table of limitations and a measurement procedure are required to keep the sails uniform.

ONE-DESIGN MEASUREMENT SPECIFICATIONS

The first thing you should understand about controlling sail specifications is the reasoning behind the controls. What should be governed and why? If a new class follows the measurement rules of an older class, there may be a dozen reasons why this formula will not work. You have to learn the purpose behind each rule before you can write the measurement specifications for a particular class.

Class rules have to be practical, and sail specifications, at best, are a compromise. They should be thought of as approaching an ideal rather than as having achieved it. Most existing sail specifications have been worked out with care along these lines by class officials whose aim is to give you the kind of competitive conditions you want. Sometimes, however, rules that were hastily adopted lead to unforeseen problems. In other cases, there are rules that are not enforced or are outdated and need revision. Perhaps some actual cases will help you understand the difficulties involved in setting up measurement rules.

Case 1

A popular fiberglass class has no spinnaker girth dimensions in its rules. Thus, each sailmaker has been making spinnakers according to his own ideas. The class now wants to restrict the girth dimensions and intends to write a new rule by referring to specifications in other classes. The new rule will be more specific, but, without doubt, many of the present spinnakers will be oversize and therefore illegal. Everyone involved is bound to be somewhat unhappy. Having a complete spinnaker rule before the class started active racing would have helped avoid this problem.

Case 2

The class has sail restrictions which are written up and distributed to boatowners. However, the rules are not enforced. As a result, sails become larger and larger. In two instances, when sail specifications are sent to a sailmaker some distance away and sails are made to legal limitations, the boatowners are unhappy because the new sails are so much smaller than others in the fleet. These legal sails, for all practical purposes, are not competitive. The class officials rule that since so many sails are oversize, it would be difficult to enforce the rule.

Case 3

In many instances, the rule reads that sails are to be measured with only enough tension applied to smooth out the wrinkles. Frequently, a local fleet measurer decides that this is the wrong way to do it and that sails should be pulled quite hard to eliminate all wrinkles completely. This generally produces some stretch in the sailcloth. It also establishes different measurement procedures and different sizes of sails in various areas, so that there is a definite departure from the one-design concept.

Case 4

In *Yachting* some years ago, George O'Day referred to an Olympic Class spinnaker as a "horror." The sixteen specified dimensions were so binding that there was no way to make a better shape for the sail. Of course, as O'Day pointed out, everyone had to suffer the same hardship and in this sense the sails were similar. But if a spinnaker is not really efficient, it can hurt the overall performance of the boat, so that when the merits of one class are compared with another, the picture is distorted.

These examples point out two important requirements: that adequate and practical rules be written before a class begins racing; and that a uniform and universal sail measurement procedure be established so that the same sail will be measured the same way by all class measurers.

Basic sail specifications and measurement procedures should require that careful consideration be given first of all to material. In the past twenty years sails have been made from domestic cotton, imported Egyptian cotton, nylon, Orlon, and Dacron. Perhaps some day there may be better materials than those available today. Meanwhile, it is difficult to write a rule restricting the kinds of material to be used and still allow for progress. The object of many classes appears to be to prevent the use of metal sails or any rigid airfoils. Therefore, a statement accepting any flexible material similar to duck, nylon, or Dacron is put into many rules.

The weights of sailcloth are restricted in some classes and not in others. This restriction is not universal because of a rule in many classes that limits the purchase of sails to two suits with a new boat and one suit a year thereafter. Practically speaking, this eliminates experiments with different weight cloth, since the boatowner has one new suit of sails which he is stuck with for a year if it does not work out. Such a restriction is almost binding enough to eliminate the necessity for a cloth-weight rule.

The same thing applies to spinnakers. If you are only allowed one spinnaker, even though there is a wide range of cloth weights available, you are forced to choose an all-purpose weight, which is usually ¾ ounce. The Lightning Class wrote its rules when the only good spinnaker cloth available was the 1½-ounce material; this weight was written into the rule. When lighter cloth weights came out on the market, the class held to the original rule for a while because so many boatowners had the 1½-ounce spinnakers. Eventually, Lightning spinnakers of ¾ ounce were legalized. Many of the relatively new classes either have no restrictions on spinnaker cloth weights, or they require the ¾-ounce sail.

MAINSAIL SPECIFICATIONS

The major problem in the measurement of mainsails is that luff and foot construction varies from sailmaker to sailmaker. Frequently, on finished sails, luffs made to the same design dimension will measure differently when laid out on the floor. The variation results from construction techniques.

As we saw in Chapter 4, in making a sail, cloths are laid with the thread lines perpendicular to the straight-line leech. This is the strongest direction of the cloth, and it is laid this way because the leech is not reinforced by anything other than the tabling, which usually consists of extra strips of sailcloth. Therefore, along the luff and the foot the cloth terminates on the bias (its weakest direction) and requires reinforcement in the form of rope or tape to reduce excessive stretch.

When you are measuring a taped luff on the floor, it will pull out to almost full size. Some machine-roped luffs are quite difficult to pull out to full size. Thus, the most practical rules limit the length of the luff and the foot through the use of black bands on the mast at the head and at the tack, and on the boom at the outhaul.

The most important consequence of differences in luff length is in the measurement of upper and lower girth dimensions. Some rules have specified that upper and lower girth dimensions are to be measured at a certain distance down from the head and up from the tack. Small differences in the luff length can cause the girth dimensions to be measured from different points. If the luff is not pulled out to full size when the positions of the girth dimensions are marked on the luff, the upper girth dimension would be relatively farther down in the sail, where it is wider, and the lower girth would be farther up in the sail, where it is narrower. Measurements, therefore, might be larger than specified on the upper girth and smaller on the lower girth (Fig. 247). Some classes have provided for this by allowing a tackle to be used to pull the luff out to full size. Girth dimensions then are measured at the same points each time.

Fig. 247
Effects of Bolt-Rope Shrinkage.   If girths are measured at specific lengths from the head and clew, luff shrinkage can cause variations in the measured girth locations. An apparently shorter luff due to bolt-rope shrinkage will cause the upper girths to be over legal size and the lower girths to be under legal size.

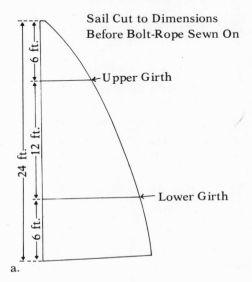

a.

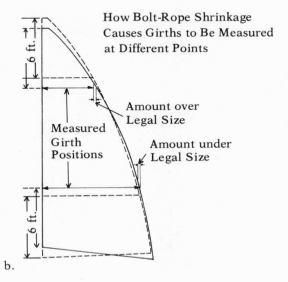

b.

Many classes use a mid-girth measurement, whereby first the luff is folded in half and then the leech is folded in half to find the mid-luff and mid-leech points. The girth dimension is then taken between these two mid-points when the sail is opened up. The rule is quite equitable, and classes using it have found few problems. It is about as simple a rule as you can devise and produces a consistency in size, providing the leech assumes a smooth curve (Fig. 248).

Fig. 248
Measuring Mainsails

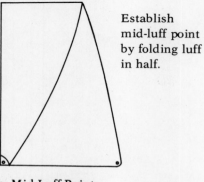

Establish
mid-luff point
by folding luff
in half.

a. Mid-Luff Point

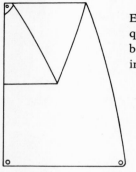

Establish
quarter-luff point
by folding luff
in half again.

b. Quarter-Luff Point

Establish
mid-leech point
by folding leech
in half.

c. Mid-Leech Point

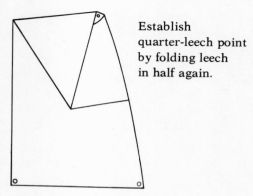

Establish
quarter-leech point
by folding leech
in half again.

d. Quarter-Leech Point

e.
The girth points are measured between
the luff fold point and the leech fold point.

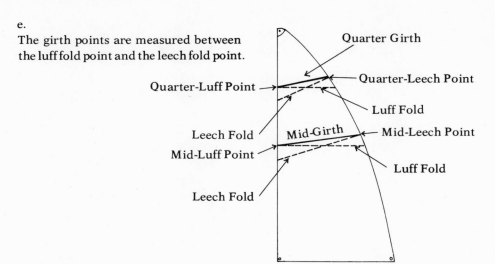

Quarter Girth

Quarter-Leech Point

Quarter-Luff Point →

Luff Fold

Leech Fold   Mid-Girth   Mid-Leech Point

Mid-Luff Point

Luff Fold

Leech Fold

If you want to find the quarter-girth measurement you simply fold
the luff and leech in half, and then fold the upper half once more in the
same way. Folding the sail is better than measuring total dimensions, since
folding keeps the same ratios up and down the luff and leech.

When considering restrictions on the mainsail, or any other sail
for that matter, a class is faced with the choice of being very restrictive
or allowing a certain amount of flexibility to provide the opportunity to
improve performance and sharpen competition. Many classes have chosen
the latter way and then sanctioned the use of draft-control devices such as
the Cunningham hole and roach reefs or zippers. (See Chapter 5.)

Mast bend, which also flattens the mainsail, is allowed under many
class rules. There is some debate about whether to restrict mast bending
devices that can be changed during a race. Bending the mast, for example,
adjusts the amount of draft to suit the breeze. The average skipper can get
more fun out of sailing a boat with a versatile rig like this than one which
is tightly restricted. If you are not quite as good a helmsman as the next
fellow, you may be able to trim your sails better and make up the difference.

Another measurement area is the mainsail's headboard. As the headboard increases in size perpendicular to the luff, the leech is also moved
outboard (Fig. 249), thus increasing the sail area. Therefore, a headboard

Fig. 249
A wider headboard adds more area on leech.

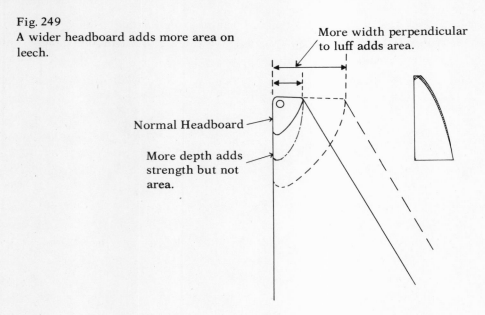

More width perpendicular to luff adds area.

Normal Headboard

More depth adds strength but not area.

rule should restrict the greatest width, measured perpendicular to the luff, to a specified dimension. (The depth of the headboard parallel to the luff has no such application as it only serves to strengthen the manner in which the board is fastened to the sail.)

Batten length is also subject to measurement rules. Battens are used to support the leech roach, and therefore the length allowed controls the amount of roach.

JIB SPECIFICATIONS

Jibs are somewhat simpler to lay out and measure than mainsails since they usually are reinforced only along the luff. The leech and foot are free edges. The exceptions are the club-footed jib or one with a wooden luff spar, and in these cases specifications similar to those used for a mainsail can be used.

Here are some thoughts to bear in mind when considering rules and procedures for measuring jibs. Some classes have rules stating that luff, foot, and leech measurements should be taken from eye to eye—that is from head eye to tack eye to clew eye. This invites rule beating, since a sailmaker could move the eyes deeper into the sail and pick up a lot of unmeasured area. But if the class restricts how far into the sail the eyes can be moved, the measuring becomes overcomplicated.

Many classes use the simple method of laying out a triangle on the floor. The three corners of the sail either fit inside the triangle or they do not, which eliminates any arguments. A limit on mid-girth and foot roach, if desired, can be met by measuring separately, although some classes simply require that the entire jib fit inside the triangle.

Some classes do not have any girth restrictions on the jib, since there are practical factors that limit size unless the jib has battens. The amount of roach, or excess cloth, in the luff cannot be excessive, or the jib will not set properly. Extra roach in the leech does not always prove effective, and many sailmakers make jibs narrower than the maximum allowed girth. So a girth restriction in class rules does not seem to be necessary. However, the leech and foot should be fair curves, and these can be projected to indicate the corner of the sail where they intersect. Foot roach on a jib also has a practical limit unless an artificial means is used to make the roach stand. As long as the foot roach has to stand by itself, there is less need to restrict its depth. Nevertheless, a commonsense limitation on foot roach for most one-design jibs would be about 6½ to 7 per cent of the length of the foot.

In classes which use maximum and minimum luff, leech, and foot measurements as the limitations on the jib, decksweeper working jibs can be fitted into the rules by intentionally using the minimum luff length and the maximum leech length. (See Fig. 157.) There are two ways to control extreme changes in clew height: the first is to limit the differences between minimum and maximum dimensions; and the second is to use the triangle-on-the-floor method. The question of whether or not to allow decksweeper jibs is one that has bothered many one-design class measurement committees. In most cases, with the introduction of the decksweeper, many classes have shown improved performance and better boat-handling qualities in all winds, so in all likelihood they are here to stay.

Battens in a jib keep the leech firm and, as with the mainsail, control the amount of positive roach that can set properly. Thus, class rules normally limit the number and size of battens.

SPINNAKER SPECIFICATIONS

While mainsails and jibs are made of Dacron, which is fairly stable, spinnakers are made of nylon, which stretches and shrinks with changes in humidity. Consequently, spinnaker measurements vary from day to day. The synthetic fibers increase in length if the moisture content in the air is increased, and they decrease in length if the moisture content is reduced (Fig. 250).

Fig. 250

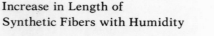

Increase in Length of
Synthetic Fibers with Humidity

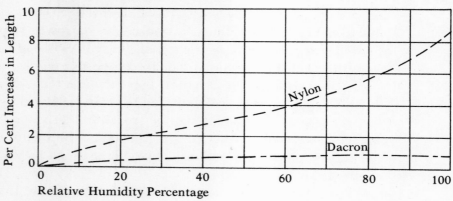

This characteristic of nylon spinnakers has produced many measurement headaches for one-design classes. At some regattas, a large percentage of spinnakers will measure too large, while at other regattas, the same sails will measure within the rules. For this reason, many skippers use laundry dryers to remove moisture from their sails before they are measured on humid days. However, after a sail has been dried, it will pick up moisture in 15 or 20 minutes and increase in size. Trying to measure a moisture-sensitive fabric with a steel tape is difficult and certainly inaccurate. The sailmaker is faced with a virtually insoluble problem. If he cuts a sail to maximum size on a dry day, the sail will then be oversized if it is measured at a regatta on a damp day. If he cuts the sail to full size on a damp day, it will measure short on a dry day. Either situation can make a boatowner unhappy. Therefore, to satisfy measurement rules, sailmakers have to make spinnakers in weather somewhere between the two extremes of moisture, or in a moisture-controlled atmosphere, which is still neither a very practical nor satisfactory solution:they don't control the humidity at the time of measurement. Sail measurements become larger when the air is generally cooler and more moist. A Lightning spinnaker, which measures 20 feet 6 inches on the luff could vary as much as 2½ per cent between a very damp day and a very dry day. According to DuPont figures, this could amount to 6 inches. And so on a damp day the 20-foot-6-inch sail might measure 21 feet. This is a ticklish problem, but as long as measurers know it exists, there should be a better understanding of the variations in spinnaker dimensions.

There is also the fact that nylon stretches (far more than Dacron), and if a measurer decides to pull out the spinnaker harder than usual, he can add several extra inches to a particular dimension. The Olympic Class spinnaker mentioned above (Case 4) had very stringent measurement restrictions. Such a rule presents inevitable problems, since it is difficult to use such close tolerances on a changeable material.

To get a practical spinnaker measurement rule, you have to reduce the number of restrictive dimensions. The more measurement points, the more complications there are and the more difficult it is to measure a large number of spinnakers at a regatta. The simplest measurement rule, and one that will produce sails that are quite alike in all cases, is merely to have luff, foot, and mid-girth restrictions. Since spinnakers are most easily measured when they are folded in half, the maximum girth can be obtained at the mid-girth by folding the sail in half from head to foot and measuring across the fold (Fig. 251a). Another system of measuring is through one or more girth dimensions whose position is controlled by arcs radiating out of the head. The girth dimension will be found between the points where the arc cuts the luffs and the centerfold. Many one-design classes require two arcs, one about one-quarter of the way down and the other halfway down from the head (Fig. 251b).

On a well-shaped spinnaker the curves formed by the leeches and the luffs should be fair and symmetrical. An upper girth dimension, if correct, will not alter the smooth-shaped profile of the spinnaker when it is laid on the floor (Fig. 252). If the upper girth is too large or too small in relation to the maximum girth, it will create an irregularity in the centerfold and luff curves in the upper half of the sail.

Fig. 251
Spinnaker Measurement Systems
NOTE: all views show the spinnaker laid
out flat, and folded to luff.

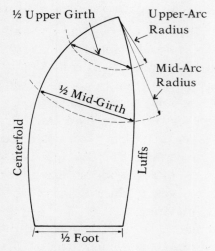

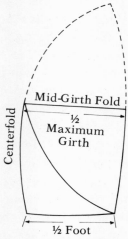

a. Girth points are found by drawing arcs

b. Mid-girth is found by folding head to clew.

Fig. 252
Effects of Upper-Girth Restrictions

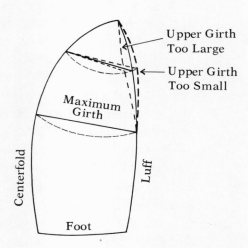

Some classes use a spinnaker head-to-mid-foot measurement to restrict foot roach but many classes omit it and do not seem to have many variations in the amount of skirt or girth at the foot (Fig. 253). Skirt is hard to control, and if the dimension given is large, owners usually demand that the spinnaker be made to full size even though it is difficult to construct an oversized skirt so that it sets well. As a result, sailmakers have had to learn to design these oversized skirts to set well.

Fig. 253
Head-to-foot measurement
restricts the amount
of skirt on a spinnaker.

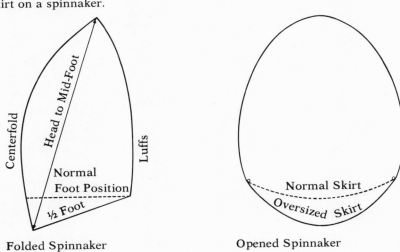

Another complication in a straight-line, head-to-mid-foot measurement is that many sails have built-in shaping in the panels, so that they will not lie flat in this dimension. If a class feels strongly that it wants to control the skirt, it might be best to measure around the vertical curve of the centerfold. However, in the long run it seems best to eliminate this measurement entirely.

In taking measurements from the head to the clew, you have to avoid measuring from eye to eye. As mentioned before, eyes can be moved into the sail to beat the rule. Consequently, measurements at any corner should be taken at the point where the two edges intersect. If a corner is rounded or cut off, the edges should be projected to their intersection and measurements made from that point (Fig. 254).

Fig. 254
How Projection of Edges
Forms a Corner

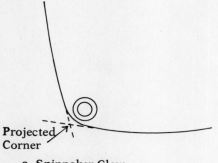

Projected
Corner

a. Spinnaker Clew

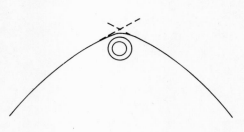

b. Spinnaker Head

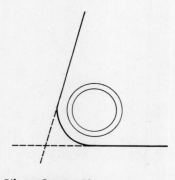

c. Jib or Genoa Clew

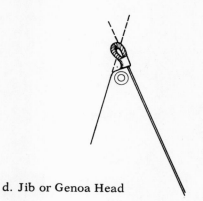

d. Jib or Genoa Head

Most meter-boat classes restrict the luff and sometimes the foot, and have no mid-girth limitation. Since there is so much freedom in design, their spinnakers look and perform very well. The smaller meter classes have running spinnakers that are sometimes as wide as they are high, which gives them a round appearance. (See Figure 123.) An average one-design spinnaker has a maximum girth dimension of 65 to 80 per cent of its luff length.

This type of sail would not be practical for some larger racing classes, because its size is too big for the boat.

International Offshore Rule or CCA spinnakers, on the other hand, are relatively narrow. They are figured to a rule where maximum girth anywhere in the spinnaker is 1.8 times the base of the foretriangle. (See pages 413 and following.) This usually works out to a girth of only 57 to 67 per cent of the luff. Although the average cruising-boat spinnakers are adequate in size under this rule, if the same rule were applied to one-design boats, the sails would look small.

Actually, the cruising spinnaker under the IOR is more difficult to make. With one maximum girth allowed from foot to shoulder, it is difficult to achieve an ideal leech curve without decreasing the foot girth to below maximum; thus you get an "S" curve that results in a bell-shaped sail, cutting down on sail area. Unless you do this, however, it neither looks nor sets as well as a spinnaker that allows a mid-girth dimension larger than the foot; the larger dimension through the center of the sail provides a smooth leech curve. You also need a generous upper girth dimension to maintain this shape. A maximum spinnaker width of about 110 to 120 per cent of the foot makes a nicely shaped sail.

You probably will never become directly involved in measuring sails, but understanding how and why they are measured should help you improve your sail power. By the same token, cruising-boatowners should have a working knowledge of the International Offshore Rule governing sail measurements, which is described next.

Chapter 19

The International Offshore Rule

One-design classes race on a boat-for-boat basis, while cruising boats, which generally are dissimilar in design, compete on a handicap basis. The handicap or time allowance is calculated on the basis of a boat's *rating* as compared to the ratings of other boats in a particular race. In theory the rating, which is translated into a time allowance (seconds per mile), puts all boats on an equal footing, so that small boats have as good a chance of winning a race as the larger boats.

Cruising boats have raced under several different measurement rules, but the most generally accepted one in the past was the rule of the Cruising Club of America (CCA). In England, boats raced under the measurement rule of the Royal Ocean Racing Club (RORC).

In recent years, ocean racing has become more and more popular, attracting boats from many countries, and so in 1960, the Offshore Rule Coordinating Committee was formed to explore the possibilities of developing an International Rule that would govern races among boats of different countries and also be used within a single country.

However, it was not until 1966 when, at the behest of the International Yacht Racing Union, the Offshore Rule Coordinating Committee, the CCA, and the RORC began to cooperate in the formulation of what is now the International Offshore Rule that has been accepted by most ocean-racing organizations as the basic measurement rule for competition at home and abroad. The IOR is administered by the Offshore Racing Council, composed of representatives from the thirteen participating nations, and generally has superseded all previous measurement rules for racing-cruising boats in most major international events, although local areas may choose their own rating rules.

MEASURING PROCEDURE

There is only one official IOR measuring body today in the United States, the office in New York City. The IOR appoints official North American Yacht Racing Union (NAYRU) measurers through the country who actually measure the boats and send input data to the IOR office. The measurer gets a completed rating certificate back for his examination and signature; it then goes to the owner for his signature, after which it becomes a valid certificate. During the program run the IOR computer also scans data in the certificate and compares it to that of similar boats. If a measurement looks unusual, it is marked for questioning, and the measurer is so notified and will double-check the dimensions.

The master IOR rating is determined by a string of formulations. The rating considers the boat's rated waterline length, draft, freeboard, beam, engine and propeller factor, and the center of gravity. All these factors are designated by symbols, and their value is determined by a subsequent formulation or string of formulations that specifically cover every variable in the hull or rig.

In the broadest terms, the rule establishes a rated length for a given boat by formula, and this rated length is then increased or decreased by the relative values of rated depth, rated beam, corrected draft, corrected freeboard, and sail area. These factors produce an initial measured rating or MR. This MR is then multiplied by the engine and propeller factor and the center of gravity factor (stability) to produce the final rating.

Here is a summary of the factors included in the IOR rating:

L — rated length of hull
$\sqrt{S}$ — square root of total rated sail area
DC — draft correction (including centerboard)
FC — freeboard correction
B — rated beam (maximum)
D — rated depth

The rule gives most weight to the rated length (L) and sail area $\sqrt{S}$, as L produces a length somewhat near the actual waterline length and $\sqrt{S}$ provides the power. The other values are small by comparison and add or subtract to the value of L. All these calculations determine a value for MR. This MR value is decreased then slightly by three percentage factors, EPF, CGF, MAF, which may vary from approximately 96 per cent to 100.75 per cent. These factors give slight credits to boats with large propellers and engines and to boats that are very tender or top heavy, and penalize boats with more than two movable parts—rudder and centerboard—under the water (MAF).

The formulas used to determine the above symbols are sometimes very complicated, as they try to include every different variable that may occur from boat to boat and also try to plug possible loopholes that may be used to gain more boat speed without equal penalty.

EPF — engine and propeller factor
CGF — center of gravity factor, which includes the tenderness ratio and righting moments
MAF — movable appendage factor

MR and final rating are shown by the following equations:

$$MR = \frac{.13\ L\ \sqrt{S}}{\sqrt{B \times D}} + .25L + .20\ \sqrt{S} + DC + FC$$

$$Rating\ (R) = MR \times EPF \times CGF \times MAF$$

None of these factors can be changed easily except the sail and rig. The hull is measured both onshore and as it floats when loaded for normal sailing. These measurements determine the draft, beam, freeboard (and overhang and girth), and these cannot be varied appreciably without major hull revisions except by redistribution of weight within the hull. However, propeller factor, for example, can be altered on the existing hull, which would then have only the propeller factor input changed. Any change in weight from ballast, such as a larger engine, changes the waterline, freeboard center of gravity factor (CGF), and so on, with the result that you have to go through the whole process of remeasurement.

The IOR has also adopted a system of standardizing hull measurements when the same class of cruising boat is produced in sufficient quantities. In this case the measurer does not measure hull shape requirements but just the possible variables such as engine and propeller factor, inclining moment (which varies with weight and rig height), and freeboard.

The sail plan (except for rig height because it adds weight and changes the center of gravity factor) can be varied easily because the change involves only the key sail dimensions; nothing else is affected and so nothing else has to be measured again. The new rig information is used as input, so that many sail combinations can be tested for subsequent rating and time allowance comparisons. It is the sail-plan variances that we will discuss in this section.

SAIL-PLAN MEASUREMENTS

For a sloop and a yawl, the basic rig dimensions and certain sails are measured. From this, individual rated sail areas are computed to get total rated sail area (RSAT); the individual rated sail areas are summarized as follows:

RSAM — rated sail area of the main
RSAY — rated sail area of the mizzen
RSAK — rated sail area of the mizzen staysail
RSAF — rated sail area of the foretriangle (including genoa and spinnakers)
SATC — rated sail area penalty that adds 10% to RSAF and subtracts 14.3% from **RSAM**

This list does not mention genoas or spinnakers as they are included in the calculations of the foretriangle. In other words, they are based on the foretriangle size and have certain limits.

Let us turn to the individual formulations first and see how they are obtained for the four basic categories: rated sail area for the mizzen (RSAY), rated sail area for the mainsail (RSAM), rated sail area for the foretriangle (RSAF), and rated sail area for mizzen staysails (RSAK).

The main, mizzen, and foretriangle all have measured height and base dimensions, such as P, E, I, Y, etc. (See Figs. 255a, 256a, and 259.)

The letter C indicates a corrected dimension, which is used when the measured dimension is increased by a penalty. This is the way that oversized battens, headboards, spinnaker pole lengths, main booms and spinnaker poles above deck, and many other variables are controlled. The rules define the limits in these categories; if the limits are exceeded, the excess is related to one of the measured dimensions. The following table shows the sail dimensions used in the rated sail areas and the dimensions that could carry the C penalty.

Sail dimension	Measured symbol	Penalized or corrected symbol
Main luff	P	PC
Main foot	E	EC
Mizzen luff	PY	PYC
Mizzen foot	EY	EYC
Foretriangle height	I	IC
Foretriangle base	J	JC
Genoa girth	LP	—
Mizzen staysail—shortest distance head to foot	YSD	—
Mizzen staysail—shortest side (foot)	YSF	—
Mizzen staysail—mid-girth	YSMG	—
Mainmast to mizzenmast	EB	—
Mainsail foot	E	—
Fore side of mizzenmast	IY	—

Since the corrected sail dimensions will always be larger, the formulations will then list the corrected symbols, unless the formula purposely uses the uncorrected or measured dimensions. It does this in certain cases when it might otherwise be advantageous to take one excess penalty to gain a nonpenalized increase in another direction.

RATED SAIL-AREA FORMULATIONS

Mizzen-Rated Sail Area—RSAY

Perhaps the easiest to calculate is the rated sail area of the mizzen (Fig. 255). This is simply the area of the mizzen triangle, which is the maximum luff dimension (PYC) multiplied by the maximum mizzen foot dimension (EYC) and divided by 2. The formula for the mizzen is

$$RSAY = \frac{EYC \times PYC}{2}$$

Fig. 255
Mizzen Measurement

a. Rated Sail Area of the Mizzen

$$(RSAY) = \frac{EYC \times PYC}{2}$$

PY = measured luff: between black bands
PYC = luff corrected for penalties
EY = measured foot: black band from
mast to clew
EYC = foot corrected for penalties

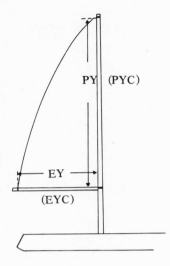

Since PY is the measured luff and EY the measured foot between their respective black bands, they can be increased to the corrected or penalized values PYC and EYC as follows:

b. Other Mizzen Measurements with Limitations, Which, If Exceeded, Are Added to Mizzen Rated Sail Area (RSAY)

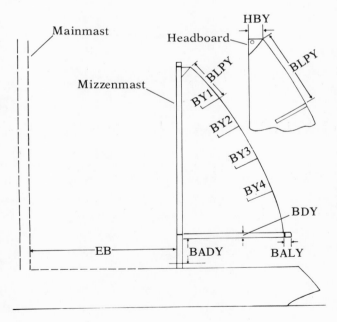

MIZZEN TABLE OF LIMITATIONS

Symbol	Description	Limit	Penalty on excess	Added to	Computed as
	Mizzen head below top of IY	.05 of IY below top of IY	Excess	PY	PYC
BADY	Mizzen tack over deck	.05 × PY + 4.0'	Excess	PY	PYC
BALY	Outer measurement of boom bale	0.5' beyond clew black band	Excess	PY	EYC
BDY	Boom depth	.05 × E	Excess	PY	PYC
BY 1	Upper batten	.10 × EY + 1.0'	All excess × PY/EY	PY	PYC
BY 2,3	Middle batten	.12 × EY + 1.0'	1/6 Excess × PY/EY	PY	PYC
BY 4	Lower batten	.10 × EY + 1.0'	1/6 Excess × PY/EY	PY	PYC
BLPY	Top batten to head	.20 × PY	Excess	BY 1	BY 1
EB	Distance between masts	—	—	—	RSAK
HBY	Headboard width	0.5 (or 0.4 × EY)	Excess × PY/EY	—	PYC
EY	Minimum mizzen foot	Minimum allowance $\dfrac{.85\,E \times PY}{P}$	Anything less illegal		EYC

Mainsail-Rated Sail Area—RSAM

To find the rated sail area for the mainsail (RSAM), you use the following formula and the dimension indicators given in Figure 256.

$$RSAM = .35\ (EC \times PC) + .2EC\ (PC - 2E)$$

This looks complicated, but it really is not. The first part represents 70 per cent of the triangular area and the second part is the aspect-ratio penalty. By multiplying the luff by the foot, you get the total area of a rectangle. If you take 35 per cent of this rectangular area, you get the equivalent of 70 per cent of a triangle. The first part of the formula says that 70 per cent of the triangular mainsail is counted as rated sail area.

The second part of the formula says that if the aspect ratio is not more than 2:1—that is, if the maximum luff length corrected (PC) is not

Fig. 256

a. Rated Sail Area of the Mainsail (RSAM)

P = luff
PC = luff corrected for any penalties
E = foot
EC = foot corrected for any penalties

b. As with the mizzen, all of the dimensions shown besides P and E are penalty sail dimensions. If these dimensions are exceeded, the excess is added to P and E to make the corrected dimensions, PC and EC respectively.

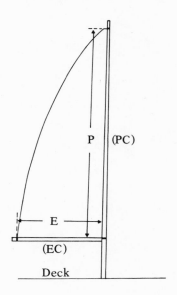

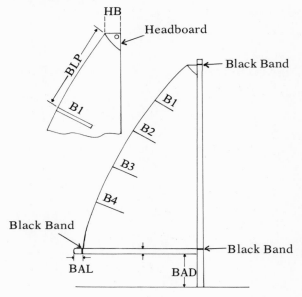

more than two times the measured foot length (E)—there is no penalty. As the corrected luff measurement increases to more than the 2:1 ratio, the excess is run through part two of the formula and added to the triangular area to give the total mainsail rated area (RSAM) (Fig. 257).

To explain this another way, the aspect-ratio penalty is obtained by multiplying the measured foot length by 2 and subtracting this figure from the corrected luff length. If the luff length is larger, this amount over 2:1 is multiplied by 20 per cent of the corrected foot measurement.

And so, the higher the aspect ratio, the more sail area penalty you get. But it is not an excessive amount. It is the amount the committee feels would compensate for the greater boat speed that results from the more efficient rig.

Fig. 257
Explanation of Mainsail Aspect-Ratio Penalty

Penalizes any amount the luff exceeds two
times the foot length. The excess over two
times the foot is multiplied by a factor of
20 per cent times foot (.20 × E).

PC = corrected luff length
EC = corrected foot length
E = measured foot length

Aspect-ratio penalty = 20% × EC × (PC—2E)
Excess over 2:1 = 3 feet
3 feet is multiplied by a factor of 20% × E.

E = 15

E × .20 = 3.0

3.0 × 3 feet = 9-foot penalty

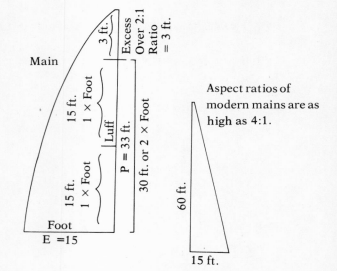

Aspect ratios of modern mains are as high as 4:1.

RSAM formulation
(1) 70% actual triangular area + aspect-ratio penalty

(2) $70\% \times \dfrac{(EC \times PC)}{2} + 20\% \times EC$ for any excess over (luff − 2 × foot)
$\qquad\qquad\qquad\qquad\qquad\qquad\qquad$ (PC) $\qquad$ (E)

(3) .35 (EC × PC) + .2EC (PC − 2E)

NOTE: aspect-ratio penalty utilizes *corrected* luff (PC) but *measured* foot (E).

MAINSAIL TABLE OF LIMITATIONS

Symbol	Description	Limit	Penalty on excess	Added to	Computed as
	Main head below top of 1	.04 below top of 1	All excess	P	PC
BAD	Main tack over deck	.05 × P + 4.0′	All excess	P	PC
BAL	OER measurement of boom bale	E + .5′	All excess	E	EC
BD	Boom depth	.05 × E	All excess	P	PC
BL 1	Upper batten	.10 × E + 1.0′	All excess × P/E	P	PC
BL 2, 3	Middle battens	.12 × E + 1.0′	1/6 excess × P/E	P	PC
BL 4	Lower batten	.10 × E + 1.0′	1/6 excess × P/E	P	PC
BLD	Top batten to head	.20 × P	All excess	P	BL 1
HB	Headboard width	.04 × E	Excess × P/E	P	PC
	Minimum rated area sail	9.49% × IC²	Anything less illegal	—	—

Foretriangle-Rated Sail Area—RSAF

The foretriangle is the most difficult rated area to understand. It is not a sail but the key dimensions upon which the genoas, spinnakers, and staysails are based. There are three dimensions in the foretriangle: the height, I or IC; the base, J or JC; and the genoa girth, LP.

The table following shows how I and J can be penalized to become IC and JC. The LP is a perpendicular from the genoa luff which intersects the clew, producing the girth of the genoa from luff to clew, and does not have a corrected dimension. The measured dimension, whatever the overlap is, is introduced directly into the formula for computing rated sail area (Fig. 258).

Fig. 258
Rated Sail Area for Foretriangle (RSAF)

J = measured foretriangle base
JC = penalized foretriangle base
(J corrected)
I = measured foretriangle height
IC = penalized foretriangle height
(I corrected)

LP = girth of largest genoa (luff to clew)

$$LP\% = \frac{LP \text{ (ft.)}}{JC \text{ (ft.)}} \times 100$$

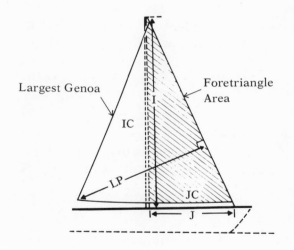

Foretriangle Penalties

I is penalized to IC if

1. The spinnaker pole is too high above deck.
2. The spinnaker luff is too long.
3. The spinnaker headboard is too wide.

J is penalized to JC if

1. The spinnaker pole is too long — pole length = JC.
2. The spinnaker girth is too wide.

There is also a dimension labeled LPIS, which is a measurement of the girth of an inner staysail plus the distance from the staysail luff to the headstay. The LPIS dimension cannot extend past the maximum girth (LP) of the largest genoa. You can get into trouble with this rule when you have a track on deck that allows the staysail tack to move so far aft that the clew of the staysail goes beyond the LPIS limitation. The tack should have a stop on the track, so that the clew is not moved beyond the genoa LP line.

The girth of a genoa is described as a percentage of the corrected base of the foretriangle. If the base is 10 feet and the girth (LP) of the genoa is 15 feet, you have a 150 per cent genoa, which is permitted under the rule without penalty. However, any girth measurement for a genoa that is less than 150 per cent of the corrected foot (JC) will still be counted as 150 per cent. And so you should be sure to have at least the minimum girth allowed under the rule (Fig. 258a).

The spinnaker height and width are functions of both I and JC (foretriangle height and corrected base). There is a penalty if the spinnaker luff exceeds $.95 \times I^2 + JC^2$ or 95 per cent of the hypotenuse formed by I and JC. The spinnaker girth or width can be 1.8 times JC without penalty (Fig. 259).

The formula for computing the rated sail area of the foretriangle (RSAF) is a bit complicated. Here is the formula itself:

$$\text{RSAF} = 50\% \ \text{IC} \times \text{JC}\left[1 + 1.1 \times \left(\frac{\text{LP} - \text{JC}}{\text{LP}}\right)\right] + 12.5\% \ \text{JC} \ (\text{IC} - 2 \times \text{JC})$$

Don't let this throw you. The whole thing breaks down into understandable components. The first part is simply 50 per cent of the height (IC) multiplied by the base (JC) of the foretriangle, which is the actual foretriangle area.

The middle part of the formula is the overlap penalty, which includes the girth measurement (LP) as the variable. The penalty increases as the overlap (LP) increases beyond 150 per cent. This works out to a figure between 1.37 and 1.49 for 150 per cent and 180 per cent, respectively.

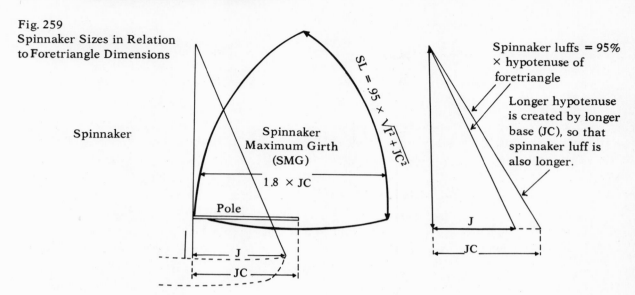

Fig. 259
Spinnaker Sizes in Relation
to Foretriangle Dimensions

Spinnaker

Spinnaker
Maximum Girth
(SMG)

$1.8 \times JC$

Pole

$SL = .95 \times \sqrt{I^2 + JC^2}$

J

JC

Spinnaker luffs = 95%
× hypotenuse of
foretriangle

Longer hypotenuse
is created by longer
base (JC), so that
spinnaker luff is
also longer.

J

JC

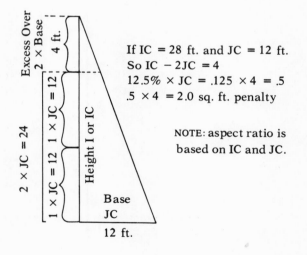

Fig. 260
Explanation of Foretriangle Aspect Ratio
Penalty.   Penalizes any amount the
height of the foretriangle exceeds two
times the base. The excess height over 2 ×
base is multiplied by a factor of 12.5% ×
base
($.125 \times JC$).
J = measured foretriangle base
JC = penalized foretriangle base
(J corrected)
I = measured foretriangle height
IC = penalized foretriangle height
(I corrected)
Aspect-ratio penalty = $12.5\% \times JC \times$
$(IC - 2JC)$

Excess Over
2 × Base

4 ft.

$2 \times JC = 24$

$1 \times JC = 12$

$1 \times JC = 12$

$1 \times JC = 12$

Height I or IC

Base
JC

12 ft.

If IC = 28 ft. and JC = 12 ft.
So IC − 2JC = 4
12.5% × JC = .125 × 4 = .5
.5 × 4 = 2.0 sq. ft. penalty

NOTE: aspect ratio is
based on IC and JC.

The third part of the formula is the aspect-ratio penalty, which is
similar to that of the mainsail except that the symbols are different (Fig.
260).

RSAF Formulation   Foretriangle

(1) Actual foretriangle triangular area × genoa-overlap factor + aspect-ratio penalty

$$\frac{IC \times JC}{2} \times 1 + 1.1 \times \frac{\text{genoa } LP - JC}{(\text{genoa } LP)} + 12.5\% \times JC \text{ for any excess over (height } - 2 \times \text{base)}$$

$$\hspace{8cm} \text{(IC)} \hspace{1.5cm} \text{(JC)}$$

$$.5 \text{ IC} \times JC \left[1 + 1.1 \times \left(\frac{LP - JC}{LP} \right) \right] + .125 \text{ JC (IC } - 2JC)$$

FORETRIANGLE TABLE OF LIMITATIONS

Symbol	Description	Limit	Penalty	Added to	Computed as
SL	Spinnaker luff	$.95 \sqrt{I^2 + JC^2}$	2 × Excess	I	IC
SF, SMW	Maximum spinnaker foot or girth	1.8 × JC	*(Already a function of JC)	—	—
SPH	Spinnaker pole height	.25 × I	All excess	I	IC
SPL	Spinnaker pole length	Same as J	Excess	J	JC
HBS	Spinnaker headboard	.05 × JC	Excess × $\frac{1.8 \times SL}{SMW}$	I	IC
SMG	Minimum spinnaker mid-girth	.75 × foot	Anything less illegal	—	—
LL	Genoa luff length	$.95 \sqrt{I^2 + JC^2}$		—	—
LPIS	Staysail girth	Staysail girth +distance from staysail luff to headstay	Excess	LP	LPG
	Maximum girth of genoa	.50 × foot	Anything more illegal		
	Spinnaker battens	Illegal			
	Maximum number of battens — jib or foresail	.08 × J	No excess allowed		
	Maximum total length of all battens		Forward end of batten, when set, must be forward		
	Pole or outrigger on lee side	Illegal	of centerline of mast		

*J is the measured foretriangle base, and the spinnaker girth can be 1.8 × J. If the spinnaker pole size is increased over the J size the pole length becomes the new penalized foretriangle base or JC. The spinnaker girth can be 1.8 × JC with no further penalty. If the spinnaker girth exceeds 1.8 × J or the spinnaker pole, then the girth is divided by 1.8 to form a larger JC.

When you put the three parts of the formula together, you multiply the foretriangle area by the overlap penalty and add the aspect-ratio penalty. For example: you have a foretriangle sail area of 500 square feet and the second part of the formula works out to 1.42. Then you have 500 times 1.42

or 710 square feet; and if the aspect ratio penalty comes to 32 feet and you add it, you have a total RSAF of 742 square feet.

$$500 \times 1.42 + 32 = 742 \text{ RSAF}$$

Mizzen-Staysail Rated Sail Area—RSAK

Before you get into measuring mizzen-staysail area, there are a couple of overall rules you should know. First, the mizzen staysail must be a three-cornered sail. Its tack or tack pendant must be secured behind the mainmast and no higher than the railcap, deck, or cabin top. There are no restrictions on the number of mizzen staysails you carry on board, but only one can be set at a time. The mizzen spinnaker is measured as a mizzen staysail. The mizzen-staysail-rated sail area (RSAK) is calculated by this formula:

$$\text{RSAK} = \text{YSD} \times \left(\frac{\text{YSF} + \text{YSMG}}{3} \right) \times .30 \, \frac{\text{EB}}{\text{E}}$$

YSD is the head-to-foot measurement, which is the dividing line between the two longest sides. YSF is the foot or shortest side, and YSMG is the mid-girth dimension which bisects YSD. EB is the measurement from the aft side of the mainmast to the forward side of the mizzenmast, and E is the measured length of the foot of the mainsail.

The first part of the formula produces an actual area for the staysail and the second part decreases this area by a factor depending on the length of the main boom in relation to the length between the main and mizzenmasts.

Turning to the actual area part of the formula, the height of the sail is multiplied by the sum of the foot and mid-girth divided by 3. This produces the triangular area of the staysail (Fig. 261). The result is multiplied by 30 per cent of the quotient obtained by dividing the distance from the mainmast to the mizzen (EB) by the length of the foot of the mainsail (E).

If the boom length is the same as the distance between the masts then EB is the same as E, producing a factor of one. Therefore, when the boom touches the mizzenmast the triangular area is multiplied by 30 per cent times a factor of one to get the rated area.

As the main boom is shorter, for instance—say, it is one half the dis-

Fig. 261
Rated Sail Area of Mizzen Staysails
(RSAK)

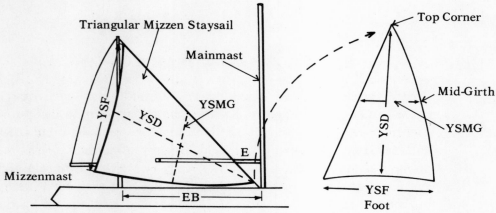

NOTE: YSD or "head-to-foot" is defined as
the dividing line between the two longest
sides. In the mizzen staysail it would be
between tack and mid-leech.

YSMG = mid-girth
YSD = shortest distance head-to-foot
YSF = shortest side "foot"
EB = distance between masts
E = mainsail foot

Spinnaker Mizzen Staysail

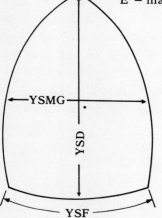

tance to the mizzenmast—then EB over E = 2 and 30% × 2 = 60%. Sixty
per cent of the triangular area is allocated to rated sail area.

Therefore, the shorter the main boom in relation to the distance between masts, the greater the per cent of actual area utilized into rated sail
area, starting with the minimum of 30 per cent of actual area.

TOTAL RATED SAIL AREA—RSAT

Now you have four rated sail area figures; foretriangle, mainsail, mizzen, and mizzen staysail.

Under the old CCA rule and the MARK I and MARK II IOR, total sail area was found by adding calculated rated sail areas. The MARK III IOR does the same thing but adds an SATC (or Sail Area Total Correction) penalty for a foretriangle that is disproportionately larger than the main (or main- and mizzensails combined). SATC is obtained by multiplying the mainsail rated area by 1.43. If this total is less than the foretriangle rated area, then 10 per cent of the difference between the two gives you the SATC. The formula is

$$SATC = .10 \, (RSAF - 1.43 \times RSAM)$$

Finding the RSAT of a sloop is simple and straightforward. It is the addition of mainsail-rated sail area (RSAM) plus foretriangle-rated sail area (RSAF) and the SATC penalty, to get the total rated sail area, RSAT. The yawl is a little more difficult because there are two combination formulas involved. It is easiest to start with the mizzen sails and work forward.

First the mizzen and mizzen staysail are compared to form the value YSAC. YSAC is simply whichever is larger: the rated sail area of the mizzen or the mizzen staysail. The YSAC and RSAM (which is the mainsail rated sail area) are then combined by a formula to produce RSAC, which is the total rated sail area of all sails aft of the mainmast and is determined by the following formula:

$$RSAC = RSAM + \frac{(YSAC)^2}{RSAM + YSAC}$$

Then, RSAC is added to RSAF and SATC to get the total rated sail area, RSAT.

SLOOP
RSAT = RSAM (main) + RSAF (foretriangle) + SATC (sail area total correction)
YAWL
RSAT = RSAC (all sails aft of mast)* + RSAF (foretriangle) + SATC (sail area total correction)

*RSAC = RSAM + $\frac{YSAC^2}{(RSAM + YSAC)}$, where YSAC = RSAY (miz) or RSAK (miz staysail), whichever is larger.

Once the RSAT total is computed under the IOR, an additional step is taken. A formula called SPIN is computed by multiplying the measured foretriangle height corrected (IC) by the corrected foretriangle base (JC) and multiplying that by 1.01 (IC $\times$ JC $\times$ 1.01). If the resultant figure is larger than RSAT, RSAT is increased to the SPIN value. SPIN would exceed RSAT when the foretriangle is disproportionately large.

Fig. 262

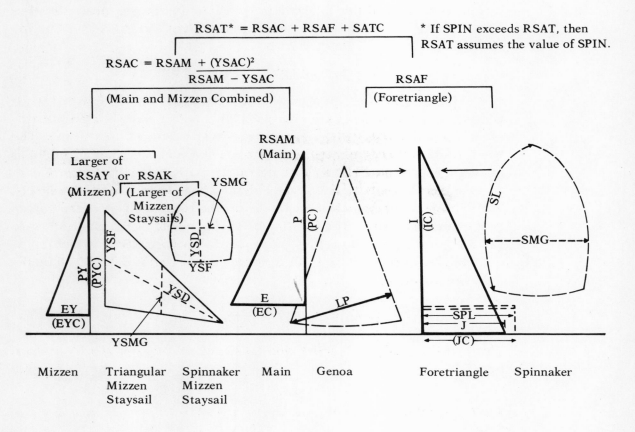

RSAT* = RSAC + RSAF + SATC   * If SPIN exceeds RSAT, then RSAT assumes the value of SPIN.

$$RSAC = RSAM \frac{+ (YSAC)^2}{RSAM - YSAC}$$

(Main and Mizzen Combined)

RSAF (Foretriangle)

HOW TO IMPROVE YOUR RATING
or Performance Through the Sail Plan

There are many ways to go about improving your rating or performance. One way is to look for hidden penalties that come from exceeding fixed tolerances. For instance, if the spinnaker luff exceeds the formula limit, two times the excess is added to I to form IC. All the dimensions listed on tables of limitations are subject to penalty when exceeded. A second way is to obtain a performance chart for all sails on the boat in various wind conditions. This will help you decide not only if too much sail exists for the conditions involved, but also if there is too little sail area. Many designers take the extra penalty in added sail area to gain the performance desired. You should look for decreased performance in various angles of sail at various ranges and then increase specific sails to help fill in the gap. For instance, in a heavy-air area such as San Francisco, a 170 per cent genoa may be too large, and a 150 per cent will be quite adequate. Or, the standard rig may be too tall; a shorter rig might be more efficient.

There are two areas which require special note. Whenever two rated sail areas are compared and the largest is used, it means that the smaller one could be brought up to the larger value at no penalty. The places this occurs are the mizzen versus mizzen staysail, and the SPIN versus RSAT. On the mizzen sails, if the RSA of the mizzen staysail is 180 square feet and the mizzen 120 square feet, the value of YSAC or the combined mizzen sails becomes the larger of the two, or 180 square feet. This means that the mizzen could be brought up to a rated sail area of 180 square feet also, without a rating increase. The same logic applies to SPIN versus RSAT. If SPIN exceeds RSAT by 200 square feet, the foretriangle should be either reduced in size or RSAM or RSAC increased until RSAT = SPIN; or reduce I and JC until SPIN = RSAT.

Otherwise, you would be sailing with a main and mizzen that could be increased, again with no increase in rating. Some designers want the SPIN always to equal RSAT. To do this, they design the sail plan as desired for windward performance. If RSAT is below SPIN, they then increase the spinnaker pole length (which is the same as increasing the foretriangle base JC) until the SPIN calculation is the same as RSAT.

The spinnaker pole penalty is common and deserves some explanation. Since the base of the foretriangle is corrected to equal the length of the pole, increasing the spinnaker pole length increases JC. Furthermore, since the spinnaker can be 1.8 times JC, the spinnaker can be wider, with the increase in JC.

Increasing JC increases the foretriangle-rated sail area and hence the rating also. From this point, however, you move in two directions.

1. The genoa LP is also a function of JC. If JC is increased, the same overlap per cent can be maintained but it will be a longer LP. If you had a 150 per cent genoa and the JC was 15, your LP would be 22½ feet. If the JC (spinnaker pole) was increased in penalty to 16 feet, the 150 per cent genoa LP would then be 24.0 with no additional penalty. If you did not increase your genoa LP and it was 150 per cent before the JC increase, the LP of 22½ would only be 141 per cent of the new 16-foot JC; and you are allowed 150 per cent without penalty, or 24.0 feet.

2. If you are sailing with a large LP, perhaps 170 per cent or 25½ feet, you may elect to maintain the same LP dimension with the longer pole. In this case the 25½-foot LP would be divided by the larger 16-foot JC and the LP per cent would be reduced to 159 per cent; this would provide some compensating credit against the spinnaker pole penalty.

Rule makers are aware of this loophole, and it is not possible to recoup the entire penalty. The pros and cons should be weighed carefully. Adding to the spinnaker pole without increasing LP adds rating and improves performance in reaching and downwind but not to windward. Increasing LP along with the spinnaker pole adds proportionately more rating and increases both reaching and windward performance.

The rule is designed with a great number of these checks and balances. You must remember that there are sailors throughout the world with computers at their disposal who have no compunction about dissecting the rule into the most minute parts to try and gain some advantage in rating for themselves. If you put yourself in the place of the rule committee, you would realize that you had to write a rule that would withstand these intense vivisections. This is a tremendous job—it is six men against the world in a technological age. But the committee does protect itself technically by having a clause dealing with the "spirit of the rule"; here it would be best to quote from the IOR rule book, which states as follows:

It is not possible for the rule to cover every eventuality and the Council therefore reserves the right to modify the rule in accordance with the following resolution of the Offshore Rating Council or to deal with any peculiarity of design and to give such rating as they consider equitable. "It is the intention of the Council that the rule should be stable, but allow for revision from time to time as research or new developments show this to be necessary."

Chapter 20

Racing:
Polar Plots,
Sail Selection, and VMG

The objective in racing is to win, and to win you have to get from mark to mark in the least amount of time. There are a lot of factors involved and books have been written about most of them: helmsmanship, fine tuning, and so on. But there are two key decision-making areas that have rarely been touched upon that, for the skipper who takes the time to study them, will produce significant increases in boat speed. These are the areas of proper sail selection and—when tacking is involved either upwind or downwind—choosing the optimum sailing angle. All the fine tuning in the world won't help if you have the wrong sails up or if you don't choose the course that will get you to the next mark in the fastest time possible. This section will deal with the ways in which the skipper can make more logical and, therefore, more accurate decisions in these areas.

The secret is first to learn how your boat goes best—on every angle and with what sails in different conditions—and then to record the vital information that will allow you to repeat this performance. You will have to note what sails were used, what the trim conditions were, and what speed was produced at which angle. Once this information is gathered, you should be able to duplicate your best speed on the race course. The key to success lies in the recording, organizing, and storing of the data: it should be easily retrievable, easily read, and as complete as possible. Theoretically, the most satisfactory method devised so far of organizing this data is the polar plot or polar diagram.

Although it may appear complicated, a polar plot is nothing more than a system for recording a boat speed achieved with a particular sail combination in a specific velocity of wind on a number of sailing angles.

Each polar diagram is designated for a specific wind velocity. Individual charts should be made for every two knots of wind up to 12 and every three knots over 12, or, if you prefer, in smaller increments. A typical polar diagram is shown in Figure 263. The circles represent boat speed and the radiating lines (radial vectors) covering approximately half of a compass rose represent the sailing angle (true-wind angle) of the boat. A dot representing boat speed produced by a sail combination is marked at each sailing angle. When the dots for boat speed at all angles for the one sail combination are connected, a polar curve results. The farther outboard the curve goes, the greater the speed produced by the sails in that sailing angle range. Thus, when a number of performance curves for various sail combinations are shown on one chart, one combination is going to emerge as the fastest at each particular sailing angle.

Obviously, having this kind of information readily at hand is a big asset for a racing sailor. However, polar plots are not easy to make and require a number of instruments. Practically speaking, their use is limited to larger cruiser-racers; small class boats must get the same information by brushing with one another, as described in Chapter 8. Since small boats have fewer sails, the results can then be recorded in a notebook or on a few key charts.* The principles are the same, however, no matter what system or what size boat you have.

PLANNING THE CHARTS

In this portion of the chapter we will restrict the discussion to sail selection. The second portion will discuss the value of polar charts as an aid to steering or to establishing the fastest course.

Preparation of the charts requires testing in the sailing conditions you may encounter and with various appropriate sail combinations at each

---

*The one design, having only one combination of upwind sails, could make one master polar chart indexed to its sail combination and could have a number of curves representing the various wind velocities. If a spinnaker were to be used, a second chart could be made under the spinnaker index for the reaching and downwind angles.

Fig. 263

Polar Diagram. Each polar diagram is geared to a specific wind velocity. The circles represent boat speed: in this case, from 1-10 knots. Each circle represents one knot of speed; the farther out the circle, the higher the speed. The radial lines represent the sailing angle (the angle from the centerline to the true wind).

Here is an analysis of what can be learned from the chart showing the relative boat speed of various sail combinations in 10 knots of true wind.

NOTE: you should read this analysis twice, before and after reading through Figure 267.

1. At 40 degrees, the No. 1 genoa produces about a quarter of a knot more than any other sail. The wind is a little too strong for the light genoa, and the angle is too acute for the double-head rig.

2. At 60 degrees, the double-head rig outperforms the genoas. Note, however, that the double-head rig is increasing in performance while the No. 1 is decreasing. The light genoa is slightly faster than the No. 1 genoa on the reaching angle because it is fuller, but it still is not so fast as the double-head rig. The star-cut can be kept full but is just below its effective range.

3. As the angle broadens to 85 degrees, additional sail area pays off. The flat star-cut spinnaker is able to draw well and is over half a knot faster than any other sail.

4. Approaching 110 degrees, the flatter and slightly smaller star-cut is gradually outperformed by the fuller, larger, and lighter ¾-ounce all-purpose spinnaker. The true wind is now far enough aft so that the genoas are no longer competitive in performance with any spinnaker: as the wind angle goes farther aft there is no way to square the genoa to the wind, so it will hang in a less effective condition.

5. At 145 degrees, the wind is quite far aft and the lighter sail weight is important in keeping the spinnaker in a lifted condition—thus, the light spinnaker performs better in the lighter air.

6. The chart goes beyond 180 degrees because often the leeward mark is a little by the lee and the chart will indicate whether a jibe is mandatory. A lot of distance can be lost with a bad jibe and it is an easy maneuver to foul up. Compare the speed on the angle to which you would jibe (say 170 degrees) to the lee angle. If there is only a very slight loss of speed by sailing 10 degrees by the lee for a short distance to the mark, a jibe might be avoided. If the mark to be rounded is on the same tack that you are already on, you might be able to avoid two jibes.

7. Depending on your inventory, you could have twenty-five or thirty sail-combination curves on a single chart; three or four staysails could be used with each of three different spinnakers and would make up nine to twelve curves alone. So some simplification has to be done. It is obvious that some sails, such as a storm spinnaker or heavy genoa, would not perform in this relatively light apparent-wind velocity, and these are left off the chart. Only use the sails practical within the wind range. The genoa curve may be omitted as soon as it clearly passes through the spinnakers, at say 110 degrees. The only time this kind of information might be needed would be in a sudden wind shift from 45 degrees to 110 degrees with 5 minutes to go to the next mark. How much would it hurt to keep that genoa? Or should you rush to put up a spinnaker? The chart will tell you if you include the complete curve for each sail.

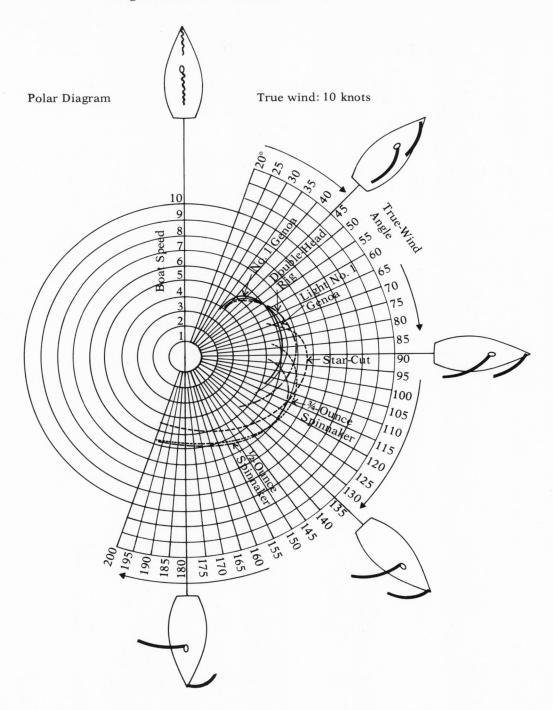

Polar Diagram

True wind: 10 knots

angle of sail in each condition. Since this is a large task, it should be simplified as much as possible. This can be done in two ways: First, by testing sails only in their obvious range—genoas do not need to be tested downwind, running spinnakers do not have to be tested upwind, etc.; also, a sail has a limit prescribed by its strength, and testing beyond these limits will only hurt the sail. Second, a decision should be made between the preparation of apparent- or true-wind charts.

With true-wind charts this can be avoided. However, they require mathematical interpolations from apparent-wind and boat-speed data (Fig. 264). True wind is the *actual* sailing condition; a true-wind chart is a steadier and much more reliable guide for selecting sails while underway.

Fig. 264
A true-wind plot is the opposite of an apparent-wind plot. To get the true-wind angle or velocity, first plot the boat speed and apparent-wind speed and direction (the length of the lines represents the velocity); then connect the top of the two vectors; this resultant line represents the speed and direction of the true wind.

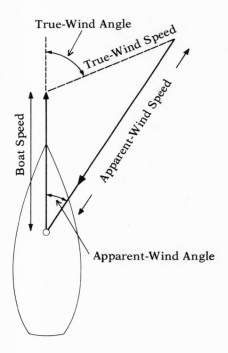

True-wind charts can also be used to select the proper sail combination for the first leg of a race. Before the start, the boat can be stopped dead in the water to measure the velocity and direction of the true wind. The course heading (corrected for any current) can be measured by compass. The difference between the two angles is the true-wind angle (or sailing angle). The true-wind speed measurement allows you to select the right chart and sailing angle to find the fastest sail combination. (If the plotted angle is within the normal tacking angle then the course is a windward leg.)

Before the turning mark, the true-wind charts again can be used to plan the fastest sail combination on the new course. As there may have been changes in true-wind speed or direction since the start, the true wind must be plotted from the present boat speed and apparent-wind input. The course for the next leg can be laid out on the navigator's chart. You select the proper true-wind velocity chart and reference the right true-wind angle for the best sails to use on the new sailing angle.

GATHERING THE DATA

The wind is variable and largely unpredictable. It is what makes boat racing so interesting and complicated. We have shown that the only accurate way to gather true-wind data is first to record the performance test data: boat speed, apparent-wind velocity, and apparent-wind speed. Then at night, after each day of testing, you can use this information to plot true-wind data in order to make your charts. The initial objective, therefore, is to assemble a large amount of test data. See the Appendix for a cross-check of true-wind data.

Ideally, you should do as much testing as you can in a non-racing condition using every possible sail combination in its maximum possible range in each wind condition. Concentrate on sailing angles about 5 to 10 degrees apart around half a compass circle, from the highest pointing angle, when the sail is barely filled away, to a slight "by the lee" downwind angle with the spinnaker. There will be critical areas for each sail to windward and to leeward where a change in sailing angle as small as 2 or 3 degrees will produce significant changes in boat speed; these areas should be tested more closely.

On each angle, trim the sail to its best advantage for that angle, hold the course for a few minutes until you reach maximum speed, then record the speed and the other pertinent information. It should only take 15 or 20 minutes to test the usable range of the sail at the different angles. If the wind stays constant, you will have one true-wind performance profile for one sail combination in one wind velocity (after you have converted to true-wind data). Then, test the next sail combination in your inventory, marking the results in the same way. Gradually, you will build up profiles of all your sail combinations in different wind velocities and at different angles.

To aid in recording information, prepare a *recording log,* which will look like that shown in Figure 265. The first three columns are for the key input of boat speed, apparent-wind speed, and apparent-wind angle. The next two are for true-wind speed and direction, which you will fill in later by plotting. Most boats have a critical angle of heel over which performance drops. A space for heel angle is suggested to compare this relationship. A figure of 23 to 25 degrees is used as a critical angle on many boats.

Sea conditions have a dramatic effect on performance and eventually your charts should be expanded to include performance data for flat and rough water. For this reason a column to note sea conditions is also suggested. Differences in sea conditions are most noticeable in two specific areas: (1) *to windward,* where in the same wind, say 20 knots, a boat will point higher and go 2 to 3 knots faster in a flat sea than in a rough seaway and (2) *offwind in strong air,* when the amount of sail and the size of the waves can make the difference between surfing and not surfing and the variance in speed can be 4 or 5 knots or more. If you race in both conditions you should test in both and, if possible, make separate polar diagrams for both.

Fig. 265
The recording log is used to input
performance data, so that
they can be used later to prepare polar
diagrams.

Recording Log

Sail Combination	Boat Speed	Apparent Wind Angle	Apparent Wind Speed	True Wind Angle	True Wind Speed	Heel Angle	Sea Condition	Sail-Trim Notes

Last, trim has almost as many variables as the wind, and in reviewing the log you will find some rather outstanding bursts of speed and some cases of the "slows." If you have some trim notes recorded, you can compare traveler settings, jib leads, etc., to see what settings should be duplicated or avoided. Or it may be the combination of heel, sea, and trim. The more information you have and the more visible you make it, the more you can understand what makes your boat go faster.

RECORDING THE DATA

To record the data the following instruments are required:

1. An apparent-wind indicator to measure the pointing angle (the angle from the boat's centerline to the apparent wind).
2. An anemometer to measure apparent-wind velocity when underway (and true-wind speed when the boat is dead in the water).
3. A speedometer to measure boat speed.
4. An inclinometer to measure heel angle.
5. A compass—which is not used for input but is used to establish sailing angle in order to reference the chart for sail selection in a race.

Many boats also carry a close-hauled apparent-wind indicator which expands the scale from 0 to 40 or 50 degrees from the bow for more accurate readability. Some close-hauled indicators will also read out an expanded scale of the downwind angles. This instrument will help you make more accurate readings for your apparent-wind-angle input. Ocean-type conditions, particularly downwind, make recording data difficult; the instruments will not stay fixed at precise numbers. For instance, in recording input, the anemometer will vary 4, 5, or even 6 knots and the apparent-wind angle will vary up to 10 or 20 degrees. This occurs because the instruments for recording wind data are located on the masthead. As the boat rocks in the seaway, the swing of the masthead will exaggerate some of the readings: as it rocks to windward the apparent-wind velocity increases and the direction changes; as it rocks to leeward the apparent-wind velocity decreases. The only remedy is to determine a median, which you can then record.

THE EFFECTS OF CURRENT

In many areas there is tidal flow that can produce a current of up to several knots, which is increasing or decreasing boat speed over the bottom and/or driving it sideways. For instance, if you had a 2 knot head current driving you backward, the boat would be moving over the bottom at 2 knots less than the boat speed registered on your instruments. This creates a problem if you have measured the true wind when anchored. If you take the true-wind reading by going head-to-wind until you are dead in the water, even though the boat is moving over the bottom at 2 knots backward, you will register the *boat's* true wind—that is, the true wind in which you are going to sail. The correction for current is automatically included. The same is true of the apparent wind; the wind the sail feels will still be whatever is read on the anemometer—it will reflect the difference caused by current. However, if you've measured the true wind when anchored, you will get the wrong actual sailing velocity, and will therefore choose the wrong polar plot.

CONSTRUCTING THE POLAR CHART

After you have accumulated and converted data representing the performance of various key sail combinations at all the appropriate wind angles and in the different velocities, you can use this data to plot your sail performance curves on the true-wind polar diagrams as shown in Figure 263.

First, index a series of blank charts for separate true-wind velocities —one chart for 2, 4, 6, 8, 10, 12, 15, 18, 21, 24, 30, and 35 knots. Next, start with one—say the 12 knot chart. From your log, select all converted true-wind data for one sail combination for velocities from 11 to 13½ knots (because not many readings will be exactly 12 knots and you have to allow for a small range). Your log should show the other two pieces of information needed for the plot, true-wind direction and resultant boat speed. If the boat is doing 5 knots at a sailing angle of 45 degrees, you would place a dot on the 45-degree radius on the fifth circle (Fig. 266). If a dot (indicating boat speed) is placed on each radius (representing the sailing angle at which

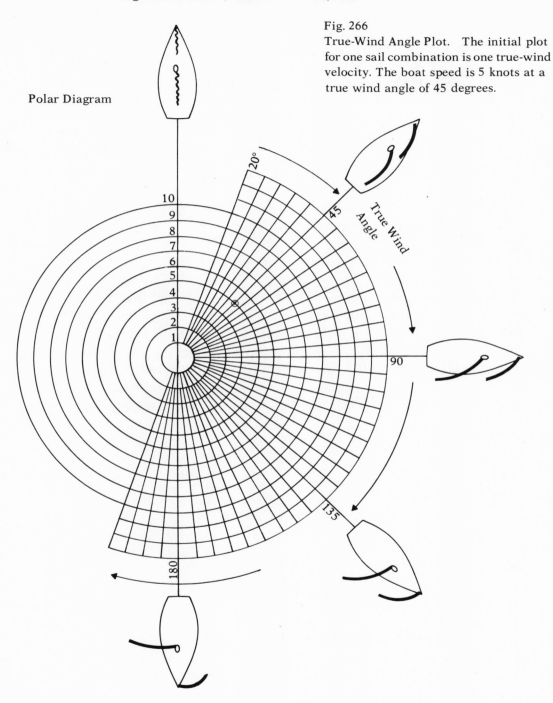

Polar Diagram

Fig. 266
True-Wind Angle Plot.   The initial plot
for one sail combination is one true-wind
velocity. The boat speed is 5 knots at a
true wind angle of 45 degrees.

that speed was reached), a polar plot or sail performance curve can be formed by connecting the dots (Fig. 267).

One curve alone is not meaningful in sail selection. But if all the sail combinations showing the same true-wind velocity are plotted on the one diagram, you have a clear visual demonstration of the relative performance for each combination. (See Fig. 263.) Each plot should be in a different color or coded in some way for easy identification. Then it will be clear which is the fastest sail combination to use for nearly every true-wind angle (sailing angle)—in other words, which combination is going to produce the greatest boat speed. When the difference is not clear-cut, further testing is indicated.

If you do not have a chart for a particular velocity when you're racing, you can tell what sails would be best by averaging the two charts above and below that velocity.

To prepare the final diagrams, draw a curve for the particular sail combination to run through the plotted points. There will inevitably be clusters of points at different spots, and you should find the average. Do the same thing for the other sail combinations on the same velocity chart and your polar diagram will be complete. Make one master drawing and photocopy as many copies as you need. Be careful to avoid the kind of duplicating process in which the image peels off when it gets wet. Keep the charts in loose-leaf notebooks. When you are ready to use them, you can quickly turn to the appropriate charts and have them ready for easy reference.

SUMMARY

Making these polar charts is a lot of work; you may not have the time or conditions to prepare them properly. You might first start with a few key velocities for your area, perhaps 5, 10, and 18 knots, and plot the key sails.* Then, because you have comparative data you can experiment with different com-

---

*Many sailmakers will give the boatowner a list of suggested wind ranges for each sail. These wind ranges are described in apparent-wind velocities; this is acceptable, if not preferable, in this one case because it offers an easy check of the sails' designed range and tells the approximate point at which a change should be considered. There is no graph or plot involved; it just lists the suggested sails for each apparent-wind velocity range and can be used as an excellent guide in organizing a testing program. On a table of this nature, the sail combinations generally overlap in wind range. The polar charts are designed to pinpoint the exact velocity (described in true wind, which can be back-plotted to apparent wind for comparison) at which the sail combination should be changed.

Polar Diagram

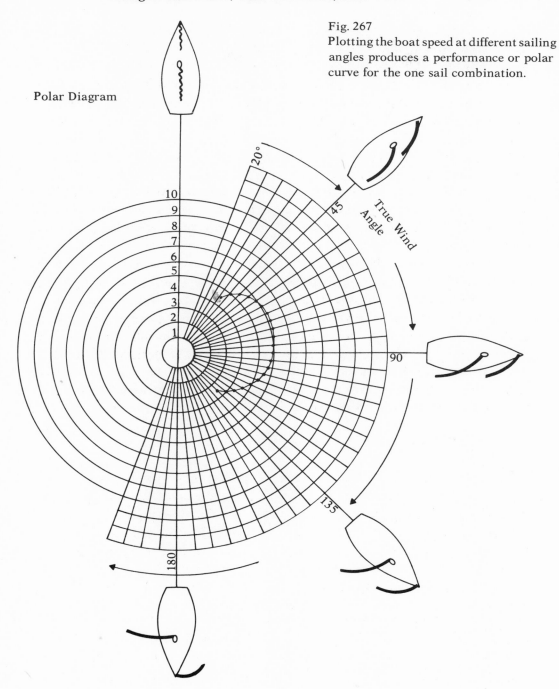

Fig. 267
Plotting the boat speed at different sailing angles produces a performance or polar curve for the one sail combination.

binations. Next, try to pinpoint the critical areas — angles and wind velocities — where sail changes are required and do more testing. Know at what wind velocity to change from the No. 1 to No. 2 genoa on the wind; when the star-cut is faster than the double-head rig; and how this varies in different velocities. These are the key decisions that help to win races.

VMG

Once the fastest sails for the particular condition in which you are sailing are known, the next thing to determine is how to use the sails that will get you to the next mark fastest; in other words, you have to choose the best course possible. If the leg is a reach, there is no problem: you just head straight for the mark. But if the mark is upwind or downwind, you have to decide which tack or sailing angle will produce the best compromise between the fastest boat speed and the shortest distance to the mark. To windward, you face the dilemma of heading up and going slower but sailing a shorter distance, or of bearing off, going faster, but covering a longer distance. Downwind, the choice is to head straight for the mark at what might be a slower sailing angle, or to tack downwind, covering more distance, but going faster. In either case, the net gain, to windward or leeward, is known as Speed Made Good or VMG where V=velocity.

Windward VMG

Tacking is a maneuver used to produce net distance to windward. Speed Made Good to windward is a measure of this gain made by computing the rate of speed in knots achieved against the true-wind direction. Theoretically, by calculating this in advance, you can choose the best pointing angle for your boat in the particular conditions in which you are sailing. However, in actual practice, it is not so simple. Since many people are currently interested in VMG to windward, and very few seem to understand exactly how it is computed or how it can and cannot be used, it seems worthwhile to explain it in detail.

The distance in feet the boat travels over a given time period can be measured by multiplying boat speed by the time interval. All of this is made very easy by the fact that 1 knot equals 100 feet per minute. For example, if a boat is traveling at the rate of 6.3 knots, it is moving 630 feet in one minute. The numbers are the same; when you plot or scale one, you can read the other.

To plot VMG, you must establish first how far the boat will move in one minute at whatever angle to the true wind you are testing. (You cannot test against the apparent wind because it does not remain constant, but changes as sailing angle changes.) Once the boat is moving at optimum speed, note the speed in knots. You can plot the true-wind direction; once you know boat speed and direction, here is how you can plot VMG. First, draw a line representing the distance traveled (Fig. 268a). (A centimeter ruler is a great help here, since it has a small scale and is broken down into tenths, making conversion of knots to feet simple.) If you were traveling at 3.2 knots, you would draw a line 3.2 centimeters long. Then, draw a line from the tip of this line to the true-wind line, intersecting it at right angles. Measure the true-wind line from the beginning of the angle to the point of intersection; this will give you the number of feet you have actually gained to windward. If you have gained 255 feet to windward even though you sailed 320 feet to get there, your VMG to windward is 2.55 knots.

One sailing angle alone will not give you much useful information; you have to compare several true-wind angles to see the one at which you

Fig. 268

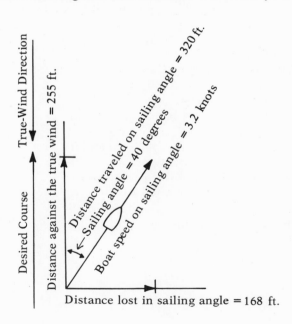

a.

Distance Made Good Against the True
Wind at Various True-Wind Angles

True-Wind Speed 10 Knots
1 knot = 100 ft. per min. or 1.66 ft. per sec.
NOTE: plots show distance traveled in
one minute.

b. As a boat sails a wider angle to the wind,
its speed increases; speed decreases as the
boat points more toward the wind. When
the distance traveled on each sailing angle
is plotted, each angle will have a distance
"wasted" to the side and a distance netted
against the true wind. When the distance
in feet against the wind is converted into
knots, you have a speed calculation
against the true wind, which is
VMG—speed made good to windward.
The plot with the fastest VMG component
is the fastest and the one you should be on.
As you can see in the diagram, the most
distance gained directly to windward for
the time period is at a sailing angle of 45
degrees. A difference of 5 degrees too high
(too close to the wind) brings the net
distance covered from 265 down to 255
feet, or 10 feet per minute. Sailing too
wide at 50 degrees brings the net gain
from 265 to 260 feet, or 5 feet per minute.
This doesn't sound like a lot, but in a
30-minute windward leg at a 10-feet-per
minute difference, you would arrive at the
windward mark 300 feet ahead of your
competitor.
NOTE: these calculations are done in a
hypothetical condition of steady air.

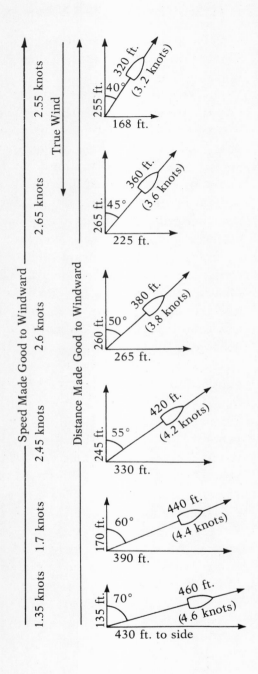

c. By putting all the vectors on one graph and drawing a perpendicular line from the vector tip to the true-wind direction, you can quickly see which is the fastest.

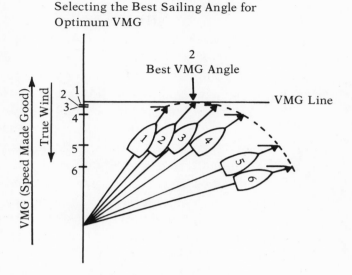

Selecting the Best Sailing Angle for Optimum VMG

are doing best. First, record the apparent-wind angles. You might take 28, 30, and 32 degrees, starting at 30 degrees, since that is the optimum sailing angle for most boats. Go degree by degree as closely as you can read your apparent-wind indicator. Once optimum speed is obtained, record boat speed on each angle. Then convert to true wind by plotting. Draw a line representing each sailing angle (Fig. 268b). The length of this vector represents the boat's speed. Then draw a perpendicular line from the true-wind line to intersect with the tip of each boat-speed line. Whichever line crosses the true-wind line the farthest to windward is the sailing angle that will give the best Speed Made Good to windward (Fig. 268c).

This is the way to plot VMG. In essence, however, you are reconstructing a polar diagram; if you went on around the compass doing this testing and measuring, you would repeat the polar diagram plot. Thus, if you've done your true-wind polar plots, the input data for VMG is at hand.

The only difference is that in our example we took some closely coupled degree readings trying to find the optimum sailing angle to windward, whereas the polar diagrams might be spaced 5 or 10 degrees apart. On the critical angles, however, more frequent readings would be advisable, as mentioned above.

If your true-wind charts have been done carefully and accurately, you will be able to select a fairly close to optimum sailing angle simply by drawing lines from the peak performance curve on different sailing angles to the true-wind line to see which gets you farthest to windward (Fig. 269). But here's the problem: this plotting will work only if you know the exact direction and velocity of the true wind in order to choose the right polar diagram. Once you're underway you have no instruments to measure the true-wind velocity or direction. But you can find the true wind by plotting back from the apparent wind and boat speed. This is not good enough to calculate differences on the close angles involved to windward; Speed Made Good readings have to be instantaneous and continuous. The only answer ultimately is to use an on-board computer, known as a "black box," which uses boat speed, apparent-wind angle, and velocity as input and gives a constant VMG read-out, taking into account the boat's leeway.*

Speed Made Good instrumentation is now undergoing serious experimentation, and very sophisticated and moderately expensive equipment is being developed. And so for the time being Speed Made Good to windward cannot be fully utilized by the ordinary cruising-boat sailor. Today, calculation of Speed Made Good to windward boils down to the ability of the helmsman, who weighs the input from his apparent-wind and boat-speed indicators. By bearing off, he knows that he can gain some speed, but his pointing angle suffers, and vice versa: if he points up too much, his boat speed drops off. After a while, the helmsman will find a "groove" in which the boat has a speed that is very close to what he thinks is maximum, at a pointing angle which is as narrow (or high) as most of the other boats in the fleet. The ultimate test is the same for both one designs and cruising boats: if two boats start at the same point and sail at slightly different angles and at slightly different speeds, one is going to end up ahead of the other when one tacks and crosses the other. One boat ends up with a greater net distance against the wind; in other words, it has had better Speed Made Good to windward.**

---

* *Leeway* is the undesirable phenomenon of side-slipping that occurs in all sailboats to a greater or lesser degree and is a factor in the calculation of VMG. For now, you will have to estimate leeway. Leeway is zero downwind, minimal on a beam reach, but it gradually increases its effect approaching the windward tacking angle, at which point it is at its maximum. Two or three degrees is an estimated average for leeway on the wind.

**Because the true wind can be estimated closely downwind, the compass is used to establish the test angles for input and the deviation from the true wind or the desired course after the plot is made. If changes in true wind are observed, then the compass headings that establish the courses should be altered by the same amounts and in the same directions.

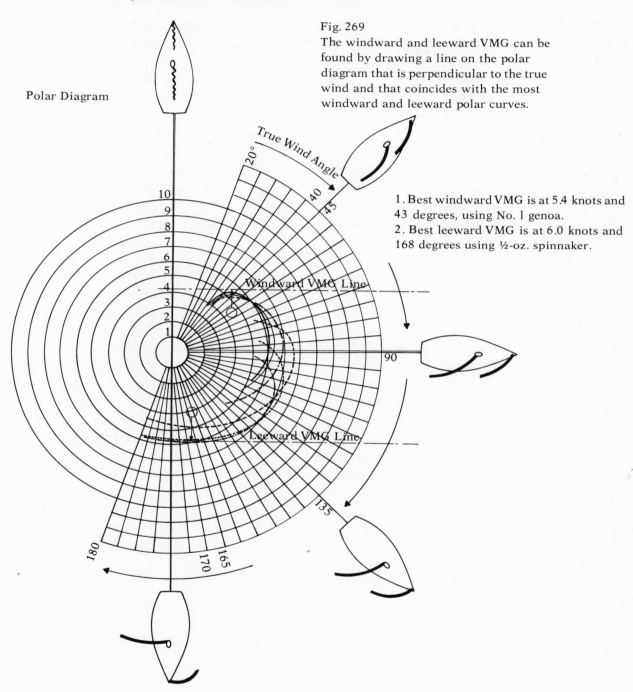

Polar Diagram

Fig. 269
The windward and leeward VMG can be
found by drawing a line on the polar
diagram that is perpendicular to the true
wind and that coincides with the most
windward and leeward polar curves.

1. Best windward VMG is at 5.4 knots and
43 degrees, using No. 1 genoa.
2. Best leeward VMG is at 6.0 knots and
168 degrees using ½-oz. spinnaker.

True Wind Angle

Windward VMG Line

Leeward VMG Line

One way for a helmsman to gain experience in judging VMG is by brushing with another identical boat; as the conditions and true wind vary, both boats are automatically responding to the changes, provided they are close enough together to be in the same wind. He must be careful that size-able shifts, particularly permanent ones, are not misread as the cause of the Speed Made Good differences.

Finding the "groove" is difficult for any but the experienced sailor. To the new sailor, or the relatively inexperienced sailor, it may not be possi-ble to gauge the optimum sailing angle within 3 to 6 degrees either side of the best course. In this case, polar diagrams and VMG plots will give him a starting point from which to experiment so he won't fall into the trap of thinking that because he is going faster he is going to get there first.

VMG to Leeward

Downwind, all a helmsman needs to know is whether his boat can point up a little higher into a reaching angle and sail the extra distance with more boat speed and less overall time, or whether he should head it straight for the mark. Computations of VMG to leeward are far easier and more practical than to windward. Downwind, the boat can be sailed at any angle, since the wind comes from behind. Boat speed, particularly in light airs, is generally minimal on a dead downwind course. A slight reaching angle will usually produce a significant increase in boat speed—but at a penalty. You will have to cover more distance and you will have to jibe to get back to the mark. This is called downwind tacking. However, if you can sail a longer course in less total time than your competitor, you will get to the next mark first, even though your reaching angles require one or more jibes. Thus, VMG to leeward becomes an important calculation.

To calculate downwind VMG, polar charts can be used, or simple plots can be prepared showing differences in boat speed for given true-wind velocities for sailing angles of every 5 degrees downwind (Fig. 270). There are also disc type course calculators (Fig. 271); these tell you the speed increase required to compensate for the increase in distance with each degree of change in sailing angle.

On the downwind angles however the differences in speed are so much larger that they make even greater differences in VMG. Also, unlike windward work, downwind you are physically able to estimate the true-

Fig. 270
Differences in Boat Speed at Various
Downwind Sailing Angles

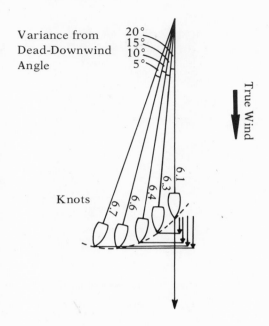

wind direction within a couple of degrees even though underway. Dead downwind, the true wind will be in the same direction as the apparent wind. For any other downwind situation, the most reliable indicator of true wind will be the wind pattern on the waves or the small cat's-paws that ruffle the surface of the water. In medium or heavy air, if the wind has been holding steady, the waves will generally come from the direction of the true wind. But if there is a wind shift, the waves cannot change direction quickly, so the cat's-paws or small ripples will indicate the new direction of the wind. Another reliable true-wind indicator is a flag on a boat dead in the water (but not anchored) nearby. Smoke from buildings on shore or other fixed aids are usually too far away to be helpful.

In heavy air, the differences in speed due to slight reaching angles are minimal and in fact may not be desirable. The angulation increases the flow of wind over the sails; in light air this increase is helpful but in heavy air it may not be to your advantage: the boat has enough wind to handle. Thus, tacking downwind is a lesser consideration in heavy air.

Once you have true-wind direction, you can plot downwind VMG. On a polar diagram simply take a ruler and draw a perpendicular from the

Fig. 271
The disc-type course calculator will tell
the approximate change in boat speed
with each change in downwind sailing
angle for a given wind velocity.

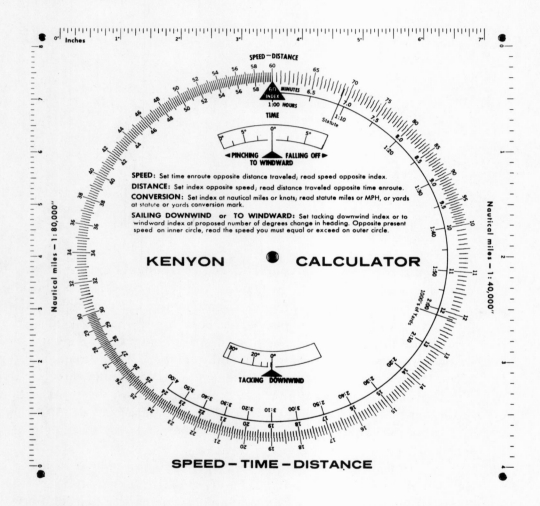

line representing true wind to the point of peak downwind performance as
represented by the performance curve on your polar diagram. This will give
the true-wind angle to steer. (See Fig. 269.) If you do not have a polar diagram you can make a simple plot for a particular true-wind velocity. First

sail dead downwind and record your speed. Next alter course to head up 5 degrees and take another reading of boat speed. Continue this procedure and record the speed at each 5-degree change to an angle of about 30 degrees away from the original course. Then, on your diagram, plot the amount of distance to be traveled on each angle (Fig. 272a). There will be one angle that

Fig. 272
Downwind VMG Chart

a. Distance vs. time on a run can be precalculated for each wind condition to achieve the optimum sailing angle. Each sailing angle has a difference in speed and distance, which can be calculated in percentage figures. The best VMG would be the course that produces the greatest difference between per cent speed increase and per cent distance increase. This occurs at both 15 degrees and 20 degrees from downwind course.

TABLE

Angle from downwind course	Distance	Speed	Difference
5°	+ 1%	+ 4%	+ 3% gain
10°	+ 2%	+10%	+ 8% gain
15°	+ 4%	+13%	+ 9% gain
20°	+ 7%	+16%	+ 9% gain
25°	+11%	+17%	+ 6% gain

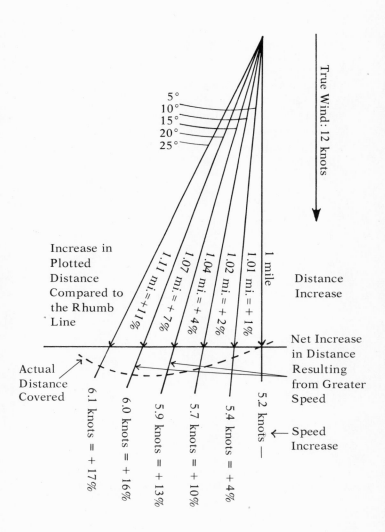

will clearly give you a faster time to the next mark (Fig. 272b). The quickest way to see this is to calculate the per cent increase in distance and measure it against the per cent increase in speed. If you go 20 per cent farther and only have a 15 per cent increase in boat speed, downwind tacking will not be worthwhile. These percentages are calculated from the simple ratio of angular distance divided by straight distance and faster boat speed divided by slower speed.

When the best sailing angle has been chosen, remember that once you tack out on that angle, you will have to tack back. If you determine from your

Change from Dead Downwind Angle

b. If five identical boats with identical sails were sailing at different angles, presuming they started at the same time and then all jibed at mid-course all of them would arrive at the next mark at different times. The one with the best downwind VMG would get to the mark first.

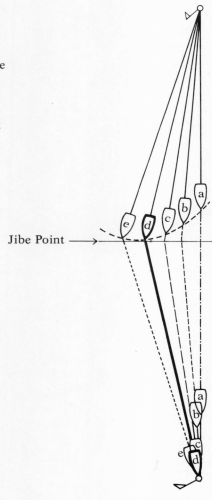

Jibe Point ——>

charts that 15 degrees is the fastest sailing angle, you will then sail to the point on that tack from which you can jibe over and sail for the mark at 15 degrees on the other tack. If the wind shifts while you are out to one side of the course, you have to reassess the optimum angle. You may even be forced to sail dead downwind for the mark.

When the true wind is shifting, you must continually evaluate your position. The optimum angle may have been 15 degrees from the rhumb-line course, but if you stick to it after the wind shifts, you might find yourself on a course 30 degrees from the rhumb line (Fig. 273). This could be highly inefficient. If the wind is quite variable, but averaging dead downwind, you can sail to a fairly close downwind course because each new wind shift

Fig. 273
If the fastest sailing angle downwind is 15 degrees from the true wind and the rhumb line to the mark is 10 degrees from the true wind, you would have to sail on an angle of 5 degrees from the course to sail the fastest sailing angle. This means, however, that you will have a short jibe to the mark at the slower angle of 25 degrees (including the 10 degrees for the difference between the true wind and the rhumb line, and the 15-degree optimum sailing angle).

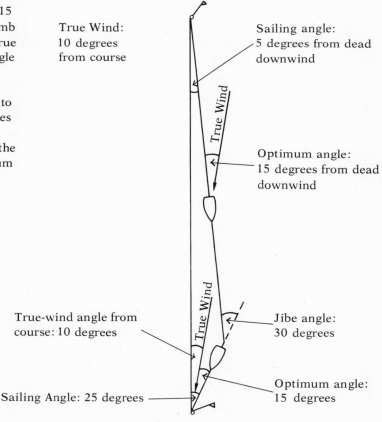

True Wind:
10 degrees
from course

Sailing angle:
5 degrees from dead
downwind

Optimum angle:
15 degrees from dead
downwind

True-wind angle from
course: 10 degrees

Jibe angle:
30 degrees

Optimum angle:
15 degrees

Sailing Angle: 25 degrees

provides angulation. You may have to jibe on shifts, however, to take advantage of the new wind direction, to keep your optimum angle, and to keep the boat headed closer to the mark.

In all downwind tacking the one major consideration is what the wind is going to do during the leg. For instance, if the wind is directly in line with the course and you think it is going to shift, you should anticipate it. If you think the wind will shift clockwise during the leg, steer to the right of course for a sharper reaching angle and a faster speed after jibing on the new shift. Conversely, if the wind backs counterclockwise, steer to the port side so that, once again, you have a better reaching angle back to the turning mark when the shift hits you (Fig. 274).

Sometimes downwind tacking can be successful if the course requires a very broad reach. The technique is to sail a long reach headed up slightly above course and then—though it may be almost square to the course—to make a short jibe at the end. Ideally, the extra distance covered by the closer reaching angle will be more than the "wasted" distance in the small jibing leg. The game is the same: to find the course that gets you to the mark the fastest. Figure 275 shows the type of course plotting that would be required for determining whether downwind tacking is justified and, if so, finding the best tacking angle for a broad reach. Only the broad reach is in the VMG category; for all others, one sails directly for the mark at a constant sailing angle. The optimum speed when sailing to the next mark is a matter of sail selection and, of course, sail trim.

Brushing, and sail-testing techniques other than polar plots, most often concentrate on windward comparisons. On most courses, the windward leg is usually less than half the total length of the course. On a one-design boat such as a Star, which has no spinnaker and uses one sail combination for the entire race, the fullness and shape of the main and jib have to account for maximum boat speed on all legs. A sail that is fairly full may go a little slower to windward and a lot faster to leeward—more than offsetting the windward deficiency. The flexible rig allows the best of both worlds; a fuller mainsail for downwind work and a flexible spar that removes some of the draft for upwind work. Such performance highlights the importance of comparative testing on reaches and runs as well as on windward legs.

There are three keys to being a winner: first, you have to choose the right sail combination; second, you have to optimize the speed of the sail

Fig. 274
Adjustment of Downwind Course in
Shifting Conditions.   In shifting
conditions, you must constantly adjust
your course to maintain the optimum
sailing angle to the true wind.

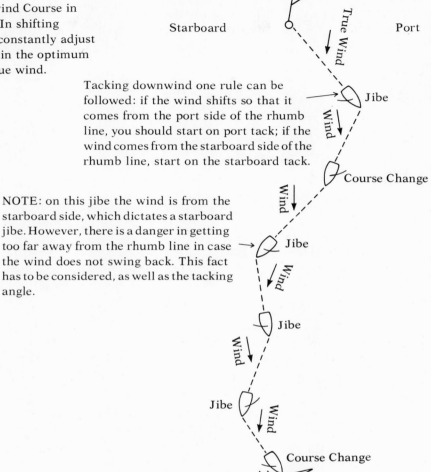

Tacking downwind one rule can be
followed: if the wind shifts so that it
comes from the port side of the rhumb
line, you should start on port tack; if the
wind comes from the starboard side of the
rhumb line, start on the starboard tack.

NOTE: on this jibe the wind is from the
starboard side, which dictates a starboard
jibe. However, there is a danger in getting
too far away from the rhumb line in case
the wind does not swing back. This fact
has to be considered, as well as the tacking
angle.

selected by trimming; and third, you have to get the best VMG possible to
the next mark. Not only do you have to record the data of your boat's performance on different sailing angles, you also have to record the trim marks
on the sheets and block positions so that you can duplicate your best trim.
In other words, everything should be done systematically. If you have a base
reference point, you can experiment from there; if you do achieve an in-

crease in speed, you will know why it happened; and if it is marked down properly, you will know how to duplicate it. The key is in recording all phases of the test results.

Fig. 275
Plot to Determine If Downwind Tacking Is
Faster on a Broad Reach

In the plot, boat "C" will reach the mark first. Therefore, tacking is justified and C's angle is fastest.

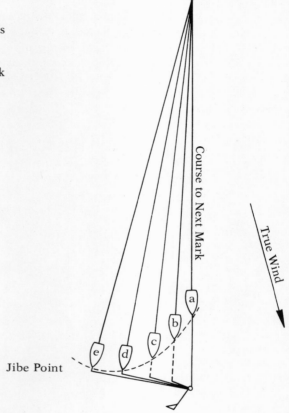

Speed Made Good by Computer

Now that we have described the purpose of the VMG plots and polar diagrams, let us examine the impact of a commercially produced "black box" —the on-board computer. Though it is only used by 12-Meters so far, this VMG instrument will soon replace polar charts as a steering aid. Technology is advancing about as fast as articles can be written; and instruments discussed today as being of the future can soon become a reality.

What can the "black box" do for you? Many things: in some areas it may be of incalculable help, in others its usefulness may be exaggerated.

1. The VMG formulation requires that the computer first calculate true wind. Therefore, a true-wind-direction indicator and the true-wind anemometer are instruments that will be developed simultaneously. Once the true-wind instruments are on board your boat, the problem of converting back and forth from true to apparent will be over. Steering will be guided by a VMG needle, a true-wind-angle needle or by an apparent-wind-direction indicator. The polar diagrams will then be relegated to the job of sail selection.

2. The computer will have the capability of either inputting a leeway factor or, if a satisfactory underwater indicator is found, calculating the actual leeway in order to find the exact course of the boat through the water in both speed and direction.

3. It will have the capability of producing infinite electrical dampening for any instrument in the system. The greatest advantage will be in sailing by a steady needle on a broad reach or run. The leading edge of a spinnaker has the same narrow tolerance between luffing and stalling as the edges of a windward sail but keeping this sail on edge could heretofore be done only by watching the shoulder "curl." Electrical dampening will hold the apparent- or true-wind needle to a very small variance, so its use will become much more valuable in offwind work, particularly at night. Needless to say, any input for the preparation of polar plots will be much more accurate.

4. The computer system can be linked to an electromagnetic compass to do dead reckoning, including giving a course to the next mark. When desired, the estimated current can also be input for compensation.

Current opinion about VMG instruments is that they are absolutely essential devices that will do everything—and this is basically true because of the capabilities we have discussed. But you may be surprised to find that the instrument's maximum value may not be as a windward steering aid. There are many excellent sailors who have learned to sail to windward by "feel" in the many varying seas and wind conditions. Their mental "computer" may do as good a job as the "black box."

The computer does offer many opportunities such as working with true-wind instruments, which will be a whole new experience. Steering to the true-wind angle may become more exacting than either the apparent-wind angle or the VMG instrument, although eventually boat speed, true-wind angle and VMG instruments will probably be used as a group as a combination steering aid. Moreover, even though we feel that steering aids will become associated with true-wind instruments, sail trim will still be based on apparent-wind angle. (Maximum loading on a particular sail will continue to be described in terms of apparent-wind velocity, whereas selection of the fastest sail combinations will be made by reference to true-wind polar diagrams.)

All of this just adds another dimension to the already complicated business of sailing. Sailing should still be fun and all of your charts and instrumentation should be well organized in advance of the racing season: they should be true aids and not distractions. This book does not concentrate on racing tactics since there are many good books on the subject. But tactics are as important as sail handling, and efficient preorganization will let you attend to all three key areas: sail handling, boat-speed devices, and racing maneuvers. In getting together a well-organized crew, "practice makes perfect" is advice that cannot be overstated—it is an essential ingredient. None of these many, complex elements is enough alone. But together they are what win races.

Appendix

VMG: Instruments and Tables

Instrumentation can be very valuable when it is accurate, but it should not become a crutch. The output is only as good as the instruments recording the data; if inaccuracies sometimes develop, they can spell disaster. Before any testing or racing, you should be quite sure that your instruments are accurate. Here are some considerations.

Speedometer. Timed runs between buoys are not always effective because buoys may not be located as marked. The effects of current are difficult to compensate for in most areas. A point-to-point check against land points is best and at least twelve runs are needed before the average speed will be meaningful. A speed-recording towing log, which is extremely accurate, could be used to check boat speed; this would eliminate any consideration of current.

Apparent-wind-angle indicator. Masthead units are usually too close to the masthead and the induced flow in the masthead area may alter the actual apparent-wind direction by as much as 10 or 12 degrees. Getting the wind-direction vane up and forward 3 to 4 feet from the masthead on a smaller boat and 6 to 7 feet away on a larger boat will reduce the error to within 2 or 3 degrees. Moving the anemometer cups farther away will also get them into a steadier air flow.

To assist you further in calculating true wind and also help you to check your instruments for accuracy, this appendix contains a set of tables that convert apparent-wind data for different boat speeds into true-wind angle and velocity. There is a separate table for each knot of boat speed from 2 to 9 knots.

On each table, the apparent-wind speed is shown across the top. The apparent-wind angle is on the left vertical index. To use the table, pull out the chart representing your boat speed. Then cross-reference any apparent-wind speed and apparent-wind angle, and you will get the resultant true-wind speed and angle, and VMG.

You will probably find that your true-wind plots still do not match the figures in the table. The most likely cause is leeway. If you know your instruments are correct, then leeway would be the difference between the plotted and computed true-wind angle. (If leeway is more than 4 or 5 per cent upwind, then there is still some error in the input from your instruments.)

An example of how to use the charts to extract the VMG is shown on the 6-knot apparent-wind speed table. Here is the input data:

Apparent-wind speed	6	knots
Boat speed	5	knots
Apparent-wind angle	30	degrees

The lines drawn vertically and horizontally to correspond to the input data give you a boxed square that lists the output data:

True-wind angle (TW$\angle$)	86	degrees
True-wind speed (TWS)	3	knots
Speed made good (VMG)	.32	knots

Study the large variances that are possible in the VMG column with just small changes in boat speed, apparent-wind angle, or apparent-wind speed. These VMG numbers are the true index of your actual progress with or against the true wind. Studying the variances gives you an acute awareness of the need for the utmost concentration at all times in simultaneously steering to the most exacting angle of attack, holding the best boat speed and having correct sail trim.

APPARENT-WIND SPEED= 6 KNOTS

Boatspeed	2	3	4	5	6	7	8	9	Knots
Apparent-wind Angle									
20	29	38	51	73	100	124	139	149	TW∠
	4.2	3.3	2.6	2.1	2.1	2.5	3.1	3.9	TWS
	1.74	2.36	2.49	1.48	−1.05	−3.88	−6.04	−7.69	VMG
25	36	46	60	80	102	122	135	145	
	4.3	3.5	2.9	2.6	2.6	3	3.6	4.4	
	1.6	2.07	1.97	.85	−1.3	−3.68	−5.69	−7.34	
30	43	54	68	86	105	121	133	142	
	4.4	3.7	3.2	3	3.1	3.5	4.1	4.8	
	1.45	1.77	1.48	.32	−1.56	−3.61	−5.47	−7.07	
32	46	57	71	88	106	121	132	141	
	4.4	3.8	3.4	3.2	3.3	3.7	4.3	5	
	1.39	1.64	1.29	.13	−1.66	−3.61	−5.41	−6.99	
34	48	60	74	90	107	121	132	140	
	4.5	3.9	3.5	3.4	3.5	3.9	4.5	5.2	
	1.32	1.52	1.11	−.04	−1.76	−3.62	−5.36	−6.92	
36	51	62	76	92	108	121	132	140	
	4.5	4	3.6	3.5	3.7	4.1	4.7	5.4	
	1.25	1.39	.94	−.21	−1.86	−3.64	−5.33	−6.86	
38	54	65	79	94	109	122	132	139	
	4.6	4.1	3.8	3.7	3.9	4.3	4.9	5.6	
	1.18	1.27	.77	−.37	−1.96	−3.67	−5.31	−6.81	

APPARENT-WIND SPEED = 4 KNOTS

Boatspeed	2	3	4	5	6	7	8	9	Knots
Apparent-wind Angle									
20	38	61	100	132	149	157	162	165	TW∠
	2.2	1.6	1.4	1.8	2.6	3.5	4.5	5.4	TWS
	1.57	1.45	−.7	−3.36	−5.13	−6.45	−7.62	−8.71	VMG
25	46	70	102	129	145	153	159	163	
	2.3	1.8	1.7	2.2	2.9	3.8	4.7	5.6	
	1.38	1.04	−.87	−3.16	−4.89	−6.26	−7.47	−8.59	
30	54	77	105	128	142	151	156	160	
	2.5	2.1	2.1	2.5	3.2	4.1	5	5.9	
	1.18	.67	−1.04	−3.05	−4.72	−6.1	−7.32	−8.47	
32	57	80	106	127	141	150	155	159	
	2.5	2.2	2.2	2.7	3.4	4.2	5.1	6	
	1.09	.54	−1.11	−3.03	−4.66	−6.04	−7.27	−8.42	
34	60	82	107	127	140	149	154	159	
	2.6	2.3	2.3	2.8	3.5	4.3	5.2	6.1	
	1.01	.41	−1.17	−3.01	−4.61	−5.99	−7.22	−8.38	
36	62	84	108	127	140	148	154	158	
	2.7	2.4	2.5	2.9	3.6	4.4	5.3	6.2	
	.93	.29	−1.24	−3.01	−4.58	−5.94	−7.18	−8.34	
38	65	86	109	127	139	147	153	157	
	2.7	2.5	2.6	3.1	3.8	4.6	5.4	6.3	
	.84	.18	−1.31	−3.01	−4.54	−5.9	−7.14	−8.3	
40	68	89	110	127	139	147	152	157	
	2.8	2.6	2.7	3.2	3.9	4.7	5.6	6.5	
	.76	.07	−1.37	−3.01	−4.52	−5.87	−7.1	−8.26	
45	74	93	112	128	138	146	151	155	
	2.9	2.8	3.1	3.6	4.2	5	5.9	6.8	
	.56	−.19	−1.54	−3.05	−4.48	−5.8	−7.02	−8.19	
50	79	98	115	128	138	145	151	155	
	3.1	3.1	3.4	3.9	4.6	5.4	6.2	7.1	
	.36	−.42	−1.7	−3.11	−4.48	−5.76	−6.97	−8.13	

457   **Appendix**

APPARENT-WIND SPEED = 4 KNOTS

Boatspeed	2	3	4	5	6	7	8	9	Knots
Apparent-wind Angle									
60	90	106	120	131	139	145	150	154	
	3.5	3.6	4	4.6	5.3	6.1	6.9	7.8	
	0	−.84	−2	−3.28	−4.54	−5.76	−6.93	−8.07	
70	100	113	125	134	141	146	150	154	
	3.8	4.1	4.6	5.2	6	6.8	7.6	8.5	
	−.34	−1.2	−2.3	−3.48	−4.66	−5.83	−6.96	−8.08	
80	108	120	130	138	143	148	152	155	
	4.1	4.6	5.1	5.8	6.6	7.4	8.3	9.2	
	−.63	−1.52	−2.58	−3.69	−4.82	−5.94	−7.05	−8.14	
90	117	127	135	141	146	150	153	156	
	4.5	5	5.7	6.4	7.2	8.1	8.9	9.8	
	−.9	−1.8	−2.83	−3.91	−5	−6.08	−7.16	−8.23	
100	124	133	140	145	150	153	156	158	
	4.8	5.4	6.1	6.9	7.8	8.6	9.5	10.5	
	−1.13	−2.06	−3.07	−4.12	−5.18	−6.24	−7.29	−8.34	
110	132	139	145	149	153	156	158	160	
	5	5.8	6.6	7.4	8.3	9.2	10.1	11	
	−1.34	−2.28	−3.28	−4.31	−5.35	−6.39	−7.43	−8.47	
120	139	145	150	154	157	159	161	163	
	5.3	6.1	6.9	7.8	8.7	9.6	10.6	11.5	
	−1.52	−2.47	−3.47	−4.49	−5.51	−6.54	−7.56	−8.59	
130	146	151	155	158	160	162	164	165	
	5.5	6.4	7.3	8.2	9.1	10	11	12	
	−1.67	−2.63	−3.63	−4.64	−5.65	−6.67	−7.69	−8.71	
140	153	157	160	162	164	166	167	168	
	5.7	6.6	7.5	8.5	9.4	10.4	11.4	12.3	
	−1.79	−2.77	−3.76	−4.77	−5.78	−6.79	−7.8	−8.81	
150	160	163	165	167	168	169	170	171	
	5.8	6.8	7.7	8.7	9.7	10.7	11.6	12.6	
	−1.88	−2.87	−3.87	−4.87	−5.88	−6.88	−7.89	−8.89	

APPARENT-WIND SPEED = 4 KNOTS

Boatspeed	2	3	4	5	6	7	8	9	Knots
Apparent-wind Angle									
160	167	169	170	171	172	173	173	174	
	5.9	6.9	7.9	8.9	9.9	10.8	11.8	12.8	
	−1.95	−2.95	−3.94	−4.95	−5.95	−6.95	−7.95	−8.95	
165	170	171	172	173	174	175	175	175	
	6	6.9	7.9	8.9	9.9	10.9	11.9	12.9	
	−1.97	−2.97	−3.97	−4.97	−5.97	−6.97	−7.97	−8.98	
170	173	174	175	176	176	176	177	177	
	6	7	8	9	10	11	12	13	
	−1.99	−2.99	−3.99	−4.99	−5.99	−6.99	−7.99	−8.99	
175	177	177	177	178	178	178	178	178	
	6	7	8	9	10	11	12	13	
	−2	−3	−4	−5	−6	−7	−8	−9	
180	180	180	180	180	180	180	180	180	
	6	7	8	9	10	11	12	13	
	−2	−3	−4	−5	−6	−7	−8	−9	

APPARENT-WIND SPEED= 6 KNOTS

Boatspeed	2	3	4	5	6	7	8	9	Knots
Apparent-wind Angle									
20	29	38	51	73	100	124	139	149	TW∠
	4.2	3.3	2.6	2.1	2.1	2.5	3.1	3.9	TWS
	1.74	2.36	2.49	1.48	−1.05	−3.88	−6.04	−7.69	VMG
25	36	46	60	80	102	122	135	145	
	4.3	3.5	2.9	2.6	2.6	3	3.6	4.4	
	1.6	2.07	1.97	.85	−1.3	−3.68	−5.69	−7.34	
30	43	54	68	86	105	121	133	142	
	4.4	3.7	3.2	3	3.1	3.5	4.1	4.8	
	1.45	1.77	1.48	.32	−1.56	−3.61	−5.47	−7.07	
32	46	57	71	88	106	121	132	141	
	4.4	3.8	3.4	3.2	3.3	3.7	4.3	5	
	1.39	1.64	1.29	.13	−1.66	−3.61	−5.41	−6.99	
34	48	60	74	90	107	121	132	140	
	4.5	3.9	3.5	3.4	3.5	3.9	4.5	5.2	
	1.32	1.52	1.11	−.04	−1.76	−3.62	−5.36	−6.92	
36	51	62	76	92	108	121	132	140	
	4.5	4	3.6	3.5	3.7	4.1	4.7	5.4	
	1.25	1.39	.94	−.21	−1.86	−3.64	−5.33	−6.86	
38	54	65	79	94	109	122	132	139	
	4.6	4.1	3.8	3.7	3.9	4.3	4.9	5.6	
	1.18	1.27	.77	−.37	−1.96	−3.67	−5.31	−6.81	
40	56	68	81	96	110	122	131	139	
	4.6	4.2	3.9	3.9	4.1	4.5	5.1	5.9	
	1.11	1.14	.61	−.53	−2.06	−3.71	−5.3	−6.78	
45	62	74	87	100	112	123	132	138	
	4.8	4.4	4.2	4.3	4.6	5.1	5.7	6.4	
	.93	.84	.22	−.88	−2.3	−3.82	−5.31	−6.72	
50	68	79	92	104	115	124	132	138	
	5	4.7	4.6	4.7	5.1	5.6	6.2	6.9	
	.74	.54	−.13	−1.21	−2.54	−3.96	−5.36	−6.72	

APPARENT-WIND SPEED= 6 KNOTS

Boatspeed	2	3	4	5	6	7	8	9	Knots
Apparent-wind Angle									
60	79	90	101	111	120	128	134	139	
	5.3	5.2	5.3	5.6	6	6.6	7.2	7.9	
	.37	0	−.76	−1.8	−3	−4.27	−5.55	−6.81	
70	89	100	109	118	125	131	137	141	
	5.6	5.7	6	6.4	6.9	7.5	8.2	8.9	
	.01	−.5	−1.31	−2.32	−3.45	−4.62	−5.81	−6.99	
80	99	108	117	124	130	135	140	143	
	6	6.2	6.6	7.1	7.7	8.4	9.1	9.9	
	−.33	−.95	−1.8	−2.79	−3.86	−4.98	−6.1	−7.23	
90	108	117	124	130	135	139	143	146	
	6.3	6.7	7.2	7.8	8.5	9.2	10	10.8	
	−.64	−1.35	−2.22	−3.21	−4.25	−5.32	−6.4	−7.49	
100	117	124	130	136	140	144	147	150	
	6.6	7.2	7.8	8.5	9.2	10	10.8	11.7	
	−.92	−1.7	−2.6	−3.58	−4.6	−5.65	−6.7	−7.76	
110	126	132	137	141	145	148	151	153	
	6.9	7.6	8.3	9	9.8	10.7	11.5	12.4	
	−1.17	−2.01	−2.93	−3.91	−4.92	−5.95	−6.98	−8.02	
120	134	139	143	147	150	153	155	157	
	7.2	7.9	8.7	9.5	10.4	11.3	12.2	13.1	
	−1.39	−2.27	−3.22	−4.2	−5.2	−6.22	−7.24	−8.26	
130	142	146	150	153	155	157	159	160	
	7.4	8.3	9.1	10	10.9	11.8	12.7	13.7	
	−1.58	−2.5	−3.46	−4.44	−5.44	−6.45	−7.46	−8.48	
140	150	153	156	158	160	162	163	164	
	7.6	8.5	9.4	10.3	11.3	12.2	13.2	14.1	
	−1.73	−2.68	−3.65	−4.64	−5.64	−6.65	−7.65	−8.66	
150	157	160	162	164	165	166	167	168	
	7.8	8.7	9.7	10.6	11.6	12.6	13.5	14.5	
	−1.85	−2.82	−3.81	−4.8	−5.8	−6.8	−7.81	−8.81	

APPARENT-WIND SPEED= 6 KNOTS

Boatspeed	2	3	4	5	6	7	8	9	Knots
Apparent-wind Angle									
160	165	167	168	169	170	171	171	172	
	7.9	8.9	9.9	10.8	11.8	12.8	13.8	14.8	
	−1.94	−2.92	−3.92	−4.91	−5.91	−6.91	−7.92	−8.92	
165	169	170	171	172	172	173	174	174	
	7.9	8.9	9.9	10.9	11.9	12.9	13.9	14.9	
	−1.97	−2.96	−3.96	−4.95	−5.95	−6.95	−7.95	−8.96	
170	172	173	174	175	175	175	176	176	
	8	9	10	11	12	13	13.9	14.9	
	−1.99	−2.98	−3.98	−4.98	−5.98	−6.98	−7.98	−8.98	
175	176	177	177	177	177	178	178	178	
	8	9	10	11	12	13	14	15	
	−2	−3	−4	−5	−6	−7	−8	−9	
180	180	180	180	180	180	180	180	180	
	8	9	10	11	12	13	14	15	
	−2	−3	−4	−5	−6	−7	−8	−9	

APPARENT-WIND SPEED = 8 KNOTS

Boatspeed	2	3	4	5	6	7	8	9	Knots
Apparent-wind Angle									
20	26	31	38	47	61	79	100	118	TW∠
	6.2	5.3	4.5	3.7	3.1	2.8	2.8	3.1	TWS
	1.79	2.56	3.15	3.38	2.91	1.3	−1.39	−4.29	VMG
25	33	38	46	56	70	86	102	117	
	6.2	5.4	4.7	4.1	3.6	3.4	3.5	3.8	
	1.68	2.34	2.77	2.77	2.08	.51	−1.74	−4.14	
30	39	46	54	64	77	91	105	117	
	6.3	5.6	5	4.4	4.1	4	4.1	4.5	
	1.55	2.1	2.36	2.17	1.35	−.13	−2.08	−4.14	
32	42	48	57	67	80	93	106	118	
	6.4	5.7	5.1	4.6	4.3	4.2	4.4	4.8	
	1.49	1.99	2.19	1.93	1.09	−.36	−2.21	−4.17	
34	44	51	60	70	82	95	107	118	
	6.4	5.8	5.2	4.8	4.5	4.5	4.7	5.1	
	1.43	1.89	2.02	1.71	.83	−.58	−2.34	−4.22	
36	46	54	62	73	84	96	108	118	
	6.5	5.8	5.3	4.9	4.7	4.7	4.9	5.3	
	1.37	1.78	1.86	1.49	.59	−.79	−2.48	−4.27	
38	49	56	65	75	86	98	109	119	
	6.5	5.9	5.4	5.1	4.9	5	5.2	5.6	
	1.31	1.67	1.69	1.27	.36	−.98	−2.61	−4.33	
40	51	59	68	78	89	100	110	119	
	6.6	6	5.6	5.3	5.1	5.2	5.5	5.9	
	1.25	1.55	1.52	1.07	.14	−1.17	−2.74	−4.39	
45	57	65	74	83	93	103	112	121	
	6.7	6.2	5.9	5.7	5.7	5.8	6.1	6.6	
	1.08	1.27	1.12	.57	−.37	−1.62	−3.07	−4.58	
50	63	71	79	89	98	107	115	122	
	6.9	6.5	6.2	6.1	6.2	6.4	6.8	7.2	
	.91	.98	.73	.11	−.84	−2.04	−3.39	−4.8	

APPARENT-WIND SPEED = 8 KNOTS

Boatspeed	2	3	4	5	6	7	8	9	Knots
Apparent-wind Angle									
60	74	82	90	98	106	113	120	126	
	7.2	7	6.9	7	7.2	7.5	8	8.5	
	.55	.42	0	−.72	−1.67	−2.79	−4	−5.27	
70	84	92	100	107	113	120	125	130	
	7.6	7.5	7.6	7.9	8.2	8.6	9.2	9.8	
	.19	−.11	−.67	−1.45	−2.39	−3.46	−4.59	−5.77	
80	94	102	108	115	120	125	130	134	
	7.9	8	8.3	8.7	9.1	9.7	10.3	11	
	−.16	−.61	−1.26	−2.09	−3.04	−4.07	−5.15	−6.26	
90	104	111	117	122	127	131	135	138	
	8.2	8.5	8.9	9.4	10	10.6	11.3	12	
	−.49	−1.06	−1.79	−2.65	−3.6	−4.61	−5.66	−6.73	
100	113	119	124	129	133	137	140	143	
	8.6	9	9.5	10.1	10.8	11.5	12.3	13	
	−.8	−1.47	−2.26	−3.15	−4.11	−5.11	−6.13	−7.18	
110	122	127	132	136	139	142	145	147	
	8.9	9.5	10.1	10.8	11.5	12.3	13.1	13.9	
	−1.07	−1.82	−2.67	−3.59	−4.55	−5.55	−6.56	−7.58	
120	131	135	139	142	145	148	150	152	
	9.2	9.8	10.6	11.4	12.2	13	13.9	14.7	
	−1.31	−2.14	−3.03	−3.97	−4.94	−5.93	−6.93	−7.95	
130	139	143	146	149	151	153	155	157	
	9.4	10.2	11	11.9	12.7	13.6	14.5	15.4	
	−1.52	−2.4	−3.33	−4.28	−5.26	−6.25	−7.26	−8.26	
140	148	151	153	155	157	159	160	161	
	9.6	10.5	11.4	12.3	13.2	14.1	15	16	
	−1.7	−2.62	−3.57	−4.54	−5.53	−6.52	−7.52	−8.53	
150	156	158	160	161	163	164	165	166	
	9.8	10.7	11.6	12.6	13.5	14.5	15.5	16.4	
	−1.83	−2.79	−3.76	−4.75	−5.74	−6.73	−7.73	−8.73	

APPARENT-WIND SPEED = 8 KNOTS

Boatspeed	2	3	4	5	6	7	8	9	Knots
Apparent-wind Angle									
160	164	165	167	168	169	169	170	171	
	9.9	10.9	11.8	12.8	13.8	14.8	15.8	16.7	
	−1.93	−2.91	−3.9	−4.89	−5.89	−6.88	−7.88	−8.88	
165	168	169	170	171	171	172	172	173	
	9.9	10.9	11.9	12.9	13.9	14.9	15.9	16.9	
	−1.96	−2.95	−3.94	−4.94	−5.94	−6.94	−7.94	−8.94	
170	172	173	173	174	174	175	175	175	
	10	11	12	13	13.9	14.9	15.9	16.9	
	−1.99	−2.98	−3.98	−4.98	−5.98	−6.97	−7.97	−8.97	
175	176	176	177	177	177	177	177	178	
	10	11	12	13	14	15	16	17	
	−2	−3	−4	−5	−6	−7	−8	−9	
180	180	180	180	180	180	180	180	180	
	10	11	12	13	14	15	16	17	
	−2	−3	−4	−5	−6	−7	−8	−9	

APPARENT-WIND SPEED = 10 KNOTS

Boatspeed	2	3	4	5	6	7	8	9	Knots
Apparent-wind Angle									
20	25	28	32	38	45	55	68	83	TW∠
	8.1	7.3	6.4	5.6	4.8	4.2	3.7	3.4	TWS
	1.81	2.64	3.37	3.94	4.22	4.01	3.02	1.03	VMG
25	31	35	40	46	54	64	76	89	
	8.2	7.4	6.6	5.9	5.2	4.7	4.4	4.2	
	1.71	2.46	3.07	3.46	3.52	3.07	1.95	.13	
30	37	41	47	54	62	72	82	94	
	8.3	7.6	6.8	6.2	5.7	5.3	5	5	
	1.59	2.24	2.72	2.95	2.81	2.2	1.04	−.62	
32	39	44	50	57	65	74	85	96	
	8.4	7.6	6.9	6.3	5.9	5.5	5.3	5.3	
	1.54	2.15	2.58	2.74	2.54	1.88	.72	−.88	
34	42	47	53	60	68	77	87	97	
	8.4	7.7	7	6.5	6	5.7	5.6	5.6	
	1.49	2.06	2.43	2.53	2.27	1.57	.41	−1.14	
36	44	49	55	62	70	79	89	99	
	8.5	7.8	7.2	6.6	6.2	6	5.9	5.9	
	1.43	1.96	2.28	2.32	2.01	1.27	.12	−1.38	
38	46	52	58	65	73	82	91	100	
	8.5	7.9	7.3	6.8	6.4	6.2	6.2	6.3	
	1.38	1.86	2.13	2.11	1.75	.99	−.16	−1.62	
40	49	54	60	68	76	84	93	102	
	8.6	7.9	7.4	7	6.6	6.5	6.4	6.6	
	1.32	1.76	1.97	1.91	1.5	.71	−.43	−1.84	
45	54	60	67	74	81	89	97	105	
	8.7	8.2	7.7	7.4	7.2	7.1	7.1	7.3	
	1.16	1.49	1.59	1.4	.89	.07	−1.05	−2.37	
50	60	66	72	79	87	94	102	109	
	8.8	8.4	8	7.8	7.7	7.7	7.8	8.1	
	1	1.22	1.2	.91	.33	−.53	−1.61	−2.87	

APPARENT-WIND SPEED = 10 KNOTS

Boatspeed	2	3	4	5	6	7	8	9	Knots
Apparent-wind Angle									
60	71	77	83	90	97.	103	109	115	
	9.2	8.9	8.7	8.7	8.7	8.9	9.2	9.5	
	.65	.67	.45	0	−.69	−1.58	−2.62	−3.78	
70	81	87	94	100	105	111	116	121	
	9.5	9.4	9.4	9.5	9.7	10.1	10.5	10.9	
	.29	.13	−.25	−.83	−1.59	−2.5	−3.51	−4.6	
80	92	97	103	108	113	118	122	126	
	9.9	9.9	10.1	10.4	10.7	11.2	11.7	12.2	
	−.06	−.39	−.9	−1.58	−2.39	−3.3	−4.3	−5.35	
90	101	107	112	117	121	125	129	132	
	10.2	10.4	10.8	11.2	11.7	12.2	12.8	13.5	
	−.4	−.87	−1.49	−2.24	−3.09	−4.02	−5	−6.03	
100	111	116	120	124	128	132	135	137	
	10.5	10.9	11.4	11.9	12.5	13.2	13.8	14.6	
	−.71	−1.31	−2.02	−2.83	−3.71	−4.65	−5.63	−6.64	
110	120	124	128	132	135	138	141	143	
	10.8	11.4	12	12.6	13.3	14	14.8	15.6	
	−1	−1.7	−2.48	−3.34	−4.25	−5.2	−6.18	−7.18	
120	129	133	136	139	142	144	146	148	
	11.1	11.8	12.5	13.2	14	14.8	15.6	16.5	
	−1.26	−2.04	−2.89	−3.78	−4.72	−5.68	−6.66	−7.66	
130	138	141	144	146	148	150	152	154	
	11.4	12.1	12.9	13.8	14.6	15.5	16.3	17.2	
	−1.48	−2.33	−3.23	−4.16	−5.11	−6.09	−7.07	−8.07	
140	146	149	151	153	155	156	158	159	
	11.6	12.4	13.3	14.2	15.1	16	16.9	17.9	
	−1.67	−2.57	−3.51	−4.46	−5.43	−6.42	−7.41	−8.4	
150	155	157	158	160	161	162	163	164	
	11.8	12.7	13.6	14.5	15.5	16.4	17.4	18.4	
	−1.82	−2.76	−3.73	−4.7	−5.68	−6.67	−7.67	−8.66	

APPARENT-WIND SPEED = 10 KNOTS

Boatspeed	2	3	4	5	6	7	8	9	Knots
Apparent-wind Angle									
160	163	165	166	167	167	168	169	169	
	11.9	12.9	13.8	14.8	15.8	16.7	17.7	18.7	
	−1.92	−2.9	−3.88	−4.87	−5.86	−6.86	−7.85	−8.85	
165	167	168	169	170	171	171	172	172	
	11.9	12.9	13.9	14.9	15.9	16.9	17.8	18.8	
	−1.96	−2.94	−3.94	−4.93	−5.92	−6.92	−7.92	−8.92	
170	172	172	173	173	174	174	174	175	
	12	13	14	14.9	15.9	16.9	17.9	18.9	
	−1.98	−2.98	−3.97	−4.97	−5.97	−6.97	−7.97	−8.97	
175	176	176	176	177	177	177	177	177	
	12	13	14	15	16	17	18	19	
	−2	−3	−4	−5	−6	−7	−8	−9	
180	180	180	180	180	180	180	180	180	
	12	13	14	15	16	17	18	19	
	−2	−3	−4	−5	−6	−7	−8	−9	

APPARENT-WIND SPEED = 12 KNOTS

Boatspeed	2	3	4	5	6	7	8	9	Knots
Apparent-wind Angle									
20	24	26	29	33	38	44	51	61	AW∠
	10.1	9.2	8.4	7.5	6.7	5.9	5.3	4.7	AWS
	1.82	2.68	3.48	4.18	4.73	5.05	4.99	4.36	VMG
25	30	33	36	41	46	53	60	70	
	10.2	9.4	8.5	7.8	7	6.4	5.8	5.4	
	1.73	2.52	3.21	3.78	4.15	4.25	3.94	3.12	
30	36	39	43	48	54	61	68	77	
	10.3	9.5	8.8	8.1	7.4	6.9	6.5	6.2	
	1.62	2.32	2.91	3.34	3.54	3.44	2.96	2.03	
32	38	42	46	51	57	63	71	80	
	10.4	9.6	8.9	8.2	7.6	7.1	6.7	6.5	
	1.57	2.24	2.78	3.15	3.29	3.12	2.59	1.63	
34	40	44	48	54	60	66	74	82	
	10.4	9.7	9	8.3	7.8	7.3	7	6.8	
	1.52	2.15	2.65	2.96	3.04	2.81	2.23	1.25	
36	42	46	51	56	62	69	76	84	
	10.4	9.7	9.1	8.5	8	7.6	7.3	7.1	
	1.47	2.06	2.51	2.77	2.79	2.5	1.88	.89	
38	45	49	54	59	65	72	79	86	
	10.5	9.8	9.2	8.6	8.2	7.8	7.5	7.4	
	1.42	1.97	2.37	2.58	2.54	2.2	1.54	.55	
40	47	51	56	61	68	74	81	89	
	10.5	9.9	9.3	8.8	8.3	8	7.8	7.7	
	1.36	1.87	2.23	2.38	2.29	1.91	1.22	.22	
45	53	57	62	68	74	80	87	93	
	10.7	10.1	9.6	9.2	8.8	8.6	8.5	8.5	
	1.21	1.62	1.86	1.89	1.68	1.2	.45	−.55	
50	58	63	68	74	79	86	92	98	
	10.8	10.3	9.9	9.6	9.4	9.2	9.2	9.3	
	1.05	1.36	1.49	1.41	1.09	.54	−.25	−1.25	

APPARENT-WIND SPEED = 12 KNOTS

Boatspeed	2	3	4	5	6	7	8	9	Knots
Apparent-wind Angle									
60	69	74	79	85	90	95	101	106	
	11.1	10.8	10.6	10.4	10.4	10.4	10.6	10.8	
	.71	.83	.75	.47	0	−.68	−1.52	−2.5	
70	79	84	89	95	100	104	109	113	
	11.5	11.3	11.3	11.3	11.4	11.6	11.9	12.3	
	.36	.29	.03	−.4	−1	−1.75	−2.62	−3.59	
80	90	94	99	104	108	113	117	120	
	11.8	11.9	12	12.2	12.4	12.8	13.2	13.7	
	.01	−.24	−.65	−1.2	−1.89	−2.69	−3.59	−4.55	
90	99	104	108	113	117	120	124	127	
	12.2	12.4	12.6	13	13.4	13.9	14.4	15	
	−.33	−.73	−1.27	−1.93	−2.69	−3.53	−4.44	−5.4	
100	109	113	117	121	124	128	130	133	
	12.5	12.9	13.3	13.8	14.3	14.9	15.5	16.2	
	−.66	−1.19	−1.84	−2.58	−3.39	−4.27	−5.2	−6.16	
110	118	122	126	129	132	135	137	139	
	12.8	13.3	13.9	14.5	15.1	15.8	16.5	17.3	
	−.96	−1.6	−2.34	−3.15	−4.01	−4.92	−5.86	−6.83	
120	128	131	134	137	139	141	143	145	
	13.1	13.7	14.4	15.1	15.9	16.6	17.4	18.2	
	−1.22	−1.97	−2.78	−3.64	−4.54	−5.47	−6.43	−7.4	
130	137	139	142	144	146	148	150	151	
	13.4	14.1	14.9	15.7	16.5	17.3	18.2	19.1	
	−1.46	−2.28	−3.15	−4.06	−4.99	−5.94	−6.91	−7.89	
140	145	148	150	151	153	155	156	157	
	13.6	14.4	15.3	16.2	17	17.9	18.8	19.8	
	−1.65	−2.54	−3.46	−4.4	−5.35	−6.32	−7.3	−8.29	
150	154	156	157	159	160	161	162	163	
	13.8	14.7	15.6	16.5	17.5	18.4	19.3	20.3	
	−1.81	−2.74	−3.7	−4.66	−5.64	−6.62	−7.61	−8.6	

APPARENT-WIND SPEED = 12 KNOTS

Boatspeed	2	3	4	5	6	7	8	9	Knots
Apparent-wind Angle									
160	163	164	165	166	167	167	168	169	
	13.9	14.9	15.8	16.8	17.8	18.7	19.7	20.7	
	−1.92	−2.89	−3.87	−4.85	−5.84	−6.83	−7.83	−8.83	
165	167	168	169	169	170	171	171	171	
	13.9	14.9	15.9	16.9	17.9	18.8	19.8	20.8	
	−1.95	−2.94	−3.93	−4.92	−5.91	−6.91	−7.91	−8.9	
170	171	172	172	173	173	174	174	174	
	14	15	16	16.9	17.9	18.9	19.9	20.9	
	−1.98	−2.98	−3.97	−4.97	−5.96	−6.96	−7.96	−8.96	
175	176	176	176	176	177	177	177	177	
	14	15	16	17	18	19	20	21	
	−2	−3	−4	−5	−5.99	−6.99	−7.99	−8.99	
180	180	180	180	180	180	180	180	180	
	14	15	16	17	18	19	20	21	
	−2	−3	−4	−5	−6	−7	−8	−9	

APPARENT-WIND SPEED = 15 KNOTS

Boatspeed	2	3	4	5	6	7	8	9	Knots
Apparent-wind Angle									
20	23	25	27	29	32	36	40	45	AW∠
	13.1	12.2	11.3	10.4	9.6	8.8	8	7.2	AWS
	1.84	2.72	3.56	4.35	5.06	5.67	6.12	6.34	VMG
25	29	31	33	36	40	44	49	54	
	13.2	12.3	11.5	10.7	9.9	9.1	8.5	7.8	
	1.75	2.57	3.33	4.02	4.6	5.04	5.29	5.28	
30	34	37	40	43	47	51	56	62	
	13.3	12.5	11.7	11	10.3	9.6	9	8.5	
	1.65	2.39	3.07	3.64	4.09	4.36	4.43	4.22	
32	37	39	42	46	50	54	59	65	
	13.3	12.6	11.8	11.1	10.4	9.8	9.2	8.8	
	1.6	2.32	2.95	3.48	3.87	4.08	4.08	3.81	
34	39	42	45	48	53	57	62	68	
	13.4	12.6	11.9	11.2	10.6	10	9.5	9.1	
	1.55	2.24	2.83	3.31	3.65	3.8	3.73	3.41	
36	41	44	47	51	55	60	65	70	
	13.4	12.7	12	11.3	10.7	10.2	9.7	9.4	
	1.5	2.15	2.71	3.14	3.42	3.52	3.39	3.01	
38	43	46	50	54	58	62	68	73	
	13.5	12.8	12.1	11.5	10.9	10.4	10	9.7	
	1.45	2.07	2.58	2.97	3.19	3.23	3.05	2.62	
40	45	49	52	56	60	65	70	76	
	13.5	12.8	12.2	11.6	11.1	10.6	10.3	10	
	1.4	1.98	2.45	2.79	2.96	2.95	2.72	2.25	
45	51	54	58	62	67	71	76	81	
	13.7	13.1	12.5	12	11.6	11.2	10.9	10.7	
	1.26	1.74	2.11	2.33	2.39	2.25	1.9	1.34	
50	56	60	64	68	72	77	82	87	
	13.8	13.3	12.8	12.4	12.1	11.8	11.6	11.5	
	1.1	1.5	1.76	1.87	1.81	1.56	1.13	.5	

APPARENT-WIND SPEED = 15 KNOTS

Boatspeed	2	3	4	5	6	7	8	9	Knots
Apparent-wind Angle									
60	67	71	75	79	83	88	92	97	
	14.1	13.7	13.5	13.2	13.1	13	13	13.1	
	.77	.98	1.04	.94	.68	.26	−.31	−1.04	
70	77	81	85	89	94	98	102	105	
	14.4	14.3	14.1	14.1	14.1	14.2	14.4	14.6	
	.43	.44	.31	.04	−.37	−.93	−1.6	−2.39	
80	88	92	95	99	103	107	110	113	
	14.8	14.8	14.8	15	15.2	15.4	15.7	16.1	
	.08	−.09	−.38	−.81	−1.35	−2	−2.75	−3.58	
90	98	101	105	108	112	115	118	121	
	15.1	15.3	15.5	15.8	16.2	16.6	17	17.5	
	−.27	−.59	−1.04	−1.59	−2.23	−2.97	−3.77	−4.64	
100	107	111	114	117	120	123	126	128	
	15.5	15.8	16.2	16.6	17.1	17.6	18.2	18.8	
	−.6	−1.07	−1.64	−2.29	−3.02	−3.82	−4.67	−5.56	
110	117	120	123	126	128	131	133	135	
	15.8	16.3	16.8	17.4	18	18.6	19.3	20	
	−.91	−1.5	−2.18	−2.92	−3.72	−4.57	−5.46	−6.38	
120	126	129	132	134	136	138	140	142	
	16.1	16.7	17.3	18	18.7	19.5	20.2	21	
	−1.19	−1.89	−2.66	−3.47	−4.33	−5.22	−6.14	−7.08	
130	135	138	140	142	144	145	147	148	
	16.4	17.1	17.8	18.6	19.4	20.2	21.1	21.9	
	−1.43	−2.22	−3.06	−3.94	−4.84	−5.77	−6.71	−7.67	
140	144	146	148	150	151	152	154	155	
	16.6	17.4	18.2	19.1	20	20.9	21.7	22.6	
	−1.63	−2.5	−3.4	−4.32	−5.26	−6.21	−7.18	−8.15	
150	153	155	156	157	158	159	160	161	
	16.8	17.7	18.6	19.5	20.4	21.4	22.3	23.2	
	−1.79	−2.72	−3.66	−4.62	−5.59	−6.56	−7.54	−8.52	

APPARENT-WIND SPEED = *15 KNOTS*

Boatspeed	2	3	4	5	6	7	8	9	Knots
Apparent-wind									
Angle									
160	162	163	164	165	166	166	167	167	
	16.9	17.8	18.8	19.8	20.7	21.7	22.7	23.7	
	−1.91	−2.88	−3.85	−4.83	−5.82	−6.81	−7.8	−8.79	
165	167	167	168	169	169	170	170	171	
	16.9	17.9	18.9	19.9	20.9	21.8	22.8	23.8	
	−1.95	−2.93	−3.92	−4.91	−5.9	−6.89	−7.89	−8.88	
170	171	172	172	172	173	173	173	174	
	17	18	19	19.9	20.9	21.9	22.9	23.9	
	−1.98	−2.97	−3.97	−4.96	−5.96	−6.96	−7.95	−8.95	
175	176	176	176	176	176	177	177	177	
	17	18	19	20	21	22	23	24	
	−2	−3	−4	−4.99	−5.99	−6.99	−7.99	−8.99	
180	180	180	180	180	180	180	180	180	
	17	18	19	20	21	22	23	24	
	−2	−3	−4	−5	−6	−7	−8	−9	

APPARENT-WIND SPEED = 18 KNOTS

Boatspeed	2	3	4	5	6	7	8	9	Knots
Apparent-wind Angle									
20	22	24	25	27	29	32	35	38	AW∠
	16.1	15.2	14.3	13.4	12.5	11.7	10.8	10	AWS
	1.84	2.74	3.61	4.44	5.22	5.94	6.58	7.1	VMG
25	28	30	32	34	36	39	42	46	
	16.2	15.3	14.5	13.6	12.8	12	11.3	10.6	
	1.76	2.6	3.4	4.14	4.82	5.42	5.9	6.23	
30	34	36	38	40	43	46	50	54	
	16.3	15.5	14.7	13.9	13.2	12.4	11.8	11.2	
	1.66	2.44	3.15	3.8	4.37	4.83	5.15	5.31	
32	36	38	40	43	46	49	53	57	
	16.3	15.5	14.8	14	13.3	12.6	12	11.4	
	1.62	2.36	3.05	3.66	4.18	4.58	4.84	4.94	
34	38	40	43	45	48	52	55	60	
	16.4	15.6	14.9	14.1	13.5	12.8	12.2	11.7	
	1.57	2.29	2.94	3.51	3.98	4.32	4.53	4.56	
36	40	42	45	48	51	54	58	62	
	16.4	15.7	14.9	14.3	13.6	13	12.5	12	
	1.52	2.21	2.82	3.35	3.77	4.07	4.21	4.18	
38	42	45	47	50	54	57	61	65	
	16.5	15.7	15.1	14.4	13.8	13.2	12.7	12.2	
	1.47	2.13	2.7	3.19	3.56	3.8	3.89	3.81	
40	44	47	50	53	56	60	63	68	
	16.5	15.8	15.2	14.5	13.9	13.4	12.9	12.5	
	1.42	2.04	2.58	3.02	3.35	3.54	3.57	3.44	
45	50	53	56	59	62	66	70	74	
	16.6	16	15.4	14.9	14.4	14	13.6	13.3	
	1.28	1.82	2.26	2.59	2.8	2.87	2.78	2.52	
50	55	58	61	65	68	72	75	79	
	16.8	16.2	15.7	15.3	14.9	14.5	14.2	14	
	1.14	1.58	1.92	2.15	2.24	2.2	2	1.64	

Appendix

APPARENT-WIND SPEED = 18 KNOTS

Boatspeed	2	3	4	5	6	7	8	9	Knots
Apparent-wind Angle									
60	66	68	72	76	79	83	86	90	
	17.1	16.7	16.4	16.1	15.9	15.7	15.6	15.6	
	.81	1.07	1.22	1.24	1.13	.89	.51	0	
70	76	79	83	86	89	93	96	100	
	17.4	17.2	17.1	17	16.9	16.9	17	17.2	
	.47	.55	.5	.34	.05	−.35	−.87	−1.5	
80	86	90	93	96	99	102	105	108	
	17.8	17.7	17.7	17.8	18	18.1	18.4	18.7	
	.12	.02	−.2	−.53	−.97	−1.5	−2.13	−2.84	
90	96	99	103	106	108	111	114	117	
	18.1	18.2	18.4	18.7	19	19.3	19.7	20.1	
	−.23	−.5	−.87	−1.34	−1.9	−2.54	−3.25	−4.03	
100	106	109	112	115	117	120	122	124	
	18.5	18.8	19.1	19.5	19.9	20.4	20.9	21.5	
	−.56	−.98	−1.5	−2.09	−2.75	−3.48	−4.26	−5.09	
110	116	118	121	123	126	128	130	132	
	18.8	19.2	19.7	20.3	20.8	21.4	22.1	22.7	
	−.87	−1.43	−2.06	−2.76	−3.51	−4.3	−5.14	−6.01	
120	125	128	130	132	134	136	137	139	
	19.1	19.7	20.3	21	21.6	22.3	23.1	23.8	
	−1.16	−1.83	−2.57	−3.35	−4.17	−5.02	−5.9	−6.81	
130	135	137	138	140	142	143	145	146	
	19.3	20.1	20.8	21.6	22.3	23.1	23.9	24.8	
	−1.41	−2.18	−3	−3.85	−4.73	−5.63	−6.54	−7.48	
140	144	145	147	148	150	151	152	153	
	19.6	20.4	21.2	22.1	22.9	23.8	24.7	25.6	
	−1.62	−2.48	−3.36	−4.26	−5.18	−6.12	−7.07	−8.03	
150	153	154	155	156	157	158	159	160	
	19.8	20.7	21.6	22.5	23.4	24.3	25.2	26.2	
	−1.79	−2.71	−3.64	−4.59	−5.54	−6.51	−7.48	−8.46	

APPARENT-WIND SPEED = 18 KNOTS

Boatspeed	2	3	4	5	6	7	8	9	Knots
Apparent-wind Angle									
160	162	163	164	164	165	166	166	167	
	19.9	20.8	21.8	22.8	23.7	24.7	25.7	26.6	
	−1.91	−2.87	−3.84	−4.82	−5.8	−6.78	−7.77	−8.76	
165	166	167	168	168	169	169	170	170	
	19.9	20.9	21.9	22.9	23.8	24.8	25.8	26.8	
	−1.95	−2.93	−3.91	−4.9	−5.89	−6.88	−7.87	−8.87	
170	171	171	172	172	172	173	173	173	
	20	21	22	22.9	23.9	24.9	25.9	26.9	
	−1.98	−2.97	−3.96	−4.96	−5.95	−6.95	−7.95	−8.94	
175	175	176	176	176	176	176	177	177	
	20	21	22	23	24	25	26	27	
	−2	−3	−3.99	−4.99	−5.99	−6.99	−7.99	−8.99	
180	180	180	180	180	180	180	180	180	
	20	21	22	23	24	25	26	27	
	−2	−3	−4	−5	−6	−7	−8	−9	

APPARENT-WIND SPEED = 21 KNOTS

Boatspeed	2	3	4	5	6	7	8	9	Knots
Apparent-wind Angle									
20	22	23	25	26	28	29	31	34	TW∠
	19.1	18.2	17.3	16.4	15.5	14.6	13.8	12.9	TWS
	1.85	2.75	3.63	4.49	5.31	6.09	6.82	7.47	VMG
25	28	29	31	32	34	36	39	41	
	19.2	18.3	17.5	16.6	15.8	15	14.2	13.4	
	1.77	2.62	3.44	4.22	4.95	5.63	6.23	6.74	
30	33	35	37	39	41	43	46	49	
	19.3	18.5	17.6	16.9	16.1	15.3	14.6	14	
	1.67	2.46	3.21	3.91	4.54	5.1	5.57	5.92	
32	35	37	39	41	43	46	49	52	
	19.3	18.5	17.7	17	16.2	15.5	14.8	14.2	
	1.63	2.39	3.11	3.77	4.36	4.87	5.28	5.58	
34	37	39	41	43	46	48	51	54	
	19.4	18.6	17.8	17.1	16.4	15.7	15	14.4	
	1.59	2.32	3	3.63	4.18	4.64	5	5.24	
36	39	41	44	46	48	51	54	57	
	19.4	18.7	17.9	17.2	16.5	15.9	15.3	14.7	
	1.54	2.24	2.89	3.48	3.98	4.4	4.7	4.89	
38	42	44	46	48	51	54	57	60	
	19.5	18.7	18	17.3	16.7	16.1	15.5	15	
	1.49	2.17	2.78	3.33	3.79	4.15	4.41	4.53	
40	44	46	48	51	53	56	59	62	
	19.5	18.8	18.1	17.5	16.9	16.3	15.7	15.2	
	1.44	2.08	2.66	3.17	3.59	3.9	4.11	4.18	
45	49	51	54	56	59	62	65	69	
	19.6	19	18.4	17.8	17.3	16.8	16.4	16	
	1.3	1.87	2.35	2.76	3.07	3.27	3.35	3.29	
50	54	57	59	62	65	68	71	74	
	19.8	19.2	18.7	18.2	17.7	17.3	17	16.7	
	1.16	1.63	2.03	2.33	2.53	2.62	2.58	2.42	

APPARENT-WIND SPEED = 21 KNOTS

Boatspeed	2	3	4	5	6	7	8	9	Knots
Apparent-wind Angle									
60	65	68	70	73	76	79	82	85	
	20.1	19.7	19.3	19	18.7	18.5	18.4	18.2	
	.84	1.14	1.34	1.44	1.44	1.32	1.08	.73	
70	75	78	81	84	87	89	92	95	
	20.4	20.2	20	19.9	19.8	19.7	19.8	19.8	
	.5	.62	.63	.54	.35	.06	−.34	−.83	
80	85	88	91	94	96	99	102	105	
	20.7	20.7	20.7	20.7	20.8	21	21.1	21.4	
	.15	.09	−0.7	−.33	−.68	−1.13	−1.65	−2.26	
90	95	98	101	103	106	108	111	113	
	21.1	21.2	21.4	21.6	21.8	22.1	22.5	22.8	
	−.19	−.43	−.75	−1.16	−1.65	−2.22	−2.85	−3.55	
100	105	108	110	113	115	117	119	121	
	21.4	21.7	22	22.4	22.8	23.3	23.7	24.2	
	−.53	−.92	−1.39	−1.93	−2.54	−3.21	−3.93	−4.7	
110	115	117	120	122	124	126	128	129	
	21.8	22.2	22.7	23.2	23.7	24.3	24.9	25.5	
	−.85	−1.38	−1.98	−2.63	−3.34	−4.09	−4.88	−5.71	
120	125	127	129	130	132	134	135	137	
	22.1	22.6	23.3	23.9	24.6	25.2	25.9	26.7	
	−1.14	−1.79	−2.5	−3.25	−4.04	−4.86	−5.71	−6.59	
130	134	136	137	139	140	142	143	144	
	22.3	23	23.8	24.5	25.3	26.1	26.9	27.7	
	−1.39	−2.15	−2.95	−3.78	−4.63	−5.51	−6.41	−7.33	
140	143	145	146	147	149	150	151	152	
	22.6	23.4	24.2	25	25.9	26.7	27.6	28.5	
	−1.61	−2.45	−3.32	−4.22	−5.12	−6.05	−6.98	−7.93	
150	153	154	155	156	157	157	158	159	
	22.8	23.6	24.5	25.5	26.4	27.3	28.2	29.1	
	−1.78	−2.69	−3.62	−4.56	−5.51	−6.47	−7.43	−8.4	

APPARENT-WIND SPEED = 21 KNOTS

Boatspeed	2	3	4	5	6	7	8	9	Knots
Apparent-wind Angle									
160	162	162	163	164	164	165	165	166	
	22.9	23.8	24.8	25.8	26.7	27.7	28.6	29.6	
	−1.9	−2.87	−3.83	−4.81	−5.78	−6.77	−7.75	−8.74	
165	166	167	167	168	168	169	169	169	
	22.9	23.9	24.9	25.9	26.8	27.8	28.8	29.8	
	−1.95	−2.93	−3.91	−4.89	−5.88	−6.87	−7.86	−8.85	
170	171	171	172	172	172	172	173	173	
	23	24	24.9	25.9	26.9	27.9	28.9	29.9	
	−1.98	−2.97	−3.96	−4.96	−5.95	−6.95	−7.94	−8.94	
175	175	176	176	176	176	176	176	176	
	23	24	25	26	27	28	29	30	
	−2	−3	−3.99	−4.99	−5.99	−6.99	−7.99	−8.99	
180	180	180	180	180	180	180	180	180	
	23	24	25	26	27	28	29	30	
	−2	−3	−4	−5	−6	−7	−8	−9	

APPARENT-WIND SPEED = 24 KNOTS

Boatspeed	2	3	4	5	6	7	8	9	Knots
Apparent-wind Angle									
20	22	23	24	25	26	28	29	31	TW∠
	22.1	21.2	20.3	19.4	18.5	17.6	16.7	15.8	TWS
	1.85	2.76	3.65	4.52	5.37	6.19	6.96	7.69	VMG
25	27	28	30	31	33	35	36	38	
	22.2	21.3	20.4	19.6	18.7	17.9	17.1	16.3	
	1.77	2.63	3.47	4.27	5.04	5.76	6.43	7.04	
30	33	34	36	37	39	41	43	46	
	22.3	21.5	20.6	19.8	19	18.3	17.5	16.8	
	1.68	2.48	3.25	3.98	4.65	5.27	5.83	6.3	
32	35	36	38	40	42	44	46	48	
	22.3	21.5	20.7	19.9	19.2	18.4	17.7	17	
	1.64	2.41	3.15	3.85	4.49	5.06	5.57	5.99	
34	37	38	40	42	44	46	48	51	
	22.4	21.6	20.8	20.1	19.3	18.6	17.9	17.3	
	1.6	2.34	3.05	3.71	4.31	4.85	5.3	5.67	
36	39	41	42	44	46	49	51	54	
	22.4	21.6	20.9	20.2	19.5	18.8	18.1	17.5	
	1.55	2.27	29.5	3.57	4.13	4.62	5.03	5.34	
38	41	43	45	47	49	51	54	56	
	22.5	21.7	21	20.3	19.6	19	18.4	17.8	
	1.5	2.19	2.84	3.42	3.94	4.39	4.75	5.01	
40	43	45	47	49	51	54	56	59	
	22.5	21.8	21.1	20.4	19.8	19.2	18.6	18.1	
	1.45	2.11	2.72	3.27	3.75	4.15	4.46	4.67	
45	49	51	53	55	57	60	62	65	
	22.6	22	21.4	20.8	20.2	19.7	19.2	18.7	
	1.32	1.9	2.42	2.88	3.25	3.54	3.73	3.82	
50	54	56	58	60	63	65	68	71	
	22.8	22.2	21.6	21.1	20.7	20.2	19.8	19.5	
	1.17	1.68	2.11	2.46	2.73	2.91	2.99	2.96	

APPARENT-WIND SPEED = 24 KNOTS

Boatspeed	2	3	4	5	6	7	8	9	Knots
Apparent-wind Angle									
60	64	67	69	71	74	76	79	82	
	23.1	22.6	22.3	21.9	21.6	21.4	21.2	21	
	.86	1.19	1.43	1.59	1.66	1.63	1.51	1.28	
70	75	77	79	82	84	87	89	92	
	23.4	23.1	22.9	22.8	22.7	22.6	22.6	22.6	
	.53	.67	.73	.7	.58	.37	.07	−.32	
80	85	87	90	92	94	97	99	102	
	23.7	23.7	23.6	23.7	23.7	23.8	23.9	24.1	
	.18	.14	.02	−.18	−.47	−.84	−1.29	−1.81	
90	95	97	99	102	104	106	108	111	
	24.1	24.2	24.3	24.5	24.7	25	25.3	25.6	
	−.17	−.38	−.66	−1.02	−1.46	−1.96	−2.53	−3.17	
100	105	107	109	111	113	115	117	119	
	24.4	24.7	25	25.4	25.7	26.1	26.6	27.1	
	−.51	−.88	−1.31	−1.81	−2.38	−3	−3.67	−4.39	
110	114	116	118	120	122	124	126	127	
	24.8	25.2	25.6	26.1	26.7	27.2	27.8	28.4	
	−.83	−1.34	−1.91	−2.53	−3.2	−3.92	−4.67	−5.46	
120	124	126	128	129	131	132	134	135	
	25.1	25.6	26.2	26.9	27.5	28.2	28.8	29.5	
	−1.12	−1.76	−2.44	−3.17	−3.93	−4.73	−5.55	−6.4	
130	133	135	137	138	139	141	142	143	
	25.3	26	26.7	27.5	28.2	29	29.8	30.6	
	−1.38	−2.13	−2.91	−3.72	−4.56	−5.42	−6.3	−7.2	
140	143	144	145	147	148	149	150	151	
	25.6	26.4	27.2	28	28.9	29.7	30.6	31.4	
	−1.6	−2.44	−3.3	−4.18	−5.08	−5.99	−6.91	−7.85	
150	152	153	154	155	156	157	157	158	
	25.8	26.6	27.5	28.4	29.3	30.3	31.2	32.1	
	−1.77	−2.68	−3.61	−4.54	−5.48	−6.43	−7.39	−8.35	

APPARENT-WIND SPEED = 24 KNOTS

Boatspeed	2	3	4	5	6	7	8	9	Knots
Apparent-wind									
Angle									
160	162	162	163	163	164	164	165	165	
	25.9	26.8	27.8	28.7	29.7	30.7	31.6	32.6	
	−1.9	−2.86	−3.83	−4.8	−5.77	−6.75	−7.73	−8.72	
165	166	167	167	168	168	168	169	169	
	25.9	26.9	27.9	28.9	29.8	30.8	31.8	32.8	
	−1.95	−2.92	−3.9	−4.89	−5.87	−6.86	−7.85	−8.84	
170	171	171	171	172	172	172	172	173	
	26	27	27.9	28.9	29.9	30.9	31.9	32.9	
	−1.98	−2.97	−3.96	−4.95	−5.95	−6.94	−7.94	−8.93	
175	175	176	176	176	176	176	176	176	
	26	27	28	29	30	31	32	33	
	−2	−3	−3.99	−4.99	−5.99	−6.99	−7.99	−8.99	
180	180	180	180	180	180	180	180	180	
	26	27	28	29	30	31	32	33	
	−2	−3	−4	−5	−6	−7	−8	−9	

Glossary

The following is neither a thesaurus nor a dictionary of sailing words and terms. It is specifically a compendium of some words used in this book and of definitions that will provide the reader with a more complete understanding of the book's subject matter. The definitions, in general, are confined to the context of the book.

Aback   A sail pushed back by the wind, so that it slows the forward motion of a boat; *e.g.*, a jib mistakenly trimmed to windward.

Abaft   Aft of; *e.g.*, wind abaft the beam.

Abeam   A point at right angles to the centerline of a boat and equidistant between bow and stern.

Afterguy   A line controlling the fore and aft trim of the spinnaker pole.

Airfoil   A curved shape capable of developing lift forces in the flow of a fluid medium.

Air pressure   There is a constant atmospheric pressure of about 14.7 pounds per square inch at sea level.

Air stream   The free air stream is a continuous flow of air moving generally horizontally, with a measurable direction and velocity.

Amidships   Halfway between bow and stern or halfway between port and starboard sides of a boat.

Apparent wind   The combination of true wind and the wind developed by boat speed; *i.e.*, the wind the boat "feels" and by which you sail it.

Aspect ratio   The relationship between horizontal and vertical dimensions; *e.g.*, a tall mast and short boom provide a high-aspect-ratio rig.

Athwartships   Running from side to side of a hull.

Angle of attack   Angle of a sail's chord to the apparent wind.

Bail   A "U"-shaped fitting on the main boom to which blocks are attached.

Backwind   Wind deflected from a forward sail onto the sail behind it.

Ballast   Heavy weight, usually lead, placed in or on the keel of a boat to provide stability.

Barber haul   A device for adjusting athwartships trim of jibsheets.

Batten   A thin, narrow strip of wood or plastic used to stiffen the leech of a sail.

Beam   The width of the hull; also, the term is used directionally to mean at right angles to the centerline of a boat; *e.g.*, a beam sea.

Beating   Tacking the boat back and forth to gain distance in a windward direction.

Beryllium   A high strength-to-weight metal.

Bias stretch (bias elongation)   Elongation of sailcloth on a diagonal, usually by distortion on the weave configuration.

Block   A device with a grooved pulley or sheave mounted in a framework that has a point of attachment, such as an eye or a shackle. It is used to gain directional or mechanical advantage on a line.

Bolt rope   Reinforcing rope sewn on the luff and foot of a sail.

Broach   Uncontrolled rounding up of a boat that is overpowered and knocked down while reaching or running.

Broad reaching   Sailing with the wind aft of abeam.

Bull-ring vang   A vang system with semicircular track.

By the lee   Sailing downwind at an angle greater than 180 degrees to the true wind.

Camber   Concavity of a sail; *i.e.*, draft.

Camber ratio   The relationship of the sail's depth to its chord.

Carriage   A sliding fitting on a track or traveler, to which a sheet block or vang block is attached.

Center of effort   The point at which the sum total of forces of the sails is applied.

Center of lateral resistance   The point (on the vertical plane at the centerline of the hull) representing the total hydrodynamic force that resists leeward movement of the hull.

Cheek block   A turning block with a mounting base secured to the deck or to a spar.

Chord   A hypothetical straight horizontal line from the luff to the leech of a sail; the baseline of an aerodynamic shape.

Chord depth   The perpendicular measurement from the chord to the point of maximum draft.

Cleat   A fitting for securing a line.

Clew   The point of a sail where the leech and the foot intersect.

Cringle   An external eye in the edge of a sail.

Cunningham hole   An eye at a short distance above the tack of a sail, which is used with a tackle to adjust the tension of the luff.

Curl   Excessive curvature in the luff or leech of a spinnaker, or in the leech of a mainsail or jib, or in the foot of a jib.

Decksweeper   A jib or genoa with foot flush with the deck.

Double-head rig   A combination of two sails in the foretriangle.

Downhaul   A fitting or control line at the tack of a sail that tightens the luff; also, a control line to pull down the main boom on its gooseneck slide.

Draft   The amount of curvature in a sail.

Drag   Resistance caused by a shape in a fluid medium.

Drifter   A very-light-weight spinnaker or genoa.

Ease   To slack a sheet or halyard.

Edge cut   A system of cutting sails that provides draft by putting extra cloth on the edge of the luff and foot.

Exit   An opening in the mast through which internal halyards are led.

Fill   The yarns in a bolt of cloth that go from side to side.

Filler   A compatible plastic put in or on the surface of sailcloth to stabilize the weave.

Finishing   A process that sailcloth goes through after weaving, such as scouring, heat-treating, and calendering, in order to produce stability and low stretch.

Firm-finish cloth   Cloth to which extra filler has been applied.

Fitting   An item of marine hardware.

Flat   Minimum draft in a sail—the opposite of full.

Foot   The bottom edge of a sail, extending from tack to clew.

Footing   Moving through the water to windward with good boat speed.

Foreguy   The line used as a downhaul on a spinnaker pole.

Forestay   A wire mast support leading forward to the bow; the foremost stay.

Foretriangle   The area between the mast and the forestay.

Full   A sail with a generous amount of draft—the opposite of flat.

Galling   Damaging action caused by the friction of two like metals.

Girth   The horizontal measurement of a sail from luff to leech.

Glued seams   Stitched seams in a sail are also glued to increase strength and reduce stretch.

Gooseneck   A fitting by which the boom is attached to the mast.

Grinder   A large, high-powered pedestal winch; also, the crewman who operates it.

Grommet   A metal eye in a sail used as a point of attachment for sheets, tack, and clew pins, reef points, etc.

Halyard   A wire or rope for hoisting a sail.

Hanks   Fittings, such as snap shackles, that connect the luff of a jib to the stay on which it is hoisted.

Hard spots   Areas of distortion in the smooth shape of a sail.

Head   The top of a sail.

Headboard   The reinforcing metal or plastic plate in the head of a sail.

Heading wind   A narrowing of the angle the wind makes with the centerline of a boat, usually requiring a change of course to leeward.

Headstay   A wire mast support running from the masthead to the bow.

Headway   Forward movement of a boat.

Heel   Sideways deviation from the vertical; to tip.

Hyfield lever   A quick tensioning device for wire controls.

Induced drag   Drag caused by eddies along the foot and head of a sail.

Jackline   An adjustable line threaded between the mainsail slides on the mast and cringles on the luff of a sail, so that slides can be removed when roller reefing is done.

Jam cleat   A self-securing holding device for lines.

Jerk string   A one-design system for tensioning the jib luff. (The jib luff is a sleeve that envelops the luff wire.) The wire is secured and the sail is fastened at the head, but is adjusted at the tack by a control line or jerk string acting as a downhaul.

Jibe   An altering of course to bring a following breeze on the opposite side of the mainsail; also to change a spinnaker pole from one side of the boat to the other, interchanging sheet and afterguy.

Jib topsail   A high-clewed headsail used either alone or set above the staysail in the double-head rig.

Jibstay sag   Negative curvature in the wire stay on which the jib is hoisted.

Laminar flow   Smooth air flow over the surface of a sail.

Lazy guy (or sheet)   A secondary line attached to the tack and clew of the spinnaker, which can be tensioned to free the primary line during jibing.

Lead   A block or eye controlling the direction of trim.

Leading edge   The foremost edge of a sail; the luff; more properly, the forward plane.

Leech   The aft area (from head to clew) of a sail; the trailing edge.

Leech falloff   A portion of the trailing plane of the sail bends to leeward, producing an "S" shape in cross-section.

Leech line   A line that controls the tension on the trailing edge (leech) of the mainsail.

Leeward   The opposite direction from which the wind is coming.

Leeway   Sliding to leeward, perpendicular to the course you are steering.

Lift   The "topping lift" or vertical control line for the spinnaker pole or for the end of the main boom; also, a change in wind direction allowing a boat to point higher or to ease the sail trim without changing course.

Low-stretch cloth   Firm finished sailcloth that resists stretching on the bias.

LP (LPG)   A foretriangle measurement that is the length of a perpendicular from the luff intersecting the clew.

Luff   The forward part of a sail between the head and the tack.

Luff tension   Pressure exerted on the luff to adjust the location of draft.

Mast bend   Curvature in the mast produced by the force of the wind or by mechanical means.

Mast rake   Positioning the top of the mast forward or aft of a perpendicular to the deck at the partners.

Mid-boom traveler (horse)   A sliding device located beneath the mid-point of the boom and attached to it by the mainsheet, which controls the athwart-ships position of the sail.

Miter-cut   An arrangement of sail panels so that cloths are perpendicular to the leech and to the foot of a sail.

Mizzen   A sail similar to the main in shape, but smaller and mounted on its own mast and boom-rigged near the stern of a yawl or ketch.

Mizzen spinnaker   A light sail flown from the mizzenmast when sailing off the wind.

Mizzen staysail   A triangular reaching sail flown from the mizzenmast.

Mule   A small genoa, approximately 60 per cent of the area of a maximum-size genoa.

Necking   Elongation at the narrow portion of a sail or fitting.

Negative forces   Forces on a sail in an aft direction that hinder forward movement of the hull.

One design   An organized class of identical racing boats.

Outhaul   A device for pulling the clew of a sail out on the boom.

Overlap (sail)   The extension of the foot of a genoa behind the luff of the mainsail.

"Parachute"   A spinnaker.

Partners   The framing inside the hole in the deck through which the mast is stepped.

Patches   Reinforcing layers of cloth in the corners of a sail.

Penalty   An increase in a boat's rating.

Pitching   Fore-and-aft oscillation of the hull; *i.e.,* hobby-horsing.

Platform   The deck is the trimming platform of a boat.

Pointing angle   The angle that the centerline of the boat makes with the direction of the wind.

Point-loading   Dispersed strains that become increasingly concentrated as they approach a point to which the load is applied, as in the corner of a sail.

Radial vector   A line of angle emanating from the center of the compass use.

Ratchet block   A spring-loaded block in which sheet tension engages a pawl that allows the sheave to move only in the "trim" direction.

Rating   The resolution of a measurement formula that establishes a boat's racing handicap.

Reach   The sailing angles between beating to windward and running before the wind.

Reacher   A lightweight, high-clewed headsail for reaching, or a flat spinnaker.

Reaching strut   A spar extending to windward from the mast that broadens the angle of trim on the afterguy of the spinnaker.

Reef   A system for reducing sail area.

Reef points   Short lines, attached to the mainsail, used to tie in a reef.

Roach   A convex curve in the edge of a sail, where the sailcloth extends beyond a straight line from corner to corner.

Roller furling   A mechanical system for rolling the jib around its own luff wire.

Roller reefing   A mechanical system for reducing mainsail area by rolling the sail around the boom.

Round   Extra cloth added to a sail along the luff, leech, or foot.

Rounding up   The action of the boat as it turns toward the wind—generally, a fairly large angle of change.

Rubber-banding   A method of stopping sails that has become popular on larger boats; it is used instead of a zipper for stopping a spinnaker. It is also used, instead of rotten twine, to stop a genoa.

Separation   Air flow detaching from the lee side of sail.

Sheave   The pulley wheel for turning a sheet or halyard.

Sheet   A line to control the trim of a sail.

Sheet lead   A device, such as a block, that controls the angle and direction in which the sheet is led.

Shrouds   Part of the standing rigging that supports the mast athwartships.

Side-loading   Heeling forces exerted on sails by the wind.

Skirt   The convex-curved area below a straight line from tack to clew of a spinnaker or genoa.

Slack   To ease or pay out a line.

Slat   An uncontrolled sail slapping against the mast or rigging.

Slot   The area between the aft portion of the genoa and the leeward side of the mainsail.

Snatch block   A block that is hinged at the neck so that it can be readily opened to put a line over the sheave.

Soft-finish cloth   Cloth with little or no filler but with an increased amount of bias "stretch" or elongation.

Spreaders   Projections from the mast that "spread" the shrouds to provide more favorable angle between shrouds and the mast.

Stagnation point   The point of zero pressure differential in front of the sail where the flow lines divide to go to either side; also, the first point of zero pressure behind the leech.

Stall   A breakdown of aerodynamic forces, usually caused by separation of air flow on the leeward side of a sail.

Stay   A part of the standing rigging that supports the mast in a fore-and-aft direction.

Stiff   A boat that tends to resist heeling forces and stands up relatively straight.

Square   To bring the spinnaker pole or boom more perpendicular to the centerline of the boat.

Started sheets   Eased sheets.

Step   A receptacle that holds the base of the mast; also, to install the mast.

Storm jib   A small sail of heavyweight cloth hoisted in place of the regular jib in heavy weather.

Storm trysail   A small triangular sail of heavyweight cloth hoisted in place of the mainsail in heavy weather.

Stretch   Filaments or yarns in rope or sailcloth increasing in length under tension.

Tabling   Cloth reinforcing along the edge of a sail

Tack   The corner of a sail formed by the luff and the foot.

Tailer   A man overhauling a line as it comes from a winch.

Tang   A fitting used to attach the upper ends of the standing rigging to the mast.

Tender   A boat that heels excessively in average wind conditions.

Thimble   A grooved, metal or plastic teardrop shape used inside an eye splice to protect the rope or wire.

Threadline   The direction of the yarns in the warp and fill in the weave of sailcloth. (Sails are designed to try and take strains on the threadline rather than on the bias.)

Tension curl   Wrinkle in a sail caused by excess loading.

Track   Course made good over the bottom; also, a metal strip that accommodates slide or carriage.

Transom   Athwartships section at the stern of a boat.

Traveler   A sliding device to control the athwartships position of a sail, usually the mainsail.

Trim   The adjustment of a sail relative to the centerline of a boat, or to take in on a sheet; also, to balance the weight in a hull, so that she rides on her lines.

Turbulence   Irregular air flow that is still attached to the lee side.

Turnbuckle   An adjustable screw device that controls tension on stays, shrouds, and other rigging components.

Turning block   The block on the quarter or transom that leads a sheet or guy forward to a winch.

Turtle   A device to contain a spinnaker before it is set and from which it is set.

Twist   A sail, usually a spinnaker, turned around itself so that it will not fly properly; also, falloff or curvature in the leech of a sail.

Vang   A device to pull down the main boom and tighten the leech when the mainsheet cannot perform this function.

VMG   Speed made good: the calculated rate of speed of a hull against the true-wind direction.

Weather helm   Unbalanced helm that requires pulling the tiller to windward in order to keep the boat on course on the wind. The bow tends to move to windward when the helm is held on the centerline. Opposite of lee helm.

Wind gradient   The variation in the wind velocity at different heights above the water.

Index

A NOTE ABOUT THE AUTHOR

As president of Hard Sails, Wallace Ross has made sails for over 100 national and international small-boat champions, for many of the 12-Meters, and for such winning yachts as *Phantome*, *Windigo*, *Tempest*, and *Ondine*. As founder and president of Hard's sister company, Seaboard Marine, Ross has also pioneered in the field of hardware and fittings. Among his innovations have been the radial head spinnaker, the spherical spinnaker, and the ball-bearing traveler.

A NOTE ON THE TYPE

The text of this book was set on the Alphatype in Astro, a film version of Aster, a typeface designed by Francesco Simoncini (born 1912 in Bologna, Italy) for Ludwig and Mayer, the German type foundry. Starting out with the basic old-face letterforms that can be traced back to Francesco Griffo in 1495, Simoncini emphasized the diagonal stress by the simple device of extending diagonals to the full height of the letterforms and squaring off. By modifying the weights of the individual letters to combat this stress, he has produced a type of rare balance and vigor. Introduced in 1958, Aster has steadily grown in popularity wherever type is used.

Composed by University Graphics, Inc., Shrewsbury, N.J., and Alpha Graphics, New York, N.Y. Printed by Murray Printing, Forge Village, Mass., and bound by The Haddon Craftsmen, Inc., Scranton, Pa. Typography and binding design by Virginia Tan.